BRADMAN'S WAR

BRADMAN'S
WAR

HOW THE 1948 INVINCIBLES TURNED THE CRICKET PITCH INTO A BATTLEFIELD

MALCOLM KNOX

The Robson Press

This edition published in Great Britain in 2013 by
The Robson Press (an imprint of Biteback Publishing Ltd)
Westminster Tower
3 Albert Embankment
London SE1 7SP
Text copyright © Malcolm Knox 2012

First published by Penguin Group (Australia), 2012.

ISBN 978-1-84954-571-6

10 9 8 7 6 5 4 3 2 1

A CIP catalogue record for this book is available from the British Library.

All plates © The Roger Mann Collection

Text design by Laura Thomas © Penguin Group (Australia)

Printed and bound in Great Britain by
CPI Group (UK) Ltd, Croydon CR0 4YY

CONTENTS

INTRODUCTION

It was while reading through some old cricket documents in the Marylebone Cricket Club Library that I discovered a forgotten perception of Don Bradman.

Immediately after his retirement, when Don became Sir Donald and accepted the plaudits for his cricket career, he was not the universally praised hero to whom we have become accustomed. In fact, by the early 1950s Bradman was the most controversial and divisive figure in the cricket world. It is not going too far to say that he was engaged in a bitter fight to redeem his reputation.

This image of Bradman re-emerged gradually, like a photograph being cleaned of layers of dust. I had read his retirement autobiography, *Farewell to Cricket*, which was published in 1950, two years after his poignant last Test innings. Had Bradman lived and retired today, I imagine that it would have been written in gracious receipt of the tributes to his greatness. But 1950 was a more candid time, and the curatorship of public image was left up to the individual. Bradman used *Farewell to Cricket* to release all his bottled-up desire to set the record straight.

Consequently, it is a book laced with a sour stridency that seems, from our historical viewpoint, both surprising and unnecessary. Why should the Don, of all people, have needed to fight so hard for his reputation? Immediately after his retirement, however, Bradman was many decades away from becoming The Greatest Australian. In 1950, he saw his legacy as a highly contestable matter and set about its zealous protection. No document gives as clear an insight into his motivations. It's all in his own words.

No slight was too small for Bradman's memory. He never forgot how the New South Wales selectors snubbed him when, as a boy, he had travelled from the country to trials at the Sydney Cricket Ground. He never forgot how, when he took his first interstate tours, the senior men teased him as a bumpkin. He never forgot the merciless batting of the great England team of 1928–29, when, as twelfth man – he never forgot *that* either – he spent days in the sun picking Wally Hammond's cover drives out of the gutter. He never forgot the teasing from England's spin bowler Jack White, who chided Maurice Tate for dismissing Bradman in his first Test: 'Hey, you got my bunny!'

Bradman played in retirement as he had played on the field: for keeps. From its beginning, Anglo–Australian cricket had been played as war by another means. There was never any 'gentlemen's game', from the time W.G. Grace sneaked up to run out Sammy Jones while he was gardening the Oval wicket in the most famous match of all, the 'Ashes' Test of 1882. By the 1930s, Bradman's success put Ashes cricket on an unprecedentedly hostile footing. His mathematical accumulation of 974 runs in 1930, when he hit White, among others, into submission, provoked England's counter-reaction – the infamous physical assault of Bodyline in 1932–33. Cricket wars, like real wars, are not discrete affairs with beginnings and ends; they flow into each other. After Bodyline, it is well known that Australia's outrage ended the Ashes careers of its chief prosecutor, Douglas Jardine, and its weapon, Harold Larwood. Perhaps less well known is how the next Australian team to tour England, in 1934, was booed out of Nottingham when it threatened a walk-off after Larwood's partner Bill Voce bounced them. That Australian team, with Bradman again dominant, was described as 'the silent, sneering sixteen'. Bodyline left both sides resentful: Australia for having suffered from it, England for having been de-fanged as a consequence of it.

Fifteen years and a world war later, writing his memoir, Bradman was still seething over Bodyline. He was also seething over the battles he had fought in South Australia, when he was imported from New South Wales to take over the state captaincy from the popular hero and legendary Adelaide sportsman Victor York Richardson. He was seething over his clashes with teammates when he became Australian captain in 1936: a quintet of senior men, all Roman Catholics – Bill O'Reilly, Stan McCabe, Len Darling, Chuck Fleetwood-Smith and Leo O'Brien – had been carpeted by the Australian Board of Control for 'undermining' him.

Bradman seethed, still, over the apotheosis of 1930s cricket brutality, England's 903 runs for seven wickets at The Oval in 1938. Len Hutton batted nearly three days for 364, Bradman broke his ankle, and, in the last Ashes Test before the war, the Australians were ground into the Kennington dust. Four weeks later, Neville Chamberlain came back from his summit with Adolf Hitler in Germany and declared 'Peace for our time'. In the deeper mood of cricket, just as in the deeper movements of people, there was a stronger pull towards hostility.

Years later, Bradman took out his greatest frustration on his former teammates and antagonists from the 1930s, such as Jack Fingleton and O'Reilly, who had become journalists critical of his actions. Worse than enemies, he saw them as apostates; his autobiography gave him his chance to bite them back. He missed no opportunity to vent at the 'personal spleen, naked and unashamed' of Fingleton's writing. Bradman lived by the rule, he declared, of 'You can't make people like you, but you can make them respect you.' But can respect be forced? In *Farewell to Cricket*, the peerless English cricket writer Alan Gibson concluded, Bradman 'seemed to go through every slur cast on him during his cricket career, and reject them all'. It was nothing less than a tirade.

Who was this angry man? Certainly not the Bradman we came to know in recent decades, when, having retired from a sometimes stormy life as a cricket administrator, he had become such an unquestionable Australian eminence that his vital statistics were in the questionnaire for applicants for Australian citizenship and his batting average comprised the post office box number of the Australian Broadcasting Corporation. By the time of his death, he was the nation's shy grandfather, to whose suburban Adelaide home great men went to pay homage. We knew that Bradman had had his critics – O'Reilly and Fingleton were well known, as were Ian Chappell and the protagonists of World Series Cricket – but his record of accomplishment and service to the game surely placed him above all criticism.

This was not the real Bradman, however, at least as he perceived himself. By 2001, when he died five years into the prime ministership of John Howard, who idolised him, he might have felt satisfied that his reputation had been cleared of any taint. But Bradman never forgot his *own* time, and knew better than anyone that his final iconic status was a reward for longevity. He had outlived his critics, but their ghosts were fresher in his mind than in ours.

Australians are used to thinking of his 1948 team – the Invincibles – as having conducted a triumphal march through war-ravaged Britain. It was a tour that restored cricket's supremacy as a popular entertainment, and resuscitated the mother country's battered morale. It was a gift from the triumphant new world to the shrunken old, from the coming Pacific Century to the fading Empire. Our boys delivered food parcels and speeches, played joyfully and won some of the most dramatic matches ever staged. Once they scored 729 runs – 729! – in a day. Bradman went out, truly, in a blaze of glory, and his famous duck at The Oval, stranding him with a Test cricket average of 99.94, was just a minor flaw, Japanese-style, to emphasise the perfection of the whole.

This, at least, is the orthodox view. But when I went back to the original documents, a very different picture emerged. Among Bradman's teammates, those inimitable golden boys, few spoke of the 1948 tour as their favourite. Neil Harvey, the teenaged 'baby' of the tour, said that of his four Test tours to England, his most enjoyable by far was his last, in 1961 under Richie Benaud. Arthur Morris, whose batting in the 1948 Tests eclipsed even Bradman's, preferred the 1953 tour under Lindsay Hassett. Hassett's happiest tours were in 1938 when he was a prankish youngster and 1953 when he was captain, but not 1948. The famously good-natured Bill Brown said he gained more enjoyment out of his two Ashes tours in the 1930s than in 1948. Keith Miller, after the 1948 tour, bowled bouncers at Bradman in the great man's testimonial match and was dropped from the next Australian team, which toured South Africa in 1949–50. Bradman was one of the selectors responsible, but blamed the others. When Miller approached another selector, Chappie Dwyer, and informed him that Bradman denied any part in the decision, Dwyer replied, 'Did the little — say that?' In the early 1950s, Bradman was involved in the murky blacklisting of another Invincible, Sid Barnes, who effectively sued the Australian Board for defamation. Bradman was widely believed to be behind Barnes's ostracism, though the fall was taken by Keith Johnson, a loyal Bradman retainer who had been the manager of the 1948 tour.

The contest over Bradman's legacy figured in teammates' memoirs as if it was a feature of the cricket climate that everyone knew. That some, such as Colin McCool, rose in his defence only confirms that there was a widely held body of negative opinion to be challenged. McCool had been Australia's first-choice spin bowler going into 1948, but Bradman did not pick him for one Test match. A decade later, rising above his disappointment, McCool still felt it necessary to comment on Bradman's reputation. 'Quite unjustly and irrationally, Bradman has been labelled as the man responsible for [the] depressing trend' of eradicating leg spinners, McCool said. Even the team scorer, Bill Ferguson, was moved to rebut what he called 'the legend of Bradman's unpopularity' a decade after Bradman retired.

Entertainment-hungry Britons had flocked to see Bradman and had thrown their hats in the air to celebrate him. There are famous photographs of Bradman walking onto Headingley through a tunnel of Englishmen, and of Norman Yardley leading the three cheers of Bradman in his final innings at The Oval. The world seems to have forgotten the wild scenes of celebration when, after Bradman walked through the Headingley tunnel, Dick Pollard clean-bowled him. John Arlott said the cheering at his dismissal 'rolled like thunder'; Fingleton saw 'almost indescribable scenes of bedlam'. Yes, Yardley, England's captain, did lead the three cheers at The Oval, but he said to Eric Hollies: 'That's all we'll give him – then bowl him out.' When Hollies did so, no England player spared a moment's mercy for Bradman. As Bradman walked off, Hollies quipped, 'Best f—ing ball I've bowled all season, and they're clapping *him*!'

After the series, England's champion players of 1948, such as Cyril Washbrook, Denis Compton and Bill Edrich, wrote scathingly of Bradman's sportsmanship. Yardley wrote that Bradman 'will never forget or forgive the Bodyline Tour' and 'let his relentless determination to win sometimes run away with him'. Edrich, the most outspoken, wrote that Bradman brought 'an element of grimness, savage competition and uncompromising search for victory, that no other country has equalled, and that may, I hope and believe, be reduced again to more normal proportions now that the controversial figure of Don Bradman has retired to the Olympian heights of cricket control'.

The clashes between Miller and Bradman – perhaps the most defining personal differences, because they embody the fundamental schism of life in the 1940s, between a warrior and a non-combatant, and between two opposing ideologies of how cricket ought to be played – had also seeped out of the dressing room into public knowledge over time. Most famously, Miller derided the pressure a mere cricketer faced, no matter how Bradman-like his status; real pressure was 'having a Messerschmidt up your arse'. That lay at the heart of Miller-versus-Bradman: one man, his nerves damaged by war, wishing to play cricket as a game, versus another man, who spent the war as an invalid, yet returned to the field to wage cricket as war without the shooting. It also lay at the heart of England's ambivalence over the way Bradman led his 1948 team.

The surviving participants in the 1948 tour have mellowed as their ranks have thinned, and they have taken on the guardianship of the legend of the Invincibles. I interviewed the four surviving players from 1948 when I commenced my research – Australia's Neil Harvey, Arthur Morris and Sam Loxton (in his last interview before his death in December 2011), and England's John Dewes. Dewes was quite forceful in his opinions of the Australians' ruthless attitude to cricket in 1948. Harvey and Morris maintained that the presence of Bradman made 1948 a highly pressured tour, less enjoyable perhaps than their later ones, yet they had over time recognised that they were custodians of a corporate memory, talismans of national myth-making, and this had subsumed their personal feelings. Loxton, who only made the one tour of England as a Test cricketer, was as strident as he had always been in supporting Bradman and denouncing his enemies.

Just as the passage of years mellows individuals, it reshapes the telling of history. It is not far-fetched to suggest that cricket has been as much a battleground of the contestability of history during the past fifteen years as have other fields of Australian life. Just as our participation in the two world wars is seen very differently, and more positively, than it was closer to the events themselves, the Invincibles tour has been subject to a historical spit-and-polish. Anzac and Armistice days are commemorated with a lustre that was never in the minds of the silent and grim-faced men who had recently been there and lived on with the nightmares. When it comes to Bradman, too, we live in revisionist times, when we who were not there have put aside the negative and celebrated his contribution.

The two strands of our history – the world wars and Bradman – are intertwined. The dispute over their remembrance has been wrongly simplified as positive-versus-negative, or optimistic-versus-pessimistic. John Howard took the view that 'black armband' history talked down the nation and its achievements. It is easily argued that to rediscover the negatives of the past is to denigrate it. Yet that may not be the case. When we go back to the real story of the Invincibles, we rediscover a forgotten optimism that came out of the war: an alternative vision for what postwar England and Australia, and postwar cricket, might have become. When we go back and listen to the original voices of the time, we find an undercurrent of utopian ideas that the world might be remade better than it was before the fighting. Some cricketers were tired of the brutality of the game in the 1930s, as whole populations were tired of the economic and political forces that brought a long Depression and the slaughter of millions. During the war, hopes also arose that a new Anglo–Australian cricket might be played, one that might not be just a continuation of fighting to the death. These hopes were fostered most of all by the men who saw combat. In Britain, these men came home and voted Winston Churchill out of office in an unprecedented landslide. They wanted a new world to be the fruit of all the sacrifice. Otherwise, what would the sacrifice have been for?

In cricket a new vision arose among the soldiers, fliers and sailors who played each other in services games to take minds off the fighting. Many of these men, English and Australian, had been Test cricketers in the 1930s. They wanted something different, something better, something played in the spirit of the interservices games, when the cricket was hard but the players shared dressing rooms. Among the Englishmen, this spirit promised the final breakdown of the century-old amateur–professional class division in the same way that the postwar general election promised a fairer society. For these warriors in white, a window would open up in 1945 when this better kind of cricket could be realised and exported into real Test cricket whenever it recommenced. Cricket had the potential to be not what it had been – a ritualisation of warlike behaviour – but war's antidote. The story of the 1948 Invincibles starts with those idealists and the fate of their dream.

1

WARRIORS IN WHITE

For weeks the little gunner, his head rubbed bald by the webbing of his tin helmet, had been lining up German planes from Mount Carmel. His favourite view was not of the targets in the sky, but over the dark ribbon of the Nazareth Road and the Flanders poppies a previous war's diggers had planted south of Migdal, towards Galilee's green hills. These rare splashes of cricket-field colour did not so much bring him a tear of nostalgia as keep him sane.

Sanity: another scarce wartime resource. The gunner had signed up with the 2/2 Anti-Aircraft Regiment in Melbourne and had immediately been offered a commission. He was famous, after all, and therefore valuable. He declined. He wanted to serve alongside the mates he knew from happier days; this war was only worth surviving if sportsmen could survive it together.

Arthur Lindsay Hassett could only blame himself for being in the firing line. A champion at four different sports at Geelong College, he had chosen cricket when his body refused to grow more than 160 centimetres in height. Tiny, he had struggled for credibility in his first few years playing for Victoria. He also seemed drawn to a good time more than the stern chieftains of the game liked to see. But his free-stroking talent had eventually won him a place with Bradman's 1938 Ashes tourists. His batting on the tour was commendable, but he was better remembered for his late hours. He led team renditions of 'The Bridle Hanging on the Wall' or 'Down Came a [bloody great] Blackbird', and had a dry sense of humour inherited from his father, Ted, a real-estate agent who, when congratulated on his boys doing well at cricket, replied: 'So they should. They never do anything at home.'

On the 1938 tour, Stan McCabe recalled Hassett 'knocking on my door about midnight demanding to be allowed in for a nightcap and a chat . . . He never seemed to understand that most people need seven or eight hours' sleep between long days on a cricket-field.' Once he put a dirty goat in the hotel room occupied by McCabe and O'Reilly, but in the Headingley Test match, when McCabe was too nervous to watch, Hassett steered Australia home with an innings of maturity and calm. By the time his career was cut short by the war, he was, with Bradman, Sydney's Sid Barnes and Toowoomba's Bill Brown, in the top drawer of Australian batting. He was the only man to consistently master the great O'Reilly, scoring a pair of centuries off 'the Tiger' in the last Sheffield Shield match before the competition was suspended. Not even Bradman had done that.

After Hassett enlisted, the *Mauretania* took his regiment to Suez before trains carted them to El Kantara and across the Sinai desert. Their first active ack-ack duty was in Haifa, though they were busier standing watch outside the city's brothels.

One night in a park near Mount Carmel, the little gunner came across a 1000-pound landmine. Parachuted out of a German plane, it had punched a silent divot in the earth but failed to explode. Fascinated, he took his bayonet out of its scabbard and stepped into the hole. He was sitting on the mine and cutting strips of silk from the parachute – the material could be put to any number of uses in Palestine – when a British bomb disposal squad arrived. They were stopping traffic on the nearby streets, as the vibrations of cars and trucks could have set the mine off.

A British officer loomed above the silk-cutting gunner and barked: 'Get the hell out of that hole!'

The gunner cut a last strip and obeyed. Lindsay Hassett was still getting used to taking orders from his inferiors.

Though he refused a commission, everyone knew of his batting deeds in games for the Australian Forces against the South Africans, the New Zealanders and the English on hot grounds in the Middle East. They were great occasions. For a game against the South African Forces at the Alexandria Cricket Club, team scorer Kenneth Slessor wrote: 'Every Australian in Alexandria seemed to have turned up, including a large party of hospital patients wearing black slacks and bright-red ties. A sprinkling of Australian nurses came with them. There was a little good-humoured barracking, just to bring back memories of "The Hill", but it was all done by Australians at the expense of Australians. The crowd centred most of its interest on Hassett.'

The cricket grounds in the Nile Delta were uncommonly pretty: matting wickets on green fields surrounded by jacarandas, sycamores, palms and poplars. Brass bands added a cheery soundtrack. Playing in Alexandria alongside cricket-and-army comrades such as Dick Whitington, Alec Hurwood, Ted White and Ray Robinson, Hassett failed in the first innings but made up for it with a brisk hundred, to great cheering, in the second.

Not every officer was aware of the celebrity non-com in their ranks. One overseer, 'an irritating young subaltern', unimpressed with Hassett's less than rigid routines, told him: 'If you took the trouble to clean your rifle you might just manage to become a good soldier.'

To the pompous officer, Hassett said: 'If you cleaned and oiled your cricket bat for twenty years, sir, you'd never score a run.'

Hassett always had a reply ready. This was the man who was quick enough, when he saw a Middle Eastern sheikh appear with his 199 wives, to quip: 'One more and he's entitled to a new ball.'

But cricket, as Whitington said, 'was no longer king', and

'wristwork and ball sense were [not] the answer to Rommel and Goering'. Hassett might have been a cricket star, but in wartime he was just one of the men. He might have lost an entire cricket career – he was certainly losing his prime years – but Hassett never let his regret show. Death was able to remind him, constantly, that his luck had been better than many's. Ken Farnes, England's fastest bowler in the 1938 series, had died on a night flight in 1941. South Australia's wicketkeeper and Australia's second choice, Charlie Walker, was shot down over Soltau, Germany, while Hassett was in Egypt. There were the countless others. He had no reason to feel sorry for himself. Whitington described Hassett as 'one of the merriest of warriors – especially when things were at their worst'.

Outside Cairo one day, Hassett stopped to eat a watermelon from a street stall, a practice thought unbecoming for a soldier, as a purringly important staff car pulled up.

'Just what might you be doing, gunner?'

The window was down, and Hassett beheld General Thomas Blamey, the supreme commander of the Australian forces.

'Conducting a snipers' school, sir.'

'And where might the snipers be at the moment?'

Hassett looked around: nothing but street vendors, passing foot traffic and the fields beyond.

'Hiding, sir.'

'And what might you be teaching them?'

'Cover from view, sir.'

'Really, gunner. Then I must congratulate you on the job they're doing.'

The car drove off. Two days later, Hassett was leading the Australian Forces cricket XI at the Gezirah Sporting Club. During a break, his duty was to introduce them to the VIP guest.

'Haven't I met you somewhere before, Hassett?' the general said.

Hassett's face, which would become renowned for qualities he might have learnt from the nearby Sphinx, betrayed nothing.

Once Rommel was driven into the Mediterranean, Hassett and his mates trooped through Beirut and Syria to embark on the *Strathallan* for Australia, then, on the Dutch cutter *Swardenwoerdt* ('Black Dog'), for Port Moresby. The 4000 Australian troops had for company 200 head of cattle, 2000 cases of ammunition and 4000 drums of petrol. Hassett was put on instruments under the coconut palms at Eddy Avenue in Moresby. The Japanese were creeping down New Guinea's spine. New place, new war. 'The prospect of ever playing cricket again,' said Whitington, 'seemed slim.'

But as the war drew towards its end, the military authorities recognised the potential value of cricket in raising morale. In 1919, an Australian Services team had been put together under Herbie Collins, another non-com who became a Test captain. Not only had their games helped the transition to postwar normality in England and Australia, but their personnel had formed the basis for the peerless Test teams of the early 1920s under Warwick Armstrong, whose 1921 tour of England had fallen one match short – the *last* match – of the inconceivably high achievement of going through a whole summer without loss.

In 1945, Hassett was made a sergeant in the Second AIF Reception Group, to look after repatriated prisoners of war. The Reception Group travelled to England via New York, marching down Broadway in a parade of thanks for the defence of Australia. The group consisted of 'doctors, dentists, lawyers, pay-officers, clerks and amenities personnel, plus three padres', said Whitington, but only one celebrity. Sir Eugene Gorman, the group's commanding officer, soon learnt that Hassett was not 'his sergeant', but that he, Gorman, was 'Lindsay's brigadier'. Cricket had not been forgotten, and now that the war was ending, it would be looked to for its restorative powers.

In the spring and summer of 1945, even while the war was still going, Hassett's army team began playing matches against English teams, sometimes under the drone of Lancaster bombers heading across the Channel. 'Peaceful English country-green cricket and aerial destruction,' Whitington wrote, 'combined to form an unforgettable eerie contrast.'

After VE Day, the army cricket team morphed into an AIF side. Hassett's teammates included first-class cricketers Whitington, Hurwood, Stan Sismey and Cec Pepper. They were joined by a tall, blue-eyed Victorian airman who had broken into Sheffield Shield cricket just before the war.

Keith Miller had played a handful of state games alongside Hassett, whom he had admired since his teens. Like Hassett, Miller was an aggressive top-order batsman. Miller had enlisted on 29 August 1940, going into a training camp at Caulfield with the Australian army's motor transport division. Like many top-level sportsmen, Miller was given leave to play cricket for his state and football for his club, St Kilda. For the hundreds of thousands of soldiers stationed in Australia, sport was a welcome break from the boredom. One of Miller's St Kilda clubmates was Sam Loxton, the only child of an electrician, Sam Senior, and his ambitious wife, Annie. A bustling, energetic boy of nineteen, Sam was living with his parents in Armadale when he signed up on 12 May 1941.

'My father had played cricket and baseball for Collingwood many years before,' Loxton recalled. 'He had a business in High Street, Armadale after starting in Smith Street, Fitzroy. Many's the night I got called out with him to hold the torch while he did his work. He was pretty well known in the area.

'I had no great appetite for following him into it. My mother was pretty definite in her ways, and didn't want me to be associated with the electrical business. She'd had enough of it and didn't think it was the way for me.'

Annie helped Sam get a job in bookkeeping with the ES&A Bank. 'That was more along the lines she wanted. I didn't know till many years later that my father had to put up a surety of one hundred pounds when I got the job. Anyway, he got it back!'

Sam was working at the bank when he enlisted in the Second Armoured Division. He liked the idea of being swaddled in metal.

As with Miller, Loxton's first year of armed service involved a lot of football and cricket.

> Brigadier Bill Locke was our commanding officer, and a mad St Kilda supporter. On Sundays, you played for the army against the air force or the navy. They drew pretty good crowds. If you'd happened to play league football, and a few of us had played for St Kilda, you were always in demand. I was full-forward for the army. I tell you, it was tough football. After the game, though, I'd have to catch the train straight back to the barracks. Your leave pass ran out at 11.59 on Sunday night. I had to get back to Rokeby, where divisional headquarters was, near Seymour and Puckapunyal. We had to walk from the train station to the barracks in the middle of the night. It was a funny way to spend the first part of the war. But I was so busy, I never thought about what I might be missing out on.

Loxton would not leave Australia during the war. His grand dreams of fighting the war from a tank were turning to dust and mud.

> In training, I was made a corporal and put up in the cupola with the 37mm armour-piercing gun, the smaller of the tank's guns. But by the time I was ready, the tank war was finished in North Africa. The theatre had moved to New Guinea, to stop the Japanese. They sent one tank squadron up there, but the tanks sank in the mud. So I was put in the Brisbane Line, in case the Japanese landed, in tents up at Murgon. It was a bit different from what I'd expected. I didn't know anybody. It hadn't been my choice to go there. I'd been assigned to where it was thought I'd be most useful. Not the way it turned out!

Meanwhile, Keith Miller was waging war against his officers. Within two months of enlistment he received a ten-shilling fine for using insulting language. He couldn't manage to return on time from his sporting engagements, and after a string of disciplinary problems, he quit the army reserve. He was impatient for action. He flirted with the navy, and tried to join up with a mate, but when his mate's application was rejected Miller tore up his own. In November 1941 he found his calling, and took his gamble. He joined the air force. He trained in Victor Harbor, near Adelaide, gaining his wings by the end of 1942. He met Colin McCool, a blond leg-spinning all-rounder from Queensland, and they bonded over long games of table tennis before McCool was sent to New Guinea to fly transports and train as a navigator.

Promoted to flight sergeant, Miller went for more training to Boston, where he met Peggy Wagner, a secretary at the Massachusetts Institute of Technology. Just as they became romantically involved, Miller was shipped to Scotland for further training and more run-ins with authority. He was given three weeks' hard labour after threatening to punch an officer. Fortunately, cricket provided an outlet. Miller took part in games for the RAF, the RAAF and the Dominions. When a German bomb hit a game at Bournemouth, Miller was listed as missing. In fact, he had never shown up.

He did front for a charity game at Lord's, the headquarters of cricket, with which he would enjoy a special affinity. He came across a charismatic Londoner who would become something of a soulmate.

Denis Compton, as supreme on the wing for Arsenal and England as he was with the bat in England's middle order, recalled a game which was to take 'some London minds off the air raids':

> I feel set for a big score when the ball is thrown to a tall, brush-back-haired fellow who has been racing round the boundary like a gazelle. He is the fifth bowling change. I turn to [the Dominions wicketkeeper] Stan Sismey.
>
> 'What's this chap do, Stan?'
>
> 'Oh, he's not really a bowler. Probably wants some exercise. You might find him a bit quick, though.'

A bit quick! The bowler takes a short run. When he lets the
ball go, my hair stands on end. This is the fastest ball I've faced
since I played Ernie McCormick in 1938. So do I meet Keith
Miller.

Training in England, Miller earned a reputation for luck. After
injuring his back in a wrestling match, he crashed a Beaufighter
when returning from a night training operation over France. On
its next mission, the Beaufighter malfunctioned, killing its pilot.

Soon Miller was nicknamed 'Golden Nugget', or 'Nugget'.
He missed colliding with a hangar by centimetres. On leave in
London, he was planning to go to a theatre, which was that night
hit by a V-1 flying bomb. He wasn't there; he'd been too drunk
to show up. In March 1945 he joined the RAF station at Great
Massingham and flew missions for No. 169 Squadron in Mosquito
fighters, pathfinders for the Lancaster bombers. In April he took
part in an attack on German ships in Flensburg, Denmark, and in
May, after a raid on the Danish town of Sylt, he was forced to land
with one of his unexploded bombs hanging from his wing.

When the European war ended a few days later, Miller was at
Great Massingham. He recalled: 'I simply stood there and thought,
"What the hell am I going to do now?" I'd never been so lonely.'

For the warrior-cricketers, sport was meant to fill the vacuum.
But the military quickly turned cricket into another duty. When
the war ended, the AIF team were still under orders, on meagre
military pay depending on their rank. The men were desperate
to go home, but the summer of 1945 in England was infused
with a once-in-a-generation mood of optimism. As historian
David Kynaston wrote in his study of the postwar era, *Austerity
Britain*, the immediate aftermath of the war saw a surge in utopian
hope, when workers and returned soldiers dreamed of building
a new society. Their vote for a new Labour government was not

necessarily a repudiation of the wartime heroism of Churchill, but rather expressed a belief that capitalist excess had been responsible for sixteen years of Depression and conflict. In his novel *The Linden Tree*, a J.B. Priestley character carried this hope for a new democratic socialism: 'Call us drab and dismal, if you like, and tell us we don't know how to cook our food or wear our clothes – but for Heaven's sake, recognise that we're trying to do something that is as extraordinary and wonderful as it's difficult – to have a revolution for once without the Terror, without looting mobs and secret police . . . We're fighting in the last ditch of our civilisation. If we win through, everybody wins through.'

On the cricket field, four 'Victory Tests' were scheduled between Hassett's Australians and an England Services side boasting pre-war heroes such as Wally Hammond, Compton and Hutton. The teams enjoyed a camaraderie that promised a friendly new dawn for international cricket. Whitington recalled fondly: 'The English and Australian teams shared the same dressing room, a situation surely unique in the history of matches between the two countries. They did more than change in the same room. They travelled to and from the ground in the same motor-coach and stayed at the same hotel. Nobody lost anything by this. Nor did the cricket.'

John Dewes, a left-handed opening batsman from Cheshire who was just a few weeks out of school, failed against Miller and dropped him at Lord's, but remembers the Victory Tests fondly. 'The war was over, and we felt, "Whoopee, here we are. We know they're Aussies, but they're nice!"'

Whitington, the Australian Services XI's player-chronicler, said the 'Victory Series gave the cricket-starved public almost everything it wanted from cricket'. It gave the players just as much, and they took it in good humour. One of the Australians, after a week of constant rain, looked at the barrage balloons tied to the ground and asked: 'Why don't they cut the wires and let the dump sink?'

The cricketers in the Victory Tests were uniquely placed to put the importance of the game into perspective. The warlike temper of 1930s Ashes cricket seemed stupid, almost obscene, to them now. Ghosts haunted the field. Ken Farnes was gone, and so was his partner, Yorkshire's slow left-armer Hedley Verity, the wizard who had bowled more balls to Bradman in the 1930s than any other, dismissing him ten times, eight in Tests. Neville Cardus once said that Bradman, having got out to Verity, left the field looking pensive, '[t]hinking about one of the eternal Veritys, perhaps'.

In Verity's last game of first-class cricket, the week Hitler invaded Poland, he took seven for 9 for Yorkshire against Sussex. After enlisting, he rose swiftly to the rank of captain in the army. Leading an attack on the German forces at Caserta, Sicily, in July 1943, he was hit in the chest and captured. Eleven days later he died, a prisoner of war.

With such sadness surrounding them, how could the cricketers treat their matches as if they were a war? Bodyline itself seemed so much fuss over so little. No surviving Test player had more cause to ponder the strange relationship between those two theatres of conflict, war and sport, as the nuggety Londoner Bill Edrich. One of the English Services players, Edrich had been a rising star of the 1938 series and a *Wisden* cricketer of the year in 1940. In his last prewar appearance, for Middlesex against Warwickshire, he had scored a century. As far as he knew, it would be the last county match he would ever play.

One Saturday in June 1941, Edrich, flying Blenheims out of Great Massingham, had a morning mission. His squadron lost two aircraft with all crew. He flew back to Norfolk in time to join the squadron cricket team for a 12.30 p.m. game against a village XI at Colonel Birkbeck's private ground at Massingham Hall. The immediate past bled into the present. 'I shall always remember this match,' Edrich said.

At times it seemed like a strange dream. There were the big

elms throwing grave shadows on the English grass, the wild roses in the hedges, the lazy caw of a rook passing overhead, the old village in the distance, and the quiet sound of bat and ball; then would come a sudden vision, as real as the other, of a 5000-ton ship heeling over, with pathetic little black figures scrambling up her tilting deck and trying vainly to escape the blast of the flames that belched and flickered out of her blazing hold, the drowning and burning sailors, the stab of the tracer coming up at us, the interminable roaring of engines punctuated by the heart-thud of exploding bombs . . .

Both cricket teams played well, and it was a hard and exciting game. Every now and then would come the old, accustomed cry – 'OWZATT?' – and then one's mind would flicker off to the briefing, and to joking with a pal whose broken body was now washing in the long, cold tides, and one saw again his machine cartwheeling down flaming from nose to tail; and then a ball would roll fast along the green English turf and in the distance the village clock would strike and the mellow echoes would ring through the lazy air of that perfect summer afternoon.

Sport a distraction, a pleasant pastime to take the mind off war? Such a sport had never been invented.

As I batted I wondered whether, perhaps, young Germans who had rained down death and terror on London's civilians the night before were now slowly cycling through some fairy glade of the Black Forest and thinking what I thought . . . *why, why, why?*

It is only in the RAF that such contrasts come so sharply, for the Army and Navy cannot engage in a battle and a cricket match on the same day. It is a queer feeling, bowling for a catch in the slips, and watching the batsman put a chance there which is missed; and then realising that the fieldsman with whom you have concerted so many traps of that kind is not there any more; you had been laying plans with him this morning for that very catch, but now he is dead. He – and perhaps hundreds of sailors you have never seen, with him. But that is war.

The Victory Tests began with a common resolve between the captains, Hassett and Hammond, to play 'differently'. Without putting it into words, they understood what they meant: this would be cricket without Bradman. Although the footage we see of Bradman shows a figure of uncommon lightness and *joie de jouer*, the little master cast a shadow over his contemporaries. Between 1930 and 1948, there were really two types of cricket for Australian stars: Bradman and non-Bradman. When he wasn't playing, they felt freer. The whole world wasn't watching as intently as in Bradman-cricket. The Australians who went to South Africa under Victor Richardson in 1935–36, when Bradman, who would have been captain, was fighting illness, spoke of that tour as a highpoint of camaraderie. The same would be said of the non-Bradman Test tours to New Zealand and South Africa in the 1940s. Only a madman would not want Bradman in his team; yet somehow, when he was not playing, a burden was lifted.

Undoubtedly, the unique mood of the Victory Tests could only have come about because of the enforced break and the experience of war. Australians who had fought in Europe came to a different view of cricket's place in the scheme of things from those who had stayed in uniform at home, or had not fought at all. And it would certainly be understood in a different way by the English, whose own country had been devastated by Germany's attempted invasion and ravaged by the long war's immeasurable costs.

England's Services opening batsmen, preparing to face Miller, were a mighty Roses pairing, Lancashire's Cyril Washbrook and Yorkshire's Len Hutton. Washbrook had come of cricketing age

at the most inopportune time, playing just one Test match before
the war. He enlisted as a physical trainer and endured a miserable
farewell to his home ground, Old Trafford, in 1940. 'Nobody knew
when cricket, if ever, would be played again. Normally I am not
what you might call an emotional type, and until that moment I
had not fully realised how much a part of my life Old Trafford had
become. When I turned out of the ground again, I felt sad. I was
saying "Au revoir" to an old friend.'

For Hutton, frighteningly, it had seemed like "Adieu". The
Yorkshireman had been England's answer to Bradman, scoring
364 in the Oval Test of 1938. Just married when the war broke
out, he joined the Army Physical Training Corps. On the last
day of a commando course, he lost concentration – a rare event,
his biographer A.A. Thomson wrote, 'almost to the point of
impossibility in that particular person' – while performing a 'fly
spring'. The mat slipped under him; he badly fractured his left
radius and dislocated his ulna at the wrist. He had an operation,
but remained in constant pain except when anaesthetised,
and required a series of bone grafts, a procedure still in its
experimental stage. A three-inch length of bone was taken
from his right leg and inserted into the shattered right forearm.
'The very conception of such an operation struck the patient
as miraculous, a thought which must also strike every layman,'
Thomson wrote.

Hutton's worst enemy was his own mind. 'His keen imagination,
as he lay in hospital, painted a dark picture of the future. There
was no refuge in lack of imagination because . . . he was keenly
imaginative.' After that, 'perhaps his most interesting speculation
would be confined to wondering whether his leg or his arm hurt
him the most'.

Hutton was discharged from the army fourteen months after
his accident, only to learn that he needed more operations. He
wrote: 'The uneasy thought that worried me in the long hours of
monotony and loneliness was just as human as the question each

inevitably asked himself in secret: "Shall I ever return to the old life? Shall I ever play cricket again?"'

Even if he did, his shortened right arm left doubts that he would ever recapture his prewar ability. He returned in the Victory Tests but averaged less than 40. Miller, discovering a talent and love for very fast short-pitched bowling to go with his brilliant batting, sent down bumpers at Hutton during the match at Bramall Lane, Sheffield. When he hit him in the left forearm, the crowd yelled, 'Go off, Larwood!'

Miller laughed. There was no ill will between the teams in the Victory Tests, and Hutton, far from being angry, complimented Miller's bowling. 'If I ever had the luxury of picking a side to face the proverbial Martian XI,' he wrote, 'no time would be lost in naming Miller as my first choice . . . I always prided myself, given time, that I could work out methods to play most bowlers, but Miller was an exception, partly because half the time he himself did not know what he intended to do.'

Against all expectations, inspired by Miller, the Australian Services XI drew the series 2–2. Many on both sides would say it was the happiest cricket of their life. The quality of the matches was high, but the players expressed themselves with an 'outlook that was more like that of a cavalier than a cricketer', Whitington recalled. 'Cricket was meant for making friends, not enemies; for making fun and friendly fight, not money.'

Such distinctions were evident in the continued commitment of Australian team captain Hassett to staying among the rank and file. He remained a fierce anti-snob. Whitington, a captain, was sent notes from British officers in social clubs, begging him to rescue them from unwanted conversations with non-coms – not realising that the pesky enlisted men included the great Hassett. Whitington's fealty to his leader, who did not score heavily either in the Victory Tests or when the tour continued to India, was unwavering.

'We who were his cricketing colleagues, officers and other

ranks, admired him for his refusal to win military rank from cricketing prowess; but we felt that a captain who had to lead a team of Australians against an England led by a commissioned captain [Hammond], and against India led by a millionaire, would have suffered no harm from higher military status at the close of a six-year war.'

The Services team arrived in Perth exhausted and yearning for home. The war had been over for eight months, but these men were still owned by the military. Whitington wrote: 'We were close to a fourteen-man strike in Madras. And all we wanted to do now was creep under the nearest axminster or, better still, board a Persian flying-carpet to our loved ones . . . We'd battled with wasps, flies, dysentery, autograph-hunters, Indian curry and, finally, that enervating flight over the hungry, grey Indian Ocean.'

In Perth they met Bert Oldfield, the Australian Test wicketkeeper who had played in Collins's services team in 1919. Oldfield rubbed his palms and said they were to go around Australia playing state teams featuring the cream of prewar cricket, including Bradman, O'Reilly and Barnes.

'They've given you a whole day off tomorrow,' Oldfield said.

Whitington turned to Hassett. 'Lindsay did not have to answer. His face spoke "volum's".'

They played on under protest, against six state teams filled with a mixture of men who had not served, men who had served in the Pacific theatre, and men who had served within Australia. The Services XI didn't win a game, losing two and drawing four. In Sydney, they took a battering from an inner-Sydney street urchin made good, a snappily dressed, opportunistic wheeler-dealer named Sid Barnes.

Since childhood days when he bowled to his brother Horrie for sixpence, Barnes was interested in cricket only insofar as he could make a living from it. Before the war, he switched clubs and quit wicketkeeping whenever he saw a main chance arise. He was famously cocksure. The first time he faced O'Reilly, in a St

George–Petersham match, Barnes batted well, later walking up to the great man in the showers and saying, 'You bowled very well out there, Tiger.' According to Arthur Morris, O'Reilly 'just about swallowed the soap'.

In 1938 Barnes had been the baby of Bradman's Ashes tour, but a broken wrist on the outward voyage floored him for most of the series. In the last Sheffield Shield season before the war, Barnes averaged 75 for New South Wales, persuading himself and his sceptical parents that cricket might offer fame and, more to the point, a path to fortune.

Army life was never going to suit Barnes, but still, newly married, he joined up in 1942 and was posted to an armoured division in the backwater of Greta. He had his uniforms tailored to order. Like Sam Loxton, Barnes liked the sense of security that a tank promised. The reality was equally underwhelming.

'The only thing I saw when I arrived at Greta that had any connection with a tank was a water-tank,' he would write. The individualist hated the boredom, the route marches, the discomfort, the pettiness. He was also prone to black depression. 'The inactivity of army life,' he said, 'got me down badly.' He busied himself playing in army football and cricket games, and befriended the great golfer Norman von Nida, an accomplice as much as a mate. Both were square pegs in round holes.

Barnes got a release from the army to join a firm making tank and aircraft parts. Then he worked with his brother Horrie and von Nida manufacturing mosquito oil to send to New Guinea. With O'Reilly and McCabe, Barnes taught American soldiers cricket at a camp at Warwick Farm racecourse. For Barnes, aside from a short tour of northern Australia playing for an air force team, the war involved more business, more wheeling and dealing. 'I won't say that I don't like money,' he said, 'but there's more to it than that. I like to pit my wits against those of other people.'

Through the endless summer of 1945–46, the disgruntled Servicemen began to detect, or imagine, a bias against them. It was confirmed when the Australian selectors picked a team to tour New Zealand for the first Test cricket after the war. Though exhausted, they were hoping to make the transition, like Collins's men in 1919, from AIF cricket into the Test team. The tour would be a low-key resumption, driven by Australia's obligation to its neighbour after the cancellation of a tour planned before the war. New Zealand had never played a Test against Australia, despite its first-class teams hosting tours since the 1800s.

The men from the Victory Tests were dismayed by the selection. Hassett was not even vice-captain, let alone captain. Miller was the only other member chosen. No Whitington, no Sismey, no Cristofani – none of the doughty cricketers who had drawn 2–2 with a virtual England Test team on English soil just a few months earlier.

Conspiracy theories took hold. The most unlucky omission, it seemed, was Pepper, the spin-bowling all-rounder widely acknowledged as Test class. Whitington attributed the selectors' decision to a clash between Pepper and Bradman in the Services XI's match in Adelaide. Pepper, suspecting the umpires were conspiring to keep Bradman at the wicket, cried after a rejected appeal: 'What do I have to do to get this fellow out?'

Pepper was asked to apologise. He did, but his letter was mislaid. Snubbed for the New Zealand tour, believing he would never play for Australia, he went to England to play as a professional. Whitington wrote that Pepper 'sensed the existence of what might be called "a thing" concerning those who had served abroad. It was difficult to draw any other conclusion.'

If there was a 'thing', the finger was pointed at Bradman, who helped select the New Zealand tourists. Before the war, Bradman was the undisputed driving force in Australian cricket. It would soon become clear that nothing, not even after a seven-year break, had changed.

*

Bradman was especially close to one of the England players in the Victory Tests. Walter 'Robbie' Robins, the captain of Middlesex, had sent some of his family to live with the Bradmans during the war. Bradman was godfather to one of Robins's sons. Between 1929 and 1937, Robins had played nineteen Tests, scoring 612 runs at 26.60 and taking 64 wickets at 27.46. Jack Fingleton painted this memorable portrait: 'He bustles about and barks out orders like a sergeant-major, belittling the opposition to his men, but . . . he was not impressive as a skipper, nor was he ever a capable Test performer.' Bradman, however, loved him dearly. In 1938, when Bradman had broken a bone in his foot, he recuperated at the gabled, red-brick home of Robins and his wife at Burnham, near Maidenhead, spending many pleasurable hours playing bridge and piano. It was often remarked how closely the two perky fair-haired bantamweights resembled each other.

From Adelaide during the Victory Test at Lord's, Bradman sent a telegram to the Australian Services team: 'Tell Robbie I hope he does as well in this game as he did at Lord's over Whitsun 1938.' In that match, between Australia and Robins's MCC, Bradman had made 278, Robins a duck.

The telegram was a gentle reminder, if one were needed, that the Don was watching.

War had interrupted Bradman at the absolute peak of his batting powers. Of course, he would never surpass the 974 Test runs in his magical 1930 – nobody else has surpassed it either – but eight years on he was a more complete batsman. The tour of 1938, his first as captain, was his best as a batsman: in all first-class matches, he averaged 115.66, compared with 98.66 in 1930 and 84.16 in 1934. In the Test series, his 103 at Headingley on a fiendish wicket was rated higher than most of his double- and triple-centuries. Yet just as Bradman had entertained visions of cricket's holy grail – an undefeated tour of England – his hopes had ended in injury and crushing defeat at The Oval. Up to then, the tourists were undefeated, but in that fifth Test they crashed spectacularly, losing by an innings and 574 runs, still a world-record margin, and were defeated again at the 'Festival' match at Scarborough Fair.

After recovering at Robins's house, in the 1939–40 Australian summer Bradman scored 1000 runs in a Sheffield Shield season for the first time, averaging 132.75. That season was, his biographer Irving Rosenwater wrote, 'a great summer for cricket – but for the sight of volunteers flocking to the recruiting centres, workers turning themselves over to the production of war equipment, the rationing of petrol, and the incidence of fear, rumours and strung nerves.'

Those strung nerves spurred a last gasp of enthusiasm for cricket and for Bradman. Fearing they might never see him bat again, record crowds packed the grounds. When his South Australians played in Sydney, the £4915 gate was unprecedented. Even without Bradman's presence, Sydney's three games grossed £9000 in gate receipts, nearly four times the previous year's.

Bradman was not blind to the real state of things. By June 1940, he would write, he 'felt the urge of all patriotic citizens to do my duty in a sterner sphere, and enlisted as a member of aircrew for the RAAF. At that time the supply of manpower far exceeded the number of aircraft available and training facilities. I could not be called up for some months but was placed on the reserve.'

He was nearly thirty-two years old, and by several orders of magnitude the nation's greatest sporting celebrity. The Adelaide Lord Mayor, Arthur Barrett, who had flown in World War I, said: 'Let us hope now that Don will get centuries in the air as readily as he got them on the ground.' Even if there was little chance Bradman would see combat, he wanted to underscore how seriously he took the war. The 1940–41 Ashes series was cancelled, and he wrote to Canon E.S. Hughes, the president of the Victorian Cricket Association and the minister at Bradman's wedding to Jessie Menzies in 1932, that all high-level sport should be suspended out of respect for the fighting. Not everyone agreed, and a national controversy erupted; parliamentarians spoke for and against Bradman's proposition. Could sport during war be seen as a frivolity, almost an offence? Or could it boost morale? Trying to steer a middle path, Bradman said he would only play in 'patriotic' fundraisers for the war effort.

After passing his medical, he was given the rank of lieutenant and attended training classes. When it was clear that he was surplus to the RAAF's requirements, he transferred to the army in October 1940 as a student at the School of Physical and Recreational Training at Frankston, in Victoria, joining his former Test teammate Chuck Fleetwood-Smith. The plan was for Bradman to go to the Near East as a divisional supervisor of physical training. When he wrote about being shuffled around the services, Bradman complied with the fiction that he was an ordinary 32-year-old for whom the military was trying to find an appropriate place. He said he genuinely wanted to serve, and made no mention of whether he was, instead, being protected from more onerous duties. As events would soon make clear, he had a strong motive to portray himself as someone willing to go anywhere for the war effort.

In the summer of 1940–41 he played in fundraisers only. At Richmond, where he played against the Fire Brigade, five private firms pitched in 2/6 for every run he scored: he made 109 in five hours.

From that point, though, his health went into a sudden decline. Although the army had passed him fully fit in October, during his training at Frankston he suffered 'muscular trouble which had bothered me on and off before'. Then, after the match at Richmond, he had his eyes tested. They were below par. He scored 18 runs in his next four innings. Was it that Bradman could not play cricket at half-throttle? Could he only concentrate fully if he was playing for keeps? At first, he blamed his eyes, saying he 'couldn't see the ball at all'. Suffering fibrositis, a nervous muscular complaint, he went into hospital on three occasions. He ran in an All-Services Athletics meeting in Melbourne on 14 February 1941, but then asked to be taken to the Repatriation General Hospital in Keswick, Adelaide, where he could be closer to Jessie, who was entering her last months of pregnancy.

On 2 April 1941, eleven weeks after going into full-time duty at Frankston, Bradman was taken off the army's roster. Five days later he was placed on the retired list, a week later his daughter Shirley was born with mild cerebral palsy, and three weeks after that he was given indefinite sick leave from the armed services. 'The only hope of cure,' he wrote, 'was a long convalescence and complete rest.'

He and Jessie went to their home town, Bowral, where, gulping the champagne air of her parents' farm, he had recovered from a life-threatening bout of pneumonia in 1934 and 1935. 'Anyone who has suffered the excruciating pain of muscular ailments will understand how utterly immobilizing it can be,' he wrote of his fibrositis. 'At one period I found myself quite incapable of even lifting my right arm. It was impossible even to do my own hair. I lost all feeling in the thumb and index finger of my right hand. It never returned – even when I played Test cricket.'

By the time the Allied forces evacuated Dunkirk, when Bill Edrich was suffering the double-vision of death in the morning and village cricket in the afternoon, when Lindsay Hassett was sitting on unexploded mines and Keith Miller was contemplating taking to the air, Don Bradman's war was already over. In June 1941, he was formally discharged.

After recuperating in Bowral, Bradman moved back to Adelaide to resume his job in the sharebroking offices of Harry Hodgetts. Hodgetts, a member of the South Australian Cricket Association and the state's delegate to the Board of Control for International Cricket in Australia, had lured Bradman from Sydney in 1934 with the offer of a career outside cricket. Bradman never believed in full-time professional cricket; having seen it in the English counties, he felt that it sapped the juice out of what should be a pastime. The remorseless intensity with which he played the game might, he felt, be diluted if he had to play it for a living. Hankering for a professional life that had nothing to do with cricket or its offshoots of writing, broadcasting and selling sporting equipment, he had learnt the sharebroking trade under Hodgetts.

Bradman's move to Adelaide had, for the SACA, killed two birds with one stone. It gave them the sport's greatest drawcard and also a captain to supplant the militant fifteen-season leader and champion of South Australian cricket, Victor Richardson, who had challenged the administrators' authority too often for their comfort. But the backroom mode of his recruitment and the perceived betrayal of the state's greatest sporting hero made Bradman a divisive figure in Adelaide, a mercenary working for one establishment faction against another.

After his discharge from the army, Bradman's return to civilian work in 1943 did not give him great solace, and if he ever suffered depression, it was then. 'They were dark days,' he wrote. 'Cricket, then or in the future, never crossed my mind. I am quite certain that the over-exertion of my earlier cricketing days was exacting retribution in full measure.'

In Sydney, Bradman's journalist friend A.G. 'Johnnie' Moyes heard 'stories that he had broken down very seriously in health'. Bradman wrote to Moyes, 'I'm good only for a job as an ARP Warden'. Moyes detected 'a depth of sadness behind the words . . . That he would be able to play first-class cricket again seemed impossible.'

Nonetheless, Bradman was well enough to play some golf and tennis in 1943, and on 11 May, after nearly a decade in the city, he was elected a member of the Adelaide Stock Exchange. Work was cushioning him from the disappointment of his army discharge and the likely end of his cricket career.

The last year of the war was, however, his most traumatic. He had been returning to health and acceptance in Adelaide society, being elected president of the Commonwealth Club of Adelaide, hosting functions with Dame Enid Lyons and Prime Minister John Curtin, and helping to raise £140000 as honorary secretary and organiser of the Gowrie Scholarship Fund, which had ties with Lord's. But in July 1945, Bradman's social and professional world almost collapsed around him. An affidavit was lodged in the Adelaide Bankruptcy Court showing that Harry Hodgetts had fraudulently ripped £83000 out of his sharebroking firm. As many as 238 unsecured creditors were owed £103000. Hodgetts would go to jail some years later. Bradman, described in the affidavit as a 'former employee' of the firm, was owed £762.

In his autobiography, Bradman was vague about the details of Hodgetts' scam, and indeed about Hodgetts' responsibility.

> For me personally there suddenly came a disaster. Overnight the firm by which I was employed went bankrupt. In the midst of a long struggle to regain my health, and through no fault of my own, I became the victim of another's misfortune. There was no time for reflection. I had to make an immediate decision as affecting my whole life. Despite the unprecedented difficulties there were trustworthy friends whose loyalty was responsible for my decision to commence my own business. I wasn't really fit to carry the strain of the next few months. It would be idle to try to explain the numerous troubles which had to be surmounted.

What he was referring to was how quickly he fell on his feet. Don Bradman and Company opened in Grenfell Street, in the same building as Hodgetts' firm. It inherited many of Hodgetts' clients. Bradman also took over Hodgetts' seat as SACA delegate to the Board of Control.

While there was never any proof that Bradman had known of or been involved in Hodgetts' swindle, it rankled with some in the Adelaide financial establishment that he benefited so immediately.

Bradman's application to join the Royal Adelaide Golf Club was at first turned down, and he never enjoyed full professional recognition from many in those circles.

At the end of the war, he remained unsure whether he would ever return to Test cricket. He played for South Australia against the Services team, making 112 after surviving Pepper's appeals, but was unavailable to tour New Zealand. As the incumbent Australian captain, he was part of the selection committee that put forward Bill Brown's name ahead of Hassett's as captain. Brown, the neat Queenslander who had been Australia's leading opening batsman before serving as an RAAF flight lieutenant in the Pacific, was a favourite of Bradman, who had argued for his selection ahead of Jack Fingleton on the 1934 tour and for his retention, after poor domestic form, in 1938. On both tours Brown had vindicated Bradman's faith. Given Hassett's charismatic leadership of the Services team in arduous circumstances, the choice of Brown alarmed the Services team; Whitington wondered if Bradman wanted to puncture any of the remaining *esprit de corps* among those who had fought and played in England and India. Brown was popular, but Hassett's credentials as captain were stronger – perhaps too strong for his own good. Did Bradman see him as a threat? Did he want to stop Hassett building a power base, in the event of Bradman himself returning to Test cricket? Overlooking Hassett as Test captain in 1945 was, Whitington thought, a prelude to the 'disgusting ingratitude' that saw Bradman and the Board only narrowly endorsing Hassett as captain in 1949, this time ahead of Arthur Morris.

In 1946, the captaincy was one facet of a deeper undercurrent in cricket. After the war, how was the game to be played? Was the 'cavalier' approach of Hassett's Services team the decent way to pay respect to the magnitude of what had taken place between 1939 and 1945?

Some thought it was, and should continue to be so. The strongest faction of those thinkers comprised English Test players such as Hammond, Edrich, Washbrook, Compton and Hutton. The cream of English cricket, spanning pre- and postwar eras, had played in the Victory Tests. They were citizens of a country that was embarking on building a welfare state, a new experiment in fairness that promised to shake off old ways. The crunch of repaying the war debt had still to set in; depressing postwar austerity didn't arrive until 1947. The democratic socialist plans of a National Health Service and public-owned transport were still in prospect. In foreign policy, the hawks were in retreat, and the reality of a 'cold' war with Russia, the erstwhile ally, as chief threat and enemy, had not arrived. England was yearning for a bright new dawn.

Australia, meanwhile, had a different situation off and on the field. In no way had it suffered like Britain. Its alliance with the United States, and the inevitable worldwide demand for its primary resources, promised economic prosperity. The government was stable under the Labor Party of Curtin and Ben Chifley. This comparative innocence extended to the cricket field, where the prevailing mood was to pick up where the game had left off in 1940.

When it came to who had served in the war, the cricket situation in Australia was complicated. It was not that there was a 'Services' faction and a 'non-Services' faction. The players in Hassett's Services XI were only drawn from a fraction of those who had fought. Those who had ended the war in the Pacific theatre, for example, had not been part of the Services XI. Brown, as mentioned above, flew for the RAAF in New Guinea, but was not in the Services team. Arthur Morris, Ray Lindwall, Colin McCool, Doug Ring and Ian Johnson were also in the Pacific and unavailable for the Services team. Loxton, along with Barnes and fellow top-liners Ron Hamence, Don Tallon, Ron Saggers, Ern Toshack and Bill Johnston, had enlisted in the military but had not served outside Australia. With these different categories of cricketer, there wasn't a clear demarcation between those who had 'fought' and those who had not.

The result of this was to limit what resentment existed against Bradman. No doubt Whitington, Pepper and the Services XI outcasts felt it most strongly. There was certainly something glaring about his record. For Australia's greatest sportsman, considered one of the fittest, the only periods in which his health failed were in 1934–35 and in 1941–45. The latter illness, and its timing, might seem a more striking fact now than at the time. In 1945, such murmurings as there were about how Bradman had spent the war were confined to a small number of ex-servicemen who were mostly shunted to the outer of Australian cricket. Those who had fought on the front line and played in the Services team and knew what was good for them, such as Hassett and Miller, did their best to suppress whatever resentment they felt. Hassett became a hard, pragmatic cricketer, a pared-down version of the prewar dasher. Miller had less self-discipline, but only in rare flare-ups would he let his true feelings show.

The rest were just happy to be playing cricket again. On the 1945–46 tour to New Zealand, Miller became close friends with Ray Lindwall, as adept at batting, bowling fast or chiming into the backline for his rugby league club, Canterbury-Bankstown. Muscular and self-contained, Lindwall could, like Miller, have chosen stardom in summer or winter sports. In those days, multi-sport heroes were not uncommon. Richardson, in Adelaide, was at one time a high-level representative in seven sports: cricket, football, golf, lacrosse, tennis, swimming and baseball. He continued all seven through adulthood, often going to training for two sports a night, seven nights a week. By the end of World War II, such athletes were beginning to specialise – Miller, Lindwall and Morris chose cricket. By the 1960s, the multi-sportsman was a dying breed. In all, 171 first-class cricketers have also played league-level Australian Rules football – the last to do so was Nick Jewell, a

Victorian who played one AFL game for Richmond in 1997.

After signing up, Lindwall's term in New Guinea hadn't started well. In a train arriving at Finch Haven, he had been with a schoolmaster friend who had handed a letter to a porter, hoping to get it home uncensored. A sergeant saw the letter handed over and apprehended Lindwall.

'Despite protests of my innocence I was placed under arrest and eventually brought before the CO,' Lindwall said. 'Part of my punishment entailed guard duty for fifteen of the first sixteen nights after arrival in New Guinea. I soon discovered that peering through the darkness for Japanese intruders was far from an ideal existence. They paid frequent visits and one morning five Australian soldiers, who shared a tent, were found with their throats cut.'

Ordered to shoot on sight anyone who moved, Lindwall was rattled. He nearly shot a friend, Norman Aylward, mistaking him for a Japanese soldier.

On a leave trip to Sydney in December 1944, Lindwall represented a Services XI against New South Wales; he was carved up by Sid Barnes, who was taking up a spectator's challenge of five pounds for the fastest century of the match. On his return to New Guinea, Lindwall came up against Arthur Morris in a softball match involving the Americans, one of whom slugged the last available ball so far it looked like it would disappear into the jungle, ending the game. Lindwall ran backwards with the ball's flight and, Morris says admiringly, 'took one of the greatest catches the Americans had ever seen. They couldn't believe it.'

When Hassett's Services team lost by an innings to New South Wales in 1945–46, a fateful cricket meeting took place. Miller hit 105 out of 204 in the Services' first innings, and among the bowlers was Lindwall. Immediately, Lindwall said, 'began a close friendship which has never been disturbed by even the smallest ripple.'

'I think I can claim to know him better than most people,' said Lindwall, who would room with Miller throughout the 1948 tour. 'The popular conception of Keith is that of a rather devil-may-care swashbuckling type of individual who sails happily through life without a thought for tomorrow. Having been associated with him for so long I would suggest that Keith is far more shy and self-conscious than most people realise and I am sure nearly all his mannerisms on the field spring from that.'

The tour of New Zealand delivered the greatest happiness many of the young men had known. Lindwall, who had gone through the war mostly teetotal, was given an education in the restorative powers of beer by Tiger O'Reilly, who was taking his last tour as a player.

> Bill O'Reilly talked to me on the thorny question of alcohol. I know that some people frown upon drink as something to be avoided at all costs. A few allow their objections to become almost a mania. My experience is that a few beers – beers, mark you, not spirits – are a definite help to fast bowlers, especially in hot countries. Before I went to New Zealand I had never tasted alcohol but, soon after the tour opened, Bill asked me whether I was still a teetotaller.
>
> 'Never had anything stronger than lemonade,' I told him.
>
> 'In that case I think you should start now,' he countered.

O'Reilly told him that beer during long days in the field would give him 'something to sweat off': 'If you haven't a little surplus to perspire away, you'll weaken your constitutional strength. All the best fast bowlers have taken a glass of beer or two and, as long as you make certain not to indulge in excess, it won't harm you. I suggest you have a couple of glasses a day. Try it and see.'

Lindwall 'hated the taste at first but I followed Bill's advice and have never regretted doing so . . . Whether the effect was physical or mental I cannot say but my energy and stamina seemed to increase.'

Ian Johnson, from Victoria, was among those who treated the New Zealand tour as one long celebration. The end of the war had found Johnson drinking whiskey in a slit trench on the South Pacific island of Morotai. VJ Day was a Friday, which happened to be grog day. 'What was I going to do about my cricket?' asked Johnson, who had struggled for five years after his 1935–36 debut to establish himself as an off-spinning all-rounder in the Victorian team. He had just cemented his place when the war broke out, but distinguished himself greatly as a Beaufighter pilot and flight instructor, winning a Commendation for Valuable Service in the Air and rising to the rank of flight lieutenant. From the vantage point of August 1945, though, as far as his cricket future went, 'I didn't have a clue. I had much more definite ideas as to what I was going to do with that bottle of whiskey.'

A few months later, Johnson was picked to tour New Zealand. Bradman had been good friends with Johnson's father, William, one of the Test selectors before the war. Ian Johnson would be a favourite of Bradman's into the 1948 tour and well beyond, when he became captain of Australia, ahead of Miller, in 1954. Because Johnson's playing record was only intermittently Test quality and several grades below Miller's, and because he was Bradman's first choice as spinner in 1948, he would be characterised, by some fellow players, as a Bradman pet.

The first postwar Australian team won their Test and four first-class games easily. Johnson, along with Miller, Lindwall and left-armer Ern Toshack, entered Test cricket at Wellington. Most of the team had seen service, and they flung themselves into their cricket with the joy of just-released prisoners. With a 'couldn't-care-less attitude', as Johnson put it, they 'partied' their way through New Zealand, 'a gay band to whom Test cricket was a pre-war dream'.

Six years of war seemed to have put sport into its proper place. Even international cricket was fun, for men who had witnessed its opposite. 'Cricket was very much a game after the intensity of five and more years of war,' Johnson said. 'It was a game to be enjoyed and, by golly, we did enjoy it. I doubt if first-class cricket before or since has been played in the same light-hearted atmosphere. It was a good time first, last and always.'

It was a good time, however, with a short lifespan. From Australia, Bradman was studying the team's form. Most exciting was the super-fast bowling of Miller and Lindwall, which scared the New Zealanders so much they inquired about wearing helmets. (The 'fun' side of the game had its limits!) As a child, Lindwall had been taken to the Sydney Test of the Bodyline series. His imagination was captured not by Stan McCabe's wonderful innings of 187 not out, but by Harold Larwood's express bowling. Lindwall went away and modelled his run-up and action on the Nottingham great. O'Reilly, his mentor at the St George club, urged him to bowl as fast as he could. The boy reminded the Tiger of Larwood. In fact, Lindwall reminded everyone who saw him of Larwood, and very soon he would be giving Bradman an idea for how he could finally avenge the insult of Bodyline, which had only grown sharper with the passage of time. Australia's two series of postwar joy, the non-Bradman larks in England and New Zealand, were over. Bradman cricket was about to resume.

2

'A BLOODY FINE
WAY TO START'

Since Australian representative teams first toured England in 1878, they drew great crowds. At times English umpires had found the early Australians querulous, sometimes they had been disgracefully uncouth, and on two celebrated occasions professional English players had refused to play them because the Australians took a large share of gate money while enjoying the social privileges of 'amateurs'. But the bottom line was that when Australian teams toured England, the cash registers were busy. It was said that W.G. Grace's drawing power had built half the pavilions in England, and when Grace entered the long twilight of his career, the new drawcard for cricket, the big show that put all the counties in the black, was a visit from an Australian XI.

This had, to a degree, enabled the Australian teams to dictate the terms of engagement. English cricket's status quo, and business model, rested on professional, working-class players doing the hard work of bowling, coaching, field preparation, umpiring and, if they were very good, batting, for a working man's wage, while amateurs, or gentlemen, who did not need to play cricket for a living, could bear the standard of leadership and 'fair play'. Amateurs only bowled if they particularly wanted to, and the first amateur Test team to tour Australia, in 1878–79, took two Yorkshire professionals, Tom Emmett and George Ulyett, to do most of the bowling in the hot sun for them. Since the organisation of the counties in the 1870s, which took power from the old professional 'All-England XIs' who had toured like a travelling circus, the county clubs were ruled by amateur committees and led by amateur captains. Marylebone, based at Thomas Lord's ground in north London, became the dominant amateur club and law-making authority, while professional cricket maintained a stronghold in Nottingham. The England XI was led invariably by an amateur, except briefly in the 1870s and 1880s when some all-professional teams had toured Australia. England teams gradually mixed the amateurs and professionals more, but the two castes changed clothes and ate in different rooms and travelled in different classes. An amateur and his professional batting partner might enter the game by separate gates and only meet on the pitch. This did not mean amateurs were not paid; Grace, an amateur, was the highest-paid cricketer ever, until the Indian godheads of the present day. But amateurs secured their payment under the fiction of 'expenses', often receiving far more cash in hand than the professionals, who were allocated a meagre set rate.

Since Australian teams had been coming to England, their ambiguous status had challenged what David Kynaston calls the 'class-based apartheid' of amateur-professional cricket. Australian teams were 'gentlemen', in that they held other jobs outside cricket. But they were self-funded tourists conducting their ventures as financial speculations that would live or die on how much gate money they could attract. They lunched in the gentlemen's pavilions and were feted by royalty; yet they made more money than nearly all the Englishmen they played against. Because they divvied up some of that money with the county clubs, they were able to maintain this hybrid status for their own profit.

From 1905, this arrangement was put under pressure by Australian administrators, who formed a Board and eventually seized control of the cash raised on England tours. In 1912, when six leading Australian players boycotted the tour, the seven-year-old Board of Control gained its victory. From then until 1977, Australian cricketers toured England as poorly paid Board servants. When players had owned the tours from 1878 to 1909, their profit share had been as high as £900, or enough to buy two or three houses in good suburbs of Sydney. From 1912 until the 1960s, their tour fee ranged from £400 to £800. By the 1960s, they were receiving, in real terms, a pittance, not even as much in nominal terms as the tourists of sixty to eighty years earlier.

The dismantling of player power did not mean players had no power. Theoretically individuals could still make hay, although none was really able to seize the opportunities offered by advertisers, sponsors, media organisations and other sources of income until Don Bradman. With Bradman, since 1930, power derived from the same base as for the early Australian XIs – but it was *his* pulling power, not Australia's. *He* made the counties rich. He profited, becoming the highest-paid cricketer since Grace. His popularity with the public also made him the most powerful.

The story of the Invincibles is a revelation of Bradman's influence over the lawmakers and governing bodies of cricket. That power developed during the 1930s, but back then he was *primus inter pares*. Australia boasted O'Reilly, Clarrie Grimmett, Stan McCabe, Bill Ponsford and Bill Woodfull, as well as Bradman. England had Hammond, Jack Hobbs, Herbert Sutcliffe, Maurice Tate, Larwood, Bill Voce, Verity and Farnes. These were stellar times. By 1946, on the other hand, Bradman was virtually the last man standing, the last of the titans and the biggest of all. For those populations who could remember or imagine Test cricket, Bradman *was* the game. O'Reilly's knee hadn't survived the New Zealand tour. Hammond, forty-three, was the last of the England legends still active. Cricket administrators in Australia and England knew that if the game was to resume on a firm financial footing, it needed its main attraction. This put Bradman in a bargaining position that he was not the kind of man to resist. It also quelled, and put into the margins, any mutterings about his wartime activities. Cricket, simply, needed Bradman.

Even when not playing, Bradman remained the centre of gravity of Australian and world cricket. During the Victory Tests, the Services team manager, Keith Johnson, had lobbied Lord's for an MCC Test tour of Australia in 1946–47. England would be playing home series against India and South Africa in 1946 and 1947, but the great rivalry, ever since 1876–77, was England versus Australia. Nothing else compared. Knowing how serious an Ashes contest was, and how eagerly anticipated, Lord's told Johnson that 1947–48 was more feasible. England wanted to be certain it would put up a competitive team. But when Bradman took Harry Hodgetts' Board seat, two of his closest friends, the English captains Gubby Allen and Walter Robins, became Australia's representatives on the International Cricket Conference – still, at that stage, a body comprised of Englishmen. Bradman told them he wanted the 1946–47 tour. At the ICC's meeting in January 1946, Allen and Robins swung it.

Bradman still held the power, but was he going to play again? He portrayed himself as a reluctant but dutiful invalid. 'Gradually hope returned that I might be fit to play against England the following summer,' he wrote. 'Still, there is a vast gap between reasonable health and the muscular tone required for international cricket.' His doctors told him he 'would be foolish to play'.

He didn't even plan to play for his club, Kensington, in 1945–46, but relented, telling confidants he might play for club and state but not country. For South Australia he made two half-centuries against Queensland and a century against Hassett's Services team, when Whitington said he 'batted better than anyone I have seen since I last saw Bradman', notwithstanding his difficulties with Pepper.

He was swayed, he said, to play in 1946–47 by Jessie, who said 'it would be a pity if my son John grew up without having seen me play in Test cricket'. He felt duty-bound to get cricket onto a good postwar footing, but was not contemplating anything beyond one home season.

Indeed, Bradman may not have even finished that one season if not for a most controversial on-field moment.

The first game of England's tour was against South Australia in Adelaide. Their squad contained the core of the Victory Test participants: Hammond, Hutton, Washbrook, Edrich and Compton, backed up by the Yorkshire amateur all-rounder Norman Yardley, the hearty Kent wicketkeeper Godfrey Evans, and Surrey's broad-shouldered Alec Bedser. Most of the team were youngish men who had been protected from front-line combat. Their cricket careers having been interrupted, they were as eager as the Australians to make up for lost time.

The teams at Adelaide would be led by the two colossi of the 1930s. Initially, Hammond and Bradman provided an underwhelming sight. The 43-year-old Hammond shambled out into the sun, bulky and morose beneath his fedora. His marriage was breaking down and he was estranged from his team, travelling separately in his own Jaguar.

If Hammond had expanded into a maudlin hulk, Bradman was a thin shade of his old self. When they saw him, the Englishmen were stunned. Since they had last laid eyes on him in 1938 – carried off The Oval with a broken foot – he had lost weight and hair, and during the Adelaide match he was grimacing from gastric pains. Photographer-journalist Viv Jenkins said: 'When we first saw him he looked too ill ever to play again'. Compton said: 'Some of us wondered whether or not he was due for a nursing-home rather than a cricket pitch.'

It was a shock to Compton, who had idolised Bradman. 'He

was, as it were, the most merciless of entertainers of a crowd. When I was little more than a schoolboy in the early 'thirties and he was scoring his centuries with relentless brilliance, then I hero-worshipped him.'

Throughout the 1946 spring, Bradman seemed ready to give cricket away. The tourists scored 5/506 in Adelaide and Bradman made what he called a 'very subdued' 76 and 3. 'I was a shadow of myself, physically, mentally and in cricket form. One journalist wrote of my play, "I have seen the ghost of a great cricketer and ghosts seldom come back to life." Such comments were scarcely helpful . . . I needed encouragement, not doubts.'

Bradman's comeback had an ally in the local umpiring contingent. Pepper's unavailing appeals in Adelaide the previous summer were held by many to indicate a kindly conspiracy by which some umpires, particularly Adelaide's Jack Scott, concerned that Bradman was one failure from retirement, were keen to give him every help in warding it off.

Hammond's 1946–47 venture was tagged the 'Goodwill Tour', but the tag represented hope more than reality. Australia was ready to resume Ashes cricket, but England came with equivocations. The 'goodwill' came in the form of a concession from Lord's to Bradman and Australia. If England had not toured in 1946–47, he may well have retired from cricket. This in turn would douse England's hopes of having him there in 1948, the essential ingredient, financially, to getting the counties and MCC back on their feet. So one thing led to another – if you want Bradman in 1948, come give Australia's coffers a fillip in 1946–47 – but the England players were unable to make a vibrant Ashes contest.

If Hammond was looking for England's 'goodwill' to be repaid with a new postwar kindness, Bradman soon disabused him. He made himself available for the first Test tentatively, took the field gingerly, and, on the first morning in Brisbane, showed no more goodwill to England than he had in the 1930s.

Bradman won the toss and batted. Out walked the chancer,

Barnes, and the nicest guy in cricket, Arthur Morris.

No Australian batsman, not even Bradman or Hassett or Barnes, lost as many runs to the war as Morris. In September 1939, the sandy-haired left-hander, born in Bondi, raised single-handedly by his schoolteacher father in the Hunter Valley after his mother walked out, had made a stunning entry into big cricket. He scored an unprecedented two centuries on debut for New South Wales as a teenager, and was ready to dominate England's new-ball attack in 1940–41. He was also a vibrant five-eighth, playing rugby union for Combined High Schools and St George. The NSW coach Johnny Wallace, who would coach Morris in the Combined Services rugby team, believed him the best in his position in Australia.

When all that was put on the backburner, Morris signed up without hesitation, leaving his job as a clerk in the Prosecutions Branch at Sydney Town Hall to serve as an army clerk in northern New South Wales, in the Movement Control Unit.

'We were moving troops, supplies and equipment around, and it was the hardest work I've done in my life,' says Morris, now one of the last two survivors of the Invincibles. 'The town of Casino was the last railhead before Brisbane. The Japanese were knocking off our ships, so everything was coming through Casino. A sergeant and I were doing the lot, twelve hours on and twelve off, climbing onto the trucks and reconstituting goods trains and advising Brisbane.'

Like Lindsay Hassett, Morris was content to be a non-commissioned man. Having worked for the government before the war, Morris continued to earn a public service salary on top of his army private's wage, so 'I didn't care about any promotions – I was earning officer's pay.'

Morris also had a healthy disrespect for the brass.

'Typically, just as the crisis was passing in Casino, the army brought in dozens more blokes to help us, headed by an officer. I was working under a sergeant, who told them all to piss off. They wouldn't be any better at it than we were. So they went and played bingo and saw girls in Casino while we kept on doing the work.'

By 1944, as the New Guinea campaign intensified, Morris was sent to Townsville, then Port Moresby. In the north Queensland town he met up with one of his future teammates, the tall, bluff, good-humoured leg spinner Doug Ring. In 1948, Ring would be one of those who made up for a lack of opportunities on the cricket field with his gifts at singing, socialising and morale-boosting.

'Doug and I were waiting for a pub to open one afternoon, with five hundred other blokes. Doug noticed that there were only about fifty men waiting at a smaller pub across the road. Suddenly the shout came, "It's on!" The smaller pub had been opened and everyone stampeded across. I was about to follow them when Doug grabbed me and said, "Wait, this one will open in a few minutes." We were the only ones who waited, and were able to sneak in first. We'd got our five schooners lined up before anyone knew what was going on.'

The streetwise Ring wasn't the only future teammate Morris would meet during the campaign. Bill Brown was flying DC-3s at Lei, in New Guinea, where Morris sailed on the *Canberra* with the Movement Control Unit on 14 January 1944. He went to Finch Haven, where he left a wartime secret.

'Soon after we got there, the Americans came in. You should have seen the way they looked after themselves: beautiful fresh bread, asparagus, enormous numbers of cigars.' An avid cigar smoker, Morris managed to purloin a few boxes. Before he could smoke them, he was told he was being moved to Lei. 'I buried a lot of those cigars – I wasn't going to let them go! – but I never got back to Finch Haven. As far as I know, they're still there.'

Morris would remain in New Guinea until April 1945. His war was not, in his opinion, a hard one.

I saw a bit of bombing when the Japanese planes came over at night, but not much. It wasn't a difficult life for us compared with front-line troops. Especially when the Americans joined

us, we had a soft life. My only gripe was that when leave came
up, I was never allowed to go home. Being unmarried and a
private, I never had enough points to qualify for a trip home.
Instead of sending me back to Sydney for a break, the bastards
sent me to Lei!

What had seemed such a glittering career in cricket and football
was, he thought, bound to be a victim of the conflict.

'The whole time,' Morris says, 'you thought your cricket career
was over. The Japanese were invading us, after all. It looked like
the war would go on for another ten years. Nobody knew when it
would end, so the feeling was it would go on for years and years.'

After seven years of waiting... Morris lasted eleven minutes,
caught by Hammond off Bedser. At 1/9 Bradman was at the wicket,
drained of his old zest. He scratched his way to 28 before chopping
a wide ball from Voce to Jack Ikin at second slip. The English team
were so certain it was out they didn't appeal immediately, instead
clapping and converging on the bowler and fieldsman. Only when
Bradman remained, looking to umpire George Borwick, did the
Englishmen find it necessary to ask the obvious. Bradman stood,
uncertain whether he had jammed the ball into the turf. Borwick
looked to Jack Scott at square leg. The South Australian umpire,
the same who had refused Pepper's appeals in Adelaide, said he
could not give it out. To the Englishmen's outrage, Bradman was
reprieved.

Miller, a startled witness, was one Australian who thought the
Ikin catch was beyond dispute. But, Colin McCool remarked, 'as
[Miller] at the time was sitting next to me in the pavilion, that's
the biggest mystery of the lot.'

Hammond waddled up to Bradman and growled, 'That's a
bloody fine way to start.' Hammond, at forty-three, would prove
unable to recapture his greatness, but after his reprieve, Bradman

went on to make 187 out of Australia's 645. Bill Edrich wrote, and many believed, that Bradman might have retired if he'd been given out on 28, but McCool disputed this: 'I know Bradman pretty well and I can't think he would ever have pulled up his swag and cleared off just on the strength of one failure.'

Bradman's refusal to walk was more significant for the tone it set. It was certainly within the rules of the game to wait for the umpires to decide. It was even within the spirit – at least, as the game was played in the 1930s. But this was to be the new postwar cricket, and Bradman, who hadn't seen action and spent most of the war selling stocks, playing golf and getting himself onto committees, was taking the field as grimly as ever, bearing a grudge against Hammond for not declaring until 7/903 in 1938, and against England for what they had done in Bodyline. The war seemed just a blip in his long campaign for payback.

The English players were crestfallen, not simply because they didn't get Bradman out cheaply, but because he had snuffed out all hopes of a new, Victory-Test spirit. Compton said the entire series was damaged by Bradman's not walking.

> Hammond was very angry about the decision, and in my view quite justifiably. Bradman obviously realised this, and as a result the relations, never particularly cordial, between the two captains . . . now became strained to an almost unbearable extent. I have often thought that, in consequence, Bradman's determination to win, already of the firmest kind, became still more resolute, and that there was now added to it the incentive not just of beating Hammond and his men, but of defeating them utterly.

Australia batted into the third day, whereupon sheets of summer rain coated the Gabba. England would now have to bat on a drying uncovered wicket – a nightmare. Wet wickets, as such, were advantageous to batsmen: the bowlers had trouble holding the ball, and when it bounced, it tended to skid through without cut or turn. But a drying wicket, or a 'sticky dog', when the ball was dry enough to hold and the turf gluey enough to deliver seam and bounce, was death to batsmen. Ian Johnson, one of the 'gay band' who had 'partied' their way through New Zealand a year earlier, was surprised to see Bradman cackling delightedly at the rain. When Johnson expressed his surprise, Bradman told him:

> Ian, the first time I played against England, in 1928, they scored 521, caught us on a wet wicket and got us out for about 120. With a lead of over four hundred, they batted a second time and left us over seven hundred to make in the last innings. Then they invented Bodyline for my special benefit, and the last time I played against them, in 1938, England made over nine hundred before Hammond declared and I broke my ankle while bowling and couldn't bat. Just this once, we have them in trouble. Do you really blame me for being so happy?

Not even war could dull those memories. He never forgot a thing.

In that Brisbane match, Bradman set the direction of how the war would alter the mood of Ashes cricket. His decision was: as little as possible. The war only occupied a smouldering recess in his mind behind the still-blazing memories of 1928–29, 1932–33 and 1938 – the only occasions in Bradman's era when England had hammered Australia. His saying 'Just this once', considering he had flayed the best part of four thousand runs off England in the 1930s, speaks volumes for his competitiveness and his desire for revenge. It was as if he had forgotten all the times he had defeated them. Foremost were the snubs and the losses.

England's batsmen, demoralised by Australia's 645, went out to face the most hostile pace attack since Jack Gregory and Ted McDonald had terrorised them after the previous war. Miller and Lindwall 'were a perfect combination', Johnson wrote. 'Miller, unpredictable, brilliant, was excessively fast from his first ball.

Lindwall was smoother in his approach and took a couple of overs to work to his peak, which he usually achieved in about his third over. Yet he was so accurate from the outset that he often took a wicket in his first over.'

Lindwall had a long, fluid run, tremendous strength and a low, round-arm release reminiscent of Larwood's. Something good had come out of Bodyline for Bradman. The similarities between Lindwall's action and Larwood's were, Lindwall said, 'either already in my bowling action or crept in unconsciously after I had watched him'. Compton said that in his 'loathing of batsmen', the brooding Lindwall reminded him of O'Reilly.

Miller, 'as moody and temperamental as any artist from Chelsea', had more show, a shorter approach, and often seemed to decide what to bowl as he was letting the ball go. In modern cricket, Lindwall was a prototype of Dennis Lillee: thoughtful, analytical, superbly fit and determined. Miller's heir was Ian Botham, the kind of bowler who could serve up literally anything, gold and dung, with the magical knack of taking the vital wicket.

Two war-damaged northerners faced them. Hutton said to Washbrook: 'I'll tell tha what it is. These people use Tommy guns and we use water pistols.'

Washbrook replied: 'I think you're right too.'

Then began one of the most vexed confrontations in postwar cricket. Under Bradman's supervision, the Australian pacemen proceeded to target Hutton's wounded arm. 'They had no compunction about bowling vicious bumpers,' wrote Ian Johnson, and they did so particularly at Hutton. Gerald Howat, in a biography of the great English batsman, wrote that the Australians saw Hutton as the head they wished to decapitate.

The Australian fast bowlers were at the peak of their form and he had had to readjust his reflexes to a pace not comparable with anything else he had ever met. Added to which there was the ever-nagging thought of his arm to which a further injury might put paid to his cricket for ever. The Australians regarded an attack on him at his weakest point as a legitimate weapon against the batsman they most feared. To reduce him to the ranks of mundane batsmanship was to render the whole of England's batting sterile. To remove him from the arena altogether was to create a sense of total triumph... All this made him an anxious man, concerned to adjust his batting to his own physical circumstances and conscious of the responsibilities he bore.

This view has it that the bouncers were part of a cold-blooded and deliberate plan, directed by Bradman and executed by the pacemen. Miller acknowledged Bradman's role in it: 'Ray Lindwall and I have often been asked whether Don ever asked or ordered us to bowl bumpers at Len Hutton and other England batsmen. He has never ordered me to do so, nor has he ever forbidden me to do so. Once when Hutton was well set in a Test Don did suggest to me in a very roundabout way that the selectors wouldn't drop me if by some accident I did allow a couple of flyers to slip at him.'

Bradman's view was that if the batsman didn't complain then all was fair. This was not quite how he had felt in 1932–33, but now was the time of his vengeance. Hutton had the choice of bleating or taking it. He took it. His only public comment was wry: 'I confess that I felt that taking the first brunt of the Lindwall-Miller explosions was to suffer something akin to being in the blitz.'

Johnson had observed that although Miller bowled more bouncers than Lindwall it was the quiet Sydneysider who, to his 'chagrin and the team's amusement', was nicknamed 'Killer'. The real killer, in cricket terms, was neither Lindwall nor Miller, but their captain. After the openers and Compton fell, Edrich and Hammond came together. Edrich's appearance carried heavy symbolism. Hutton might have broken his arm in the war, but it was during a training exercise. Bill Edrich was a front-line fighter, a hero, a man Miller was more likely to regard as a comrade in war.

Miller remembered 'hitting Hammond and Edrich, a gutsy little player with a DFC [Distinguished Flying Cross], from bloody pillar to post'.

> They were holding us up and Bradman came to me and said, 'Bowl faster, bowl faster. When you play Test cricket you don't give Englishmen an inch. Play it tough, all the way. Grind them into the dust.' Those were his words. I thought to myself, a war has just passed, a lot of Test cricketers and near Test ones have been killed and here we are after that war, everybody happy to be alive, and we have to grind them into the dust. So I thought bugger me, if this is Test cricket, they can stick it up their jumper. Don kept up this incessant will-to-win but it just wasn't my way of playing cricket.

As already on show against Hutton, there would be something inconsistent in Miller's attitude. At times he seemed merciful, softened by the war, unwilling to be Bradman's executioner. McCool said, 'Miller is not president of the Bradman fan club. In his playing days Miller was frequently at variance with the hard-headed Bradman over the handling of both team and tactics.' But at other times, Miller hurled down the most petulant and violent bouncer attacks, and Bradman claimed not to be able to control him.

It seems stark to us now: how Bradman, the most prominent non-soldier in the series, was the most warlike in his execution of the game. Yet at the time, his position was so unassailable, his authority so unquestioned among his young team, that there was no open resentment – or not yet. Morris says there was little or no talk about Bradman's war years because there was too strong a mood of relief to spoil it by thinking about who had or hadn't done what.

'When we were playing cricket again, we didn't talk about the war much,' Morris says. 'We were so pleased to be away from being pushed around, saying "Yes, sir" to idiot officers. I felt sorry for Don, actually, because he wasn't feeling the same relief.'

Miller, whose experience of the war was more intimate than his teammates', was bottling up his resentment. He waxed and waned, torn between two kinds of sporting instinct.

His captain never relented. Nothing if not consistent, Bradman used the 1946–47 series to instil his own ruthlessness into his players. For instance, Don Tallon, the Queensland wicketkeeper, had habitually been so quiet he was described as a mummy. Ring said, 'All he used to do was grin at you. He hardly said anything to you. He'd gamble: he and Keith Miller used to have bets on who'd hit the next four and that sort of thing. He played cards and he smoked incessantly, of course, but he rarely said anything at all.'

But on the field, under Bradman's captaincy, Tallon turned into such a vociferous appealer that the English complained that he was intimidating the umpires. Barnes, likewise, saw that if he was going to survive in Bradman's good graces, he would have to turn himself from prewar dasher into a run-grinder.

Barnes knew which side his bread was buttered; his observations of Bradman – and how he learnt from them – are instructive. On his 1938 tour of England, he said he 'didn't know much about Bradman'.

'I was only an undiscerning youth . . . and he hadn't gone out of his way to make a fuss of me. Bradman doesn't make a fuss of anybody.'

By 1946–47, having observed him more closely, Barnes saw the political importance of listening to the Don. Bradman counselled Barnes to play more cautiously. He didn't want to be going in to face the new ball. Barnes, who fancied himself as a national hero in the Bradman mould, wasn't over-keen about reining in his style. 'There was a lot of that I didn't agree with, but I could see what our skipper wanted of me as an opening batsman and I determined to fill the bill for him.'

What he didn't agree with were the lengths to which Bradman would go. In Brisbane, when England were 5/117 on the 'sticky dog' and looking at certain defeat, Barnes watched Bradman take Toshack into the middle before play, pointing at the spot on the wicket he wanted the towering left-armer to hit.

'It smacked of gallery-play to me,' Barnes wrote. 'No Test captain should find it necessary to give such a lesson in front of everybody. The Englishmen were all watching from the dressing-room and must have thought, knowing as they did that there was no future in front of them so far as the result of the game was concerned, that it was more than odd.'

In the second Test in Sydney, Barnes showed himself a good learner in the cynical arts. Having turned himself into what McCool called 'a back-foot player with no back-lift', he batted for eleven hours, seven of them with Bradman in a world-record fifth-wicket stand of 405. 'One of Barnes's secrets was his fitness,' said McCool. 'He was super fit. Sometimes he could be a bit of a problem with it, and if you fancied a smoke after you had finished a meal it was no good sitting anywhere near Sid. He wouldn't have cigarette smoke anywhere near him . . . That phase ended when he married a girl who smoked.'

In the 405-run partnership in Sydney, Barnes gained a rare insight into what it was like to bat with the great man:

> Bradman is most encouraging when you bat with him. He keeps up a running commentary in between overs and is full of information about what the other captain and his bowlers are thinking and trying to do. He never misses a beat. He is, too, a diplomat. He kept telling me during that partnership that the whole Test rested upon me. I began to feel, after a while, that I was carrying the House of Bradman as well as Australia's cricketing fortunes upon my shoulders.

Bradman was eventually out for 234. Minutes later, Barnes was caught off Bedser for the same score; he said it was intentional, so that people would remember him.

Fingleton, by then Australia's leading cricket writer, said Bradman 'gave nothing away in his captaincy'. In Sydney he used the heavy roller to break up the pitch when England batted, and in the fourth Test in Adelaide he hung on grimly for a draw, rather than accepting Hammond's declaration target of 314 on the last day, in a match when Compton and Morris both made twin centuries. 'In view of Australia's overwhelming strength in what was dubbed a goodwill series,' Fingleton wrote, 'many thought that Bradman would have accepted the challenge which Hammond made in Adelaide, but Bradman brought with him through the war years the general conception of Test cricket between England and Australia. He was grim. He gave not a ha'porth in change.'

Edrich, in the Sydney Test, 'withdrew my subscription from the Bradman fan club' when Compton was hit on the pads and Bradman appealed from point.

Edrich said to Bradman: 'That was a pretty good appeal for an Australian captain to make.'

Bradman replied: 'Why? It was plumb out.'

Edrich later reflected: 'I fancy Bradman's cricket was a different game from the one I played.'

Edrich had known fellow pilot Charlie Walker, who had played 109 games as a wicketkeeper for South Australia, many alongside Bradman, before the war. Walker was killed flying a bombing raid over Germany on 18 December 1942. While in Adelaide for the fourth Test, Edrich visited Walker's parents: a reminder of how one man retained his sense of proportion.

Australia won the series 3–0, and the great Hammond shambled off into retirement, having made no new friends and lost a few old ones. Compton was mystified by Hammond's instruction to his batsmen to defend against Lindwall and Miller. 'It tended to impose a restraint on your natural way of playing, and certainly diminished any pleasure you might get from playing the game.'

In the way Bradman led and Hammond responded, the grim attrition of the late 1930s was resumed. John Curtin, in a letter to the MCC, had written before the series: 'Australia will fight for those twenty-two yards of turf.' He was right. The spirit of the Victory Tests and the New Zealand tour had been a brief, Bradman-less, moment of relaxation. Now the real thing was back.

Hammond had played Australia for the last time, but Compton was entering his best years. He left Australia in 1947 with a head full of plans, having 'seen exactly what it was that we would have to face in the future when we were playing against Australia, even if we hadn't yet found a way to master it'.

A key, he thought, to countering Australia's batting strength was to frustrate them. '[I]t was plain that the Australian batsmen greatly disliked being tied down . . . It seemed to give them a feeling of restriction which they might attempt to break by making a stupid or hasty stroke and consequently losing their wicket. Even so good a batsman as Miller, it would seem, was prone to react in this way. It was a useful piece of information and it was duly noted, and used later on.'

England's lesson, then, was to play more defensively. Attrition would form the basis of Yardley's scheme for the 1948 series; it showed how quickly Ashes cricket had become a race towards a bottom of negativity.

The Goodwill Tour revealed how Bradman was going to use his postwar power. Would he help remake cricket in the spirit of the Services and New Zealand tours, a kinder, gentler, more celebratory game? No. He would play cricket as he always had, within the laws but hard as nails. He would inject that hardness into the young men now in his charge. He urged them, at the end of the Ashes series, not to relent. 'Don't feel you are so far on top of these boys that you can afford to give them a chance. Give them two more good players and they'll be a difficult lot to topple.'

3

BUILDING INVINCIBILITY

Among the hundreds of thousands of dreamy Australian teenagers watching Bradman's new team was Neil Harvey, who turned eighteen just before the Ashes series. Harvey had grown up in a hothouse of sport in the back lanes of Fitzroy in Melbourne. All five of his brothers played at least district-level cricket and baseball, and his sister Rita scored for their father's Fitzroy team. Among Australian cricket families, only the Gregorys, the Waughs and the Richardson-Chappells compare.

As a child, Neil, the only left-hander in the family, was taught one principle of batting: the ball is there to be hit. He honed himself on a slab of cracked concrete in the backyard of the family's terrace house, batting against a marble that nipped savagely off the cracks. When he graduated to the cobblestone lane alongside the house, his mother yelling at him to keep the ball away from her washing, he had to contend with a tennis ball jagging off the stones.

A small boy, Neil only came up to the waistband of former Australian Test bowler Maurie Sievers when he joined him at the Fitzroy club as a twelve-year-old. His coaches, Joe Plant and Arthur Liddicut, encouraged his natural inclination to take risks. Plant, an accurate off spinner, placed a coin at a good length on the wicket and challenged Neil to get to it like lightning.

On Saturday mornings the Harvey home was a madhouse of boys running in different directions getting ready for sport. Neil rode Mick's bicycle to matches with his bat and bag across the handlebars. After the thirteen-year-old scored 101 and 141 not out in a third-grade grand final, his captain asked the opposing skipper if he wanted to meet him. 'Meet him?' the man said. 'Don't you think I've seen enough of the little so-and-so out in the middle?'

During the war, the absence of top players – including his brothers, who had enlisted – allowed Neil to play first grade at fifteen. Games were reduced to one day, meaning the hard hitters prospered. On weekdays, Neil was performing maintenance work for the Melbourne City Council electrical supply, on the turbines and boilers, making flanges, using big drills and lathes and welders. 'But work got in the way of what I really wanted to do,' he says.

When Mick went to Kokoda, Neil spread maps of New Guinea spread on the kitchen table. 'I used to follow the war like anybody would follow cricket,' Neil remembers.

> I had the maps and followed who was winning, who was losing, which way things were going. Even though I wasn't in the war, I took an intense interest because Mick was right in the middle of it. We were very anxious about it. New Guinea was as bad as it got. Mick said there was nothing like it. He still doesn't want to talk about it. His best mate was killed right alongside him. It wasn't until after it all finished that he told us about that.

Mick only sent occasional letters to his family, preferring to write to his fiancée in Queensland. Neil prepared to follow him into the war. Playing cricket for Australia was inconceivable until the moment the war ended. Then, as the blockage released so much pent-up pressure, the resumption of first-class cricket accelerated Neil's career dramatically. With the Melbourne Cricket Ground still an army base in 1945, he made his Sheffield Shield debut on Princes Park, before making a hundred against Tasmania. The next season, with the servicemen back, he was good enough to make Victoria's tour of New South Wales and Queensland.

'I went to Spencer Street Station with my little Gladstone bag, which was all I had,' he says. 'I didn't have any bat, pads or batting gloves. I just had boots, a shirt, a pair of pants and socks. We went on the *Spirit of Progress*. I hardly knew anybody. I went up and introduced myself to Lindsay Hassett, who was captain.

'"I'm Neil Harvey, I believe I'm on your team."

'"Okay, you're welcome. Sam, here, you look after him."

'That's how I got passed onto Sam Loxton. He's been looking after me ever since,' Harvey said, a few months before Loxton's death.

Loxton said it wasn't accidental that he was chosen.

'His brother Merv introduced him to Hassett. Neil was only eighteen, and Merv liked a drink. Neil was a teetotaller. Lindsay knew that I didn't drink, so being a wise old head, he gave me the job of looking after him.'

The new mates would both play for Victoria against the touring Englishmen in Melbourne. Neil recalls: 'I thought I wouldn't get picked, but they did pick me to bat at number six. I made 69 against Alec Bedser and Doug Wright and Dick Pollard. Wright had a pretty good wrong'un, with a big hop at the finish, and I didn't pick it; nicked it. A voice behind me said, "Well played, son, see you in England next year." I turned around and it was Godfrey Evans.'

Harvey and Loxton would have to perform well in 1947–48 to make it that far. But the teenager was starting to believe. When Sid Barnes was injured during the 1946–47 series, Merv Harvey played what would turn out to be his only Test match. He scored 11 and 32 before giving Barnes his place back. 'We didn't talk a lot about it,' Neil recalls. 'We just took it in our stride. But it showed me what was possible. From then, playing Test cricket turned into my ambition.'

*

In the summer of 1947–48, Australia hosted its first visit from an Indian team, led by Lala Amarnath but weakened by the absence of their champion batsman Vijay Merchant.

Despite having headed the aggregates in 1946–47, Bradman was still contemplating retirement. With two young children, the younger, Shirley, suffering from cerebral palsy, and his stockbroking business in its second year, he had every reason to close his career after the bruising Ashes series.

Dick Whitington, firmly aligned with the disgruntled Services veterans, sympathetic to those such as Pepper who were leaving for England to escape the 'thing' against them, had become one of Bradman's most uncompromising critics. After watching the newly arrived Indians in Perth playing Western Australia in 'weather which would have found Bradman back in his office, buying and selling shares', Whitington wrote in the Sydney *Sun*:

> Twenty years of cricket do not seem to have taught Bradman the real British Empire meaning of the word. During most of those years Bradman as a batsman has made one of the greatest contributions to cricket in history. But unless, as Australia's captain during this Australian and the next English summers, he encourages young Australians, Indians and Englishmen to play cricket as he first played it – for sheer love of the game – he would make an even greater contribution by announcing his retirement.

Bradman might indeed have been contemplating retirement, but the acrimonious series of 1946–47 had left him with a sense of unfinished business. He was conscious that he was widely blamed for the poor spirit of the Goodwill Tour.

The servicemen's feelings about his war non-service, and his postwar attitude, were being given voice by Whitington. Bradman and the SACA sought a retraction from Whitington, unsuccessfully. Bradman now decided he would play against

India. Believing the series 'would be less exacting and that I was now better able to stand up to it, I again felt it my duty to play this one season, especially as it was to be the first tour of Australia by an Indian Team'.

He was, he said, 'still very dubious about attempting a final tour of England' in 1948. But Bradman had always been driven by the desire to shame his critics. Apart from Whitington, in the background was the 'Big Ship', Warwick Armstrong, who had written occasionally, but stridently, about the inferiority of Bradman's team to that which he had led in 1921 and the one he'd played in, under Joe Darling, in 1902. Those teams remained the gold standard: the two that had gone within a whisker of undefeated Ashes tours. Armstrong, as dyspeptic a character as ever played, had led a team unbeaten until an ambush in their last week by a Test-strength English team in a 'festival game' at the Scarborough Fair. He said that that team would have had no chance against the men of 1902. Unequivocally, in Armstrong's eyes, the old-timers were better than current players and always had been. Until 1946, he persisted in Australian cricket as an arch-critic of Bradman. Moonlighting from his day job as a whisky distributor, Armstrong wrote repeatedly that Bradman, as a batsman, was not a patch on Victor Trumper and several other pre-World War I greats. Armstrong, who had once derided Bradman as a 'cricket cocktail' who was 'scared of Larwood', would not live to see whether Bradman's team would beat his record; he died in the winter of 1947.

By leading a team to England that could win the Ashes and perhaps even surpass 1902 and 1921 by not losing a game, Bradman could finish his career on the highest note. He could confound the Whitingtons and Armstrongs in Australia. In England, he could redeem himself from the sourness of 1946–47 and blot out the horrible memory of what had become of his tour in 1938. So he began, in the summer of 1947–48, to construct an idea of invincibility.

Against the Indians, his team won easily and an Ashes squad took shape. Bill Brown was back from injury and batting well, notwithstanding his tendency to back up too far, getting himself run out twice by Vinoo Mankad at the bowler's end. Morris, Barnes, Bradman, Hassett and Miller were entrenched in the top order. Bradman's fiercely loyal South Australian underling Ron Hamence batted his way into contention, and the fast-bowling line-up of Lindwall, Miller, Bill Johnston and Toshack had no challengers. The spin-bowling positions would be fought out between leg spinners Colin McCool, Doug Ring and Bruce Dooland, while Ian Johnson's containing off spin made him a certainty. Tallon would keep wicket ('His surname tells everything,' said John Arlott, 'instinctively prehensile, naturally predatory'), with New South Wales' Ron Saggers travelling as his understudy.

Soon after Christmas, there remained two unresolved positions in the seventeen-man squad: a reserve batsman and an all-rounder. These last two would probably not play any Tests in England. Bradman was looking for a certain type of character above all else.

In November 1947, a non-Test Australian XI had played the Indians at the SCG. Thrilled to be in a Bradman team, young Neil Harvey watched from the dressing room as Bradman, batting with Miller, compiled his hundredth first-class century. Also waiting was Harvey's mate Sam Loxton. Both were nervous. Harvey made 32, while Loxton failed twice but impressed Bradman with his bustling fast-medium pacers. Given the new ball, he took four wickets in the match.

Bradman wanted a closer look, and Harvey's dynamic fielding got him the twelfth man's job for the first three Tests against India. 'It was a fillip for me to be picked,' he says, 'even as twelfth man.' They were the first Test matches he had seen. He was in awe of the Don. But there was also a cold spirit in the team: he was virtually ignored, treated as the callow teenager he was. Like Barnes nine years earlier, Harvey was discovering that in a Bradman team, the captain didn't make a fuss of anybody.

By the fourth Test in Adelaide, with the series virtually sewn up, Harvey replaced Hamence. He was beside himself with excitement. 'I'd saved up enough from my turning and fitting to buy myself my first cricket bat, a Gunn & Moore,' he remembers. Australia were 4/503 on the second day when Harvey finally made his entrance. After three overs, the handle of his brand-new bat broke. Minutes later he was lbw for 13. 'I thought, "That's my Test career finished."'

Hassett went on to score 198 not out in six hours. His old army mate Whitington wrote that the little gunner's cavalier brightness had gone, and he had become 'part of a cricketing machine, one captained by a batting machine named Bradman – a cricketing computer whose unswerving aim was victory'.

But the machine was not so rigid as to spit out Harvey after his failure. The selectors 'thought they'd seen something so they picked me again, to my surprise', he says. They also wanted a last look at Loxton.

Bradman would go to the Indians' dressing room after play and give them tips, for which they were grateful. He was in a compromising mood. When he was 57 on the first afternoon of the fifth Test, feeling an attack of fibrositis, he retired hurt. Harvey had what he thought was his last chance.

'I didn't have the money to buy another bat,' he says. 'So I borrowed one from my club at Fitzroy, an R.M. Crockett bat I'd made a few runs with. I made 153 with it, and that got me a spot in one of the best teams that ever played the game.'

Harvey was batting when Brown, backing up, was famously Mankaded. Loxton joined him, and the mates put on a vivacious 159 in 129 minutes. Lindwall and Harvey brought up the teenager's century by running a five. Loxton, buoyed by his 80, backed it up with his first three Test wickets.

Until that week, nobody knew if Bradman was going to undertake the tour of England. He was tossing up between playing, staying at home, and taking the tour as a journalist.

Fleet Street offered him Croesean riches. Fingleton later asked a London editor what the offer had been. 'Looking furtively up and down Fleet Street, he drew me up a lane and whispered the sum. It staggered me.' Bradman had refused, so they doubled the offer. Bradman refused again. The amount was said to approach $1 million in today's money.

Bradman had told his confidant Johnnie Moyes that he was leaning towards staying at home. During the 1938 tour, the strain had been so great, said Moyes, that 'more than once [Bradman] threw himself, exhausted, on my bed and dropped straight off to sleep.' Moyes had remained deeply moved by Bradman's exhaustion during that tour. From 1946 onwards, Moyes had told Bradman that 'pressure would be brought to bear to get him to England once more as captain. He replied, "I thought we settled that question in 1938."'

The other tantalising what-if relates to Bradman's application for the job of secretary of the Melbourne Cricket Club, vacated by Hugh Trumble in 1938. Bradman stood because he was told his appointment would be a foregone conclusion. He was deceived, and the club's committee voted for one of their own, the former Test batsman Vernon Ransford. Rosenwater wrote: 'Had the casting vote gone in favour of Bradman, and had he then accepted the post, the one thing that is certain above all else is that he would not have captained Australia in England in 1948.'

But something altered in Bradman during the 1947–48 summer. One was the bounty of runs, albeit against a novice international attack. Against India he made 715 runs at an average of nearly 179, a mountain even for Bradman. After the first of his four centuries in successive Tests, an English newspaper headline read: 'Our turn comes next.' More importantly, though, he discovered that most of his team, far from challenging his authority or questioning his wartime record, worshipped him. Gone were prewar stars, such as O'Reilly, Fingleton and McCabe, who saw him as a mere mortal, a contemporary with flaws just like anyone else's. In the team he now led, the older ones, such as Brown and Hassett, were pragmatically loyal. The rebellious types, such as Barnes and Miller, kept their true feelings in check. The greenhorns, who comprised the rest of the team, viewed him with awe.

The trip to England in 1948 would be different, he felt, from previous tours – a fresh start. He appreciated having 'a team of cricketers whose respect and loyalty were unquestioned, who would regard me in a fatherly sense and listen to my advice, follow my guidance and not question my handling of affairs . . . There are no longer any fears that they will query the wisdom of what you do. The result is a sense of freedom to give full rein to your own creative ability and personal judgment.'

Like many captains before and since, Bradman came into his own once he was an elder statesman. He was relaxing. Fingleton observed that 'Bradman had undoubtedly mellowed' in the summer when the Indians toured. 'He seemed to get more fun out of life; he sought the company of his fellows more than in his earlier days, when it was said of him that he was not a team man and that he was satisfied with his own company . . . He mixed more with the players than he did pre-war and he was certainly a more popular leader and man with his players and the opposition.' But if Bradman was mellowing, it was only on the surface. He had his mind on avenging a fifteen-year-old wrong, and now he had the weapons to do so.

On 5 February 1948, the eve of the final Indian Test, Bradman went for a walk in Melbourne with Bill Jeanes, the secretary of the Board of Control, and Moyes. After a general chat, they returned to Bradman's room, where he took a note from his pocket and gave it to Jeanes, who read it, then passed it without a word to the journalist.

Moyes recalled: 'It was a statement setting out that Bradman had informed his co-selectors that he was available for the English tour and that, on his return from England, he would retire from cricket of all grades, club, state and international.'

The men pondered the note in silence.

'Well?' Bradman asked Jeanes.

'I like the first part, but is the second part necessary?'

Moyes, always Bradman's adoring supporter and apologist, saw his commitment to tour as a sign of 'the bigness that was in him'. He believed Bradman was making a personal sacrifice to tour when he had 'misgivings'. 'I know that he would have preferred to have remained at home,' Moyes said, but 'his deeds made it impossible'.

Bradman liked this interpretation, for it echoed his own. 'All my impulses spurred me to go. I am a great lover of England and the English people. Their kindness to me, especially in 1934 and 1938, knew no bounds. I felt that I understood what the next Australian tour would mean to their cricket and to the people in general, and if it was possible for me to make a contribution I was anxious to discharge my duty in that direction.'

His health and business, he said, weighed against touring, but 'Finally I . . . decided it was my duty to make one last effort for the sake of cricket.'

It was a sacrifice, but he made sure he didn't miss out, either. While not as lucrative as the Fleet Street offers, his remuneration from the tour, in the form of gifts and personal subscriptions, would far exceed the paltry £600 fee – minus expenses – that he, like all the squad members, would receive. In addition, he was able to extract from the Board a promise, on the condition of touring, that he would get a testimonial match in the home summer of 1948–49. Testimonials, the public's means of thanking long-serving players and compensating them for some of their sacrifice, had been part of Australian cricket since its earliest days, but from the 1930s the Board was ruthlessly phasing them out. Bradman's – which would raise more than five times his tour fee – was among the last. He told Barnes that some on the Board had opposed a testimonial, but, using his availability for the 1948 tour as his bargaining chip, he had 'won the day'.

*

The days between the end of the Indian series and the naming of the squad were nervous. Barnes said the anxiety became painfully obsessive. Since the 1870s, a tour to England had been the only chance for a player to gain any worthwhile compensation for the time he gave to the game. Players sharing in tour profits had been stamped out by the Board's coup in 1912, but there were still fringe benefits possible for the entrepreneurial type. Postwar austerity had slashed wages. But even if the £600 tour fee left most cricketers out of pocket, the adventure in going to England would be the chance of a lifetime. So much was at stake, Barnes said, that the 'tour of England horrors are real. Many a good cricketer who has performed well over the years gets very jittery when a tour overseas is near . . . If you ask a particular batsman at any stage of an Australian season before an English tour how many runs he has, he will, if he's honest, tell you not only how many he's got but how many all his rivals have also. A great game, cricket – sometimes . . .'

Barnes was harrowed by his memories of waiting for the announcement of the 1938 Ashes team. Back then, McCabe had told him he might get on the tour if he did well in the second-last game before the selection, against Bradman's South Australia. 'What a night I had that night!' Barnes said. 'What I didn't do to Grimmett's bowling was nobody's business. I saw the members' pavilion rising to meet me in a body as I walked in after one of the best, probably the best, innings ever seen on the ground . . . I started to feel sorry for Grimmett – and then I had to get up and have a cold shower. I was in a terrific perspiration. The time was past midnight.'

In the actual game, he 'batted like an old dosser who had been sleeping the nights in the caves on the Sydney Domain. I got exactly six runs in ninety minutes.' All in front of Bradman. But he was still chosen.

In 1948, Barnes was batting well enough to feel assured – other batsmen 'were scoring their runs in bed; I was getting mine in the middle' – but he had other causes for worry. An arcane Australian rule barred players from Ashes tours if they had played for English minor-league teams. Barnes had played in the Lancashire League in 1947. Moreover, he was in bad odour with the Board of Control after some on-field showmanship, including one innings where he taunted a Melbourne crowd that was jeering him over slow scoring. In another incident, he was accosted for jumping the MCG turnstile. The fact that he was playing in the game didn't seem to mollify the stuffed shirts on the Board.

Already on thin ice, he pushed his luck even further by telling Bradman that, as his wife Alison was living in Scotland with their newborn son, Sid Junior, he would like some time off to visit them during the 1948 tour. Bradman asked for assurances that Alison wouldn't travel with the team or stay in their hotel. Bradman said it was a 'ticklish situation', but he must have been sympathetic given the stand he had taken, almost to the point of open rebellion, in demanding that Jessie be able to join the 1938 tour. Barnes 'assured him that my wife would be living in Scotland and would be nowhere near the team. He left it at that. I assumed he was the spokesman for the Board.'

The conversation with Bradman wasn't enough, however. A Board subcommittee met Barnes and asked for the same assurance.

'Then one of them said the Board was not too happy about all the clowning I indulged in on the field. Couldn't I refrain from getting spectators annoyed? This wasn't cricket, he said. That set me back a bit. This particular Board member had never played the game to my knowledge. I thought cricket badly wanted some showmanship and publicity.'

Barnes was picked, despite everything, due to Bradman's strong support and the runs he had made against England and India. 'They had reversed all their stuffy ideas and some of their most important clauses in their sacred contract,' he said. 'And they had done all this for Sidney George Barnes!'

Barnes rang Alison 'and told her the good news. I had six minutes at a guinea a minute. "I'll be seeing you very soon," I told her, "but pretend you don't know me if you see me. The Board of Control doesn't believe in wives."'

Bradman, before announcing his availability, had caused a stir by opining about some bowling candidates in an address to Adelaide's Legacy Club on 22 January. McCool, a Test regular since the war, would 'never become another Grimmett'. Bradman disparaged Queensland's Len Johnson, who had taken 3/8 and 3/66 in his one Test against India. Bruce Dooland, meanwhile, the cleverest of Australia's spinners, was in Bradman's view suffering from 'touritis', an unhealthy obsession with being chosen.

An Adelaide *News* journalist, Colin Hay, made himself known to Bradman before the lunch and reported the comments later. Bradman complained. Hay's editor-in-chief wrote: 'Bradman's conclusions on journalistic ethics are, to say the least, peculiar'. The reporter didn't have to 'come cap-in-hand to seek his permission before reporting anything of the speech'.

The cat was out of the bag regarding the spinners, however. Dooland and Johnson would not be chosen, and McCool was on tenterhooks. A few days after the fifth Indian Test, McCool 'sat and chewed my nerve-ends until the names were announced on the radio . . . I suppose you always have your biggest doubts over the things you want most in life . . . When the waiting was over I went crazy . . . We cricketers certainly take our enjoyments the hard way.'

Meanwhile another fringe candidate, Loxton, was at home in Melbourne 'with my parents listening to the news on the radio. They said the Test side would be announced at six o'clock, so we sat there and waited. I wasn't confident, though I knew I was a possible.'

At the same time, Neil Harvey was playing golf.

'When they were due to pick the side, I was like a cat on hot bricks, all pent up, so I thought, "I'm not going to stick around at home." You only found out by hearing it on the radio. There was no special call from the Board of Control. So I said to Mum, "I'm going for a game of golf." I got on my pushbike, threw my clubs over my shoulder, and pedalled the twelve kilometres to the [Yarra Glen] golf course. I played nine holes and pedalled home. Mum was leaning over the fence, smiling, and that was how I knew I'd been picked. Dad was also home, and most of the others came home soon after. I was a proud boy, but Mum and Dad were even prouder than I was.'

Adding to Harvey's thrill was that his cricketing best mate's name was also read out. Not that everyone agreed with Loxton's selection. Arthur Mailey, the great leg spinner turned journalist and cartoonist, who would be travelling with the tour, took one look at the seventeen-man squad and pronounced Loxton 'the worst Australian international cricketer ever to come to England'.

Sam would soon give him reason to apologise.

4

TO ENGLAND

Since 1878, the great names of Anglo–Australian cricket had been made in Test series played in England, not Australia. Fred Spofforth, Billy Murdoch, Jack Blackham and Victor Trumper, through to Bradman and O'Reilly, had been authenticated by their deeds 'at home'. That is, in England. The most famous matches, such as the 1882 Test match at The Oval when the 'Ashes' myth had been founded, the apotheosis of cricket's Edwardian Golden Age in 1902, and the all-at-stake Depression-era contests of the 1930s, had been staged on English soil.

One reason for this is obvious: England was the game's seat, and when Australians went to the old country it was to test themselves against the masters. Even when Australia established parity and sometimes dominance over England on the field, final validation had to take place on English turf.

Moreover, up to the 1920s, while Australia always sent full-strength teams to England, not once did England reciprocate. Early tours were speculative enterprises, very different from what they later became, promoted by private capitalists, more like travelling bands of entertainers than exalted national representatives. Even when the MCC, taking Australia more seriously, began to organise tours from 1903–04, they struggled to raise full-strength teams.

Two pillars of England's Golden Age, Stanley Jackson and Charles Fry, never toured Australia. The incomparable W.G. Grace only visited Australia once as a Test cricketer, though he played the Australians in nine Test series in England. K.S. Ranjitsinhji, the greatest stylist of the Golden Age, only toured Australia once, and vowed never to do so again due to the unruliness of the crowds. The English customarily had something to complain about in Australia. Even after full-strength English teams started touring the Antipodes in the 1920s and 1930s, the belief remained that the truest Test cricket was that played in England. It is an interesting question whether Jardine and his team of 1932–33 would have dared a Bodyline campaign 'at home'.

In 1948, a consequence of this lingering imbalance of perceptions was that even though England had toured Australia, *real* postwar Ashes cricket hadn't yet started. Even in Australia, England's visit in 1946–47 was viewed as a pipe-opener to postwar cricket. Hence the far greater nervous attacks suffered by Australian candidates before the 1948 tour selections, compared with those for Tests in Australia. Neil Harvey, though he had played his two Tests against India, was often described as someone who had yet to make his Test cricket debut – because he had not played against England in England. As Alec Bedser said later in life: 'In my youth, playing the Australians was THE Test match; the others didn't count as much.'

None of the Australian tourists was more aware of this history, of England as the proving ground, than Bradman. In preparation for his final campaign, he left nothing to chance in using his influence to tilt the odds his way.

His first victory was to lobby for a new experimental rule, brought in by the MCC, about the introduction of a second new ball. Previously, a bowling team had to concede 200 runs before it could take a second new ball. In the slow-scoring inter-war years, this meant a ball could become very old, even staying in use for more than 100 overs, before it was discarded. This in turn gave great play to spin bowlers, who obtained greater grip and turn with an older ball. After the aberration of Bodyline, the most successful bowlers of the 1930s were Australia's leg spinners O'Reilly, Grimmett and Fleetwood-Smith, while England had the great Verity and medium-pace 'cut' bowlers, such as Voce and Allen.

In 1947, the MCC altered the law so that a second new ball would become available in the fifty-sixth over. This had significant repercussions. As the ball would not now get anywhere near as scuffed up, there were fewer opportunities for attacking spin bowlers. The change greatly favoured a team which had strength in the pace department.

In the 1930s, both as a junior and as captain, Bradman had experienced a dearth of Australian speed bowlers. Since Jack Gregory's retirement in 1928–29, Australia hadn't produced one express new-ball bowler who went anywhere near matching the venom and consistency of England's Larwood, Bill Bowes and Farnes. In the home of Bodyline, Nottingham, they said in 1934 that the only reason Australia complained about the tactic was that they lacked the artillery with which to combat it.

After World War II, that situation had been turned on its head. Bradman now had, in Lindwall and Miller, the fastest bowlers since Larwood and Farnes. England, by contrast, had no-one quicker than medium-fast in the entire county system. And they had now engineered a rule that would play into Bradman's hands. As he planned for the tour, he decided on a new, openly cynical bowling strategy. He would unleash Lindwall and Miller for spells with the new ball, then go completely negative, using left-armer Toshack and off spinner Johnson to tie the batsmen down, soaking up the overs at little cost, until Lindwall and Miller were ready to return with a fresh ball. The experimental rule would be instrumental in determining the outcome of the 1948 series. Len Hutton said: 'What went into the thinking of such a patently absurd experiment is difficult to imagine.' He was not alone. O'Reilly would spend most of the 1948 tour fulminating against the rule. McCool, one of its principal victims, said it was 'just about the worst thing that happened to cricket in my time. It cost me my Test place, just as it has cost every leg-spinner his place ever since. We've been legislated out of the game.'

How had it happened? There were conspiracy theories that Bradman talked the MCC into changing the rule as a condition of him touring. Was he that powerful? Perhaps he was even more so. Lord's changed the rule without Bradman even having to represent himself. His emissaries, Robins and Allen, knew Bradman wanted the rule changed. Since 1946, his close friend Robins had been on the MCC's 'subcommittee for revision of the laws of cricket'. Robins was in constant contact with Bradman, and when his subcommittee considered changing the new ball rule, as early as October 1946, its proposed amendments would only be adopted, according to the MCC's minutes, 'in light of any comment received from Australia'. When the actual change to the new ball rule was proposed in November 1947, the minutes noted a 'considerable difference of views existed amongst overseas bodies'. It would only institute the change for the 1948 season after Australia approved. There is no smoking gun that shows Bradman prodding the MCC into changing the law in Australia's favour, but Robins's position on the subcommittee, and Allen's on the MCC's general committee, plus the minuted allusion to 'any comment from Australia', provide a circumstantial case to support the theories, that were strongly held by players in 1948, that the rule was amended for Bradman's benefit, if not at his direct instigation.

With the change in the law, Lindwall and Miller became the key players in the 1948 series. But Bradman could only control so much. Had the doctors had their way, the project could have been scuttled before it began. A medical examination of Lindwall in February 1948 'refused to guarantee' his physical soundness and declared him 'unfit for strenuous cricket' due to injuries he incurred in the India series and a bout of tonsillitis. A perturbed Bradman took Lindwall to his Melbourne masseur, Ern Saunders, and two weeks' treatment cleared him up.

Bradman still had his own health concerns. His injury in the Melbourne Test against India, an attack of fibrositis or a strained rib cartilage, suggested that 'the time has arrived to make way for younger players'. He pressed on, under Saunders' care. Just before the team left Fremantle on the SS *Strathaird*, the tour manager, Keith Johnson, told concerned Board members that Bradman's injury was not healing as quickly as hoped.

Bradman suffered a last-minute panic, harbouring 'an inward fear that my health would not stand the strain of another tour. I began to meditate on the possibility of failure. Was I taking on too much?'

After a final pre-tour match in Perth he visited a children's hospital, 'where I tried to cheer up the lives of those poor unfortunate inmates', then had 'the less pleasant task of visiting the dentist to have a wisdom tooth removed'.

His doubts were still 'haunting' him, 'but as the day for departure approached they began to recede into the background. Instead I became fired by a zeal I had not previously experienced, a burning desire to utilise my brain and my body to the utmost in the interests of cricket and the team I was to lead.'

What was changing – aside from the habitual ebbs and flows of Bradman's near-hypochondriac fretting – was that he was hatching a plan for something unprecedented.

His was the oldest team to tour England in seventy years, but that was only to be expected after the war. Harvey, at nineteen, was the youngest by seven years. The standard-setting 1921 team, when players also prolonged war-interrupted careers, was also old. Armstrong, at forty-two, had been three years older than Bradman now was in 1948. While relatively old in years, they would also be inexperienced in England. Only Bradman, Brown, Hassett and Barnes (from the 1930s), and Miller (from the Victory Tests), had played there.

Yet Bradman had supreme confidence in the pace bowling and

'an array of batsmen who could scarcely fail'. This prompted the renewal of an age-old dream. Several Australian touring squads had come within an ace of going through England undefeated, including Bradman's own 1938 team. It was too early, of course, to articulate the aim, but Bradman 'kindled in [his squad's] minds the thought that here was a team capable of going through undefeated'. In Perth, in the one team meeting Bradman held before they arrived in England, he told them they were going all-out to win. In his words, he 'tried to make them see how essential it was for the team to pull together as a unit – free of all internal bickering and strife. I instilled into them the doctrine that "happiness comes from within".'

Loxton remembered:

> There was only one team meeting! Braddles and Keith Johnson organised it. They paid for a bit of booze and some biscuits and so forth. No tactics, nothing like that. It was just, 'Here we are, we're on our way, I want it to be a happy team. Happiness comes from within. There'll be the odd problem, but we'll handle that. We'll do the talking, Keith and Lindsay and I. We want to win, and hopefully we will win.'

But Bradman was hypersensitive about his true ambitions for the tour getting out. Fingleton, one of the rare top-line cricketers who also made a top-line journalist, was on the tour 'on a strained pittance', writing for the Argus group in South Africa and *The Hindu*. He later picked up work for England's *Daily Mail*, where he was the first to write that Bradman, avid for records, aimed to go through the tour undefeated. Bradman didn't like the article and ordered his players to black-ban the former Test opener.

On the afternoon of 19 March 1948, the P&O liner *Strathaird* was loading at Fremantle for a 6 p.m. departure. The 202-metre, 22000-tonne boat was P&O's original cruise liner, the first to wear the company's distinctive white hull and gold funnels. It had recently undergone a refurbishment after sixteen years of service, including six years evacuating the Middle East of troops bound for Plymouth.

Among its 573 first-class passengers were the seventeen Australian cricketers; their support staff of Keith Johnson, scorer/baggageman Bill Ferguson, and masseur Arthur James; as well as a media corps that included Fingleton, O'Reilly, commercial broadcaster Andy Flanagan, and the veterans Mailey and Neville Cardus (returning to England after a stint at the *Sydney Morning Herald*), both of whom had told Bradman this would be their last Ashes trip.

Several hours before 6 p.m., Fingleton heard a voice cry: 'He's on!' Its 'unmistakeable excitement' could only mean one thing. Bradman, hoping to avoid land-based media, had boarded early.

On his way to his cabin, Bradman received a good luck omen: a seagull defecated on his brand-new hat. Sensitive to signs, he overheard 'a woman violently arguing with, I presume, her husband, and saying with great vehemence, "What more could I do?"'

'For me I knew this was definitely my last trip as a player. Her words came back to me. "What more could I do?" I had returned to cricket in 1946–7 against the advice of my doctors, and now I was going to England against my own judgment – risking personal failure and other possibilities. But my conscience was clear that I was discharging what I believed to be my final obligation as a player to the game of cricket and its myriads [sic] of supporters.'

The first days of the voyage brought some sights Flanagan would never forget: the lighthouse at Rottnest Island, flying fish in the Indian Ocean, 'their silvered bodies and diaphanous wings glinting in the sparkling sunlight', and the wreck of the *Emden* at the Cocos Islands.

The *Strathaird*'s captain was nicknamed 'High-Brow' Allan. Flanagan said passengers claimed his eyebrows 'were cultivated, for they spiral up his forehead, and then stand out like the questing antennae of a Swedish black beetle'. On 21 March, the captain gave a welcoming cocktail party on the bridge. On this warm, starry night, the bridge was 'picked out with hundreds of coloured lights, lending an atmosphere of fantasy to the scene of bright, ebullient-spirited team members revelling in the companionship of the ship's officers who excelled in their hospitality'.

Hassett went dressed as an Arab, but there were limits to the allowable levity. One guest went with huge artificial eyebrows, only to be taken away by an officer and told to remove them.

Bradman meanwhile took shelter in his cabin, from which he would emerge, in the next five weeks, only when necessary. Some passengers wondered if he was aboard at all. Flanagan heard comments that 'were apt to miscontrue his reserve as aloofness, or conceit'. But Bradman had learnt from 1938 that the welter of speeches he would have to deliver in England could not be prepared on the run.

Morris quickly understood that Bradman would not be seen much socially. 'How could he? In the toilet, he had to use cubicles rather than urinals, because if he went to use a urinal, someone would say, "Are you Don Bradman?" and turn and face him! He got sick of having his shoes splashed.'

For the others, the voyage meant time for fun, an aim promoted by the daily routine. Morning tea took place at 7.30 a.m., followed by breakfast at 9 a.m. and deck games from 10 to 11.30 a.m. These might include quoits, shuffleboard, 'tick tennis' (a game of throwing and catching quoits over a net), or even an occasional game of cricket played with a ball made of coiled, wettened rope. Or, wrote Flanagan, 'some may prefer to recline in a comfortable deck chair with a book, or just watch the fascinating roll of the sea, with a drink steward constantly at hand ready to attend to your every want.'

Every twenty-four hours, bets were taken on the ship's run; at noon, results and dividends were announced. Passengers would throw a cocktail or sherry party for the cricketers, followed by lunch at 1.30 p.m., and more games or sunbaking. By 5.30 p.m., cocktail hour, the players converged on the Veranda Café Bar, where they would socialise until the ship's bugle sounded for dinner at 8 p.m. The bugle, wrote Flanagan, 'was a welcome sound and found most of the team in evening dress anxious to enter the dining saloon in order to take in the vision of beauty and youthful enchantment provided by the surprising number of young girls who were privileged to make the voyage to England on the same ship as the cricketers, at a time when even important businessmen found it difficult to get a passage'.

After dinner came coffee and liqueurs, dancing, games and movies. Then some singing would be led, usually by Hassett with his favourite 'Down Came a Blackbird', in the Veranda Café. Sometimes, late at night, Bradman would show up in the forward lounge to play piano. Said Fingleton: 'In 1948 [Bradman] was fortunate to have a vice in Lindsay Hassett who took the entertaining out of his hands. I can see Hassett again, an elfish grin on his Irish face, standing on high in the lounge . . . and leading the whole lounge-full in community singing, conducting with a pencil and doing actions when needed. But Hassett was the complete extrovert. That was just not in Bradman's make-up. Neither was a night out with the boys in his conception of things. Yet he was not a prude. He never tried to stop anybody else from enjoying himself.'

Socially, says Morris, the team had a blend of military discipline and sheer postwar relief. 'Discipline wasn't a problem for us, because we had those wartime habits. Having been through all the nonsense that goes on in the army, we had a certain amount of experience and were just pleased to be free.'

Rest, play, drink, dance: this was the routine, more or less, every day. There had always been some fitness fanatics on the tours – the great South Australian all-rounder George Giffen had spent his voyages getting fit by shovelling coal into the ships' furnaces – but they tended to be in the minority. Six weeks on the ocean were for socialising and bonding. Little wonder that Miller and

Toshack, the 'film stars' of the team, were observed to enjoy the ladies' company to the full.

Though the ex-servicemen in the team did not talk a lot about their wartime experiences, having been a soldier still accentuated every pleasure of being a civilian. Johnson said: 'It was such a relief to be away from the war and going on a tour. The attitude of the team was one of celebration at being away and doing something pleasant for a change. I think that had a lot to do with the spirit of the team . . . You don't want to give any credit to war, but to have to live together [as soldiers] helps to gel a team together.'

All the squad, except for Bradman, Hassett and Keith Johnson, shared cabins. Most were decided by friendship and affinity. Lindwall and Miller were paired. 'We slept late in the morning, took practically no exercise, and every afternoon went down for a siesta,' Lindwall wrote. 'To all appearances we might have been sailing on a rest cruise.'

The spearhead had special reasons, early on, to take it easy. He was recovering from his injuries and a tonsillectomy, which had produced complications including a blood clot in his throat, an abscess in his ear and gastroenteritis.

Morris shared a cabin with Barnes, a marriage of opposites that Bradman hoped would flourish as an opening partnership.

Barnes's voyage was always going to be eventful. Alison and Sid Junior were waiting for him in the UK, and he took a cargo of commercial size.

'Many of my friends there had not had a good feed of steak, butter and the like for years and I had a long list of people who had done me good turns. They had to be looked after and, also, I wanted to take a lot of provisions for my own family. Altogether, I loaded half a ton of food onto the liner.'

At the time of departure, a policeman came up saying blood was dripping out of his wardrobe trunk. The stewards 'had a look on their faces that suggested they were in the midst of some terrible crime. The policemen, too, I noticed, had a pretty grim look about them.'

Barnes had packed several bottles of cherry brandy 'and the worst had happened'. They had broken inside his trunk. 'My soft dress-shirts were a mess of red; my sharkskin mess-jackets were horrible to see.'

The commercial motive was seldom far from Barnes's thinking, and it cost him goodwill. Before the tour, a cigarette company had asked for permission to print his photo on a calendar, for a fee of five pounds. 'Don't insult me,' Barnes said. 'If you are so keen to get the photographs of all the players, it must be worth more than £5 each to you. But I'm a reasonable fellow. Make it £50.'

The calendar was produced, without Barnes.

One of the most onerous duties was signing autograph sheets. Barnes had learnt in 1938 how much of the voyage was taken up with this, and thousands of the sheets had been discarded unused. So in Perth, he had a stamp made with his signature. He wasn't just being lazy: he didn't agree with team sheets.

'The autograph-hunters didn't like them,' he wrote. 'In the first place, the pasting of them into a book doesn't appeal to them and they prefer the intimate touch of the personal name.

'Some of the boys took that signing very seriously. They sat down and slaved away for hour after hour. But not Sidney George Barnes. My first 5000 cost me exactly two bottles of ginger beer. I found an enthusiastic lad on board who was only too eager to do the job for me and so he just sat down and planked my stamp on the list.'

When his shortcut was discovered, Barnes had to appear before Bradman and Keith Johnson to explain himself. Bradman conceded the point but opined that there was little else to do on the ship, so Barnes might as well sign the sheets. Barnes compromised by paying his lad another bottle of ginger beer, and telling him to be more careful to stamp in exactly the right place.

(Five months later, on the return trip, a hatbox was found with 'thousands of these autograph slips, unwanted and undelivered', Barnes wrote. 'I still have over a thousand of them from each of the 1938 and 1948 trips to England.')

But even if he felt vindicated in his way, Barnes's act was remembered fifty years later by one disappointed fan, who told Barnes's biographer Rick Smith: 'To have used a rubber stamp says it all. I do not feel my comments are unworthy; over the years many people who have looked at my collection have had likewise thoughts. It just isn't done.'

Barnes wasn't, incidentally, the only player to pull a swiftie. Toshack had a young girl sign his name on the sheets until he was also caught out by Keith Johnson, who asked: 'Since when have you started spelling your name without a "c"?'

While Barnes was the streetwise opportunist, Morris was just looking to relax after his years in New Guinea and two intense seasons of Test cricket.

'My routine was, have breakfast, get up at ten, read for a while, go to the bar at midday, have lunch, have a snooze afterwards, wake up and put on the black tie for the first cocktail party, then the evening. That was my exercise!'

He had earned a break. Morris's father had been transferred from Bondi to Dungog in the Hunter Valley when Arthur was young. His mother was much younger, and English, and 'reckoned anything outside Bondi was not for her. She took one look at Dungog and packed up and left.' Aside from train trips to the city to see her during holidays, Arthur was raised by his father. 'It was hard for me, but harder for Dad. He was wonderful. Men didn't often get custody.'

A country upbringing suited Morris. When he was eight or nine years old, the local cricket club held an afternoon tea for Don Bradman, who was visiting as a sales rep for the Mick Simmons sporting goods company.

'The old man was invited, being a keen fast bowler, although he had an injured knee by then. I had no shoes and Dad called me over to meet Don. I was very shy, shuffled up and said hello, then shuffled off. I could never have dreamed that one day I'd be playing under his captaincy.'

Moving around with his father, Morris had attended high school in Newcastle and Canterbury, where he joined the famous St George club, once the home of Bradman, now led by Tiger O'Reilly. The up-and-coming star was Lindwall. 'Coming from the country,' Morris says, 'you're very shy. I thought I had no chance. I was still very small, not strong enough to hit the ball against mature bowlers. Bowling my leg spinners, though, I took fifty-five wickets in six games at an average of five. They'd bring Lindwall on early to remove the shine so I could bowl my spinners!'

O'Reilly, who knew a bit about the subject, advised Morris to concentrate on his batting, just as he'd counselled Lindwall to give up his dreams of being a batting all-rounder and instead let his bowling rip. Early on the *Strathaird*'s voyage, Morris often bumped into his old mentor. 'The journalists were at a table near us. One of them was drinking so much, he ended up putting on a tie over his black tie. We were laughingly pointing it out. Tiger said, "I'll see enough of you bastards on this trip," and went off to another table.'

O'Reilly had his own sense of humour and his own ways. The cohabitation of players and ex-players could be strained. Fingleton and O'Reilly (who had given up teaching maths at school for the life of a cricket journalist) would be the Rosencrantz and Gildenstern of the 1948 tour. Both would write books about it, and both would earn reputations as Bradman's harshest critics. They had been part of the Roman Catholic clique that Bradman felt caused so much internal unrest in the teams of the 1930s, but it is too simplistic to say O'Reilly and Fingleton were reading from the same script. O'Reilly, the rambunctious, gregarious Tiger, was saturated with the aggression of the 1930s. He, in fact, supported Bradman's ruthlessness and criticised those players who put ideals

mortgaging their home to send their only child to Wesley College, one of Melbourne's top private schools.

'I loved it at Wesley: more sport! Whenever you were out of class, you did fielding practice for half an hour. That used up some energy! You practised pretty near every night too. I had great coaches there and at my club, Prahran, so I was well prepared for this life where all you thought about was sport.'

For the first eight days at sea, the cricket gear was stowed in the hold. The best the players could do for a hit was an occasional game with cut-down bats and the wet rope balls skidding off the polished deck. But on 27 March, the *Strathaird* entered the harbour at Colombo, where the team was scheduled to play a match. A flotilla of Ceylonese craft rowed out to catch sight of the cricketers. Hundreds lined the wharf when the ship moored at the breakwater.

Fingleton and O'Reilly, among the first to be rowed ashore, hopped into a brand-new taxi. Horns tooted, crows circled overhead, and the driver boasted that the local jail, which they passed, was 'full to overflowing'. The cheering crowds surrounding the Colombo Cricket Ground called out, 'O'Reilly! O'Reilly!' Fingleton observed that 'the Big Fellow, looking rather like a Cabinet Minister, with his big attaché-case, gave them a wave.'

At the ground, a stately female curator issued orders to a crew of boys dressed in white. Twenty-five thousand filled the ground to see the Australians bat on what was turning out to be a sweltering day. They struggled. After Brown was out for 3, Bradman (in a pith helmet) and Barnes battled in the growing heat. Their running between wickets was diabolical. Fingleton said they both had 'rather a reputation for being at the other end at the end of an over', and Barnes tried to out-hog the Don, sending his captain back when he was trying to steal a single. Bradman 'wasn't having any' of Barnes's trickery, and a midwicket conference 'adjusted everything'.

Bradman was out for 20 and Barnes retired, vomiting with heatstroke, on 49. He recalled:

When I arrived in the dressing room, I told the attendant to turn on the shower and, pads, batting gloves and all, I slumped under the shower and stayed there for half an hour . . . I don't think my creams and pads ever recovered. I never saw them again after that day. I gave them to the attendants when at last I emerged from the shower, and I have never seen such pleasure as on the faces of those attendants. One of them sidled up to me just before we left the ground and said, 'Massa take me with him as his servant. I be very good servant to Massa.' He would have been very handy but I had to turn him down.

The Australians batted moderately, finding the bowlers unexpectedly quick and only making 184 in sixty overs. Miller and Loxton took the new ball, and could not break through.

'I bowled six full-tosses,' Loxton said. 'I hit this bloke on the full, and at the end of the over Braddles came up to me and said, "Sammy, I hope by the time we arrive in the old country that your length has improved."

'I said, "George, the pitch is short!" There was no reply. I don't know if he thought I was being cheeky.

'At lunchtime he had the lady curator measure it, and it was two yards short.'

Bradman wasn't surprised. 'We thought,' he wrote, 'their bowlers came off the pitch rather quickly.'

To compensate, the Australian bowlers began releasing the ball two yards behind the crease, but a downpour ended the game early in the afternoon. O'Reilly and Fingleton enjoyed the most expensive drinks they had ever bought – sixteen shillings for two gin and tonics – while the exhausted players headed back to the *Strathaird*. There they enjoyed a recharge, as Flanagan observed: 'The enervating tropical heat had tired out most members of the team but so stimulating is shipboard life that even many of those who had played that day were able to dance on deck until the music ended around midnight.'

*

As the *Strathaird* motored around the Indian coast towards Bombay, Bradman sat in his cabin and wrote the speeches he would deliver in England. His spies brought him gossip from the team. He maintained his black-ban on Fingleton. The voyage would be no holiday for a leader who was already concentrating every ounce of his energy on the task of playing thirty-four matches without defeat.

Rumours circulated of smallpox and bubonic plague in Bombay. Bradman was one of several team members unwilling to risk their health by going ashore. Fingleton thought this 'was regrettable from the Indian viewpoint but understandable from the Australian angle'.

The Cricket Club of India invited Australia for at least a practice session, if not a one-day match, at the Brabourne Stadium. The locals were 'greatly disappointed' when only Keith Johnson and five players turned up for a reception. They refused to eat, though Fingleton said he enjoyed the best coffee of the entire tour. He and Ray Robinson met Vijay Merchant, who walked them out to a harder-rolled wicket than they saw anywhere in the world. Fingleton noticed vultures circling high in the steel-girdered stands, but found the Brabourne the best-appointed cricket ground he had known. 'It was the locker-rooms, the baths and showers, the grandstand view from behind the wickets, the squash courts, the swimming bath and the general air of comfort around [the] Brabourne that so impressed us.'

The one unfenced part of the ground was the CCI's club, where members lounged in wicker chairs sipping drinks brought by uniformed waiters and listened to an orchestra playing European classics. The club's facilities included bars, lounges, libraries, a double-storey wing for accommodating guests and a mobile dance floor that was laid on the ground at the end of a day's play.

Seeing such effort and luxury, Miller said the non-appearance of Bradman and most of the team 'caused Australians embarrassment'. In the end, Merchant 'swallowed his pride' and came onto the *Strathaird*, where a reception was held in the forward lounge. Merchant and Pankaj Gupta, the administrator who had quelled a riot at the ground alongside Hassett in 1945, came aboard and presented the team with ties and Bradman with a blazer. On the wharf, crowds chanted: 'We want Bradman!' When he appeared at the rail, they cheered him as if for a mighty innings.

The *Strathaird* continued across the Indian Ocean and Arabian Gulf to Aden and Port Said before entering the Mediterranean. In Aden, naked boys swam nearly a mile out to the liner. The players were told these boys were sometimes taken by sharks as they dived for pennies thrown off visiting ships.

Barnes remembered 'a bad business deal' he'd done in Aden in 1938, when he purchased what he was told were 'the best English cigarettes you can buy'. He intended to use them for tips in England, but as the tour went on, 'porters and taxi-drivers turned their noses up at them'. He offered a thousand of them to the porter at the Piccadilly Hotel, and the porter replied, 'If you don't mind, I'd rather have 2/-.'

English military men serving in Aden came aboard to renew acquaintance with Hassett and Miller, who had played there during the Services tour. Fingleton admired 'the most luxurious moustaches imaginable, their points almost touching their ears', while some of the men 'bore scars of injuries when trying to quell Arab-Jew riots; others of their type, who would have loved this fraternizing, were no longer alive'. Hassett introduced his teammates to one Colonel Swayn, who in 1945 had 'performed the rather notable feat of having sight-boards carried all the way from Haifa to Palestine for a game of cricket'. Again, though, Bradman was not in evidence.

Port Said in Egypt was surprisingly lush after the barrenness of Aden. Flanagan likened the mountain ranges to the coast of

Broken Bay, just north of Sydney, and the lit-up shore at night to Rose Bay. As a reminder of Britain's reasons for occupying Middle Eastern ports, the *Strathaird* was stopped by a British destroyer asking for credentials; each week it was stopping boatloads of illegal immigrants from sub-Saharan Africa.

As the *Strathaird* approached England, Bradman took Lindwall into his cabin for a private talk about one matter that was concerning them both. It would be another area where Bradman used his pull with English administrators to bend the odds his way.

The no-ball rule stated that bowlers had to land their back foot behind the bowling crease, instead of today's rule where the front foot must land behind the popping crease. Like many fast bowlers of the time, Lindwall exploited the no-ball rule by landing, in his delivery stride, with his back foot behind the bowling crease but dragging it forward so that it was past the crease by the time he released the ball. Umpires tended to ignore this, as they would have to look up towards the batsman as the ball was released. But English journalists and players had complained about it during the 1946–47 series, when, Bradman wrote, 'a sort of whispering campaign was started about Lindwall dragging over the line – the critics claiming that he should be no-balled. I don't know who started it. I am sure the English players did not suppress the idea. Some of them had clearly shown that they disliked very fast bowling, and anything to curb his speed would naturally be to their advantage.'

During the Adelaide Test of 1946–47, English pressmen had started writing about it, 'inspired', Bradman said, 'by senior members of the England side'.

It was interesting, in the shadow still cast by Bodyline, to have Bradman insinuating that batsmen calling on a fast bowler to observe the spirit and letter of the law reflected poorly on their courage.

After they had returned home, some England players speculated that Lindwall might be no-balled by English umpires in 1948. After newsreel film was shot of him in the first Queensland–NSW game of 1947–48, New South Wales officials invited him to a private screening. 'From time to time the projector was stopped,' Lindwall said, 'so that we could look at still photographs of my foot at the instant of releasing the ball.'

A law change in May 1947 gave an umpire more latitude to no-ball bowlers 'if he is not satisfied that at the instant of delivery the bowler has at least some part of one foot behind the bowling crease'. In other words, Lindwall might potentially be no-balled out of the game.

The NSWCA executives were worried, and Lindwall agreed to land his foot four or five inches further back, though not without protest – he said if the new interpretation was applied equally, every fast bowler could be no-balled. O'Reilly got into his ear after the meeting, telling him to continue bowling as he was and let the umpires judge. So Lindwall went back to his usual practice. When a NSWCA official asked him how he was going with the 'new method', Lindwall said, 'All right, thanks'.

Another film was taken during the fourth Test of 1947–48 against India, in Adelaide, and another private showing was attended by Bradman and Board members. 'My feelings in the matter may be imagined,' Lindwall said. But Bradman went public, stating his satisfaction with Lindwall's foot placement, and privately told Lindwall to keep going as he was.

There wasn't much question that Lindwall did drag, and Bradman gave it his own somewhat tortured logic: 'I don't think one fast bowler in ten would bowl fairly (according to the camera) if he were to put his back foot just behind the bowling crease in the act of delivery. The momentum of his run and body swing must drag him across the line before the ball leaves the hand. Nevertheless, I maintain that the spirit of the law is being observed providing the foot is placed clearly behind the line.'

He well knew that it wasn't a matter of objective truth so much as politics. Would the English umpires, in England, single

Lindwall out? Was it fair to single him out because he was the only dragger who bowled fast enough to gain a noticeable advantage?

Lindwall would recall Bradman's anxiety that English umpires would 'be prejudiced before seeing me bowl'. O'Reilly was also concerned by Lindwall's 'terrific drag' that was 'easily discernible even from the boundary seats', and wrote that there was 'a general consensus' in England that the umpires would call him.

Such strife could be catastrophic to Bradman's plans. Lindwall was not as fast as Larwood had been – most informed estimates would put his pace at around 130 to 135 kilometres per hour, whereas Larwood was probably closer to 145 – but pace is relative to what batsmen are used to. As John Dewes says, whatever Lindwall's actual pace, he was at least a metre or two faster than any bowler the English batsmen were accustomed to facing. No Lindwall firing at full pace, no Invincibles. It was that simple. In 1938, Bradman's one express bowler, Ernie McCormick, had been shattered by no-ball problems.

So, while imbuing Lindwall with his total confidence, Bradman counselled a canny political game: start the tour bowling from well behind the crease and at limited pace, get passed by umpires, and then step it up.

'I want you to know, Ray, that even if you don't take a wicket beforehand your place in the Test team is assured,' Bradman told him. 'The important thing before the first Test is to concentrate on passing the umpires. Taking wickets must be a secondary consideration for the time being.'

Even as thoughts turned to cricket, shipboard life continued. Hassett led songs and crocodile marches in the Veranda Café each night, Bradman kept to his cabin, Miller and Lindwall manned the bar, Morris snoozed, and Harvey and Loxton played tick tennis until they were teak-hard. Captain Allan once took a spectacular one-handed catch off a ball Lindwall hit from the deck to the bridge.

Among the journalists, O'Reilly often joined the players in deck games. He, Fingleton and Bradman met Allan on the bridge at Gibraltar, watching the radar showing the ship's course. General Sir Oliver Leese came aboard and told them about the 1943 attack on Cassino, which he had headed. Some film was shot of the Australians on board, then taken ashore and forwarded to English cinemas for advance publicity.

Mailey won the deck quoits championship and rebuffed a passenger who wanted an introduction to Bradman. 'Why?' the man asked. Mailey said: 'Because no-one introduced you to me.' The loner Cardus, meanwhile, was walking the deck at five o'clock each afternoon before retiring to his cabin, more of an ascetic than any of the sportsmen.

At 8 a.m. on Thursday, 15 April, the *Strathaird* picked up the channel pilot at Torbay. Late that night it passed the white cliffs of Dover. The players and passengers, enjoying one last party, went out to see the cliffs 'looking ghostly in the silvery light of a full moon', as Flanagan remembered it.

They entered the Thames estuary at midnight, the players 'busily engaged in leave-takings, pledging friendships made on board, and making appointments for future meetings. In the Veranda Café, Lindsay Hassett, for the last time on the voyage, filled his now familiar role of conductor of the community singing, and headed the crocodile marches up and down the decks in and out the various saloons. The last of the revellers did not settle down until just before dawn.'

As day broke, some players rushed to the rail to see England for the first time. Ring said: 'I thought, "Well, Mrs Ring's little boy, this is amazing, here he is . . ."'

For Harvey, who was still his mum's little boy, the ocean voyage itself was a rite of passage – into adulthood and into the team.

> You get off at the other end, you're all mates. Everyone knows each other backwards. It was the best way to go. I always felt

sorry for players who missed out on that experience. We had a great social life, we really did. I remember getting out very early in the morning to get a first glimpse of the Old Dart. Sam and I got up way before breakfast; it was a great thrill. I'll never forget it. It was one of the highlights of my cricketing life – we were in England!

5

MIND GAMES IN
AUSTERITY ENGLAND

Though affected by the Depression and war, the country the Australians had left was a lucky one. Meat and petrol rationing was being phased out, and a government attempt to extend wartime controls over prices and rents had been defeated. The High Court had overturned the nationalisation of banks and Australia was charging headlong towards normality, albeit a norm that now included unprecedented numbers of European immigrants. Holden was producing its first cars, and Ruth Park and Patrick White were publishing books. Eugene Goossens, Joan Hammond and Chips Rafferty were the torchbearers of Australian culture. For the first time Australians had a reason to look upon the old country with pity. Not even World War I had so diminished the British Empire. The Pacific Century was underway, and Australia was part of it.

So when the *Strathaird* docked at Tilbury Wharf, near Southampton, at 6 a.m. on Friday, 16 April under overcast skies, it disgorged a cricket team entitled to see itself as a benefactor. The war had reversed the flow of need. In England, times were at their toughest. Rationing had increased and the surge of optimism with the election of the Attlee Labour government had become bogged down in the mire of war debt. All the vivid brightness of 1945 had faded, and by 1948 it was a pinched and grey-faced nation. Compared with Australia's, Britain's was still a wartime economy, crumbling from the war just finished and fearing the new spectre of Soviet aggression. Its most notable cultural artefact of the year was George Orwell's dystopian *1984*. David Kynaston, in his social history of postwar Britain, provides an evocative list of absences and presences:

> No supermarkets, no motorways, no teabags, no sliced bread, no frozen food, no flavoured crisps, no lager, no microwaves, no dishwashers, no Formica, no vinyl, no CDs, no computers, no mobiles, no duvets, no Pill, no trainers, no hoodies, no Starbucks. Four Indian restaurants. Shops on every corner, pubs on every corner, cinemas in every high street, red telephone boxes, Lyons Corner Houses, trams, trolley-buses, steam trains. Woodbines, Craven 'A', Senior Service, smoke, smog, Vapex inhalant.

And so on, until:

> Heavy coins, heavy shoes, heavy suitcases, heavy tweed coats, heavy leather footballs, no unbearable lightness of being. Meat rationed, butter rationed, lard rationed, margarine rationed, sugar rationed, tea rationed, cheese rationed, jam rationed, eggs rationed, sweets rationed, soap rationed, clothes rationed. Make do and mend.

Before anything could be built, Britain had to repay its debts. Its brave social experiment was being strangled by over-regulation and the pessimistic conservatism of those charged with running the programs designed by optimists. Basic necessities were in shorter supply and daily life was harder in 1948 than it had been in the war. Of the 1947–48 period, Anthony Heap, an English diarist quoted by Kynaston, wrote: 'I can remember few years I've been happier to see the end of.'

Test cricket had been played in the two postwar summers, with India and South Africa touring, but by 1948 the real opponent – Australia and Bradman – was looked upon as a potential saviour. The South African tour had brought an unexpectedly handy profit of £9208 and 'very exceptional' receipts, according to the MCC's annual report, but was small beer compared to the Ashes series of 1946–47 in Australia, which had attracted 850000 spectators and returned £18100 to Lord's. If such crowds came to watch the Australians in England, the finances and spirit of the game 'at home' could be set on the road to recovery.

At Tilbury, the Australians were met by what Bradman called 'a terrific battery' of cameras and a cricketing delegation including prewar heroes Maurice Tate, Charles Fry and Bill Bowes, and the leading current bowler, Alec Bedser, along with newspaper posters exclaiming: 'Aussies are here!' The Earl of Gowrie, president of the MCC, came on board the *Straithaird*, and the BBC telecast his and Bradman's speeches.

The Australians peered curiously out of their train on the way to London. Though the weather was beautiful, Fingleton noting 'soft, warm sunshine, unusual for England in April, but typical of a spring day on Bondi Beach', many buildings were still war-damaged. 'To see what those people suffered, it was terrible, the holes in the ground and in the buildings,' Loxton recalled.

The novelist Fay Weldon had arrived as a fifteen-year-old two years earlier. 'Where were the green fields, rippling brooks and church towers?' she asked. 'Here was a grey harbour and a grey hillside, shrouded in a kind of murky, badly woven cloth, which as the day grew lighter proved to be a mass of tiny, dirty houses pressed up against one another, with holes gaping where bombs had fallen . . . I could not believe that people actually chose to live like this. "It's just Tilbury," my mother said. "It's always like this."'

Of London, novelist Christopher Isherwood would later reflect:

'Plaster was peeling from even the most fashionable squares and crescents; hardly a building was freshly painted. In the Reform Club, the wallpaper was hanging down in tatters . . . London remembered its past and was ashamed of its present appearance. Several Londoners I talked to at that time believed it would never recover. "This is a dying city," one of them told me.'

But the capital stirred the young Australian men. Fingleton saw wild flowers growing out of 'soil, much of it seeing its first London light for centuries . . . Wild flowers in the middle of London!' O'Reilly, sitting beside him, commented that he knew he was seeing Englishmen by the manner in which they thrust out their chests. 'It was a glorious sight, indeed, not ruffled even by the trails of planes high in the sky and naval vessels on manoeuvres and talk of war again in the air.'

When the team and press checked in at the Piccadilly Hotel in central London, and set off for walks in the city, what they saw evoked a mixture of admiration and sympathy. Fingleton said, 'London still looked magnificently good . . . It had been battered and purged but it was still pulsating in resilient manner'. He was reassured by the persistence of the Londoners he had known in 1938: Cockney cabbies, proud Chelsea warriors, top-hatted bank messengers, bobbies, 'varied London types – a little frayed in dress, perhaps, a little tired-looking, some of the girls a little prematurely grey but still the same old lovable London types'.

What Harvey saw, he never forgot.

'It was pretty well unscathed around the hotel, but when Sam and I walked to St Paul's we couldn't believe it. All the buildings around it were flattened, and only St Paul's was standing. God only knows how that happened – He's the only one who does.'

On those walks, Harvey developed a lifelong love for London.

'London was the best city I've ever seen. It wasn't overcrowded, and it felt very safe, day or night. It had the greatest theatre stars in the world on stage every night. We'd wander around, Sam and I, just looking at things, thinking the same way, wanting to learn about the city we were in. Even recovering from war, it was a great city.'

In one of his speeches, Bradman joked about 'a young chap named Allen on trial in the West Indies'. He was teasing his friend Gubby Allen, who had been summoned from retirement in 1947 to lead England on what turned out to be a catastrophic tour of the Caribbean.

The English side that awaited Bradman's 1948 Australians has been described as war-weakened and understrength. This might have been true of the counties, but the Test XI would be anything but weak. Five of Bradman's team would be named in an Australian 'Team of the Century': Bradman, Morris, Harvey, Miller and Lindwall. Yet four of the 1948 Englishmen were of the same exalted calibre: Hutton, Compton, Evans and Bedser. In Washbrook and Edrich, they had top-order batsmen only just below that level. Off spinner Jim Laker and leg spinner Doug Wright promised to turn into world-class slow bowlers. On paper, England only lacked in one respect, which was a top-class fast bowler, but playing at home they had every hope of beating Australia.

England had some cricketers for the future, but the institution of the captaincy remained shackled to the past. Politically, the war had convinced Britain to break with Tory traditions, and even Churchill's Conservative Party, punted out of office in 1945, was embracing the open society. Not cricket. The English captain, Norman Yardley, came from an old-style amateur background: St Peter's school in York, then Cambridge. Though he was the first Yorkshireman to lead England since Stanley Jackson, he had been, wrote Alan Gibson, 'destined to the succession before the war': because Yardley was a gentleman. In Australia in 1946–47, Yardley had been the de facto leader in place of the remote Hammond. One of the rare playing successes of that tour, Yardley was nicknamed 'Spof' by his teammates – a reference to Fred 'the

Demon' Spofforth – when he took Bradman's wicket three times with his wrong-footed medium pacers. 'Norman Yardley was, and is, immensely liked and respected. I have hardly ever heard an unkind word said of him,' Gibson said. He was considered the best of the county captains, though he did not bully his men like his Yorkshire predecessor Brian Sellars and had a disdain for cricket politics. If an amateur had to lead England – and one still did – the steady hand at the tiller was Yardley.

But there was optimism in England. O'Reilly wrote that 'there must have been many English hearts beating quietly but confidently'. They expected Australia to be weaker than in 1946–47, when England had been just out of war and the umpiring had gone against them. 'Bradman was growing no younger with the years and sooner or later his speed of hand, eye and foot must slow down.' The other Australians were inexperienced in English conditions. In 1947, the 'Middlesex twins', Compton and Edrich, had both broken Tom Hayward's forty-year-old record for the most runs in a summer. In the Tests, England had beaten South Africa convincingly, Compton and Edrich reaping six centuries between them while Wright and Edrich bagged the majority of the wickets. Edrich, Compton and Washbrook all averaged more than 68, while in the five Test matches the Hutton–Washbrook opening stands were 40, 20, 75, 26*, 40, 63, 141, 47*, 63 and 73. Compton's eighteen centuries broke all records, but it was his panache that excited England most, a rare splash of colour in the greyness. As Cardus wrote, 'There were no rations in an innings by Compton.'

But then, in the West Indies, a depleted English team had lost a four-Test series 2–0. Compton, Edrich, Washbrook, Wright, Bedser and Yardley had rested from the tour, which was led by the 45-year-old Allen. England was utterly overwhelmed by a West Indian team that was surging out of the war years with the prodigies Walcott, Weekes and Worrell. Hutton's forgettable series in the West Indies, where he had been called up as a late reinforcement, left many to question whether his talents were on the permanent fade. Had his confidence been ruined by the assault on his arm in Australia? If the pre-eminent opening batsman could not blunt Lindwall and Miller in 1948, England would be exposed and Bradman's ruthlessness would, in cricketing terms at least, be vindicated.

More optimism rested with the improving Surrey swinger Bedser. In a speech at the Savoy Hotel, Bradman had praised the right-armer and wondered, humorously, why Bedser had sent him a telegram congratulating him for deciding to tour.

Bradman was an unabashed fan ever since Bedser had bowled him in the Adelaide Test of 1946–47. The ball was, Bradman thought, 'the finest ever to take my wicket. It must have come three quarters of the way straight on the off stump then suddenly dipped to pitch on the leg stump, only to turn off the pitch and hit the middle and off stumps. It was Bedser's misfortune to bowl quite a few more of this type which [narrowly missed] the off stump.'

The next day, a boy approached Bedser on Glenelg Beach and said: 'You've spoilt my weekend. I could hit you. Why did you bowl out Don Bradman for a duck?'

Bedser's leg-cutter had been unplayable for more batsmen than the Don. When he had beaten Barnes with one, the opener called out: 'Eh, what the hell's going on?'

Not everyone was pleased with the way Bradman was building Bedser up. Miller had been batting at the other end in Adelaide, and he thought the 'wonder ball' was a straight one that Bradman simply missed. Miller said it was unnerving the other batsmen to hear Bradman praising Bedser so highly.

As for Bedser, he was taking it humbly. Fingleton bumped into him at the Piccadilly Hotel and mentioned Bradman's Savoy speech. Bedser, characteristically modest, smiled and blushed.

'It was just one of those things that happened,' said Bedser. 'The ball floated away in the air and turned back. I don't know how I did it.'

*

Six weeks of first-class games lay between Bradman's Australians and the first Test in Nottingham, on 10 June. This long period reflected a time when many of the English counties had been a match for a full-strength Australia. In the earliest tours, Australia only played England once; three dozen matches spread over four months against counties and invitation XIs were considered a sufficient test. The Gloucestershire teams bursting with Graces; the glorious Cambridge students of the 1870s and 1880s; the Surrey bowling batteries of George Lohmann, Bill Lockwood and Tom Richardson; Archie MacLaren's Lancashire; Kent and Yorkshire, led by the potentates of early cricket, Lords Harris and Hawke; and, of course, the Marylebone Cricket Club provided as fierce a contest as scratch All-England teams.

By 1948, however, the counties were in decline and the Test matches had long been the proving ground. It would soon be apparent that the war had accelerated the weakening of many county teams, leaving only Yorkshire, Lancashire, Hampshire, Derbyshire, Glamorgan and Middlesex as serious threats. Therefore, Bradman could look at the six-week pre-Test program as a psychological phase, in which he could build up the confidence of his inexperienced men and, correspondingly, niggle away at the mentality of the opponent.

The schedule called for ten days in London, filled with functions and, if possible, some practice, before the team would open its campaign in Worcester on 27 April. At a function at Australia House, they met past England players such as Hammond, Jack Hobbs, Herbert Sutcliffe, Percy Chapman and Arthur Gilligan. Douglas Jardine, the architect of Bodyline, chatted with several Australian players but not Bradman.

Bradman, a man who never forgot how New South Wales selectors omitted him from a team when he was seventeen, was hardly going to let the memory of Bodyline fade. Fingleton said someone at the reception asked Jardine if he had owned a copy of Bradman's book *How to Play Cricket*. Jardine said no. The man said, 'Ah, it must have been a forgery then.' He had found a copy second-hand, signed by Bradman affectionately, 'To Douglas'.

For Bradman, crossing paths with Jardine was the least of his stresses. At Australia House, he wrote, 'I had to receive some 200 guests and after shaking hands with them I suddenly acquired a new-found respect for the duties of royalty, together with a fear that my right hand would not recover prior to the first match at Worcester.'

Receptions crowded the first week; the team could only accept a small fraction of their invitations. Bradman had to make a speech at every one. He agreed to sign menus as souvenirs, but asked in return for a donation to the Spastic Centre of the Adelaide Crippled Children's Hospital, which had helped treat his daughter Shirley. For a man who felt hemmed in when out in public, these days 'were a nightmare . . . Suddenly [I] had to rub shoulders with leaders of the Empire . . . be the principal guest and speaker when all around are the most brilliant orators in the land. It is a frightening prospect.'

Everyone wanted a piece of him, and he found it an 'ordeal'. Functions were thrown by the Royal Empire Society, the British Sportsmen's Club, the Institute of Journalists and the Cricket Writers' Club. London's Lord Mayor invited the team to a private dinner at Mansion House. 'For weeks in advance I worried about each and every function. Would I make an unholy mess of my speech – say the wrong thing – repeat myself?'

His anxiety having driven him to prepare with the utmost thoroughness during the voyage, his speeches now won due praise. Having faced the prospect of losing him, the cricket establishment was savouring him. He ranged from the light-hearted – recommending England choose the Duke of Edinburgh for his off spinners – to the semi-serious, dodging questions about the controversies of 1946–47 and Lindwall's drag. He chided O'Reilly for criticising Australia's over-appealing 'when you taught our boys to do it', and warned the press not to beat up 'incidents or sensations'. He refuted suggestions that Australia played cricket too seriously and defensively, saying the three batsmen who had scored centuries before lunch on the first day of an Ashes Test – Victor Trumper, Charlie Macartney and himself – were all Australian.

The BBC interrupted its normal programming to broadcast his 22 April speech to the Cricket Writers' Club, as well as those of Canon Gillingham, who noted the front-page headlines from the past week ('Four Murderers Reprieved', 'Gangsters Charter', 'Australian Cricketers Arrive'), and Justice Sir Norman Birkett, who spoke for many when he hoped Bradman's decision to retire might not be final, as 'life always gives opportunities for repentance'.

Australia's military participation in the war had increased the cricketers' prestige. Fingleton was moved by the spirit of the early gatherings, writing: 'There was about the receptions to the Australian cricketers this time a warmness not equalled, indeed, by those of pre-war years. It was good to be in England again.'

Loxton remembered: 'It was fascinating, the people you'd meet at those receptions. We were given every privilege you could possibly think of. Those of us who'd been in the army and air force, we'd roughed it a bit and were now being treated magnificently.'

One side benefit of the opulent luncheons and dinners was that the team ate better than in their hotel. Breakfast at the Piccadilly was half a piece of toast and one mushroom. There was rarely red meat, just chicken, fish and bad sausages. Even in the House of Commons, the only meat on the menu was seal or whale steak.

'The food was pretty nasty,' Harvey says. 'We sneaked an occasional good meal. I remember going to the Cornhill Chophouse in the Bank area and being served lamb chops. It felt like Christmas. Everything was rationed. Keith Johnson gave you ration books to get chocolate, and when you'd used them up, you were gone. We just ate what the English people ate.'

What did the English eat? Bedser recalled: 'We had rations until 1952–53. Breakfast before I went out and bowled was half a sausage, half a tomato, a pat of butter, two slices of bread. I used to go down to Old Trafford and find the old lady doing the catering, because they got extra rations, and I'd scrounge two cheese rolls. That was what it was.'

To spread goodwill, the Australians distributed tinned fruit and other food – 200 cases, including fifty cases of Ballantyne's beef dripping – that had been loaded onto the *Strathaird* in Fremantle. State cricket associations had contributed fifty pounds per Board of Control seat to the Food for Britain campaign. A tin of food would be distributed to the campaign for every run scored in the Trent Bridge Test. The Victorian government also gave £5000 sterling worth of food aid. On 26 April, Bradman and Keith Johnson presented Food Minister Strachey with a food consignment from the Australian Board. The Australians were the picture of beneficence, bringing the bounty of the Antipodes to the war-ravaged north. Bradman was conscious that he was also projecting a picture of his men as bursting with good health, as opposed to their Spam-fed, ration-eking rivals.

Strachey took Bradman and Johnson to the Silver Jubilee Service in St Paul's Cathedral. Their car got stuck in the crowds, Bradman said, 'with the result that Mr and Mrs Strachey, Keith Johnson and I found ourselves in the middle of the road on Ludgate Hill with rows of fixed bayonets on either side, walking in a procession of glittering cars containing famous people. It was somewhat embarrassing, especially as here and there a small coterie of people would recognise us.' At the end of the service, they sang 'God Save the Queen', 'in which the Cathedral Grand Organ and the trumpets of the Heralders joined to produce music of indescribable beauty. It made one's heart swell with pride.'

In that first week and a half, the team also saw *Annie Get Your Gun* at the Coliseum Theatre and the FA Cup final, in which Manchester United beat Blackpool 4–2, in seats beside the Royal Box at Wembley. In defiance of austerity, Britain's dance halls, live theatres and cinemas were enjoying levels of popularity never seen before or since. Morris went off and played squash. Barnes plied his wares in the Piccadilly; so busy was he that his roommate, Brown, applied for a transfer when he couldn't get any sleep. 'Sid was a bit different from everybody else,' Harvey says.

> Sid was a bit for Sid, unfortunately. A one-man band. People were good to us in England: they gave us shirts and boots and bats and other presents; in Scotland they gave us cashmere sweaters, which they'd then photograph us in, to advertise them. We were an advertising tool. Simpsons of Piccadilly gave us pairs of pads. There were always gifts, but Sid set up shop in his hotel room and flogged them off to the public.

Morris, who became Barnes's roommate, says: 'They'd call him bipolar nowadays. He could be very funny, but also very low. He was the best batsman I'd seen outside Bradman, but unfortunately the war intervened. Now the war was over, he was determined to make some money, and got on the wrong side of the administration. It shouldn't have happened. But it was probably bound to, because Sid was an individual.'

Flanagan wrote perceptively of Barnes: 'At heart, and in disposition, Sid Barnes is a fellow of infinite generosity and kindness. Yet he wages constant war against those innate qualities to assume an antic temperament, believing it gives him a status which ordinarily he imagines he does not possess . . . A lone wolf, Sid Barnes seldom mixes in with the crowd, or joins in with mass celebrations.'

The Australians of 1948 were far from a homogeneous bunch. While Barnes was wheeling and dealing and Harvey was gaping at the sights, Miller caught up with girlfriends he had made during the war – including 'Christine from Putney', who he was distressed to find had been admitted to a psychiatric ward since his previous visit. Bradman and others had a round of golf with Walter Robins at the Burnham Beeches club in Buckinghamshire. Tallon took on the locals in a snooker game for money (and won), while Bradman took great relief from the golf, which permitted him 'to become an ordinary mortal, to be envious of some other fellow's ability, but above all to get the mental relaxation which golf so peculiarly affords'. Still, he thought his game was adversely affected by cricket. 'There is the tendency to bend the left arm and slice the ball over the "covers" which is a splendid method of getting in the rough.' Back at the Piccadilly, he sat up most of the night answering the hundreds of letters that poured in each day.

He also had to deal with personal matters, such as when Barnes asked if he could drive up to Scotland to see his wife Alison and his son. Sid Junior had only been a few days old when Barnes had last seen him, in October 1947. To Barnes's great joy, Bradman assented.

'My wife had a furnished cottage just out of Edinburgh and we had a grand family reunion,' Barnes said. 'I determined then that I would never again travel without them. Cricket could take a back seat if it affected my family life.'

On his way back, he was pulled over for speeding, but when he explained who he was, the policeman gave him a high-speed escort into London.

Barnes was one of seventeen Australians who were beginning to chafe to play some cricket. He didn't enjoy the endless functions. 'You itch to be at the practice nets but you have to sit still for hour after hour, listening to some old boys talking about the bonds that bind Empires together. It is always the same old line, every tour.'

Even Harvey, while not as irreverent as Barnes, was growing jittery. 'We'd try to get some practice in; it'd be raining. We'd have to go to an official luncheon; that'd finish at three, then there'd be dinner at seven.'

On the first Saturday afternoon, they had a net at the Nursery End at Lord's. Otherwise they 'sandwiched' in practice, as Bradman put it, between functions and April showers. Whether they were returning to Lord's or seeing it for the first time, the Australians felt at home. In the roofed Nursery, the professionals were teaching young boys. A new concrete pitch had been laid. Bradman chatted with Field Marshal Lord Alexander, whose son was receiving a batting lesson. Fingleton wrote:

> Lord's had barely changed at all. It was drab and stood in much need of paint, but then this applied to most of London – indeed, it did to the cities of Australia. We saw Lord's again in the soft sunlight of an English spring day. There was freshness in the trees and on the grass, though the scoreboard had run amok in its winter's hibernation. It showed forty wickets down for no runs, the last man inconceivably made 82, and the same bowler had performed the amazing feat of bowling from both ends.

Curious crowds gathered to watch the Australians, particularly to see Bradman and Lindwall. In this psychological phoney war period, Bradman was keen to promote the mystique of Lindwall and his thunderbolts. When the paceman flattened Ring's stumps with successive balls, Ring left them lying down to emphasise Lindwall's destructiveness. When photographers gathered to try to shoot Lindwall's action close-up, Bradman stood in their way.

Barnes was in a three-way selection battle with Morris and Brown. He felt it keenly and was not happy with his form in the nets. 'I had put on weight in the wrong places on the ship. I determined not to take the risks on shipboard that I had in 1938. I didn't take any chances of a broken wrist this time and the inactivity left me somewhat porky. I knew at the nets at Lord's that I would have to work hard to get down to my playing weight.'

There was a bit of history between Barnes and Lord's. The previous summer, when visiting with his wife during his Lancashire League stint, he had been denied a request for a net. 'I was barred at Lord's! This was a smack in the eye, if you like. Six weeks before, I was making big scores in Australia against the English Test team, and now, here in London, Lord's could not offer me the courtesy of a net. Fine talk, all that business about cricket binding countries and people together. The home of cricket was deliberately high-hatting me.'

Now, in 1948, Barnes was alive to the irony of being treated as 'Mr Barnes of the Australian Eleven'. 'That made a difference and the red carpet was out with handshakes and smiles on all sides.' He set himself with inimitable Barnesian grit to make a century in the Lord's Test match.

Slowly, the team was emerging from its chrysalis of voyage and tuxedo. In the nets, little was lost on what Fingleton called 'the critics and the cynics of the game, noting this and demonstrating that, already certain in the first five minutes that A would be a complete success on the tour and B an utter flop. There can be no other sound in England to equal the first hit of a new season at Lord's.'

Some said Bradman was not the same as in 1938. Others questioned Barnes's back-foot style and Morris's footwork. One of the Australian journalists nodded towards the big, bald, bounding left-armer Bill Johnston and said to John Arlott, 'I don't know why on earth they picked him.' In a newspaper interview, Hutton commented: 'It's a very strong side viewed from every angle.' Wally Hammond called for the 'sporting' kind of wickets that had been prepared for the Victory Tests.

Everyone had a speculation about this Australian side. In a matter of days, opinion would be tested against fact.

On 27 April, Bradman's team boarded a train at Paddington for the 225-kilometre trip to Shrub Hill station in Worcester. They travelled in suits and ties. The balding little gunner, the blue-eyed Victorian, the wheeler-dealer Sydney street urchin, the silent Queenslander with the stomach ulcers, the pair of blond St George footballers. Side by side were the neat little teenager from the alleys of Fitzroy and his ever-present 'big brother' from Armadale. All of what they thought of this critic were better expressed verbally than in print.'

By claiming his own feelings for Fingleton were shared by the other players, Bradman might have been drawing a long bow. Hassett, for instance, remained a good friend of Fingleton's. While Bradman stayed in his cabin, another world was going on outside. When he saw Fingleton and Hassett strolling around the deck of the *Strathaird* together, he sent his cease-and-desist message through a peeved Miller, who wrote later: 'Bradman, who had not got on particularly well with Fingleton for a long time, asked me – on my first trip to England – to speak to Lindsay. "Tell Lindsay not to knock about with that chap," said Bradman. "He's one of the Press!"'

Miller refused, but Bradman found more sympathetic ears when he warned the youngsters Harvey and Loxton against Fingleton. One day during the voyage, Fingleton approached the young pair.

'You two will know you've been playing cricket after this tour,' he said.

Loxton and Harvey had never met Fingleton personally, and were on the defensive. Loxton said, 'We're looking forward to it.'

'This Bradman,' Fingleton went on, 'he'll walk over the top of you. He's not interested in you, he's only interested in winning. He couldn't care less about you.'

'I'm in the side and I suppose I've got a job to do,' Loxton bristled.

'You don't understand. I played with him. I know what he's like. I fielded in the O'Reilly leg trap. O'Reilly bowled a half-pitcher . . .'

Loxton thought, 'Hello, there's something wrong with this story. O'Reilly never bowled a half-pitcher in his life. O'Reilly was a genius.'

Fingleton went on: '[A] tail-ender laid back his ears and middled it, right into my head. All I can remember is this squeaky little voice in the covers saying, "Catch it!" Bradman was more of sportsmanship and gentlemanly behaviour above the job of beating England. Fingleton, a better writer than O'Reilly, had a more subtle personality, cagey, intelligent, and more resolutely anti-Bradman. Whereas O'Reilly and Bradman shared a mutual respect since boyhood days in the Southern Highlands of New South Wales – they were the paramount Australian Test players of the 1930s – Fingleton and Bradman had not got on well since the Bodyline series, when Bradman inferred that Fingleton was the notorious 'dressing room leaker' – the player who had repeated to a journalist Bill Woodfull's line to Pelham Warner about 'two sides out there and only one is playing cricket'. Fingleton denied it, and counter-accused Bradman. Fingleton was never Bradman's 'rival' as a cricketer; he was the first to acknowledge that Bradman had no rivals, except perhaps Hammond. The undercurrent of sectarianism flowed strongly in Australian cricket, as throughout society, in the 1930s. It had died out during the war, when Catholics and Protestants discovered that their blood was the same colour; nevertheless, Fingleton's presence on the 1948 tour was a reminder for Bradman of those bitter years. Sectarianism was another facet of Bradman's ingrained worldview that had emerged from the war untouched.

From the outset, Fingleton was unafraid to be personal in his criticism. In his tour preview for London's *Daily Mail* (in which he disclosed Bradman's aim to go undefeated), he also wrote: 'There are things for which we count the game most blessed that Bradman seems to have missed. We have always had a spirit of comradeship between us that, in my personal experience, has been unknown to Bradman. He thinks we are jealous and resentful of him. He's wrong. A lot of us only think he has sacrificed much for runs and records.'

A livid Bradman told Keith Johnson that Fingleton would 'not receive any further privileges on the tour as far as I am concerned'. Bradman said his players expressed 'their disgust at what was obviously a personal tirade against me ... Their references to them, together, and the thing was starting at last.

Bradman took, among the creams and kit and prepared speeches, 'a large suitcase full of unopened letters'. He didn't converse much with the team. For at least three hours in the train he opened letters. In Worcester he opened letters for an hour before dinner, and another two hours after. He was helped by the team's masseur, Arthur James (who surely needed a massage himself afterwards), and an unnamed teammate. 'All that just to open and read the letters,' Bradman said. 'Not answer them.'

Bradman resembled a modern St Paul, conscientiously dashing off correspondence. He estimated receiving 100 personal letters a day, up to 600 at peak times. The result was a deepening reputation for unsociability. Andy Flanagan observed: 'You see very little of him on tour, except on the field. He comes in to the dining room for breakfast and dinner and joins the other players wherever there may be a vacant seat. But then he seems to disappear.'

His younger players understood, and admired, his dedication. For his attentiveness to this correspondence, Harvey calls Bradman 'a champion bloke'. 'And it wasn't just Bradman who had the letters,' Harvey adds. 'We'd all get our fair share of personal mail. Often it was just addressed to, "Australian team, Leicester" or wherever, but sometimes it was to us as individuals.'

Harvey is coy about his own mail, but Flanagan outed him as a pin-up boy. 'Young English girls, and Scotch lassies, too, wrote imploringly to Neil Harvey for an autographed photo of himself and he had scores of photos of attractive young ladies crowding his dressing-table.'

There is no gainsaying the diplomatic impact of Bradman's efforts. Never accused of doing things by halves, he appeared set on winning cricket fans one at a time.

The team sailed along in his slipstream. Flanagan noted an almost regal reception: 'To travel throughout England with Bradman is a unique experience. Cities, towns and hotels are beflagged, carpets set down, and dignitaries wait to extend an official welcome. He is the Prince of Cricketers.' Bradman was presented with a bat made of marigolds and green leaves, the word 'Don' woven into the blade.

On their first night in Worcester, the team inspected the cathedral, with its chime of twelve bells and the tomb of King John. Worcester had been a Cromwell town; Fingleton recalled how O'Reilly, in 1938, had bowled at his fieriest against Worcestershire when the tolling carillion reminded him of the Roundheads.

All this, though, was preamble. That night, the young journalist John Arlott captured the unique spell of anticipation, bottled up by ten years, six of them in war, that would be broken the next day. Arlott had been a poor cricketer, a Southampton policeman and a BBC poetry producer before emerging, fully formed, as England's favourite cricket commentator in 1947.

> Tomorrow we shall see him again. What will his opening gambit be? . . . English cricket, since the war, has been building up to this season. The visits of the Indian and South African teams made happy summers. This one, however, will be grimmer . . . No cricketer is to blame for the fact that this year people will try to make cricket something other than a game.

Something other than a game? George Orwell had coined the phrase 'war minus the shooting' when shocked by the bitterness of Dynamo Moscow's football matches in England in 1945, the first autumn of peace. The anticipation of the coming cricket tour contained as much fear as joy, a tingling worry that the celebration of cricket would renew the edge of real combat from the 1946–47 series in Australia.

Wednesday, 28 April dawned cold upon the queues formed in the dark. Schoolchildren, given a half-day off, followed their parents into the red-and-white-striped marquees and the grandstand built on stilts to withstand the Severn's floods.

Bradman selected his team like a card player with a handful of trumps: why bother foxing? He wanted to win, or at least avoid losing, all of the thirty-two scheduled first-class games. Simple. So he chose his first-draft Test team for the first game. Morris and Barnes won the opening jobs ahead of Brown, who moved down the order to add commonsense between Miller and the tail. Lindwall, Toshack, Ian Johnson and McCool would be the bowlers. Bradman still fancied two spinners, a legacy of having been undefeated in Ashes series in England in the 1930s on the arms of Grimmett and O'Reilly.

In 1938 Bradman had called tails in all the non-Test matches, with great success, and heads in the Tests – losing all five. This time he decided to call heads in every match. Allan White tossed, Bradman called heads, and the coin fell tails.

In 1878, the first representative Australian team in England had been so underdressed for their opening game they had shivered in their silk shirts and talked about going home. With seventy years of learning behind them, the 1948 Australians took the field wearing several sweaters each.

Lindwall, who always took a while to warm up, was still slippery enough to pin Don Kenyon on his crease with the second ball of the tour. Not a bad start, but Bradman continued to restrain his paceman.

His management of the dragging issue is a textbook example of his political savoir-faire and deployment of power. At Lord's, Bradman had addressed an umpires' conference, 'noticing their obvious desire to cooperate with the players, and to be scrupulously fair'. Another way of putting it is that he was buttering them up. He planned to neutralise the dragging issue by holding Lindwall back, and by mollifying Lord's. After Bradman's speech, the MCC chose two of England's senior umpires, probable Test officials Fred Root and Dai Davies, to control the Worcester match. Nobody wanted a scene. Root later told Lindwall that he'd come away from the London meeting 'with the strong feeling that the authorities at Lord's hoped that the match would not contain any sensations'.

But Root, one of the game's eccentrics, could not necessarily be bought. The son of Leicestershire's groundsman, he had decided from childhood to be a cricketer, even asking his vicar for a reference at the local club. In France, in 1916, he was shot in the chest. His army doctor told him he wouldn't play cricket again, but from his hospital bed Root arranged a Bradford League professional contract. Bowling at a commercial medium pace, he knew better than to hurl it down fast. He counselled other young professionals to do likewise – a conservatism for which England was about to pay a high price. That said, Root was no percentage player. He was ever ready to take a crack at the hypocrisy of amateurs who accepted gifts and 'expenses'. He urged attacking, crowd-pleasing cricket (from batsmen) and once told Lord Harris to stop talking in the slips cordon.

But the key to Root being chosen as umpire was that he was a dragger himself. After playing in the 1926 Test series against Australia, he had stated in a film that all pace bowlers dragged. He might have been a rebellious type – he later lost his Test umpiring position because he wrote for the press – but on dragging he was a liberal. His appointment at Worcester, where Ernie McCormick had been no-balled thirty-five times in 1938, torpedoing Bradman's plans, 'presaged smooth sailing for Lindwall', Fingleton said.

Lindwall bowled fifteen overs on the first day without incident. It was Bradman's first victory of the tour, and proof of the unspoken sway he held over Lord's. The MCC knew that the success of the summer, financially and morale-wise, depended on Bradman playing. But to get him to come to England, they had to cooperate. They had already pleased him greatly with the experimental 55-over new-ball law. The quid for the pro quo was simple: no 'controversies'. For the next five months, he felt umpires adopted 'a very sensible attitude' to the drag. In cricket's best tradition, it was a victory of politics over law.

*

It took just the one day for the Australians to witness the best innings by a non-Test English player they would see from April to September. The slight, bespectacled schoolteacher Charles Palmer showed 'a rich flow of strokes', sharp footwork and 'plenty of time in which to do things' that had Fingleton marking him down 'as a class player'.

Class, however, remained the operative word. Palmer's 85 was a beautiful knock, but he would not be seriously considered for England because as an amateur he could only turn out on weekends and holidays. His school needed him more than his country.

In turn, England was fascinated by every one of these Australians. Among the crowd was a young Glamorgan all-rounder, Allan Watkins, whose county captain Wilfred Wooller had sent him to Worcester with a specific brief: 'Watch Toshack.'

He was worth watching. Bradman called Toshack 'a player unique in every way. I cannot remember another of the same type. His normal delivery was medium-pace left arm over the wicket, and he would cut the ball from, say, a right-hander's off stump to his leg stump. Then he would spin one from leg to off, bowl a faster one straight through and occasionally just drift one either to off or leg.'

Watkins would go back to Wales and imitate Toshack's tight line so successfully that his teammates nicknamed him 'Tosh'. Not only did Glamorgan begin to march up the county table towards their first-ever title, but Watkins would get the chance to play Test cricket against the Australians before the end of the summer.

The Australians, as Australians always had and would, appealed a lot. Toshack raised both hands to the umpire and cried 'Ow whizz 'e?' To go with Toshack's other nicknames – 'The Black Prince', 'The Film Star' – Fingleton christened him 'The Voice', for the way his appeals 'float across the ground and penetrate every nook'.

Fred Root was less impressed, replying to Toshack, 'I don't know. Is that an appeal?'

No doubt the appeals were excessive. Fingleton said some 'came from fantastically situated positions, but perhaps the boys wanted to keep warm'.

The cold surprised everyone. While the players were able to crouch by the fire in the pavilion, the press had no heat in a shed 'that admitted all breezes without question or visa', Fingleton said, noting that these were the coldest days he'd ever spent at a cricket ground, 'though Leicester and Bradford, particularly the latter, were still looming ahead like icebergs in the Atlantic'.

Morris says, 'It was too cold to do much outdoors, and you didn't realise at the start what a long six months it was going to be. And it was cold. At Worcester, you'd put two or three sweaters on and hope the ball didn't come near you.'

Worcester made 233, three runs fewer than Bradman in his only innings there in 1930. Four years later he'd made 206. As captain in 1938, he'd scored 258.

Now he joined Morris after Barnes was out for 44. The focus was on Bradman, of course – was he as good as before the war? – and Bradman duly did his Worcester thing. His driving drew gasps of recognition. Then it was the glides and dabs and cuts; always, his busyness, his effervescence, his placement. Thousands of letters and autographs, all those speeches, the garlands and red carpets – but here he was again, on his stage. The rumours were misplaced. 'We had read by suggestion that something had been lost, or slightly diminished, of his past glory,' said *The Times*. 'That is not true, for yesterday we were privileged once again to see the batsman who is the complete proof that a bowler can bowl only so well as the striker allows him to do . . . If any man can believe that Bradman is past his best he is welcome to spend an hour or so in bowling to him.'

Bradman got to 99 ahead of Morris, who kept the strike. Bradman shook his fist, feigning anger.

'I beat him to it!' Morris laughs. 'I probably smirked at him.' More seriously, he remembers having a point to prove. 'It was a great relief, because according to some journalists I wouldn't get a run, playing off the back foot as I did. But [Stan] McCabe never played forward. Bradman and Barnes were back-foot players. Once you lunge forward with that foot there's nowhere to go. There was nothing to say you couldn't score runs in England as a back-foot player.'

Bradman passed his hundred the next over, waking Arlott from a revery. The important thing, for Bradman, was to foster gloom in English cricketers' minds. Arlott felt it: 'There it was, happening under our very eyes again – a Bradman century to start the tour. To be sure there was a suggestion of stiffness which was new, a hint of the batsman's anxiety to score yet another hundred on this ground. But there was no encouragement for English bowlers in this same superb and merciless confidence.'

He showed his age, however, by eschewing the double ton. To save his strength and his fragile intercostal, he threw his wicket away after a two-and-a-half-hour 107. Morris, 138, would outscore if not outshine him.

Miller had an attractive slog, but Hassett, Brown and McCool were short of practice. It didn't matter for the match, the spinners ensuring an innings win on a wearing pitch speckled with saw-dust. Brown heard a spectator cry out to the ground staff: 'Go easy with yon sawdust! That's wasting a full month's ration of ruddy sausage meat!'

All in all, a job well done. The record three-day crowd of 32000 contributed £4000, double the 1938 gate. A guildhall dinner produced eight courses, each supplied by a local councillor from his farm, and mercifully no speeches.

But there was also a hollowness in the victory, Fingleton opining that the crowd was 'the most unresponsive one I have known'. After all the anticipation, perhaps a certain flatness was predictable. Perhaps the Australians' superiority had too much inevitability about it. Perhaps Bradman, having proved his point, also had too much inevitability. Across England, hope began its slow slide towards self-doubt.

Miller considered himself a true rival to Bradman as a batsman and an entertainer. In the next game in Leicester, he answered his captain's century with a sumptuous 202 not out, what he thought would be the first of many big innings on tour. Bradman had other plans for him, however.

In more cold, damp weather, the other Australian batsmen faltered against the spin of Vic Jackson and Jack Walsh, two former Sydney bowlers. O'Reilly said, 'If the [England] selectors had seen the way in which Walsh mesmerized the Australian batsmen I feel certain that England would have placed much more hope on spin bowling than she did.'

But England's best two county spinners were Australians. Bradman missed a ball from Walsh by two feet, in Fingleton's estimation. 'I had never before seen Bradman so completely beaten.'

Harvey, finally getting a bat in England, looked like a lost boy. Said Arlott: 'Neil Harvey was completely baffled by Walsh's googly, which struck back at him while he was playing it as the ball that leaves him . . . It is rare to see the first-class batsman so utterly without an idea what the ball is doing.' Thanks to wickets from Ring and Johnson, Australia again won by an innings, but as keenly as Bradman wanted to win, he must have been disturbed by the lack of serious batting opposition. Bill Johnston couldn't control his swing, while Loxton couldn't swing the ball at all. None of the bowlers got better than a fair rating.

More entertaining was Barnes, who told the umpire Alec Skelding he needed a guide dog. Skelding, keen to join in the fun, later sent Barnes a note saying he had three pairs of spectacles: one for lbws, one for run-outs and one for catches behind. He said he had left his white cane in the pavilion and guide dog outside the ground.

Miller, typically, enjoyed the roguish Skelding, who, he recalled, 'always wears white boots, reminding me of umpires at home, and he generally carries a flask of something which, he maintains, "keeps out the cold and helps me to see straighter".' One day Harvey threw down the wicket. 'In that husky sergeant-major parade-ground bark that every man who has played first-class cricket in England in recent times knows, Skelding called out: "It's a photo finish, but we can't wait for the photo, so he's not out."'

On the matter of the dog, Barnes would have the last laugh.

Bradman's plan to intimidate the English players suffered its first setback in the next match, in Bradford. Disappointing Yorkshire officials, he stayed in London with Barnes. It wasn't unusual for resting players to take time out from travelling; on this tour, Harvey became, he believes, the first and only Australian cricketer to buck the tradition and stick with the team for every single match. Bradman and Barnes went to the London Exhibition, where Barnes bought movie equipment, Bradman a grand piano, and they listened for scores. The game would provide the first challenge to Bradman's grand plan, and the first sight of a weakness he did not want seen.

The start of the three-day game was delayed by rain until 2.30 p.m., but no amount of waiting, or hearing 'Waltzing Matilda' over the public address, was going to warm Fingleton's bones. 'This was the coldest day, surely, that cricket has ever known. The sunshine came in watery, rationed patches and a chill wind froze us in our open-air seats. I swear I once saw snow.'

Flanagan was appalled by what the paying public had to put up with. This was an unnecessary example, he thought, of the slogan 'Britain Can Take It'. The public had queued for hours to pay their 5/- to 7/6.

[And] when they got inside what were they offered? Not cushioned seats and covered stands, but bare boards, at Bradford bare stone, and the damp earth, and no covering whatever above them. They were ruthlessly exposed to the elements, and as they entered the grounds they were confronted with a sign which told them savagely that if, due to rain, there should be no play, not a penny of their admittance money would be refunded . . . I thought, what a pity Hitler didn't travel. Had he gone to England and seen these people he would never have attempted the impossible task of subduing their spirit or conquering their resolve.

The Australians huddled by their log fire and finally emerged, after Hassett lost the toss, not in two sweaters but three. Yorkshire had not been playing well since the war, Middlesex overshadowing them as the power county. But Yorkshire meant Hutton. His first single, taking the new ball, 'was cheered as lustily as if it were the winning run', said Fingleton. But he took another fifty-eight minutes to get his second, against Miller and Johnston, who were bowling slow-medium cutters and tweakers. Yorkshire was the only county not to cover its wickets overnight, and Hassett had his bowlers reduce their pace rather than risk injury. He held Lindwall back entirely. Loxton, who could never be held back, tore his groin slipping on the pitch in his first over.

On a dog of a wicket, Yorkshire fell for 71. At tea, the youth of Bradford poured onto the surface for football, cricket and other games. A child asked Yorkshire players for their autographs. Not wanting to attract a crowd, the players refused. Instead, Don Tallon offered his. 'No,' the boy said, 'I doon't want Australians. I want Yorkshire players.'

Yorkshire being Yorkshire, they expected to win. No county had beaten an Australian side since 1912, and the closest since had been the Yorkshire team of 1938. Forget England; Yorkshire had unfinished business.

Hassett opted against the heavy roller, which Fingleton thought might have been a mistake 'because whenever there was rain about in England the heavy roller seemed to knock any nonsense out of the pitch'. If not for Miller's 34, with two brazen sixes, Australia might have conceded a lead instead of edging ahead by 30. Johnston and Miller went through Yorkshire (and Hutton) again on the second morning, leaving precisely 60 to get. A Yorkshire committeeman remarked dismally to Hutton, 'If only Keith Miller had been born a Yorkshireman.'

On that wicket, anything could happen and soon did. John Wardle and Frank Smailes were too wily not to find the right pace and length. Brown was lbw padding up, Morris shuffled and popped one to Hutton, and Miller survived an lbw appeal but was caught on the fence trying to move things along. Hamence ran too slowly and Hassett skied a pull. Five for 20 became 6/31 when McCool spooned a short one back to Wardle. On 1, Harvey turned a ball to Hutton at short leg. Hutton got a hand under it but spilt it as he was falling. Harvey swept the next ball for four. *Wisden* thought Hutton's miss cost Yorkshire victory.

The eighth man, Tallon, went out preceded by a small dog as a hard sunlight broke through. He – Tallon, not the dog – was lucky to survive an lbw appeal.

In the dressing room Lindwall swung his bat vigorously to warm up and ease his tension. Hassett sat with his head in his hands and moaned, not even half in jest, 'Why me? Why is it always me?'

At the Piccadilly Hotel in London, Bradman and Barnes were sweating on telegraphed news of the match. According to Barnes, who was not averse to promoting his place in the scheme of things, Bradman said: 'This is the last time you and I will be out of this team together.'

Witnessing Bradman's despair, Barnes gained an insight into what was driving his captain.

'No Australian captain had ever gone through a tour unbeaten. Don, I knew, wished to finish this, his last tour, in a blaze of glory and had that unbeaten record marked out early. That is understandable but it meant there could be no let-up.'

Bradman had talked vaguely about going through the tour undefeated, but now, three matches in, on the precipice of losing any hope, impotent and half a day's travel from the scene, he resolved to leave nothing to chance.

In the last overs before tea, Harvey and Tallon survived their crises. Then Wardle dropped short and Tallon hit him for two fours. He spooned one out of the glue, but it fell short of the diving fieldsman. The flow of fortune was turning. By tea Australia were 6/47, Harvey and Tallon's chancy hitting having cut the target from 29 runs to 13.

The boys and girls came out again, one youth staring at the pitch, trying to divine its mysteries, until a policeman led him away. The players came out too early, and waited amid great tension for the clock to tick over.

Harvey charged Smailes and missed, but the wicketkeeper Don Brennan missed the stumping. Every piece of luck had to go Australia's way, and it did.

Harvey admits to being completely at sea:

> I couldn't get used to the seaming ball. It hadn't done so much in Australia. I'd borrowed this R.M. Crockett bat from my club to take to England, but it wasn't working. Nothing was! The Bradford wicket was such a wet, horrible thing. Seventy to win and we kept losing wickets. Eventually we needed four to win. Smailes was a big tall off-spin bowler. I hopped on a half volley, I don't know what made me do it – I was a rash teenager – and I hit the ball over the mid-on fence. I didn't hit six sixes in my life, but there it was!

After the tautness of thirty-six wickets falling in four sessions, the game was over in three overs after tea. Harvey's six let the air out of the Yorkshire crowd.

O'Reilly said any signs of 'invincibility' were 'dispersed' by Yorkshire's spin bowlers. The Australians, he said, were 'allergic to good-length spin bowling. They were to demonstrate this weakness many more times during their tour . . .'

Any previous Yorkshire team, O'Reilly felt, would have beaten the Australians 'as a pipe-opening job'. 'The weakest White Rose team perhaps in living memory almost did the trick.'

Fingleton sent Hassett a hoax telegram with Bradman's name on it: 'You nearly lost our record for me!' They could have a laugh now, but they knew the captain would return, after such a near miss and the attendant criticism, with a sharpened blade.

'It was probably a good thing to have been so hard pressed by a County early in the tour,' Bradman wrote. 'Such lessons are a valuable brake on complacency which can so easily arise when the opposition isn't too strong.'

In other words – never again.

The near-catastrophe at Bradford closed a first, vulnerable phase of the tour. Rusty from their voyage, cold, short on practice, Bradman's team was there for the taking on soft springtime wickets. That Worcestershire, Leicestershire and Yorkshire were unable to do so made a first statement about the general weakness of county cricket.

How much the war had depleted playing stocks remains an open question. Leaving aside the insoluble mystery of lives lost, young men were still required for compulsory national service in 1948, and overall nutrition in England since 1939 had fallen behind Australia's. More tangibly, the war's effect, as in the early 1920s, was to prolong the careers of cricketers well past their prime. For all Bradman's seniority, he was still the right side of forty. In 1948, nearly fifty players on the wrong side of it played first-class cricket for English teams.

Bradman, who dined at the Savoy in London while the team

was in Bradford, and met the pianist Carroll Gibbons while playing backstage with Gibbons' band, gave the team a day off on 7 May. They continued to remark on Londoners' spirit. Bill Brown said 'there was a tremendous sense of relief and of new life beginning, particularly in London which had been bombed so heavily during the war.'

If Bradman needed a spur to get serious (which he didn't), he had it at the next venue. The Oval appeared more barren than ever. Still scarred from its wartime use as military accommodation and storage, and briefly a POW camp, now its 'father, mother and baby' gasometers were being painted a murky green to brighten them up from military grey. Bradman, who arrived in a chauffeur-driven car and walked through the Hobbs Gates in a dark blue suit on 8 May, was thinking of another miserable experience: fielding for three days in the Test in 1938 while Hutton made 364 and England 903, and being carried off the field with a bone broken while bowling. During the war, Bradman believed that had been his ignominious finale in Test cricket.

Thousands poured out of the Tube to see the Australians play Surrey. The sun shone on a new wicket, apparently slower and drier than prewar. A gloomy Bedser said: 'Since the war, the wicket seems to have altered, and few people but the batsmen think it is for the better.' Fingleton was struck by the wear and tear on the ground: 'The war gave The Oval a hammering. Bowlers, the world wide, would have given three cheers had a bomb hit the somnolent pitch area and dug it up, but fires had badly damaged the pavilion and surrounding buildings, and as he entered the dressing-room a player had to watch his flannels from brushing against the black, burnt sides of the woodwork.'

Bradman won the toss and made a point of asserting himself over Bedser and the broad-shouldered young off spinner Jim Laker. He, Barnes and Hassett made centuries. A cocky Barnes gave the premier English seamer a cheeky pat on the rear with his bat after hitting one of his seventeen boundaries. Bradman was visibly jaunty. He 'enjoyed himself immensely', wrote Fingleton. 'Once he rushed through for a quick two, grabbed slip and did a turn around him, laughed, turned back smartly, tapped the pitch, hit the ball five yards and sped off for another short run.' In the pavilion, Toshack was eating a bread roll when a Surrey member asked him, 'What would happen if you bowled that to Bradman?' Toshack replied: 'He'd hit it clean over the bakery, I suspect.'

Australia made 632, bracketed around a Sunday off for golf. O'Reilly and Fingleton spent the day at Gravesend playing in a benefit match for Leslie Ames, the great Kent wicketkeeper-batsman of the 1930s, at the ground where George Bonnor had deposited a ball on the workhouse roof in 1886. The team were dinner guests at Armourers and Braziers Hall, Lord Rosebery presiding, for the cricket patron H.D.G. 'Shrimp' Leveson-Gower's seventy-fifth birthday. The birthday boy thanked the 'Supreme Umpire' for giving him 'the benefit of the doubt for 75 years'.

Bradman's men returned to The Oval on the Monday and Tuesday to rumble Surrey twice. Bradman had one anxious moment with Lindwall. One of the umpires was Harry Baldwin, who had changed the complexion of the 1938 tour by no-balling Ernie McCormick thirty-five times at Worcester. Baldwin now called Lindwall for his first no-ball of the tour. Otherwise, though, he restrained himself, as did Lindwall, and the match passed without controversy.

Harvey and Barnes provided different kinds of memorable moments in the field. Near the end of Surrey's first innings in the twilight on the Monday, Stuart Surridge was facing Ian Johnson. Harvey, who had failed again with the bat, was fielding on the wide long-on boundary.

'Stuart clobbered this thing,' Harvey says. 'I could just see it coming and started to gallop around the boundary. I jumped, grabbed it, fortunately it stuck, and I put the ball in my pocket. The boys didn't know I'd caught it. I ran in and said, "Here it is."'

Greatness always seems matter-of-fact to the actor himself;

so here is Bradman's view from the infield:

> I unhesitatingly rate [the catch] as the greatest of its kind I've
> ever seen. A towering drive seemed certain to go for 6, but
> Neil, running flat out to the left, took the catch high above
> his head and wide on his left side as he jumped into the air.
> The ball would have gone well over the ropes, and it was some
> seconds before even the players realized he had made the catch
> – it seemed an impossibility that he could even reach it.

The opponents were equally dazzled. Bedser said Harvey's was 'a
catch of incredible brilliance', and the belief began to grow that
Australia could effortlessly produce even teenagers who were a
species of supermen.

Barnes, meanwhile, had more in common with Bradman than
a superlative batting eye: he took special delight in payback. Alec
Skelding, the 'blind' umpire from the Leicester game, was again
officiating. A mongrel Jack Russell-fox terrier ran onto The Oval
while Surrey were batting. Johnson took it off, but it returned.
Bradman threw a ball at it, but the dog thought the Don was
playing a game with him. 'On came a dignified policeman,'
Fingleton observed, 'but the dog knew his policemen and gave
him a wide berth. Barnes trapped it with the ball as bait and
then marched it up to umpire Skelding, who got in a great flurry.
Skelding refused to take the dog, backed away and, with Barnes
persisting in his offer, hurriedly took the bails off and made for
the pavilion.'

Poor Skelding was terrified of dogs.

The start of the cricket had by no means stopped the eternal
banqueting. After the Surrey match, the Australians were guests of
honour for dinner at the House of Commons with the cabinet and
shadow cabinet. Labour Prime Minister Clement Attlee was their

host, having won an unprecedented majority in 1945. Winston Churchill, the Tory opposition leader, was in no mood to meet the Australians. 'At least he was honest,' says Morris.

Military bands, sunshine, oaks, walnuts, horse chestnuts, laburnum and a crowd of 10000 students on bicycles watched an easy Australian win, Bradman resting again, on the patterned turf of Fenner's at Cambridge. The university had once been the strongest first-class team in England, thrashing Dave Gregory's 1878 tourists, but no longer. Many of their audience were crippled ex-servicemen back in study, making up for lost time, stumping into Fenner's on artificial legs.

John Dewes, the left-handed Cambridge opener, had to face something of a nemesis in Miller. In the third 1945 Victory Test, Dewes had come into the England team as a teenage prodigy, having scored heavily for the university, where he was doing a short course after enlisting in the navy. But Miller's bouncers seemed magnetised to Dewes's ribs and thighs, and then Dewes went on to drop Miller at square leg. Whitington had written encouragingly: 'The eighteen-year-old Dewes revealed temperament, determination and defensive skill until Miller, bowling from a full run at what a member described as the fastest pace he had seen since he first saw Larwood, crashed through the youngster's guard.'

Since then, Dewes had served as a sub-lieutenant on minesweepers off the Faroe Islands, suffering constant seasickness, but at least eating well ('you ate better in the navy than as a civilian'), and batted for the Combined Services during a two-and-a-half-year stint. 'The Combined Services played here, there and everywhere,' he says. 'I got great experience from players who'd been county cricketers before the war.'

By 1948 he was back at Cambridge to study law, and again scoring runs. But Miller was back too. 'I'd never played anybody like that,' Dewes says. 'Nobody was that fast, and when he pitched it on a good length it would rear up. I couldn't play it at all.' As a precaution, he stuffed his shirt with a towel. Miller bounced him, then yorked him for 6, though Dewes made 40 in his second dig. 'Miller hit me but didn't hurt me so much,' he says. 'With a towel I thought I'd be a bit safer. Nobody else was doing it.'

Cambridge capitulated badly, the young Trevor Bailey and Doug Insole giving no hint of their future influence on England cricket by becoming involved in a comical mix-up. When they were stranded at the same end, Bailey said, 'I made the mistake of asking Doug where we went from there. His reply has always been extremely fast and he merely said, "You go back to the pavilion."'

Another of the Cambridge youngsters was Hubert Doggart. A future Test player and MCC president, Doggart was playing his third first-class game after a brief career in the army. 'I was only in the war for five weeks,' he says. 'I liberated Holland, with the help of a few others.'

In his first game for Cambridge, Doggart had scored a record unbeaten 215, sharing a big partnership with Insole. 'My third game for Cambridge was against the Australians. What a thrill! It was disappointing that Bradman wasn't there, because we wanted to see him.'

A double-century from Brown, 92 from Hamence and wickets from Miller and McCool sealed another easy win. 'The Australians treated us a bit kindly at Fenner's,' Dewes says. 'They didn't bust themselves.'

Doggart, who as a boy had collected the autographs of the 1934 Australian tourists, remembers a sociable touring group – one in particular. 'The thing that stands out is the party we gave at Emmanuel College, and how wonderful Keith Miller was, encouraging, interested. This went on after the tour with telephone calls, not only to Denis [Compton], but even to the chap in the Lord's pavilion, who he'd call on his birthday. He called me to keep up. Amazing. I eventually went and met him in Australia, and was introduced to his wife. We didn't know he had a wife, because he had a different one in England – a lovely nurse from St Mary's Hospital!'

In Cambridge's second innings, Doggart stroked a bright 33.

> I hit Lindwall through the covers and Fingleton wrote very
> kindly about my prospects. Having got through Lindwall and
> Miller, I had to face Toshack. I'd never faced anyone like that,
> bowling left arm over the wicket. At Selsey, where I grew up, my
> father had laid a concrete wicket that we covered with matting.
> Cricket was an off-side game as I learnt it. Toshack was very
> tall, bowled slow-medium. He got his wickets because people
> weren't used to his angle. Bill Johnston was more athletic and
> whippy. Both demanded that you have more of a leg-side game.
> Against Toshack, I was stumped but given not out, and then he
> gave me a little full toss. I was so surprised I hit it to Lindsay.

For Trevor Bailey, this and the next match would confirm what was
becoming obvious: the difference in pace between the countries'
fastest bowlers was unbreachable.

'There were no genuinely fast bowlers in England,' Bailey said,
'and until 1948, as one of the fastest around, I still cherished the
hope that I would become a bowler of real pace who would be
able to blast out the opposition. The arrival of Ray Lindwall and
Keith Miller changed all that, as their pace was yards faster; while
the third member of what was essentially a three-pronged attack,
Bill Johnston, was not only a much better bowler than myself, but
also quicker.'

Bailey, still considered too green for Tests but on his way
to becoming one of England's best all-rounders of the next
decade, scored 66 not out at Fenner's and hitched a ride with the
Australians to the next venue, Southend, where his county, Essex,
would host them.

'We let him on the bus because we all had to play the next day,'
Loxton recalled. 'Keith Johnson arranged it, and smuggled him
aboard. It was a nice gesture, but of course the next thing we knew,
Trevor was writing how we were "most peculiar people".'

In an article after the event, Bailey seemed shocked by the Australians' risqué limericks. Loxton staunchly defended his teammates: 'Hamence and Ring had lovely voices. They were the leaders of the communal singing. Lovely voices.'

Harvey, who would clash competitively with Bailey throughout the next decade, says:

> Trevor wasn't the most popular fellow to play against. He had that Cambridge demeanour about him, a pompous young cricketer, although, as we all know, he turned out to be a handy all-rounder for England. He came down in the bus with us after the Cambridge game and played against us at Southend for Essex. He got a hammering, of course, from Barnes and Bradman and co. I dare say it must have been good for him. When you think you're that good, and you get hammered by the best, it's got to do you good in the long run.

Johnson was another to take exception to Bailey, saying he was 'very much that of the caricatured Englishman lording it over the "Colonials", and not all Colonials are that thick-skinned. Trevor has been heard to say, in Australia, that he dislikes us. That's fair enough because he means it and no Australian minds anybody talking straight . . . [But] with Trevor's background and education, he should show more self-control, in the interests both of his team and his country.'

While sitting out the Cambridge match, Bradman was courted by the directors of Imperial Chemical Industries – with whom he would begin a business relationship – and played a mock cricket game on the floor of the London Stock Exchange. One broker dressed as W.G. Grace. Bradman remembered skying a ball that was lost 'in some far corner of the building from which, so far as I know, neither the bulls nor the bears returned it'. He was offered a whisky and soda, Grace-style, but, although he enjoyed an occasional drink, oiling up for batting was not a strategy Bradman had in common with the earlier champion.

The aura of invincibility that travelled in advance of this team can be traced to what happened at Southend on 15 May. Bradman had not played Essex on his three previous tours, so he joined his men who were sampling the carnival atmosphere and jellied eels at Southend Pier. He expected a tough opponent and wanted to make a statement. Bailey, he said, was 'rated the best bowler at Cambridge and one of the most promising fast-medium boys in England'. Ray Smith was 'a very useful fast-medium who bowled in-swingers to a leg field, a type of bowling hard to score from'. Peter Smith was 'one of *Wisden*'s 5 Cricketers of the year in 1946 who was brought to Australia in 1946–7 as understudy to Doug Wright and rated then as the second best slow in England'. And Tom Pearce 'was selected as a member of one of England's Test Trial teams in the same year'.

Four weeks of cricket had produced injuries – Lindwall had a leg strain, Tallon had hurt his hands, and McCool's spinning finger had blistered badly – so Bradman was pleased to bat first.

The 16000 crammed into Southchurch Park gave a great cheer when Barnes off-drove Bailey to the rope in the first over. They thought they were watching a normal day's cricket. They were not. Barnes and Brown put on 100 in 74 minutes, and that was just taking the shine off the ball.

Their biggest problem soon emerged to be not the bowling but each other. Barnes liked to monopolise the strike, and his stoush with Bradman in Colombo was no one-off. When Barnes had first seen Bradman in 1936–37, he 'noticed that [Bradman] seemed to get much more of the strike than other batsmen'.

> Was it accidental? Whether it was or not it gave me the impression that to be a great batsman you had to dominate the game and the strike . . . He took, I noticed, about two of every three balls that were bowled. This didn't just happen. Bradman made it happen. He judged his running between

wickets accordingly and got more singles off the last ball of the
over than any other batsman I've seen before or since – with
the possible exception of myself. I copied him in this and many
a few words we had in the middle, and other places, about
who was to get most of the strike . . . I refused to be a running
partner for anybody. Not even Bradman.

Now, against Essex, Brown 'rightly refused to be [Barnes's] running
hack', said Fingleton. At stumps, Bradman would sit them down
and tell them 'if anything like that happened again, he would
stand them down for two matches – which was hard on Bill.'

Before long, running between wickets became superfluous. The
spectators were watching boundary after boundary in complete
silence. They would be glutted by eighty-seven fours in the
day. *Wisden* said Australia batted in a 'light-hearted vein'. The
actual spectacle of such batting is usually less appealing than the
mythology that flows from it. Invincibility, at its apogee, often
throws the flattening brutal light of a noonday sun. Bailey said:
'They never accelerated. They just kept plodding along at just
under 250 runs per session.'

Sydney broadcaster Flanagan was, at least, enjoying himself.

It was real festival cricket. This seaside ground with the dew-
tipped turf fairly sparkling in the brilliant sunshine, the white
railing fence contrasting harmoniously with the emerald
playing area, and the huge red and white striped marquees
occupied as temporary club premises by such bodies as the
Conservative Club, the Rotary Club, the Services' Club and
the Yacht Club, had about it the appearance and atmosphere
of joyous festival and carnival.

He saw it as the best of England, but it was even better to be
Australian. While Barnes and Brown were motoring along, an
Essex man said to Flanagan, 'We'll never get Bradman out.'

Flanagan replied: 'I don't think you'll ever get him in.'

They did, when Barnes, 79, knocked over his wicket. Bradman went out and annihilated the attack with a precision, speed and conviction that not even O'Reilly, who had seen all of Bradman worth seeing since boyhood, had witnessed.

When Frank Vigar lobbed up his leg breaks, Bradman turned them into full-tosses and hit four straight fours, and then asked Brown, 'What does this fellow do, Bill? Does he turn them much?'

Bailey, who had never seen Bradman bat, could measure reality against legend. He felt 'slight disappointment, because [Bradman] did not produce a series of spectacular strokes. Indeed, he did not appear to be scoring especially quickly, until I happened to glance at the scoreboard.' Thomas Moult, reporting on the innings, was more impressed: 'There were spells in which he seemed to be trying new variations of stroke-play, interesting and even fascinating to students of batsmanship.'

Throughout his career, Bradman was a master of efficiency and concentration more than a showy stylist or hitter. But he was not above mischief. When he hit four fours to the point fence in one Eric Price over, he issued what Loxton called 'Bradman's only sledge of the tour'.

'Bradman's first shot made a dint in the fence. The second one enlarged the dint. The third one stuck in there. A spectator took his boot off and hit the dint out with his heel. Brownie's at the other end. He says, "I want a piece of this." He runs down the wicket trying to get the strike, but he can't. He hears the wicketkeeper, Frank Rist, say to Bradman, "Sir, is that the only shot you've got?"

'Not a word was said. Not a word.

'The last ball of the over, Braddles goes down the wicket and hits it past mid-off. It crashes into the fence there. As he turns to walk off for lunch, he says to Rist: "That's another one."'

The statistics, as happens with Bradman more than anyone, are worth contemplation. In twenty-two minutes before lunch, he made 42. In fifty-two minutes after the break, he went from 42 to 100. He scored his next 87 runs in fifty minutes. In one hour, Australia scored 148. Bradman's 187, in two hours, was the fastest big innings of his career. There were always records to break, somewhere, and this time it was Warren Bardsley's tally of centuries against eleven different counties. Essex, whom Bradman had previously spared, became the twelfth county against which he scored three figures.

Brown was out next, for 153, sparking another episode of Miller mythology.

Miller, who had been enjoying a postprandial siesta, was evidently displeased when he was woken to bat. Fingleton said he 'showed his boredom as he walked to the wickets . . . He likes a fight – or nothing at all.'

The chief propagandist of what came next was Miller himself.

'I walked in to bat, did not take guard, made a sleep-walking stroke and was bowled. I turned to the wicketkeeper, said "Thank God that's over", and walked away.' Miller maintained that he was protesting at Bradman's refusal to promote Hamence, who could have done with a bat.

Watching Miller saunter off, Bradman apparently said to the bowler, Bailey: 'He'll learn.'

Miller's account was hotly disputed by Ian Johnson. (Bear in mind that Johnson would later clash with Miller, his unchosen rival for the Australian captaincy, after 1954.) Johnson said:

> Keith is said to have made no attempt to score but just lifted his bat and allowed himself to be bowled first ball, indicating that he thought there were more than enough runs on the board without his having to make an effort. That is nonsense, and is unfair both to Miller and the team. What happened was that Keith had been sitting in the dressing-room through a long partnership and, when he was suddenly summoned to the middle, the first ball he received from Trevor Bailey was

a yorker. Just as with many other batsmen, the yorker got through before he could get his bat down.

Nobody but Miller can have known which version was correct, and he, a self-mythologiser of the first rank, could not necessarily be trusted. Miller was a poet's cricketer, and the poets were more inspired by the image of his throwing his wicket away than by his being beaten by a Bailey yorker.

Arlott endorsed the Miller version that has been accepted, perhaps by too many romantics, as fact: 'Only Keith Miller took no part in the carnage. Such a situation does not attract him as a cricketer. He looks for worlds to conquer, not for the already conquered lying open for his exploitation.'

Another explanation is that Miller, who truly saw himself as Bradman's rival as Australia's best batsman, was peeved that he was going in when all the damage had been done. Whitington, Miller's teammate in the Victory Tests and later his co-writer and friend, said this rivalry was at the heart of the Bradman–Miller friction. When Bradman declared his desire to go through England undefeated, Pelham Warner had replied: 'Give us Keith Miller and we'll beat Australia.' Whitington wrote that Bradman's 'reactions can well be imagined, especially by those who know him. "Give us Keith Miller", not "Give us Don Bradman". This was heresy.'

This may surprise, given Miller's greatness as an all-rounder, but in 1948 he saw himself as a batsman who could compete with Bradman. His bowling, in his own mind, was secondary. Whether from rivalry or as an honest assessment, Bradman simply didn't share Miller's opinion. Gubby Allen once said: 'The Don and I don't agree on a lot of things. But on one thing we are agreed. Keith was no better than no. 6 in a good batting side.'

Miller was aware of Bradman's opinion of his batting, and believed Bradman was jealous of him. Each man knew where the other stood. Now they had to get through a five-month tour without blowing up over it.

*

Half an hour before stumps at Southend, Australia passed Middlesex's year-old record of 663 runs in a day. When Loxton and Saggers were thrashing 166 in an hour, the scoreboard could not keep up. Here, for the record, is the Australians' scoring rate:

0–100 in 74 minutes
100–200 in 44
200–300 in 52
300–350 in 19
350–450 in 31
450–500 in 27
500–600 in 39
600–700 in 52
700–721 in 12

When Toshack was out – thrashing intemperately! – right on stumps, Tom Pearce was congratulated for being the first captain to bowl out the Australians inside a day. (In fact he was the second, after Yorkshire's Brian Sellars, but it's a good story.)

These occasions give an opportunity for cricket's gallows humour. Bailey said: '[W]e managed somehow to bowl 129 overs, which was remarkable in six hours of play considering the amount of time spent retrieving the ball from the boundary'.

For all its carnivalesque, 15 May was a day when some questioned whether the Australians had taken things too far. Mixed feelings, rather than praise, followed the performance. O'Reilly spoke for many in the ground when he said:

It nauseated me . . . I felt Essex might have been spared some of the indignity of the tremendous blow they sustained . . . The colossal score meant nothing to me so far as assessing the batting ability of the Australians went. It did show, however,

that Bradman, unlike some other touring captains, had no
intention of getting the easy matches over as quickly as possible
so as to give his bowlers a holiday.

Even Bill Ferguson, Australia's faithful scorer and baggage-master
since 1909, felt uneasy. It was, he wrote, 'a fantastic day of cricket,
I will admit, but treated, nevertheless, by Bradman as an ordinary
match, and part of his team's normal chores'.

Bradman's almost inhuman mercilessness was noticed in the
local press. Crawford White's match report in the *News Chronicle*
said: 'It was all part of his deliberate, merciless, efficient plan, brilliant
in its execution, to build up the biggest possible psychological
advantage for the Australians over English bowlers as a whole.'

It seems churlish to castigate Bradman for being too attacking
when Australia's reputation in England had historically been for
dour, defensive batting. As twenty-first century cricket fans have
found in abbreviated versions of the game, big-hitting batfests can
become so entertaining that they are tedious. The contest is the
thing. But if there is no contest, the victor is hardly to blame.

Yet controversy is part of cricket. Perhaps the great West Indian
Learie Constantine summed it up best, in his book *Cricketers'
Carnival*, which came out the same week as Australia's 721 and
therefore has an air of prophecy as well as summary. He wrote:

> [Bradman] pities none. If he can make any bowler look foolish,
> he will do it. If he can smash a man's averages so much that the
> man is dropped from big games for the season, he will spend
> his last ounce of energy and strain his wonderful sighting to
> do just that. No room for mercy, no standing back while a
> disarmed rival picks up his fallen weapon; the best of modern
> cricket is like that; and if you ask me, that is how the best
> cricket has always been.

Even O'Reilly, the hardest of hard men, had to concede that.

*

After a Sunday off, Essex's flag was noticed to be flying upside-down. Another record crowd – nauseated but addicted? – watched Miller, Toshack and Johnson rip through the home team twice.

After his desultory batting, Miller fired up with the ball, precisely as Bradman wanted. Bradman had enough batsmen; he wanted to exploit Miller as a bowler. O'Reilly was among many to feel deprived of a great spectacle, saying Miller's batting was steadily being 'wrecked' by Bradman's demands on him as a bowler. If entertainment were the aim of the tour, O'Reilly was right. But it wasn't.

After the match Arlott, seeking the glass half-full, wrote: 'Despite the immensity of the Australian victory, no depression was to be observed in those salubrious cellar-haunts near Southend pier, where the attractions range from the democratic winkle to an economically priced but elegant oyster.'

Not everyone was overlooking another example of Bradman pushing the laws of cricket to their limit. Barnes was developing a reputation for standing closer to the bat than any other silly mid-on. In Essex's first innings, Ray Smith swished and nearly hit him.

'That won't drive me away,' Barnes said.

An over later, Smith got him in the chest.

'I told you,' Barnes said, 'it wouldn't drive me away.'

Nonetheless, he needed treatment to his chest and also his foot from blows he sustained. They would not be the last.

The Australians still had six matches before the first Test in Nottingham, and the second of those would be a Test rehearsal against the MCC at Lord's from 22 May.

Bradman stayed in London while Hassett took the team 185 kilometres to Oxford to play at Christ Church college amid the deckchairs and bandsmen, the chiming bells and the slap of oars;

what Fingleton called a 'country-house atmosphere'. The students included an Indian (Hafeez Kardar), a South African (Clive Van Ryneveld) and even an Australian, the future Shore school headmaster Basil 'Jika' Travers. They still lost by an innings.

In London, Morris and Miller dined with their new friend Jardine, who was 'charming', Morris says. 'You had these stereotypes, but he was a very charming man. Don wasn't with us. He and Jardine didn't get on too well. We didn't talk about Bodyline. It was a delightful night. We just talked about current players and how we were enjoying the tour.'

Bradman was dining at Grosvenor House with Sir Norman and Lady Brookes. There he had his most frightening experience of the tour. '[W]e were travelling in the lift to the dining-room when for some reason it got out of control and crashed to the bottom . . . I can assure you it is a somewhat terrifying experience and one which I don't recommend for pleasure.'

After five weeks of patchy opposition, the MCC was putting up the real thing: the Middlesex twins Compton and Edrich, who had just come off a 424 stand against Somerset, Hutton, the likely Test captain Yardley, just back from a bout of lumbago, and the Test finger-spinners, right-armer Laker and left-armer Jack Young. Also included were the in-form opener Jack Robertson, who had represented England the previous summer, and Martin Donnelly, the New Zealand left-hander rated as highly as any of the local product. This was the game, said Arlott, 'when the major paths of England and Australian cricket first crossed'.

Bradman chose his notional Test XI, with Barnes and Morris opening and Brown at six, while Toshack, Johnson and McCool backed up Lindwall and Miller. The tour selectors were nominally Bradman, Hassett and Morris, but Morris says: 'Bradman picked the teams, really. We were trying to move people around in games to make sure the Test team was well prepared and fit. But they were Don's teams.'

The gates at Lord's were locked with more outside than in. Some of the young Australians, including Morris, were underwhelmed by Lord's: its small boundaries, its idiosyncratic slope. 'Lord's was the headquarters of cricket, but it wasn't a great ground,' Morris admits.

From the players' balcony, Loxton and Harvey were confused. 'It was our first time at Lord's for a game,' Harvey says, 'and we looked out to the wicket – or where we thought the wicket was. The creases weren't marked and the stumps weren't marked. I said to Sam, "Where the bloody hell are we meant to play?" It was so green, the pitch and outfield looked exactly the same.'

Suspicious of the rain-dampened wicket, Morris was soon out. Barnes, Bradman and Hassett made half-centuries. Bradman's dismissal on 98 was the closest he ever fell short of three figures in Test or first-class cricket. He 'seemed very disappointed', Fingleton observed, 'and lingered momentarily at the pitch as if disbelieving that such a thing could happen when so close to a century.' Hassett made what Fingleton called 'the prettiest half century we saw in the whole summer'. But generally, the little gunner was changing. His mate Whitington wrote: 'Those laughing feet, of the late 1930s and of New Delhi in November 1945, were becoming shackled. That old willingness to take a tilt at providence was toning down. We who played with and under Lindsay in that 'Happy Series' and across India and Australia have always realised why.'

After going to the rest day at 5/407, the Australians resumed in what Arlott called a 'gaily murderous' mood. Miller's 163, in four hours, included three sixes and twenty boundaries. Johnson also hit three sixes and helped Miller put on 155 in 105 minutes. It was a slaughter, targeting Laker in particular. Lindwall hit Laker for another three sixes, and even Tallon plonked one over the ropes. Ten sixes, nine off Laker, were hit in eighty-two minutes that morning. Barnes said, 'Some of the noisy [spectators] in the Tavern bar, and just outside it, did more fielding that morning than many of the fieldsmen.'

When they were done, Australia had 552 on the board – a perfect fortress from which to assail Hutton. Bradman really wanted his man. It's fair to say that since 1938 Bradman had set himself upon Hutton's ruin. There had been the bouncer assault in 1946–47, and now, in a cab on the way to Lord's, he conscripted a very willing Barnes.

'You know, Sid,' Bradman said in the cab, 'we can't afford to let Hutton get control of us. I've got an idea that if you can worry him by fielding up close, on top of his bat almost, we might rattle him. What do you think?'

'That's all right with me,' said Barnes, who had fielded and even bowled during Hutton's 364 at The Oval.

'Do you mind how close you field to him?'

'Not a bit. I don't think he can knock my head off.'

Barnes would ridicule Hutton's batting against express pace, writing that 'he dropped to earth like a felled log when the ball was flying. He was no lover of fast bowling – in fact, he disliked it very much and we knew, also, that he helped our cause very much in the England dressing-room. He would paint a gloomy, depressing picture of how hard it was in the middle against our fast bowlers and this, naturally, did not help the morale of those to follow.'

So when Hutton batted, Barnes moved in close, 'not frightened', although he knew a hit on the temple 'would bring the Barnes bones to their rest at last in some English cemetery. That is the risk a close-in fieldsman must always take but I am a fatalist. If your end comes, it comes and you cannot do anything about it. Finally, and I placed much reliance on this, I didn't think Hutton could play the hook stroke.'

Hutton would top-score with 52, but the Australians didn't mind that, as he spent long enough at the wicket to get a nightmarish taste of the rising ball and the hovering short leg. 'It was obvious,' said Barnes, 'that Hutton, and some of the other batsmen, were not too keen about me fielding up so close. I could see that in Hutton's face.'

Irrepressible, Barnes began teasing the umpire, Frank Chester, who he knew was watching him closely. 'As the bowler was running up, I would turn towards [Chester] with my left toe raised and suspended over the pitch. I could see Chester begin to stop the bowler and, quickly, I would turn back and put my toe down well clear of the pitch.'

Though targeting Hutton, Barnes found that 'others seemed to resent me being there, [so] it looked as if I would be up close for all the series'. Unless, of course, someone belted him out of the way.

Some of the leading English batsmen found Barnes's placement objectionable. '[It] was a fine piece of showmanship, apart from anything else,' Compton said, 'but I thought it unfair to the batsman because as he faced the bowler he couldn't help being conscious of Barnes almost at his elbow. You saw him out of the corner of your eye, and it hindered concentration. As you watched the bowler, Barnes came most unhelpfully into your vision as well.'

Edrich said:

> [Barnes] employed a technique of ostentatious gesture and behaviour apparently to scare batsmen from moving too far forward in defensive play – his every movement and facial expression indicated that he would pick the ball off the bat if they did so. This sort of thing can be amusing up to a point; it can also be disturbing in times of great concentration. All down the history of the game, it has been customary for batsmen to hit hard at fieldsmen who crowd the bat, to make them (or their captain) take a hint and give a bit more space . . . Denis and I several times gave Barnes this hint, but his captain stared impassively and Barnes himself was more aggressive than before.

If Bradman was pushing his men to the limit, he was also testing the boundaries of good sportsmanship. Brian Chapman, in the

Daily Express, wrote an open letter to Bradman saying: 'Sidney Barnes stood repeatedly on the actual playing area. There can be no dispute about this – one foot was clearly placed across the edge of the prepared wicket . . . often he was moving – unintentionally, no doubt – after the bowlers started his run.' Another journalist wrote: 'Bradman will continue to get English wickets in any way that is within the rules. They, not the higher ethics, are his guide to conduct in cricket.'

Bradman took Chapman's article to Barnes and said, 'Read this and then tear it up. Forget about it.'

Bradman, suspecting he was being lured into controversy, maintained a public silence, though he said later that he 'badly wanted to refute' Chapman's letter, as it 'deserved a very harsh reply'. Two years later, Bradman wrote that 'the umpires were clearly of the opinion no unfair play had occurred. Barnes never stood with one foot on the prepared wicket – he never distracted batsmen by moving as the bowler came up [even though Barnes admitted that he did]. But the damage was done. The public who read the article believed there was a case against Barnes.'

If Bradman had taken up the issue in public, he would, ironically, have had support from his two *bêtes noires*, O'Reilly and Fingleton. O'Reilly wrote that Barnes was the one taking all the risk, and if the batsmen didn't like it they could hit him out of position. Fingleton said Barnes's closeness was only intimidatory 'if the batsman allows it'. Fingleton's criticism of the position was a pragmatic one: he was concerned that Barnes was too close to react to the sharpest chances.

The MCC lost by an innings and 158. Hutton passed 50 again, but Arlott noticed that 'he hooked Miller badly – alarmingly badly', almost in desperation. 'The Australians regarded Hutton's batting as a major problem of the 1948 series. To the end of solving the problem, Miller and Lindwall, at their freshest, employed the short ball rising along the line of Hutton's body.' Hutton decided to sway from it. 'In this aim, however, one of Hutton's chief merits as a batsman contributed to his difficulties. He moves automatically into the line of the bowled ball . . . [and the bouncer] was bowled to Hutton more than to any other batsman in the English team.'

And Hutton was the success story of the batting in that match at Lord's. The Middlesex Marvels failed, as did Yardley, about whom O'Reilly was scathing: 'I for one was not prepared for the shock of his first innings display. It would be unkind to describe my reactions to Yardley's first encounter with the Australians. He had been a sick man and looked far from well. But the point that was hard to understand was the reason why he should have been spoken about as the logical English captain when he was so palpably out of form.'

The match, said O'Reilly, 'was a tremendous blow to English cricket'.

Bradman and the batsmen were demoralising England's best bowlers one by one. He was spooking their batsmen by holding Lindwall back in the shadows and letting Miller loose for brief assaults. In the field, Barnes was creeping into their eyeline. In the committee rooms, Bradman had already won all the key arguments over the laws of the game and their policing. And beyond all this, Bradman had his men exude a New World cockiness that, far from acknowledging the pain England had suffered during the war, exploited it as a competitive edge. *We are young and free*, he had his men humming, *and you are a spent Empire*. Laurence Kitchin, another Hutton biographer, was a bewitched young boy watching the Australians at Lord's.

[Their] surplus energy became a psychological weapon. From the time of their first public practice at Lord's (admission 1s. 6d.), they looked more like an army of occupation than a beatable side, and the only word to describe their coming out to field in the Test dress rehearsal against MCC is 'annexation'. At the fall of a wicket they would bowl one another leg-breaks or practise catching, as if cricket were a newly invented form of amusement. Bradman watched them indulgently, when he wasn't taking part in the fun himself. His face reminded me so much of the more ruthless Renaissance prelates, that I wondered whether he'd been keeping a photograph of Jardine on his desk, and caught some of its expression. While Miller larked about and Hassett grinned, Bradman's card-index mind was brooding over criminal records.

If the Australians were showing signs of invincibility on the field, perhaps they could be got at elsewhere. Rather than burying the acrimony of 1946–47, the tour was soon renewing it. During the MCC match, the former England captain Lord Lionel Tennyson came from the hosts' dressing room to the door of the Australians' and asked to meet Bradman. Australia's room attendant told Bradman that Tennyson, fifty-nine years old and enjoying his retirement, had been 'drinking rather heavily', and Bradman passed back the message that he was indisposed.

The story – Bradman snubbing a peer – did not appear at first in the English press (nor in Bradman's autobiography), but a week after the match it surfaced in Australian papers. An outraged Tennyson had told the Sydney *Daily Telegraph*'s blazer-loving David McNicoll that he had immediately written to Bradman: 'I told him I thought that as a former captain of England and a son of a former Governor-General of Australia he [sic] might have seen fit to spare me a moment. I also told him that I had merely wanted to congratulate him and to ask him and Hassett, Brown and Miller to dine with me at White's Club. I was so furious that I added that good manners cost nothing.'

To Bradman's discomfort, the story bounced back to England, where a *Sunday Pictorial* cartoon showed a top-hatted Tennyson waiting and Bradman holding a phone. It was captioned, apparently without irony, 'He hasn't yet phoned to apologise.'

Bradman's 'needless brusqueness and lack of tact' prompted

more 'Bradlines' than usual, and he didn't get support from the usual quarters. Flanagan, forced to choose whom to toady to, bowed to the upper class: 'I considered Bradman was justified in refusing to give audience then and there to Lord Tennyson but he was definitely wrong in the manner of his refusal. After all, Lord Tennyson is a person of high rank and his position as an ex-captain of the English team should have prompted Bradman at least to have spoken to him personally and perhaps apologised for his inability to entertain him at that moment.'

To balance the scales, England's *Sporting Record* defended Bradman: 'In our opinion [the criticism] was an uncalled-for reflection on a captain who has done everything possible to make the tour a happy one. And you can take it that all his players almost worship the turf he treads on.'

Bradman wore the criticism, refusing to comment when it must have been tempting to point out that Tennyson had been drunk (something the peer had omitted to tell McNicoll). In fact, even two years later, when Tennyson published a book, *Sticky Wickets*, continuing to call Bradman 'this mannerless little man', it was still not publicly known why Bradman had avoided greeting him. It wasn't until 1972 that Ted Swanton, in *Sort of a Cricket Person*, revealed Tennyson's state, and that Bradman had refused his entry because 'he did not want his team to meet the great man in these particular circumstances.' By not defending himself publicly, in fact, Bradman showed this Colonel Blimp-like character more courtesy than his actions merited.

One Australian player, meanwhile, ended the match in a particularly good mood. Miller, having renewed his love affair with Lord's, had also enlisted the MCC to help him see off a challenge for breach of contract by the league club Rawtenstall, with whom he had signed but was now reneging. (Rawtenstall then opened talks with McCool.) While Miller was combing his hair after the game, a gentleman told him: 'Margaret would like you to join her at the Embassy Club.'

'Margaret who?'

'Princess Margaret. I'm the Princess's equerry.'

'Really? What was that club again?'

That night, Miller, in cravat and sports jacket, bumped into Bradman on their way out of the Piccadilly.

'Where are you off to, Braddles?'

'Dinner at Buckingham Palace. And where are you headed, Nugget?'

'Well, Princess Margaret has asked me out. And I'm late!'

'Good to know you don't make an exception with royalty, Nugget.'

It wouldn't be the last time Miller saw the princess. But his sublime 163 would be his last century of the tour.

The MCC's loss cast a pall over English followers. Arlott wrote glumly that 'the poor Australian bowling form of the early matches was becoming no more than a false impression or English wishful thinking.'

But nor had the pieces, for the self-confessed 'calculatingly pessimistic' Bradman, quite fallen into place. Lindwall was yet to hit top speed, Morris had slumped after his Worcester century, and McCool, in taking 4/35 in the MCC's second innings, had re-split his spinning finger. Bradman said 'the constant friction had set up a small callus or corn which in turn appeared to tear away, thus exposing the raw flesh. The wound would heal quickly, but that was not much compensation, as we obviously couldn't risk it happening in the middle of a Test . . . We could never make up our minds whether the cure was to harden the skin so that it would stand the strain or to soften the skin and thereby prevent the hard callus forming.'

O'Reilly, ever ready to take up an outrage on a leg spinner's behalf, believed this was all poppycock and an excuse for a pre-formed strategy to take only the off spinner Johnson into the Tests. '[E]ven if [McCool's] finger had been as solid as a diamond drill he would still have been asked to keep the dressing-room attendant company during the Tests,' O'Reilly said. He blamed the 55-over new-ball rule, the 'legislative monstrosity' that would 'bump the slow bowler out of the big-game reckoning'.

McCool was not picked for the next match, against Lancashire at Old Trafford. Bradman said the Queenslander was 'downcast at the prospect' of being left out of the Test team but 'deserves great praise for the fortitude he displayed and the light-hearted way in which he cloaked his own disappointment in order not to disturb the general harmony of the team'. McCool said he became 'a philosopher (the alternative was to become a nervous wreck'. Friends told him he'd 'got a raw deal', he said, 'But it wasn't true. I was disappointed, naturally, but there were no chips on my shoulder.'

If Bradman could be said to have had a bogey ground, it was Old Trafford. The pitch was the best in England for seamers, and in two Test matches there he had totalled 44 runs.

On the morning of 26 May, he went to a Manchester school to present a panoramic photograph of the SCG, a gift from Sir William McKell, the NSW Governor. He gave a well-received speech and went to the ground, but the day was rained off.

Old Trafford, like The Oval, had done its war service, bombed and then restored by German POWs. 'To give the "Jerries" their due,' wrote Whitington, 'they did an excellent job on Old Trafford, despite their ignorance of, and contempt for, their recent enemies' national summer game.'

The rain eased on 27 May, and Lancashire's Ken Cranston sent the Australians in on a drying wicket. Morris was out early, and Bradman was hit on the chest by his third ball from the redheaded workhorse Dick Pollard. Fingleton observed Bradman's concern with the difficult wicket, and 'noticed that he did not seem at all keen' to face Pollard.

Pollard wasn't to be his nemesis, however. In a country full of old cricketers, nineteen-year-old left-arm orthodox spinner Malcolm Hilton, in his third match, was a novelty. He had left his father's building and decorating business at Werneth to become a professional, and that morning his fiancée had told him, 'I don't care if you only get one wicket, as long as it is Don's.'

Hilton walked onto the field, said O'Reilly, 'unnoticed and unknown. He could not have dreamed that by the time he was to walk off the field again he would be surrounded by Pressmen eager to get the story of his life.'

Hilton's moment came when Bradman, 11, played forward and inside-edged onto his stumps. 'Well bowled,' said Bradman to England's newly minted celebrity.

Hilton and the veteran Bill Roberts went accurately about their work and dismissed Australia for a paltry 204. The wicket was still damp, however, and Lancashire's response was only 189. Cyril Washbrook, the likely England opener, hit a ball into Barnes, bringing cheers from the crowd and cries of 'That'll shift him!' Barnes took a step closer.

The master Lancashire professional was disconcerted, but not angered, by Barnes's positioning. 'I cannot recollect having seen anybody else field as close to the bat as this. [But] as long as the fieldsman stands still and does not put himself into the line of flight of the ball, there can be no complaint by the batsman, and I saw nothing wrong in the tactics Barnes adopted.'

Washbrook was extremely impressed with the Australians' fielding. 'One of the main reasons for Australians being such fine fieldsmen is that nearly all their cricketers play baseball as well, and many participate in Australian rules football, a queer 18-a-side game which I could never understand.' He noted how they 'loved some "theatre"' on the field while they waited for a new batsman to come in.

'It was quite common to see them throwing the ball around to each other, like a crowd of excited young schoolboys and for them to glance at the incoming batsmen with an almost patronising air, as if they were saying to themselves: "What's he doing, interrupting our little game? Get him out quickly, anyway. He won't be much trouble."' It was more of the gamesmanship for which the 1948 Australians were becoming recognised.

When Australia batted in their second innings, Morris again failed and Bradman came out, to murmurs. Was he just trying to get some batting practice, or did he want to assert himself over the young Malcolm Hilton? As Whitington once wrote, 'Don's first name should really have been Drama.'

Bradman seemed nervous. Off the last ball of an over, he hit the ball through the field and called Barnes for three. Barnes jogged two and kept the strike. Fingleton saw what unfolded: 'Bradman summoned Barnes at the end of the over and was obviously castigating him for not running a 3. Johnny Ikin overheard the conversation and told us about it afterwards. "All right," Barnes had said, "you have the bloody lot and I'll have none."'

In a tense mood, Bradman wanted to make another point, as Fingleton saw it: 'Bradman has never allowed any bowler to think for long that he enjoys mastery. In all his years, he has gone out of his way to give particular attention to any bowler who has had temporary success with him, and I felt rather sorry for Hilton when I saw Bradman walk out to bat.' After Barnes was out for 31, Bradman took on Hilton. The teenager spun the ball away to a tight-set off-side field, and Bradman tried to hit him to leg. On 43, he missed one, was nearly bowled next ball, then 'rushed wildly down the pitch, swung furiously to leg with a cross-bat, missed, swung about and fell flat on the pitch with the momentum . . . This was, I think, with the exception of the bodyline days, the only time I have seen Bradman behave in such a manner. Usually, when he sets out to "kill" a bowler he does it with calm intent. This was clearly a case of over-anxiety.'

O'Reilly described Bradman's humiliation with a gleeful detail that probably says more about the writer than the subject:

When the Australian captain walked to the wicket it seemed to
be written all over him that he intended to make the boy pay
dearly for his first innings' presumptuousness. His method of
dealing with Hilton left nothing to doubt about this course.
Bradman made a crude agricultural swipe of the rusty-gate
variety at a leg-break which eluded the bat, hit his pads and
was fielded in the slips; then he played forward in defence with
meticulous care at one which missed his bat and his stumps by
the proverbial coat of varnish. The breathtaking show finished
with Bradman flat on his back, legs pointing towards heaven
and arms in knots, with the keeper quietly removing the bails.
Another almighty haymaker had gone haywire. Bradman's
efforts to square his account with the boy were as undignified
as they were unsuccessful.

It might have been worth going into the detail because it happened
so seldom. Even the stumping, by Eric Edrich – one of Bill's two
brothers playing for Lancashire – had its share of theatre. Edrich
didn't take the bails off straight away, teasing Bradman by letting
him turn and try to get back. Geoffrey Edrich said, 'If he'd taken
them off straight away he'd have missed half the fun.' Eric said,
mischievously, 'I was just a bit slow getting them off.' The summer
wouldn't be a particularly happy one for their brother Bill, so they
were taking their fun where they could get it.

In Bradman's forty-six first-class games after the war, this was
the only time he was twice dismissed for less than 50, and it was
the last time he was stumped. In the papers the next day, diagrams
explained the genius of England's most famous teenager.

Loxton, the batsman at the other end, had a novel interpretation,
characteristically kind to Bradman: 'You felt like it was all a joke to
kid the England selectors into picking Hilton for the Tests.'

Bradman himself was circumspect, praising Hilton's 'impressive
performance' but chiding the press for losing 'proper perspective'.
He didn't think Hilton was good enough for Test cricket in good

batting conditions, and the England selectors, not for the first or last time and not, perhaps, coincidentally, agreed with Bradman's judgment. By the time of Lancashire's return match with Australia later in the season, Hilton would not even be in his county's team, let alone his country's. Barnes said: 'I think Hilton would have had his heart broken had he played in the Tests.' Hilton did eventually make four Test appearances between 1950 and 1952.

After pleas from Nottinghamshire officials, Bradman decided to play the county match at what would be the venue of the first Test. Trent Bridge, the home of Larwood and Voce, was where Bradman let Lindwall off his leash. Having recovered from his ailments and injuries, Lindwall was primed.

He understood the symbolism too, looking backward as well as forward. When the Australians arrived at the train station, locals chirped: 'Look out, here comes Larwood!'

Lindwall retorted: 'Why not? He was the master!'

Nottinghamshire was the home of English cricket professionalism, the county of Alfred Shaw, Fred Morley and Arthur Shrewsbury, and its pride had been turned into anger by the scapegoating of Larwood after Bodyline. When Voce had bowled short at the Australian team of 1934, provoking a protest and near walk-off, the Nottingham crowd vented their fury. On Larwood's behalf, they didn't know who they resented more, the plaintive Australians or the complaisant MCC.

Landing carefully eighteen inches behind the bowling crease, Lindwall removed both Notts openers in his first overs. He rested while Reg Simpson and Joe Hardstaff, both Test candidates, retrieved the home side's situation, but came back to break the partnership and ended with 6/14 off 15.1 overs. He gave himself a bruise on his chest, a good sign: 'I have a simple way of knowing whether I am going flat out and making a complete follow-through. When I put everything into my bowling, my left hand flaps against my chest just as the right arm swings over. In time a small bruise forms on my chest.'

Typically, he saved his bumper for shock value, and his three bowled victims were all yorked. His display gave Bradman a warm feeling.

Lindwall had come a long way with Bradman, traversing the distance from fan to teammate. He recalled:

> The first time I saw Don Bradman bat, I was one of the scores of small boys who formed a lane on the field, through which he had to pass to reach the wicket, and I was a proud lad when I managed to get near enough to spur him on his way with a pat on the back. Normally St George matches drew a crowd of about 2000, but when Don was due to play a 10000 gate became guaranteed. Before I even set eyes on him I was a Bradman fan . . . In too many instances boyhood idols have feet of clay, but nothing in the passing years has caused me to lose any of my youthful admiration for Australia's only cricketing knight.

Now, in England, while Bradman 'remained a hero to me . . . as a cricketer he had treated me exactly as an equal'.

Bradman was gentle with him. With field placings, the most Bradman would say was, 'Why don't you have him somewhere else, Ray?' If Lindwall resisted, Bradman said: 'All right, you're the bowler. You have them where you want.'

Lindwall added: 'If subsequent events proved to me that he was right, as they usually did, he would come up again and ask, "What about it now, Ray?", but he never attempted to say "I told you so".'

Brown, 122, and Bradman, 86, underpinned Australia's reply. After striking the former Test opener Walter Keeton in the chest, Lindwall took it easier in the second innings, as Simpson made his second 70 and Hardstaff, with the first century against Australia in 1948, sealed his Test selection.

On their day off, the Australians were entertained by the Duke and Duchess of Portland at Welbeck Abbey, north of Nottingham. Bradman had stayed there while recuperating from appendicitis in 1934, as a guest of the Duke's father. Sherwood Forest had been clear-felled for the war effort, and the Portlands' finances were in decline, the Duke having had to cede residence of the Abbey to the military while he moved into a smaller house.

Bradman wrote sorrowfully: 'The lovely dining-room, the walls of which had been decorated by glorious Rembrandts, was now an officers' mess – coconut matting on the floor. Where picturesque lawns and flower gardens formerly existed was now to a large extent natural growth.' The dowager's quarters were still intact, and she was 'still a beautiful woman, and her intellect razor-keen'. But the passing of a way of life 'left a deep pang of remorse'.

It still had its humorous moments. When the Australians' bus arrived at the property gate, the Duke asked the gatekeeper to open it. From the bus Bradman saw 'a dear old pensioner, legs and back bent with age and walking by the aid of a stick, [sally] forth to open the gate'.

The Duke had an exchange with him and came back to the bus. Bradman asked if the Duke had admonished the gatekeeper. He had, said the Duke. And had the man been chastened? Far from it. He had replied: 'And what about you putting in a pane of glass in my window like you promised?'

'The boys,' Bradman said, 'were convulsed with laughter.'

Hampshire, without a Test player, looked a safe match for Bradman to miss. He stayed in London rather than take the 300-kilometre trip to Southampton, where rain had wettened the pitch. Hassett gladly sent Hampshire in, and they were no match for the bounding left-arm cut and swing of Bill Johnston, backed up by Johnson's off breaks.

From two down and 141 behind at stumps on the first day,

Australia collapsed abjectly on the second. Again spin was their downfall, though their batsmen's minds might have already drifted towards the following week's Test match. Miller swished three sixes; without his 39, Australia would not have reached three figures.

Hassett's misery was even greater than at Bradford. The dream was slipping away at the hands of one of the weakest counties. Mailey, who was tootling around the countryside in a new maroon Austin 10, the Peter Pan of cricket on his tenth and last visit to England, sent Hassett a telegram: 'Good luck, but why must you always be carrying the baby when it's wet?'

Any laughter was doused by Bradman's missive that followed: 'Bradford was bad enough but this is unbearable. Heads up and chin down.'

Over the second afternoon and third morning, Miller demonstrated his powers as an impact player. His overall statistics on the tour would be moderate. But he had an uncanny ability to deliver when needed, whether in the Test series or, here, to prevent the ultimate embarrassment. Leading by 78, Hampshire could have put the result beyond doubt with 150. Against Miller's hostility and Johnston's guile, they barely mustered 100. 'Every hour would bring a telegram from Don asking us what was going on and to tell us to pull up our sox,' said Barnes.

Miller and Johnston were making his fretting unnecessary. Like Lindwall, Johnston had become Miller's friend before they played for Australia. The pair had met during the war training for the RAAF. 'Bill,' Miller reminisced, 'could not land Tiger Moths, so he was "scrubbed" as a pilot. Then he tried to qualify as a navigator, but when he started to suffer from air-sickness both he and the Air Force were reluctantly forced to agree that he could best help the war effort in a ground-staff capacity.'

On tour they knocked around together, enjoying a portagaff (a mixture of stout and lemonade) and visiting the dog track at Belle Vue, Manchester. While Miller provoked admiration and frustration, Johnston was one of the most popular men in cricket.

The tall, balding left-armer was double-jointed, able to wrap his legs around his neck. One night at the Albany Club he did his trick too close to a flight of stairs and overbalanced. 'Bumpity-bumpity-bump,' Miller recalled, 'Bill bounced down the stairs just like a rubber ball – and got away without as much as a bruise.'

With his 11/117 at Southampton, Johnston completed a successful six-week campaign to bowl himself into the Test XI. From the Worcester game to the first Test, Bradman would only make the one change to his preferred team: Johnston in for McCool. He viewed Johnston as a containment bowler alongside Toshack and Johnson, tying down the batting while Lindwall and Miller freshened up for the next new ball. Johnston would turn into a lot more than that.

Miller thought Johnston deserved the promotion, but felt McCool was hard done by and Bradman 'wanted [Ian Johnson] to do well'. Johnson, Miller believed, got 'chance after chance to bowl at nine-ten-jack. There was a remarkably high percentage of tail-enders among Johnson's haul of victims. Colin McCool used to get bitter about this, and it was understandable. Ray Lindwall, Bill Johnston, Ernie Toshack, Colin and I might have worked hard to get the first six out and then had to make way time after time so that Ian could have a go at the "rabbits". It was very galling.'

Miller and others gave Johnson, Bradman's pet, a new nickname: 'Mixomatosis'.

A day later, the troupe was up the coast in Hove. Lindwall roared into town with six wickets on the first fast, grassy wicket of the summer, hitting the off stump five times, rumbling Sussex for 86 and leaving ample time for batting practice.

Although so many of the Test preparations had gone to plan, two batsmen were enduring personal crises.

Morris, since his century against Worcester, had scored 223 runs at an average of 25. His two rivals in the bat-off for the opening slots, Brown and Barnes, were in fine fettle. Brown had made a double-century and three centuries; why should he have to make way at the top for Morris?

Doubts were raised about Morris's unorthodox technique. He shuffled sideways to get front-on and behind the line, but Fingleton, who described it as a 'double-shuffle', felt Morris's head was still in motion as he played the ball. What made things even more ticklish was that Morris was a tour selector.

'I wasn't going too well,' he admits. 'I said to Don and Lindsay that they could drop me. I didn't want to put them in the uncomfortable position of having to drop me, so I gave them the opportunity. They said, "No, no, you'll settle in." They were right and I was wrong.'

He might have forced the issue and stood down from the Test, he says, but for his 184, alongside Bradman's 109, at Hove. From that point he was able to enjoy the atmosphere – the Rolls-Royces parked at the 'aristocratic' end of the ground, the chill water at the beach – and re-boot his tour.

Padded by a 463-run lead, Lindwall destroyed Sussex again, bowling faster still and taking two wickets before a run was scored. And so the preparations were complete: twelve matches, ten wins – eight by an innings – and two draws.

England's early confidence had evaporated. Nobody, Swanton wrote, 'can have been sanguine about England's prospect of winning back the Ashes . . . But that for the present was a minor consideration. Cricket euphoria ran at its peak.'

6

NOTTINGHAM:
THE RACE TO THE BOTTOM

The Test matches of 1948 would each have a distinctive character, a narrative pattern that gives the five-day game its enduring appeal. There would be moments of drama, grace, violence, joy, controversy and poignancy throughout a summer that was far, far more closely contested than the final scoreline indicates. Each Test was a unique gem.

There is no doubt that the competitive fever was at its hottest in the first Test, in Nottingham. And what that fever produced was one of the most negative, bitter Test matches ever played.

Such was the fear that Bradman's team had spread in their first six weeks, England's selectors were, by the first week of June, already searching for a Plan B. The top four of Hutton, Washbrook, Edrich and Compton were a settled affair, notwithstanding the latter three's failures against Australia so far. Number five would be Hardstaff, after his home-ground century. He had also scored 169 in the 1938 Oval slaughter, so was a proven Test batsman. Godfrey Evans was wicketkeeper.

It was in the bottom half that England's troubles began. Rain had ruined an England vs The Rest trial at Birmingham, robbing bowlers of a chance to press their claims. Bedser was the only certainty. Doug Wright, the dangerous, looping, but sometimes loose leg spinner, was injured. With too many similar-quality in-swing bowlers to choose from – Lancashire's Dick Pollard, Yorkshire's Alec Coxon, Derbyshire's Fred Pope, Cambridge's Phil Whitcombe – the selectors went for none. On the defensive, they stacked the team with two batting all-rounders, the veteran Charlie Barnett and the captain Yardley, and two finger-spinners, Laker and Jack Young.

With just three specialist bowlers, it was an unbalanced team chosen for a draw. Arlott commented that the selectors were admitting 'that England had no real chance of winning a Test against these 1948 Australians if the game was played on equal terms. Therefore they backed the batting as a defensive measure.' He endorsed this defensiveness: 'I thought at the time, and think now, that the English selectors were entirely right . . . They realised that England's best team – and there is little doubt that it was the best team – must hope for the rub of the green to win . . . Without rain the eleven best bowlers in England could hardly hope to bowl out the 1948 Australians twice in five days for headable totals.'

The elephant in the selection room was, from our distance, more obvious. Yardley was not quite a good enough batsman, or a bowler, to be chosen as a specialist, but had to be in the team because he was captain. He had to be captain because the only other amateur in the team was Edrich, who had no captaincy experience. The tail wagged the dog.

The gentlemen–players division was never more absurd than when it was in its dying days. When English society was undergoing a wholesale postwar democratisation, amateur and professional cricketers were still using separate facilities. Only Leicestershire of the counties had a professional captain, and Surrey's, in 1947, was Nigel Bennett, a club cricketer who got the job when his committee mistook his achievements for those of another Bennett, a professional. The two classes' names were still noted differently on scoresheets: amateurs with honorifics, professionals plain. Snobbery, as it always must, bred inverse snobbery. John

Dewes, an amateur, says the 'pros called us "jazz hats". When you realised that was what they thought of you, it was difficult to get matey with them.' Not since the 1880s had a professional, Arthur Shrewsbury, been England captain – and he led an all-professional team. No professional had ever told an amateur how to bowl or where to field for England.

The stipulation of an amateur captain had already led England into blind alleys since the war. England's postwar captains had been Hammond, Yardley, Gubby Allen, George Mann and Freddie Brown. All were of advanced age and questionable quality. Allen, moreover, had been feuding with the professional Hardstaff during the West Indian tour, and bet him he would never play for England again. When Hardstaff was picked for Trent Bridge, Allen wrote him a cheque to honour the bet. Hardstaff tore it up.

Yardley, the Yorkshire gentleman and peacemaker, had played well in Australia in 1946–47, and it was on this basis that he was chosen as captain against South Africa in 1947. He didn't bowl in that series, and scored 273 runs at 39, fifth in the aggregates. Since then he had missed the tour of the West Indies and the Yorkshire– Australia game with lumbago, and brought no decent form to the table. But he was the right kind of chap, a popular, well-liked leader who could be trusted to pass the port the correct way.

Before the Test, a last push was made to give the captaincy to another aged amateur, Bradman's mate Walter Robins, who celebrated his forty-second birthday that week. Temperamentally Bradman and Robins were similar: dry, tightly wound, purposeful. Rosenwater wrote: 'It was an interesting coincidence how closely Bradman and Robins resembled each other in physical appearance. Someone once suggested that they might well go to a fancy-dress ball together as the two Dromios in "The Comedy of Errors"!'

Among Robins's other fans was Ian Peebles, the England Test spinner of the 1930s, who called him 'the most enthusiastic and joyful cricketer I played with'. There was no doubting Robins's commitment to action on the cricket field. Doug Insole, who played under him as a young man, said Robins was 'the greatest ever exponent of "brighter cricket", though not for its own sake'. When a selector again, from 1962 to 1964, Robins issued an edict: 'Play aggressively at all times; otherwise you will not be chosen for England.'

But Robins was not universally liked. Alan Gibson wrote that one of Robins's problems was that he 'did not get on very well with the press' or young players. 'He was not very popular with cricketers of the succeeding generation, was Robins. I dare say he deserved it, because he never troubled to understand them.' Even the writer David Foot, who nominated Robins as one of his cricket heroes in his book *Fragments of Idolatry*, couldn't quite work out why he liked a man who was 'quintessentially a cold fish. He could be brusque, impatient, dismissive. It helped if you agreed with him.' As a selector, Robins 'spoke his piece forcefully; he knew no other way. There was an undeniable logic behind many of his ideas, however dogmatically they were expressed.'

What makes Robins's position in 1948 particularly interesting is that, as well as being Australia's liaison officer, he was one of England's selectors, along with A.J. Holmes, Yardley and Jack Clay. Gubby Allen, another friend of Bradman's, had a non-voting advisory role on the panel. It seems strange, and almost sinister, from this distance, that Bradman was so intimate with two of England's selectors. Harvey says, 'Quite often after a game, Don would disappear with Walter and they'd have dinner together while the rest of us sat around in the dressing room.'

But it was for neither of these reasons – being so close to the Australians and being an England selector – that Robins turned down the captaincy. Having seen Allen go one series too far in the Caribbean, Robins decided, no doubt correctly, that he was not up to it. The very idea of him trying to handle the three roles – captain, liaison officer and selector – astonishes. Even with his two roles he would soon find himself in a curious position.

*

The Englishmen checked into Nottingham's best hotel, the Black
Boy. For the first time they were coming together two days before
a domestic Test match. Previously, they came straight from county
matches on Test eve. Yardley felt that 'modern Tests cannot be
won that way'. At Nottingham, they practised at 3 p.m. on the
Wednesday followed by a dinner in the hotel, which the selectors
and ground secretary attended before leaving the team alone to
discuss tactics.

That night, Yardley said, England hatched the 'Bedser–Hutton
Plan' for Bradman, to exploit 'his weakness to make an opening
single by tickling the ball round behind to the leg'. The plan had
a history – Hammond had tried it in Adelaide in 1946–47 – but
now 'Alec suggested that he should vary his bowling, sometimes
letting one dip in to Don so that he was always feeling for that
tickle behind the wicket; and when we had got him looking for it,
Alec proposed to send down one that left the batsman a bit, in the
hope of clean-bowling him.'

Yardley's memoir reveals a meticulousness in planning for which
the 1948 English team is not often given credit. It also shows that
Australia's dominance in the early matches of the tour, particularly
against Essex and the MCC, outweighed any of the chinks that
were shown up by Yorkshire and Hampshire. Yardley and his team
were scared of Bradman's team, and they responded with a game
plan that was wholly negative. The selection was defensive, and
now the planning would be equally constrained. It was as if they
had swallowed, hook line and sinker, all the cocky propaganda
Bradman had projected. Picking up on what they had learnt in
1946–47 about frustrating the Australians into error, they aimed
to clog the legside, the strength of most Australian batsmen. 'A
strange psychological effect is produced on a batsman when his
scoring shots do not produce runs,' Yardley said. 'My strategy
was that, if they played to leg, it would reduce their scoring rate

and suit us; but if they took risks to score on the offside and lost wickets, it would suit us even better.'

Yardley would also set an extra gully for Morris, to capitalise on his tendency to 'throw' his bat at full balls outside off stump, and leave cover open to tempt him to drive the new ball. Miller, on the other hand, was strong on the off side, so they would attack his leg stump. Hassett they would target with Doug Wright, when he was fit again. Brown could be caught at leg slip. Barnes scored heavily between square leg and mid-off, so they set about blocking this area. There was no shortage of thinking on England's side, all of it aimed at the containment, frustration and neutralisation of an opponent they already seemed to regard as their superior.

The Australians stayed in Nottingham's second-best hotel, the Victoria. O'Reilly's fears for the guild of leg spinners were borne out in the Australian selection: overlooking both McCool and Ring, Bradman plumped for Johnston and Johnson. Barnes had food poisoning, raising the possibility that Brown might move to the top and Harvey come in at six, but he quickly recovered. The team seemed impregnable. When Loxton saw the team sheet he said to Harvey: 'Have a look at this line-up! There's no way we'll ever get a Test match.'

The staff at the Victoria, said Flanagan, 'did everything possible to fete the Australians. The Australian flag hung over the doorway, flags and bunting festooned the entrance hall, and a fleet of cars was made available for the team. Crowds lined the roadway and milled around the entrance. On the Wednesday night, the eve of the Test, several of the English Test Team were noticed in the lounge of our hotel fraternising with the Australians, proving that in sport, as in law, it is possible to "strive mightily, but eat and drink as friends"'.

By the weekend, that amity would be strained to the limit.

*

Thursday, 10 June dawned damp, cold and cloudy. At 11.25 a.m.
Bradman and Yardley, in heavy street clothes, followed by a
photographic pack, inspected the wicket. Nottinghamshire was
one of the counties that covered its wickets after dark, so, despite
overnight rain, the wicket was good enough for Bill Voce, on
behalf of bowlers, to give Fingleton an 'unprintable' opinion on it.

Twenty-five minutes later, the captains emerged in blazers
and flannels, and poked at the pitch and sawdust-sprinkled
surrounds,while the public address played canned music. Yardley
tossed, Bradman called his now customary heads, and the coin
showed tails. Bradman pulled his blazer down over his shoulders,
to signal to his team that they would bowl. He would have batted
too. He said later, 'I am certain we won the 1948 Nottingham Test
because I lost the toss.'

At midday the Australian team took the field, behind umpires
Chester and Ernest Cooke. Behind them came Hutton and
Washbrook, York and Lancaster, the hardest front line England
presented in the twentieth century. They had made three century
partnerships in 1946–47, blunting if not dominating Lindwall and
Miller. Arlott observed:

> As the pair go out to the wicket, Hutton is likely to be looking
> down at the ground. At the crease he is more obviously nervous
> than Washbrook. He touches his cap to the bowler, turns his
> bat in his hand, picks at the chest of his shirt and taps the
> crease in quick nervous pats. Yet between delivery of the ball
> and playing of stroke his degree of cool concentration and
> thought, as opposed to pure reflex, is striking – it results in his
> being able to play extremely late and on fuller evidence than
> most batsmen.

Lindwall scattered sawdust over his approach and ignored the
batsmen. While Miller would chat with anyone, Lindwall had
put the freeze on the English during social functions. To Hutton's

request for an introduction, Lindwall had offered a simple expletive. Hutton would get to know Lindwall over the next decade, but little changed. Hutton wrote: 'We were not the chatting type. Once Lindwall drove me the fifteen minutes from the Sydney ground to the city centre and barely a word was spoken. A stranger might have been excused for thinking we were not on good terms, but that was far from the case.'

As for Washbrook, Lindwall just didn't like him in 1948, considering him 'rather a standoffish Englishman with an aggravating swagger in his walk'. Over the next five years, Lindwall changed his view:

> On further and deeper acquaintance I found that he came right from the top drawer. He did not greatly enjoy idle gossip but he was a very sincere man who spoke his mind, and his word was his bond . . . I realized more than ever that Cyril's style of walking is nothing but an unconscious mannerism. One day on [the 1953] tour he brought along to the ground his three-year-old son who, with the same high shoulders and determined step, could not be mistaken for anyone but Cyril Washbrook's boy.

Lindwall performed his stretches. Hutton waited. The light, Fingleton said, was so dim that 'an immediate appeal against it might have been upheld'. But Trent Bridge was full; Arlott said the match was a 'symbol'. 'The atmosphere of a Day – more than just another opening day of another Test Match – was present at Trent Bridge, and not even the smoke-sombre cloak of the clouds nor the skirts of the rain could hide it.'

Feeling confident about his drag, as Chester and Cooke had already passed him, Lindwall bowled his first over at three-quarter pace.

Miller did no stretches and bowled full tilt. Washbrook snicked him short of slips. Bradman, at cover, urged his cordon to move

closer. 'Better drop a catch than not be in a position to attempt
it,' he would say. 'I have always been very particular about the
position of fieldsmen. I might even have been called fussy. But it
is important. One might just as well miss a catch by ten feet as
three inches.'

With the first ball of his second over, Miller bowled a good-
length ball to which Hutton, 3, pressed forward, too slowly. Miller
would only take thirteen wickets in the series; most were as vital
as this.

A pre-lunch downpour sent the players off. During the break,
O'Reilly was scandalised by the lack of cover in the cheap seats.
'To those of us who have seen Australian crowds commandeer
refuge in the members' reserve during wet weather, the sight of
Nottingham sitting out and just "taking it" was sad commentary
on the initiative of those who have been responsible for the conduct
of the business side of the game in this country.'

On resumption, Lindwall and Miller were, said Arlott, 'driving
like a gale'. On 4, Edrich flashed at a Lindwall riser but Johnson
dropped the high chance at first slip. Lindwall scrutinised Edrich
for weaknesses. Bradman wandered over and said: 'Have you
noticed anything about him yet?'

Lindwall said he hadn't.

'Well,' Bradman said, 'I think you'll see he doesn't often play
a forcing shot to the ball just short of length on the off stump. It
may not get him out but it will tie him down. Try it and see.'

Containment worked, and Edrich was soon, to Arlott's anxious
eye, 'a struggling fury'.

Washbrook's weakness was his compulsive hooking. Lindwall
waited for his moment and sent down his surprise 'throat ball'.
Taking the bait, Washbrook top-edged to fine leg, and Brown,
running around the white line, caught it assuredly.

Yardley would say that the series was decided within that first
half-hour, when Miller and Lindwall were more 'warmed up to
the fight' than the English batsmen. He wasn't alone, sensing 'the

cold pessimism creeping about the ground'. In 1948 England, it wouldn't have taken a lot to unstopper cold pessimism. But when Compton joined Edrich, England remembered their record-breaking glories of 1947. They did not bat with the same panache, but 'struggled with hope towards command and ease', said Arlott.

Passing train passengers hung out the windows for a look at the Middlesex Marvels. Compton suppressed his exuberance and his favourite on-side flicks. He square-drove his mate Miller for four, to which the Australian responded with a series of short balls. The crowd jeered; Miller's bouncer attacks always resembled temper tantrums.

Then, a first victory for England: Lindwall slipped on the greasy pitch and strained his groin. Bradman replaced him with Johnston.

With the pressure relieved, the reversal soon came: friendly, balding, harmless-looking Johnston wobbled one through Edrich. Johnston kept bounding up, all arms and legs and head and teeth, left-armed, his awkwardness somehow infecting the batsman. Thanks to the 55-over law, he 'was like a child with a whole hamperful of new toys', said Arlott. His wobbling floater that dismissed Edrich would be one of the most damaging variations of the summer. 'With a bucking and plunging run-up, he bowled from a good height to an honest length. He bowled one particular ball sparingly but most effectively – a ball pitched up almost to the bat at slower than his usual pace, which floated away sharply and dipped. This ball was constantly mistimed by the best batsmen in England.'

At 3/46 the gate was open. Hardstaff, the local hero, came in. As he walked down the steps, Bradman passed him, running into the pavilion. A substitute was not sent out, as Bradman said he had been asked to attend to an urgent matter that would only take a minute. The effect was that Hardstaff, fresh from his 107 on the same ground against Australia, but understandably nervous, had to wait for several minutes for Bradman to come back. Some observers said Bradman had gone off as an act of gamesmanship. 'This was a most unfair suggestion,' Lindwall said, 'and, I would emphasise, would have been out of character with Australia's captain.'

Whatever Bradman's reasons, the delay worked. Hardstaff was a jittery starter, gripping the bat near the top of the handle which, O'Reilly said, 'makes him prone to flick at the offside stuff in such exasperating fashion'. Young Joe flashed airily at his second ball and was well caught in the gully by Miller.

'Great catch, Nugget,' Bradman said. 'Now see if you can clean up your mate [Compton].'

Nobody could have been happier than Johnston, who now had two wickets for no runs in Test cricket. O'Reilly was a convert to 'the extraordinary improvement in Johnston's bowling since the beginning of the tour. The confidence and experience coming from continuous match play combined to make him one of the most valuable stock bowlers I have seen.'

Miller was not the most eager Test bowler, but rose to meet the crisis produced by Lindwall's injury. Miller bowled so fast to Compton that the 'Prince of Cricket' was jumping across his off stump to cover the line. He went too far, and Miller bowled him behind his legs.

After a session of hope, the Middlesex Marvels and the only man to take a century off the Australian bowlers had fallen within a few balls. Fingleton wondered 'if England has known a more sickening ten minutes in Test history than this!'

Yardley came out with a forced smile. Charlie Barnett's frame had filled out since the 1930s. The pair played their shots against Johnston and Toshack, but Bradman's field was thoughtfully placed. Both were soon out. Bradman then dropped Evans twice in one Johnston over – the first going through his hands for four, the second hitting him in the stomach – and exclaimed to the batsman: 'I don't mind you giving me a catch, but why hit the ball so darned hard?'

England's keeper was soon out to a sharp catch by Morris on the leg side, and England, on a 400-run wicket, were 8/75. Evans came across Morris during the tea break and said: 'Like picking cherries, wasn't it?'

'As a matter of fact,' Morris replied, 'I was having a little doze at the time. I sensed the ball coming, stuck out my hand, and lo and behold, there it was!'

At tea, Arlott said, England's supporters were 'downcast indeed; there was no hope left: this was not only defeat, but defeat without a shred of credit'. Nobody could blame the pitch. O'Reilly thought the 'exhilarating' Australian fast bowling was 'fit to be classed with any match-winning bowling performance in the story of Test cricket'.

But Lindwall was gone, for the day and perhaps the match, and Miller was spent. The Surrey bowlers, Bedser and Laker, counterattacked in the last session with a stand of 89. Perhaps there was hope after all. A dismayed Brown said to Bedser: 'Ray is three-quarters of our bowling.' Whatever happened now, if Lindwall's injury was as bad as it seemed, the Australians knew that this match had taken a dramatic turn that would manifest itself when England batted again.

'From a completely hopeless position,' O'Reilly said, Bedser and Laker 'hit back with such two-fisted virility that England was placed in the position where a good shower of rain overnight could have had the Australians floundering and foundering'.

Bedser was drily impressed by his Surrey teammate's batting. '[T]o me it was rather amusing to watch him hooking a short ball from Keith Miller in a way that would have done credit to any of the early batsmen. I have never seen him make such a stroke before – and at least once Jim did not look at the ball quite as much as he should have done!'

England's 165 was worse than it should have been but better than it might have been. 'A relief,' Arlott said, 'after the *mauvais quart d'heure* of tea-time'. For Australia, Johnston's 5/36 not only justified his place for this Test but cemented it for the series.

Bradman was worried about the quarter-hour Barnes and

Morris had to face before stumps. Edrich's first ball was a wide. Barnes walked up to Chester and said, 'Eh – the light!'

Chester, said Fingleton, 'almost had a stroke' to be so addressed, and the Australian pair were obliged to bat out the remaining minutes, which they did without mishap.

A rueful Yardley, like Bradman, felt that 'England's greatest misfortune was my winning the toss! The wicket was perfect, and I had no option but to bat first. Within five or ten minutes of starting play there was heavy rain, and another shower fell during the morning, completely altering conditions to a bowler's wicket . . . Had the Australians been batting, they might quite probably have fared even worse.'

In damage control, Yardley prepared to enact his plan on day two. Under a lighter cloud cover, Morris and Barnes showed no hurry against Bedser and Edrich. A depressed Arlott watched them walk 'about their creases with the air of men pottering comfortably at home in their own back-gardens'. The press box ran a sweep on Australia's likely score. Guesses ranged from 302 to 904.

With only 165 to defend, the folly of giving Edrich new-ball duties lay exposed. O'Reilly was scathing: 'Edrich's bowling has seldom had a feature about it worthy of notice. He certainly can be described as an enthusiastic trundler. He does not spare himself in his desire to get at the enemy. He rushes up apace and flings himself and the ball with reckless abandon into the firing line; but there all his bowling attributes disappear.'

Morris's Hove century hadn't fully restored his confidence. He was dropped by Evans off Bedser, then, after a laboured 31, played Laker into his pads, the ball rebounding onto the stumps.

At 12.50 p.m., Bradman came onto a Test ground in England for the first time in a decade: a sight many would not have believed until they saw it. They recorded their relief with a 'hail of cheering', said Arlott, 'such as would have disturbed most men'.

Concentrating on the problems of Laker and Bedser, Bradman began shakily. Flanagan 'noticed he was struggling desperately to keep the ball out of his wicket. Bedser repeatedly got the edge of his bat.'

With a leg-side field, Bedser attacked his pads. Bradman wobbled and poked. Edrich came on for Laker and bounced Bradman, giving him a taste of how Miller might be without sightscreens. Later, Bradman would record his annoyance: 'English authorities are very casual about such details. They don't always appear to regard the player's requirements as Priority No. 1 . . . it may enable a few more spectators to see the game – in other words it may add a few pounds to the gate money – but that won't compensate for somebody getting cracked on the head one day.' He was, of course, less concerned about English batsmen's heads.

If a postwar weakness revealed itself in Bradman's stuttering start, Yardley's defensive plan and a still-ingrained fear of the Australian's invulnerability stopped England from capitalising. As Arlott put it: 'Perhaps Bradman of 1948 takes longer to consolidate than he did in his prodigy days: the entry of the full artillery is delayed if he is judged by his old standard. There is that spell when Bradman is frankly, humanly and unashamedly, scratching himself an emplacement. Catch him then and he will go uncomplaining. Fail and you have the Bradman of old to deal with.' By lunch he was more comfortable; correspondingly, England went to that 'well-ordered meal' with an 'apathy fitting a game whose issue was virtually settled after it had run only a quarter of its way'.

Barnes, meanwhile, was thinking three figures, if not four. But on 62, he went back to Laker and under-edged a cut. It struck Evans's thigh and looped over the keeper's head in the direction of fine leg. Here are four eyewitness versions of what occurred in the next two seconds:

Bradman: 'Evans' catching of Barnes [was] one of the most miraculous feats of recovery as well as acrobatics one would see in a long time.'

Fingleton: 'Evans dived back like a Rugby winger going for the line in an international . . .'

O'Reilly: '. . . a corkscrew backward dive, sizing up to Olympic Games standards.'

Evans: 'I just saw this little blob in the sun and dived towards it instinctively and caught it one-handed.'

So astounding was Evans's effort, umpire Cooke couldn't decide if it was a catch. He referred it to Chester, who gave it out.

Barnes said to Evans: 'I didn't believe you had caught me – I didn't think you COULD have caught that ball.'

Evans's catch precipitated a brief England comeback. Miller stretched forward to a Laker arm ball, didn't read it, and edged to slip. Brown came in ahead of Hassett, following Bradman's instruction: the second new ball was due. Yardley might have thwarted the plan by continuing with Laker, who had now taken three quick wickets, but, as if beguiled by Bradman, he threw the new ball to Bedser. Brown survived, and Bradman, having been pinned down by spin, hit his first boundary in eighty-three minutes.

Australia ground past England's 165, Bedser and Edrich unable to break the partnership. Yardley, who later admitted he had erred by taking the new ball, put himself on for his wrong-footed dibbly-dobblers. O'Reilly detected 'an apologetic air about him'. Yardley's fourth ball was, however, good enough to trap Brown. One more wicket and England would be almost on terms. They didn't get it; they didn't even try for it. The ensuing session would be one of the most discussed of the summer.

Hassett came in, and a squad of Hurricanes flew low overhead. He spooned a Bedser ball over Evans, but thereafter batted, in Arlott's estimation, 'cold-bloodedly'. As we have seen, Whitington held the view that the dasher was bent out of shape by Bradman's insistence that he bat like a machine. But this might overstate Hassett's puckishness and understate his will to win. When necessary, Hassett could dig in with the worst of them. Once, during Hassett's 'carefree' 1930s, he had defended O'Reilly so numbingly that when he made a firmer push at the ball the Tiger cried: 'Good God, it's alive!'

In any case, Bradman and Hassett had little opportunity to brighten the Nottingham gloom because Yardley didn't give them one.

Barnett came on and bowled seventeen straight overs, nearly every ball aimed outside leg stump, with six men on the leg side. Barnes, in the pavilion, was livid about Barnett, 'who would be a fair bowler in a Sunday-school game', bowling leg theory. 'And this in a Test match! . . . This is not bowling; it is not cricket at all. Just a waste of time.'

Bradman stood between overs with a hand on his hip and his ankles crossed, as if surely some cricket would resume soon. He faced one Yardley over barely moving from his stance as each ball passed outside his legs. Blaming the batsmen, the crowd booed and slow-handclapped. Someone played 'Land of Hope and Glory' on a recorder and Yardley 'wondered if it was cynical or serious'.

Hassett, taking twenty minutes to progress from 30 to 31, was jeered by schoolboys. Ray Robinson, sketching a neat contrast between Bradman and Hassett, had time to study something other than strokeplay: 'Lindsay is more relaxed at the crease than Bradman. Chewing gum while batting, Bradman's jaw would stop soon after the bowler began his run. Hassett would chew on calmly until the ball was in the air on the way to him.'

O'Reilly said 'the most outstanding feature of the batting was its unlimited capacity as a crowd-boring agency'. Spectators voted with their feet; Arlott said 'more than one spectator considered honour satisfied and the price of his seat money well spent' and left. Real cricket for the day had finished.

O'Reilly, like most of Nottinghamshire, sheeted the blame to Bradman and Hassett, saying Yardley's tactics were 'completely legal and what is more they were completely praiseworthy. He was fighting a delaying action and it was up to the Australians to take the initiative.'

Bradman was unmoved. 'It was purely negative cricket. We

were not going to be stupid enough to throw our wickets away, but neither could we score more than an occasional run.'

It went on, for over after over – a slow-motion game of chicken – but the Australians did not flinch. Seventy minutes after passing 70, Bradman raised his century, at 211 minutes the slowest of his twenty-nine in Tests.

'I cannot say that I enjoyed bowling in this fashion,' Bedser said, 'but what is one to do? If the bowler cannot stop the flow of runs he is criticised, so he gets it in the neck either way.'

England might have tried to take a wicket by normal means, but they were unified behind Yardley's plan. Fingleton wrote approvingly: 'This was the period, in the innings of his career, when Bradman commenced his onslaught and rapidly changed the whole nature of the game. Yardley was simply determined to have none of that.' He thought Yardley's captaincy emerged 'with high honours'.

This kind of leg theory was another anti-Bradman plan: frustrate him out. It frustrated him, but not out. It also suited the Australians to bat for time and hope some rain might fall for England's second innings. A Nottingham drought, O'Reilly commented, had now lasted an unheard-of twenty-four hours. If Bradman's and Hassett's concentration lasted, Yardley's negativity could backfire horribly.

Compton's account of the day betrays an undercurrent of strong feeling from the England players that they rarely let show in public. The leg theory, Compton wrote later, was giving Bradman 'some of his own medicine . . . It was very obvious that he didn't like it one little bit, and he made it almost equally obvious that he didn't think that it was the way to play cricket. For Bradman's side to bowl bouncers or to perpetrate negative cricket was, it almost seemed, perfectly all right; for anyone else to do so was a serious cricketing offence.'

Bogged down, Bradman said venomously to Edrich: 'This game is developing into a farce!'

Edrich replied: 'You've got yourself to blame. You started it.'

Bradman turned away. 'Sad to say,' Edrich reflected, 'my great admiration for him as a batsman did not extend to the rest of his cricketing make-up.'

Edrich's argument was based on Bradman's negative use of Toshack, in particular, with the old ball. '[T]he whole bias towards leg-theory bowling in post-war cricket was started by him during the 1948 series,' Edrich said. 'It was the first time in my career I had met it used on such an elaborate scale.'

Whoever started it, the victory at Trent Bridge belonged to Bradman and Hassett. They kept their patience, they survived to the end of Friday, and they managed to score some runs. 'They scored with legitimate shots,' Harvey says. 'They trusted their technique to get the ball through the onside field. Bedser was one of the best inswing bowlers ever seen, but they still got him away. It wasn't flashy, but it was marvellous batting.'

Two days in, and the match-eve spirit of 'eat and drink as friends' was gone. It wasn't quite Hammond's 'that's a bloody fine way to start' of 1946–47, but the friction was manifest.

That night, O'Reilly went to the Black Boy Hotel for a drink with Bedser. The Tiger had a history of helping opponents. Back in the mid-1930s, Victoria's Jack Ledward was struggling against him until O'Reilly advised him to play back more. Ledward was grateful: 'Fancy a bowler helping his opponent. That's just how generous Bill is. He has always put cricket ahead of himself.' O'Reilly said he drank with Bedser at the Black Boy as part of 'a genuine freemasonry amongst bowlers'. Arthur Mailey, defending O'Reilly against a charge tantamount to cricketing treason, recalled how he had shown Ian Peebles his googly grip in the 1930s. 'Cricket is like art,' Mailey said. 'It is international.' (Bradman was himself quite prepared to indulge in the same kind of freemasonry. During the Sydney Test in 1946–47, he had Compton to dinner and gave him a lesson on how to play certain shots on Australian wickets. 'I found it all very instructive,' said Compton, 'especially from the Australian captain in the middle of the Second Test of the series.')

Writing on the margin of an evening newspaper, O'Reilly showed Bedser how to have his cake and eat it too – bowl leg theory in a way that would attack as well as contain. He suggested moving Hutton from leg slip to a fine-leg position twelve yards from the bat, bringing in a mid-on as well as a short leg, and bowling a faster ball rising into the space between Bradman's left hip and ribcage. Bedser was happy to learn. 'I have always found it profitable to talk as much as possible to the giants of the game.'

Never short of an opinion, O'Reilly also asked Bedser why he, Edrich and Young had been fielding in slips: 'It is risky to ask a hardworking bowler to go there, as his natural inclination is to stop concentrating as soon as he vacates the bowling crease.'

The next morning brought sunshine and the prospect of a 'daddy' century from Bradman, perhaps a double or triple; 904, anyone?

He cruised to his thousandth run for the season, beating Middlesex's Jack Robertson by precisely thirteen minutes, then, in Bedser's second over of the day, on 138 he glanced a ball off the space between his left hip and his ribcage straight to the chest of Hutton twelve yards from the bat at short fine leg. It popped out, then in again. Bradman considered himself unlucky. 'Had the ball gone a few inches either side it would never have been caught as he would not have had time to pick up its flight.' He called it an 'accidental' wicket. Bedser gave a wave to O'Reilly.

Three minutes later, a passing train let off a 'cock-a-doodle-doo' whistle to celebrate. England loved to watch Bradman, but loved getting him out even more.

Bedser's wave to O'Reilly alerted the Australians, some of whom accused the Tiger of betraying Bradman. Interestingly, Yardley said England had devised the leg trap themselves:

[T]his theory was first attempted, under Wally Hammond's direction and advice, in the fourth Test in Australia in the previous rubber, and we got Don for a duck with it there, but it was not then formulated in such detail. Now we had seen it tried, and were able to modify it a bit, it worked extremely well . . . The great man's apprehensive feeling until he was fairly well off the mark was about the single weak joint in his shining armour!

Whoever took credit, perhaps the main point was that Bradman had scored 138 runs before the plan worked. He and Hassett would not be the dominant batsmen of the series, but their Trent Bridge stand crushed England's first Test hopes. Consider: Hassett came in when Australia were four down and 20 runs ahead. They could easily have been held back to a lead of 100 or so, which England were fully capable of nullifying. Instead, by the time Bradman and Hassett were parted, only one team could win the match.

Hassett played what would be his sole critical innings in the series. An adoring Arlott wrote: 'Hassett made his runs so slowly that only his grace and concealed humour made his innings tolerable . . . Perhaps he was amused by his own disguise, by the contrast between the style he had assumed and his style as it would have been if Australia had needed quick runs.' For the most part, Hassett 'was light-footedly passive, pushing the ball away or deflecting it neatly. On the other hand, when Yardley called for the new ball, Hassett was violent with it to the disturbance of the shine and any offensive plan which England's captain may have entertained.'

Bradman's century had been slow by his standards; Hassett's was slow by anybody's, coming in five hours and five minutes. He did hit the first six of the match, off Laker, but was also primarily responsible for Young bowling eleven straight maidens, a Test record, in his eye-watering analysis of 60-28-79-1. Young, said Arlott, 'is a small man but, as he comes up to bowl, there is dominance about him . . . Jack Young accepts no batsman as his master . . . He is a good average bowler who bowls a length and spins and who is twice the man all day long because he believes he is twice the man.'

Hassett was finally out for 137 to, McCool said, 'what a lot of people rate the best ball [Bedser] ever bowled. Lindsay, they say, was batting well at the time when Alec Bedser pitched the ball on his leg-stump and hit the top of his off! Hassett was not only bowled but bewildered as well. He looked curiously down at his wicket to make sure all was above board, and then called "Well bowled!" down the pitch to Bedser.'

After Hassett's dismissal, Johnson and Tallon increased the lead, and Lindwall, batting without a runner, scored 42. When the ninth wicket fell at 476 and Toshack joined Johnston, the Englishmen were looking for a cool-down, not a comedy act. But the tailenders went on for another 33 runs. Arlott wrote:

> [Johnston] makes a number of powerful strokes, some of which call for last-minute adjustments of several limbs if the bat is to continue upon the course [he] has chosen for it . . . Toshack, one feels, bats because he will not otherwise be allowed to bowl. He has an earnest, almost helpful air as of one not unwilling to co-operate with the bowler. His strokes are executed with less than the maximum co-ordination of limbs. But both Toshack and Johnston scored more runs than several recognised batsmen on the England side – and they made them in a manner calculated to interest and amuse.

Having seen Australia to a lead 'safe beyond the normal requirements of safety', Toshack gave Bedser his third wicket.

The Australians' task might have looked straightforward when they took the field again, but they were without their spearhead.

Lindwall's place in the field was taken by the quicksilver Harvey. This raised eyebrows, considering Lindwall's bright innings just an hour earlier and the fact that Bradman had not informed Yardley of the substitution. Fingleton thought that, having batted, Lindwall should have had to field; 'if [he was] restrained from getting to a catch because of his ailment, then England was entitled to that advantage.'

Where Fingleton was inclined to blame Bradman for sharp practice, O'Reilly slated Yardley for allowing it to happen when Test cricket teams should always be 'flat out' to win. '[C]an a man be said to be incapacitated and yet come out and score a valuable forty runs or more at a time when the pressure was on? I say no and that Yardley . . . must be condemned for carrying his concepts of sportsmanship too far.'

Lindwall himself said he might have 'aggravated the injury' had he fielded, and 'bowling would have been absolutely impossible.' Why, then, had he not used a runner? 'I had to limp when running but only a very bad injury would have influenced me to ask for a runner. I cannot settle down to my normal game if I have to think of a runner with me.'

It seems that the injury lay in a grey area between the physical demands of batting and fielding. In any case, Bradman's discourteous failure to inform Yardley suggests that some ill feeling lingered from the English captain's leg-theory tactics.

Hutton and Washbrook walked out to a plumb wicket knowing two days of batting were needed to save the match. Yardley had told them to bat like Bradman and Hassett: defensively. Within minutes, their hopes of setting a platform were dashed, controversially. Miller bowled a chest-high bouncer to Washbrook, who hooked. Tallon took a fine leg-side catch and Washbrook was out. In the dressing room, furious, he showed his teammates a red mark on his shirt.

England's vaunted top order was tottering again when Johnson had Edrich playing down the wrong line of an arm ball. 'The price of reserved tickets for the fifth day's play,' Arlott remarked, 'at once dropped several more points.'

Exhausted by two days in the field, the hosts were throwing it away. Compton walked out. Miller sauntered towards him and wished him luck. Compton then 'almost turned everybody's hair white', said Fingleton, 'by marching up the pitch to the first ball before it was bowled'. He survived an lbw appeal off Johnson that was so close he seemed ready to walk.

Hutton saved his partner's, and England's, honour. In an innings that ranked with his rearguard efforts in 1946–47, Hutton shielded the slapdash Compton and exposed Australia's weakness without Lindwall. His counterattack was orthodox, thrilling and risk-free. Soon, Arlott said, Compton settled down and 'depression lifted from the crowd like mist before the sun'. Hutton and Compton scored at more than a run a minute 'with power and delight . . . Now, with the game apparently within their grasp, Australia were threatened by two great batsmen batting at their greatest.'

It had taken nine sessions, but England was competitive at last. Hutton and Compton, like Lindwall and Miller, were a study in contrasts: Hutton the classicist, Compton the improviser, Hutton the buttoned-down pro from Pudsey, Compton the playboy Londoner. On the field, Miller said, 'Len hardly spoke and Denis never stopped talking.'

Perhaps it was because Miller was talking to him. Whenever Compton hit Miller for four, Miller would 'pause and look at me and say, a little ominously: "Good shot, Denis." Then the next ball would come down, fiery and awkward and hostile, and I would call back: "Well bowled, Keith." With us that sort of thing was a continuous performance.'

During this stand, Evans, in the pavilion, thought he saw Bradman the tactician at his best. He 'relied solely on himself, and asked no one's advice. He knew the game so well and had studied the players so thoroughly that he didn't need any counsel but his own.' He set men to block the batsmen's favourite shots:

Compton's sweep and Hutton's cover drive and leg glide. 'He knew Len had a very clever trick of twisting the bat a little when making his on drive off the back foot so that the ball would go slightly wide of mid-on, and he blocked that too.'

But no matter how cleverly Bradman foiled them, for a session Hutton and Compton prevailed. Without Lindwall, Miller had to exercise his mind. 'What I used to do, bowling to Hutton, was to say, right, the conditions are such and such, now if I was batting what would I not like now? Then I'd try and bowl it. That's the way I bowled to Hutton, and to Compton; they made me think more. It was like chess, bowling to those two. With others, I'd just run up and bowl.'

He had an idea: he started bowling off spin. Hutton went for him. 'The two fours with which he reached 50,' wrote A.A. Thomson, 'were gems of purest ray serene.'

Hutton, however, knew he had tempted a devil. 'The worst mistake a batsman could make against [Miller] was to hit him for 4,' he said. 'At Trent Bridge in 1948, he was trundling away with medium-pace off breaks when I took two successive boundaries and 14 in the over. That was too much for Keith, but what else can a batsman do with the gift of half-volleys? I knew what to expect . . .'

It was time, under Bradman's steerage, for Miller to retaliate. In fading light, he switched back to pace and bounced Compton. Trent Bridge heckled him with shouts of 'Bodyline!' Miller responded by imitating a hook shot – how he would have dealt with the ball. Laughing, Bradman said to Compton, 'I can't understand why you fellows don't step inside them and hit them to the leg fence.'

But had Bradman gone too far in choosing this moment on this venue? 'Trent Bridge,' said Arlott, 'is the last pitch in the world on which an Australian should bowl a bouncer if he wishes to retain the affection of the crowd.' Or, as McCool put it in an Australian accent: 'Trent Bridge has got a Larwood complex about Australia.' Nottingham was unlike anywhere else in England. Whereas elsewhere there might have been disapproval of bouncers because to aim at batsmen was distastefully warlike, crossing a line between ritualised and actual hostility, in Nottingham the Australians' use of bouncers aroused local passions and memories. Nottingham was where Larwood came from, and where Arthur Carr, the county captain, had first hatched the Bodyline plan and passed it to Jardine. Nottingham was where the players had gone on strike back in 1880 and 1884 because they were outraged at the money Australian teams had taken from the game. The colliers didn't forget how Larwood had been made the fall guy after Bodyline, to appease Bradman's and Australia's hurt feelings – and when Voce had bounced the Australians in 1934, Woodfull had threatened to walk away from the game. Nowhere else was like Nottingham; here, the response to violence was violence. The colliers' great frustration was not so much that Miller bowled bouncers, but that they had once had a fast bowler who could retaliate, and that man had been drummed out of the game. In Nottingham, a bumper attack was taken personally.

But popularity was not Miller's aim, and he was just getting started. For the last thirty-five minutes of play, he sent down an average of four bouncers an over at Hutton and Compton. It was, in its ferocious way, the most exciting spell in the series: Miller, on his own, against the two England greats; Bradman, fifteen years after Bodyline, condoning a bumper attack in the twilight at Trent Bridge.

Miller's bouncers were far from harmless. Hutton, said Thomson, 'looked hard put to it to defend his face'. Hutton wrote that 'in eight balls I had five bouncers, one of which left the manufacturer's imprint on my left shoulder. Two others leaped at my throat from just short of a length as if they had been bowled from no more than ten yards away with a tennis ball.'

With the fourth ball of his last over, Miller hit Hutton's shoulder. The crowd turned feral. Flanagan, usually a 'my country right or wrong' broadcaster, said Miller 'was largely to blame for any demonstrations against him, for he rather truculently and, I thought, foolishly, unfailingly sent down a bumper whenever a boundary was scored off him.'

There was something about Miller's manner and intent that particularly riled the Nottingham crowd. Reg Hayter wrote in *Wisden* that, compared with Lindwall's, Miller's bumpers 'created more annoyance to those spectators and cricket-lovers who disliked this type of bowling'.

> His habit of wheeling round, flying into an abnormally fast start and tossing back his head before releasing the ball gave an impression that petulance more than cricket tactics dictated his methods at such times. To many people it seemed a pity that such a fine player and one of the game's personalities should have caused the only sign of displeasure, minor as it was, by crowds during the tour; but he could not expect otherwise when he bowled five bumpers in eight balls . . .

Miller said he couldn't help his quirks.

> Flicking back the hair or flinging my hands about does not constitute conscious exhibitionism. If I do something like that I find it liberates nervous tension. Different players express their emotions in different ways. Before he went into bat, Arthur Morris would not talk to anyone if he could help it. He liked just to sit and smoke. When he got out in the middle he was casualness personified. Bradman and Hassett looked casual and carefree, but behind the poker faces they cared an awful lot. I'm the same. If this pose of casualness can be successfully simulated it brings a better performance, because a player becomes more relaxed and therefore loose and natural. Don't let any mannerism of mine fool you.

He certainly wanted to soften up Hutton and Compton. Hutton, he thought, 'never knew what to do with the bumper – hook, duck or try to parry the ball'. In retirement, Hutton would admit: 'Generally, once I had a sight of the ball I did not fear being hit, but Miller was the exception. I never felt physically safe against him.'

Bradman flogged Miller as if it was the last day of the last Test with the Ashes on the line. Fingleton observed wrily that 'though he holds more field conferences than any captain I've known, [he] had remarkably few with Miller'.

From Bradman's point of view, there was no need to bring Miller under control – because Miller was causing no harm:

> Miller was, on this occasion, not above fast medium, the wicket was easy paced with no lift in it, and there were never more than three men on the leg side. The batsmen were not in any danger. Hutton certainly got hit on the arm, but it was a ball to which he ducked but which he could have comfortably played, scarcely more than waist high, by standing erect.
>
> [Miller's] mannerisms caused the crowd to think he resented it. The result was one of the most hostile demonstrations against a bowler that I've ever heard. Even the members' pavilion was the scene of vigorous booing of our team but especially Miller, as we left the field. It was a senseless and embarrassing demonstration on behalf of people who allowed their feelings to be swayed by sentiment not judgment.

Lindwall also stuck up for his best mate: 'Watching from the dressing room, I could vouch that Keith did not bowl at his top pace . . . The roar from the spectators was staggering and when the players left the field an outburst of booing, not a little from the Members' Pavilion, swept the ground.'

Miller also had his supporters among the universal guild of bowlers, even the English. Remembering how O'Reilly had crossed national lines to help him in the Black Boy, Bedser defended

Miller, saying 'the public seemed to be confused over the issue. If the umpire is satisfied that there is no attempt at intimidation then the bumper or the short-pitched ball is perfectly legitimate.'

But perhaps this is an occasion where the testimony of the man at the other end of the pitch should be given the decisive weight. Compton's account is arguably the most revealing piece of evidence about Bradman's motives and character. His recollection is worth reproducing at length.

> For about thirty-five minutes before half-past six, Keith Miller bowled bouncers at the rate of four an over. It was in its way a wonderful piece of bowling, by someone who was very fit indeed. Keith would follow right through with a run round to cover-point, pick the ball up almost without stopping, turn and run back and come up again, with his effective, unorganised run, and deliver, probably another bouncer . . . Hutton was hit on a number of occasions, but I managed, I remember, to get out of the way. Before very long I became very conscious of Bradman at cover-point, grinning his head off. It was bad enough trying to get my head out of the way of the flying ball, but it was very, very much worse to see Bradman apparently deriving so much pleasure from my antics.

At the close of play, Compton approached Bradman.

> 'Well, Don,' I said, probably with more than a touch of sarcasm in my voice, 'I saw you enjoying yourself just now. I can't really understand why and how you were . . . I thought you used to say that this wasn't the right way to play cricket – bouncers and all that . . .'
>
> He wasn't smiling any more. From his answer I had the impression that he was a little uncomfortable but, being Bradman, was very definitely not going to show it. 'You've got a bat in your hand, haven't you?' he answered. 'You should be

able to get out of the way of them anyway . . . I used to love it when I played against bouncers. I used to hook them . . .'

I don't remember any more of the conversation. Equally, I can't remember Bradman, the target of bouncers in the 'thirties, ever before having expressed such tolerant and amiable views on the matter.

The Trent Bridge crowd weren't holding a debate; they'd already decided. When stumps were called and the Australians walked off, thousands converged on the pavilion. There was a distinct menace in the air. 'No one,' said Arlott, 'not even the crowd itself, I fancy, was sure what would happen. This was a deeply angry and bitter crowd.'

They closed in, continuing to heckle Miller, who said, 'I certainly did not object to the boos until, as I walked through a throng of members up the pavilion steps, someone booed and said nasty words in my ear. I picked him up, took him inside the pavilion, shook him inside out and then sent him packing with some naughty words of my own!'

Just behind him, Johnson's recollection was vivid:

'[O]ne member, about five feet tall, vented all his wrath on Miller. He was extremely rude, and his language was abusive. Keith stopped, picked up the man and said, "You come with me and we'll settle this right away." Like a startled jack-rabbit, the man, who could never have expected this turn of events and thought he was on "safe" ground with the players disappearing into the pavilion, pleaded, "It wasn't me, Mr Miller. I didn't say anything." Miller laughed, and released his grip, and the little fellow was able to make good his escape.'

Loxton's derisive response sixty-three years later showed that all of the Australians, even the most junior, were well aware of the history behind the confrontation: 'The Nottingham crowd had nothing to complain about. They started it all!'

The prevailing English view was expressed by Yardley: 'The only thing one can say is that it would have reached much greater proportions in Australia had the boot been on the other foot.'

The physical confrontation between Miller and the spectator took the sting out of the 'poisonous atmosphere of mob-anger' that Arlott saw. He forgave the 'honest indignation' at Miller's bowling, which was merely a case of a cricket crowd getting involved passionately in the game. Even though 'proportion was restored', however, 'a sickness remained with me'.

The rest day, Sunday, 13 June, couldn't have been better timed. Bradman held talks with Nottingham officials, and their response is another indication of his influence over English administrators. Now was the time to call in the debt from his decision to play the county match at Trent Bridge, putting the Nottinghamshire County Cricket Club's accounts in the black for the summer.

Sir Douglas McCraith, chairman of the Notts committee, personally apologised to Bradman for the barracking of Miller and blamed 'colliers from Larwood's former district'.

The next morning, before play started, the club secretary, Captain H.A. Brown, appealed to spectators to 'keep Nottingham a place where Test Matches can continue to be played'. He reminded them that Miller was one of those who 'stood by the Empire in the war'. Given a choice between siding with the Australians or their own coal miners, the amateurs chose the former, just as they had in 1934, when Nottingham's amateur committee had overruled its working-class players and spectators and ordered Voce to stop bowling bouncers. In English committee rooms, it had become more important to appease Bradman than to uphold any principle of fair play or solidarity with the working man.

Amusingly, Brown's lecture managed to turn O'Reilly's opinion on his head. After Saturday's play, the Tiger fully endorsed Miller's bowling as the type of rugged combat that distinguished Test cricket from 'glee clubs and what-nots . . . It no more resembled bodyline . . . than Alec Bedser resembled Lindsay Hassett in stature. It was well-directed and planned bowling.' But if there was one thing that riled the Tiger more than whingers, it was the nanny state. 'The atmosphere created by the "good talking to" was strangely reminiscent of the schoolroom.' O'Reilly thought Captain Brown's address – over a loudspeaker, a device O'Reilly hated – was 'just another method of bringing cricket into line with the modern method of regimenting us all like flocks of sheep'.

Fingleton was, as usual, more consistent, and more stringent on Bradman's role.

'[I]n showing their displeasure the Nottingham spectators were doing only what the Australian crowds had done in the Jardine-Larwood tour. I think they were fully entitled to show their displeasure and should not have been coerced from doing so by the threat of Nottingham losing a Test or by introducing the Australian war effort . . . The principle of freedom of expression must hold good in all places.'

Fingleton had heard about Bradman's 'You've got a bat in your hands, don't you?' line to Compton. As a Bodyline veteran, Fingleton was appalled by Bradman's hypocrisy.

'We hadn't thought much of that when it was said to us in 1932–33 . . . The Don, it appears, had two views of bouncers – one when they were bowled against him and the other when bowled by his side with no fear of retaliation.'

After all that, Miller took the new ball on the Monday – and bowled no bouncers. Hutton and Compton, starting at 2/126, had every hope of saving the game, particularly when the weather closed in. Their appeal against the light was turned down in the first half-hour before a thunderstorm chased them off.

The hour after the resumption would, Fingleton thought, 'be one of the most vital in English Test history'. And so it was. On 74, Hutton was beaten by a Miller ball that skidded off the wet wicket. Thomson said it was 'probably the most devilish ball of the match'. This was Miller's trick: not his hostility so much as his subtlety. 'The secret of Miller's success as a bowler,' said O'Reilly, 'is his ability to bowl the occasional beauty which moves off the pitch and leaves the batsman flatfooted. That power to make the ball do that extra bit is the hallmark of the gifted bowler.'

Miller produced two samplings of his greatness in this series, with the ball at Trent Bridge and with the bat at Leeds. They were instrumental in both results. He was not a statistics-builder, but a match-winner.

Leaving aside the controversy around his bumpers, his toil at Trent Bridge was lion-hearted. He had cut short Hutton and Compton after a 111-run partnership that was as 'valuable to England', said Fingleton, 'as a large splash of Marshall aid'. It was, remarkably, one of only two century partnerships they ever put on, the other being 228 against the West Indies in 1939. They were never a well-matched pair. Alan Gibson wrote:

> The relationship between Compton and Hutton was never of the easiest . . . When Compton was captain in a state match [in Australia in 1950–51], and MCC were in trouble, he consulted Hutton, and received the advice, 'Send home for another bowler.' I am sure Keith Miller is right when he says that this was no more than an example of Hutton's dry sense of humour, but it was a style of humour which Compton did not share. It is no disparagement of either man to say that they could never have become kindred spirits.

Hardstaff replaced Hutton and batted with more fibre than in his first innings. He was dropped by Morris at slip, then smacked a ball within an inch of Barnes's ear. Yardley was amazed that Barnes stayed 'dangerously near the bat and rather unpleasantly near the pitch of the ball . . . Bradman didn't move him and Barnes was unperturbed. I would not have liked the responsibility of leaving a man there in bad light.'

After lunch, the light got even worse, as a fog settled on the ground. In O'Reilly's opinion, it was 'completely ludicrous to call the game at that stage a Test match'.

Bradman put on Johnson and Toshack, less to allow the batsmen to see the ball than to thwart English hopes of scrambling some runs before the expected downpour. Compton's innings, throughout, was a Test cricket classic. In such a hopeless position, amid the darkness, 'his grit and determination, his confidence and concentration must have gone a long way to restore the prestige of English cricket,' O'Reilly said. 'Every run that he scored was worth two in ordinary circumstances.'

McCool provided an insight into what made Compton so hard to bowl to. Compton 'was an unorthodox player with a strange twist of the wrists which sent the ball scuttling between cover and point. But his technique was all right, and the very fact that he was unorthodox was a help in itself. It is a weakness of the coached player that he can be tied down when runs are needed at their fastest. Not so with Compton. He could go for any bowling.'

Harvey, who 'fielded quite a bit' at Trent Bridge, describes Compton's as 'one of the greatest innings I've ever seen'.

> At Nottingham, you have to understand, with the members' stands behind the wicket – they wouldn't allow sightscreens – you really struggled to see the ball. This day was pretty bleak, and I think it got the bowlers extra wickets. But Compton, not only could he play, but he had a lot of guts as well. I thought his bat was twenty-four inches wide. Our boys couldn't get the ball past him. From that moment I'd rate him among the three best English players I played against, along with Hutton and Peter May.

When the second new ball arrived, Hardstaff played and missed and looked inquiringly at the umpires. The power to stop the game now rested entirely with them, as England had exhausted its one permitted appeal against the light. Chester and Cooke gave Hardstaff no joy. Then he clipped Toshack to backward square where Hassett 'did a great job to follow the course of the ball through the fog', O'Reilly said. When Compton was 97, in 'perhaps the worst light in which Test cricket has ever been played', the fog thickened into rain and stopped the game for an hour. On resumption, in light Arlott described as 'barely more than a half candle-power' better than before, the prankster Hassett made things even harder for Miller by hiding the ball in his sawdust heap.

Not for the first time, the rules were shaping the game in Bradman's favour. Few on the ground thought the light was playable. *Wisden* said: 'rarely can a Test Match have been played under such appalling conditions.' But England weren't allowed to appeal against it. Evans said: 'I think we can be forgiven for saying that the rule beat us'.

Barnett failed, but Yardley assisted Compton towards his hundred, which he reached at 4.30 p.m., a day after he had come in. Miller had him dropped at slip by Johnson – who didn't see the ball – and then, when Compton cut him again, Miller bounced him. Amid the jeers, he tried a slower ball but it slipped and flew over Compton's head.

Yardley machine-gunned Barnes with his bat, as if to clear him away. Distracted, the English captain then popped a return catch to Johnston. Evans joined Compton, who asked him which end he wanted to take. The aim was for each batsman to take his preferred bowler. Evans cried: 'Denis, I couldn't care less!'

The wicketkeeper's arrival brightened things up. He enjoyed his batting, and Arlott enjoyed watching him as he 'walked with a taut, balanced, impatient, flickering half-trot, and held himself with a brisk uprightness. Beside him Denis Compton was apparently thinking of other more pleasant things; trailing his bat behind him as if his possession of it were an afterthought of which he was not yet fully convinced.'

Towards stumps, Miller bounced Evans, nearly knocking his cap off.

'What the hell are you doing?' Evans said.

'Sorry, old boy. Things were getting a bit dull. Had to liven it up a bit.'

Things were a lot less heated than on Saturday. The colliers were back at work, and the Notts committee had done its job. By the end of play, Compton, 154, and Evans, 10, had taken England to a 1-run lead. That Compton was still there spoke to Fingleton of 'one of the grandest Test days I have known. Apart from Compton's superb innings, there was a constant battle of wits going on between Bradman and the Englishmen.'

This game was not yet over. A storm was predicted, and Bradman had been squinting at the clouds all afternoon. He knew that Yardley hoped to eke out a few more runs, then get the Australians in on a sticky. Rain on this five-day-old wicket could make even a chase of 80 or 100 no foregone conclusion. Bradman, the calculating pessimist, was well cognisant of the worst that could happen. 'All day long,' said Fingleton, 'the battle revolved around these points.'

More gloom and drizzle gladdened English hearts on Tuesday, the last day. Compton and Evans held out through two rain interruptions, Miller's titanic stamina and Johnston's endlessly enthusiastic swing and cut. 'The crowd was quiet,' said Arlott, 'sensing the final dominant of the game; matches flared like tiny beacons as men lit their pipes in the backs of the stands.'

It was again very dark. 'We shouldn't have been out there,' Evans said simply.

Ten minutes before lunch, Compton was no longer out there. Miller bowled a bouncer, which, on 184, Compton shaped to hook. He reconsidered, then, said Arlott, 'simultaneously ducked, pulled back his bat, and moved across the wicket. This triple operation was too much for him on the slippery turf, and he fell, delightfully comically, on to his wicket.'

'You bastard!' Compton yelled at the grinning Miller.

Compton later told Fingleton he had lost sight of the ball against the dark pavilion. He told Evans, 'If I hadn't got my head out of the way, Godfrey, that ball would have hit me in the face.'

Tallon said it 'was the fastest ball Miller had then bowled on the tour. So the bouncer had once again been Australia's greatest shock weapon.'

Given the feeling on the Saturday, a Miller bouncer was an incendiary end to one of the great Test innings. The ball was the decisive one in the entire series, for if Compton had lasted another hour, England would have saved the match and sent the Ashes contest on an entirely different course. The ironies multiplied beneath the surface: Bradman's sway over the county committee enabled his most hostile fast bowler to put a tragic end to a great innings, and set the direction of the Ashes rubber, with a vicious bouncer. Bradman's vengeance for Bodyline couldn't have found more satisfying expression.

The Australian dressing room was unapologetic. Lindwall, letting his friendship for Miller assume somewhat ludicrous proportions, maintained that 'it could have been only the second or third bouncer Keith gave [Compton] in his long innings'.

Bradman was equally selective: '[L]et me record that in an innings which extended over some 6 and a half hours, only two real bumpers were sent down to him, one of which got him out. If that is transgressing the spirit of cricket, I am a very poor judge.'

The innings of the summer was over, and England were out at 2.40 p.m., just 97 ahead. Johnston and Miller had bowled 113 overs between them to take eight of the wickets. Miller, as a bowler, was broken. Australia's series hopes hinged almost entirely now on Lindwall's recovery.

Chasing 98 in three hours could have been a challenge in the gloom, but Barnes went out and batted as if, Fingleton said, 'he had an urgent appointment immediately after tea.' He hit three fours in Bedser's first over. O'Reilly thought 'the Australians had decided to catch an early train'.

Barnes's aggression was necessary, for Morris was bowled by Bedser for 9, and then a huge black cloud swelled up, containing, Arlott said hopefully, 'half a summer's rain'. Bradman was toey. When Barnes pushed a ball down the wicket and umpire Chester put his foot out to stop it, Bradman rebuked him. 'Although there might not have been a run in it, this was the type of breach of cricket conduct no umpire should commit,' Johnson said. '[I]t emphasised his rather arrogant manner.'

Johnson said that 'Chester did not like the Australians in 1948, and the feeling was fully reciprocated. It was his attitude that annoyed them, although one or two decisions he made were a little perplexing and, at times, somewhat aggravating. He was far too theatrical and over-demonstrative . . . He had a habit of ignoring appeals completely, by just swinging his back to the bowler and gazing dramatically skywards.'

Distracted, Bradman made his first duck in a Test in England. Bedser bowled the perfect hip-high riser, and Bradman guided it to Hutton in what was now becoming known as 'O'Reilly's Spot'. After a gesture of disgust at his dismissal, Bradman waved to Barnes and Hassett to hurry up. Arlott joked that England might save the match if Barnes 'should forget himself and, from sheer force of habit, appeal against the light'.

Jokes aside, Barnes's belligerent knock (he said he played 'like a German band') was absolutely vital. Flanagan called it 'an epic innings, an unfinished symphony' at a time when runs had to be scored quickly and Bedser and Laker were bowling with confidence and menace.

Yardley, who was beginning to show an unhealthy interest in the vicissitudes of fortune, complained that the lack of rain had robbed his team of an honourable draw. 'At four o'clock on the last day, when the Australians still needed about 50 to win, the sky became so black that it seemed as if the whole Bench of Bishops must have prayed for rain and now the Deluge was coming! . . . but there must have been something wrong with the Bishops after all, for though it rained tremendously at that time everywhere around Trent Bridge, the cricket ground itself was miraculously preserved.'

With the score on 93, Barnes hit a four off Young, grabbed a handful of souvenir stumps and sprinted to the pavilion. No-one followed him.

'Several people performed counting operations on their fingers, Denis Compton smiled at the world in general, and the other players remained on the field,' said Arlott. In the pavilion, one of the Australian players told Barnes to go back, as Australia needed another run.

Barnes reappeared, O'Reilly said, 'preceded by the stump which he hurled out on to the field, and on picking it up he proceeded to the wicket and shaped up with it as he handed his bat to the umpire to place in the ground'.

Hassett hit the winning shot, and because he had to complete the run, Barnes was beaten by the English players to the souvenir stumps. He threw his bat down in anger, as if the whole episode had been a trick at his expense.

Trent Bridge was dubbed 'Compton's match', as if cricket were about individual feats. It was truly Australia's match, a convincing team effort that swung on the bowling partnership of Miller–Johnston and the batting partnership of Bradman–Hassett. Bradman could be satisfied with winning despite Lindwall's breakdown, but was anxious over what would happen next. Hutton and Compton had revealed their character; Bedser was brimming with confidence after getting Bradman twice since his meeting with O'Reilly. The eight-wicket margin did not mask what had been a grimly fought, tense, acrimonious Test match.

4

When he had arrived in England, Bradman had been told, by the *Sporting Chronicle*, 'Relax, Mr Bradman – Test Cricket is Only a Game'. Bradman would find it even harder to relax after the first Test until he saw how his fast bowlers pulled up.

For Miller, the pivotal actor in the game, and his sidekick Johnston, relaxation was easier.

> [We] hopped into the not over-big bath at Trent Bridge [and Johnston] started clowning to express his high spirits. He was long-limbed and double-jointed, so he had no difficulty in putting his feet behind his head, and as we got into the bath he did his dressing-room party piece. It was great fun – until he slid under the water on the soap on the bottom of the bath. When we saw the bubbles coming up we thought it was all part of the act, but by the time Bill disentangled himself and broke [the] surface he was half drowned. But he quickly recovered and was laughing and whooping away in glee again for Australia's victory. Bill has won a lot of money in bets and free drinks by kicking objects above his head with his long and tremendous high kick, but after the bath incident he never did it again anywhere near water!

7

LORD'S:
HUTTON DEMORALISED,
MILLER OSTRACISED

On 15 June, Barnes tore open the newspapers, looking for reports on his spanking unbeaten 64. Instead the talk was all about Bradman's duck. Barnes thought: 'What's the use? Whether Don gets a hundred or a "duck" he still gets the publicity. The rest of us are only there to make up the team.'

Barnes cared greatly about publicity, and parlaying it into an income. The following day, he travelled to Northampton with the team for the next county match, minus the exhausted Miller, the injured Lindwall and Bradman, who was resting after that 'nerve-racking "something" about the opening Test of a series which is not apparent in the remaining games unless it so happens that one match becomes the decider. It was not that we were ever near defeat at Nottingham, but the suspense persisted right to the end as to whether we could force a win against time and elements combined.'

Barnes fielded restlessly as the Australians bowled out a weak Northamptonshire, then failed with the bat and went to the boot and shoe factory to pick up stocks while Hassett scored a century. For Barnes, a deal was in the offing: 'The factories are exceptionally kind to us and some of them are close to the ground which enables even the twelfth man to have a try-on for shoes and still be on call for emergencies.'

The twelfth man, Toshack, was not, however, as available as the team wanted. Barnes took him to the tennis court behind the pavilion for a hit. When Keith Johnson called for Toshack, the big left-armer was nowhere to be found. Barnes would pay the price for Toshack's absence – not during the tour, but four years later, in sensational circumstances.

An easy innings win was a tonic for the Australians after their turbulent Test match. But six-day-a-week cricket gave them no rest; a day after beating Northants they had to again face the Yorkshire team that had run them so close a few weeks earlier. The return match was at Bramall Lane, Sheffield, the soot-filled amphitheatre where, it was said, word would go around, 'Stoke up the furnaces, lads, the Aussies are batting.' A huge overcoated crowd snaked through the streets. Bradman, who had a career-long love of Leeds, considered their neighbours in Sheffield even more knowledgeable. 'Long before the first ball was bowled one could sense the "atmosphere",' he said. 'It was like a Test Match but more intimate and concentrated.'

The cutlery city's crowd were nicknamed the 'Grinders'. Fingleton said they 'believe that once inside the ground they are part of the game'.

They had plenty of excitement on the Saturday. Barnes, now fully out of sorts, was bowled third ball of the match and Bradman joined Brown. 'As I walked out to bat,' he said, 'the air was electric. The Yorkshire crowd was right on its toes, sensing something sensational, and if it were possible to capture the feeling of a gladiator entering a bull-ring, I'm sure this was the nearest I'll ever get to it.'

Brown was out, and then, on Yardley's orders, Barnes's conqueror Roy Aspinall flung down successive bouncers at Bradman. Interesting idea. Both were pulled for four. Bradman strolled down the pitch to new batsman Miller and said, 'Looks as if we are going to have a bit of fun here. This fellow's going to bowl bumpers, those terrible bumpers.'

Aspinall bowled another. Bradman pulled it, too, to the fence. 'I hope nobody complains that he's bowling too many,' he quipped to Miller.

This was, aside from anything else, a cruel comment to make in a match in which Hutton was participating. Bradman showed an unnecessary meanness of spirit by joking about 'complaints' on Hutton's home turf, when Hutton's dignified silence was all that stood between the Australians and another threatening mob.

The impotence of Aspinall's response pointed to England's real problem. The first Test had shown up a lack of leadership, a lack of youth and, above all, a lack of speed. 'At all the functions we attended,' Flanagan said, 'the same mournful dirge was repeated to which was added the lamentation: "We have no chance of beating you; we have no fast bowler."'

Yorkshire did have a steaming ball of aggression, though, in Alec Coxon, who wasn't fast but bustled in with his elbows out, sometimes almost knocking over the umpire, before hurling the ball with great energy. He dismissed Miller, Harvey, Hamence and McCool, while John Wardle, who Bradman said 'worried us with flight' more than any other spinner, also took four in Australia's 249, which would have been fewer if Yorkshire hadn't dropped seven chances.

The Australians were entertained that night at an eastern banquet hosted by an Indian steel magnate named Dr Chapra. It rained for most of the Sunday and Monday, Bradman taking advantage of the break with a lightning train trip to London to sign 3600 bats.

Unwilling to risk defeat and hoping to maintain all-out pressure on Hutton, Bradman asked Miller to open the bowling. After a spray of bouncers, Miller broke down. Bradman showed no mercy to his other Test bowlers. He gave Johnston and Toshack more than eighty overs, Hamence three, McCool and Ring none at all. It was harsh treatment, but Bradman would take no chances.

Brown laboured to a century in Australia's second innings, while Bradman was again caught in the leg trap, for 86. O'Reilly observed: 'In all Bradman's career, and I had seen a great deal of it, I had never known him to be guilty of falling into the same trap twice.' Hammond wrote that Bradman was slipping into the ranks of the mortals.

The Grinders showed him no sympathy. As he delayed his declaration, they heckled him. With only his leg spinners available, Bradman had no interest in making a match of it. In the end, stumps were called two hours ahead of schedule so the Australians could take an afternoon train to London. If Bradman's tactics had annoyed the Grinders, his presence certainly pleased the Yorkshire CCC. At Bradford, where he hadn't played, receipts were £534 on a gate of 12 128. At Sheffield, £2757 was gleaned from 51 824 spectators.

But the Bradman effect sometimes had a double edge. The game had ended sourly, with Yardley giving his batsmen a bowl and his bowlers a bat, in mockery of Bradman's refusal to try for a result. 'The Yorkshire people are the last in the world to put up with any nonsense at cricket,' said Fingleton. 'It was a poor finish to what could easily have been the county game of the season.' It also showed that the combative atmosphere of Trent Bridge was flowing over towards the second Test at Lord's.

England's selectors dropped Young and Barnett and omitted Hardstaff, who had a poisoned toe. In came Coxon, whose hustle had impressed at Sheffield, the recuperated leg spinner Wright, and Warwickshire's middle-order right-hander Tom Dollery.

Coxon's inclusion, necessitated by the thinness of the new-ball attack at Trent Bridge, incited most commentary. Arlott was dubious about yet another all-rounder, saying Coxon was 'a game and hardworking bowler, a plucky and dour batsman and a keen field anywhere . . . [but] not of Test standard in any department'. Still, he was 'a man of good heart and experience'.

O'Reilly was more complimentary, saying Coxon 'possesses the invaluable ability to make the ball swing away from the bat', and of course praised the recall of Wright, whose spell at Melbourne eighteen months earlier, where he took ten wickets in a match against Victoria, had been 'the best piece of spin bowling I have seen since the war'. The re-balanced team, with one fewer batsman, showed 'that England had at last realised that attack was the best method of defence'.

For all the criticism England's selectors would receive, especially after this match and generally throughout the series, it would be worth noting that they were only fiddling around the edges. As with most cricket teams, six of England's XI, plus the captain Yardley, selected themselves. Those seven, said Arlott, 'were so clearly the best men in England at their particular cricketing jobs that if we could not beat Australia with them, we should certainly not do so with any of the available alternative choices'.

There was, nonetheless, hot debate about the other four, who would be drawn, through the summer, from a movable feast composed of Young, Coxon, Hardstaff, Barnett, Dewes, Allan Watkins of Glamorgan, Pollard, Dollery, Lancashire captain Ken Cranston, and the Gloucestershire batsmen Jack Crapp and George Emmett. As so often in England, an apparent oversupply of qualified players only led to confusion. As the summer became more desperate, said Arlott, 'A tired bowler had only to return good analyses on two or three bowlers' wickets, or a batsman need but score three centuries against weak bowling on plumb wickets and everyone even remotely connected with first-class cricket was swamped with letters demanding those players' inclusion in the Test side.'

But too much can be made of the peripherals. If England were going to win, they needed their seven-man core to rise to the standard Compton had set in Nottingham. They needed more from Hutton, Washbrook, Edrich, Yardley, Evans and Bedser.

On the Australian side, although Bradman retained the Trent Bridge winning XI, he was not without worry. The three batsmen involved in the openers' shoot-out, Morris, Barnes and Brown, were unsettled. Morris was still out of touch, Barnes was in a funk and Brown was never happy in the middle-order. O'Reilly wrote that Harvey and Loxton now had 'better claims for inclusion than had Brown. His selection was regarded as a tribute to his great career in the game, but it was certainly not a good selection, and no one recognised that fact quicker than did Brown himself.' Harvey's fielding and exuberance were promising, while Loxton could be seen as a potential stopgap with three fast bowlers in suspect condition.

Miller felt burnt out after Trent Bridge, and Toshack's bad knee wasn't helped by his forty unchanged overs at Bramall Lane. But the big worry was Lindwall, who hadn't set foot on a cricket ground since his controversial turn with the bat in Nottingham. At Lord's on match eve, an anxious Bradman gave Lindwall a long net bowling session. Lindwall said he felt 'fine'.

Bradman said: 'You know, I don't like it. We can't afford to run risks of losing a bowler early in the match, and I can't get out of my head that you damaged a muscle badly only a few days ago. Muscles don't heal as quickly as all that. We'll wait until the morning and see how you are then.'

Barnes, meanwhile, had beaten everyone to the nets. He had to admit it: his mood since Nottingham had something to do with the tension he felt about coming back to Lord's. He asked for two hours of bowling from the ground staff before the rest of the Australians arrived. This time Lord's gave it to him. At a dinner at the Tavern that night, he declared to his teammates, 'I'm going to make a hundred on this ground.' Nobody doubted his desire; but there was a danger of wanting something too much.

*

Sun-up on 24 June revealed queues of thousands in St John's Wood. As the morning wore on, 20 000 were let in and as many left on the pavements. Symbolically, on that day in faraway Australia, the rationing of meat and clothing came to an end. In England, such relaxation of postwar austerity remained a dream.

The Australians arrived in their bus to a morning that had turned cold and squally. Ian Johnson said, 'I refuse to go on the bus. I'll walk through here.' He set off through the W.G. Grace Gates. Lord's on a Test match day felt different. 'It wasn't a great ground,' says Morris, 'but it was special.'

Lord's was the home of the MCC and the seat of cricketing power, but in terms of tradition, The Oval was more important. Surrey had been a more influential club than Middlesex in the early years of the county championship. The first Test match had been played at The Oval, as well as the most famous Test of all, in 1882. Lord's, on the other hand, was an idiosyncratic surface, with a sloping pitch and an outfield that used to be kept short by grazing sheep. The first Australian Test team, in 1880, had been refused games at Lord's. After their first Test there, in 1884, Australia had suffered a string of losses until, in 1934, they began a winning run that would last into the twenty-first century. Given the Australians' success there and naturally fond memories of winning, the elevation of Lord's mythology is one example of how the narrative of Ashes cricket moved, through the decades, from the northern hemisphere to the southern. Lord's became Australia's favourite ground before it was England's, if it ever was. It is ironic, though, that a ground and a club that preserved anachronistic class distinctions should have found its greatest fans and myth-makers in Australia.

In the dressing room, Bradman approached Lindwall.

'I've been thinking about it again, and I'm still doubtful whether we should take the chance with you.'

Lindwall, very upset, played what he called 'my last card'.

'Look, Don, I'm absolutely sure I shall be all right. Leave me out on form if you want to – but not on fitness.'

Faced with such vehemence, Bradman backed off. 'All right, keep your hair on, you've talked me into it. We'll take the gamble.'

Had Lindwall been fully fit, Bradman might have considered bowling first. He spent a long time poking and prodding the damp green wicket. The groundsman told him it would play 'slow and easy'. Bradman wasn't sure. But nor did he want to risk putting England in and giving them the advantage, particularly with Lindwall's unproven fitness. Having called correctly, Bradman tapped his legs to the pavilion. In the England dressing room, Wright said to Evans, 'That means two days in the field, Godfrey.'

Barnes's wife Alison and her sister, down from Scotland, were at that moment riding a taxi to Lord's. The cabbie sighed, 'Oh, yes, down to the slaughter.' They hoped so. Sid, though needing no extra incentive, had laid eight pounds on himself at 15/1 to score a century. He did not consider himself a betting man, but his friend Norman von Nida 'once told me never to be afraid to back my sporting ability with a little money. He says it gives you extra confidence.'

Morris took Bedser, and Barnes faced Coxon, who rumbled up, nearly knocked down the umpire and followed through straight down the wicket. Arlott said he planted his feet down very hard and looked very fierce, but his delivery was 'not so fast as the preliminaries promise'.

Barnes's resolve was almost bursting through the top of his head. He was 'determined not to take a risk until the ball was as "big as a pumpkin"'. The first ball of Coxon's second over was a poor one, down the leg side, which 'ordinarily, I would have tried to hit out of the ground. With the motto "safety first" for the first hour, I gently pushed at the ball and glided it down Hutton's neck.'

A year of drama at Lord's, a solemn vow, a wager, a wife down from Scotland – and now a duck.

He didn't hide his feelings, responding to his poor shot with what O'Reilly called a 'petulant flourish of his bat'. As he came off, he called out sarcastically to the applauding members, 'Anyone want a bat?'

One of Barnes's frustrations with life was that he knew that whatever the scale of his personal dramas, good or bad, they were only a curtain raiser to the main show. Bradman came in to an ovation that consigned Barnes's dismissal to history.

Bradman found Bedser and Coxon extremely hard to handle. An amazed Arlott recorded his first balls: 'Bradman made so stammering a start, even for him, that many spectators had to take a second look to be sure that it was indeed *le maître*. He almost played his first ball into his wicket, and immediately afterwards he was thumped upon the pad, and at the instant-roared appeal for lbw he looked up with the air of one who has enough troubles already without outsiders presuming to add to them.'

Bounced by Edrich, Bradman spooned the ball just out of gully's reach. On 13, he edged into the leg trap and was dropped by Hutton, although, *Wisden* said, Hutton 'deserved more praise for getting his hands to the ball than blame for not holding it'.

Thirty-two runs were scored in the first hour. The ball, Bradman said, 'came off at different heights and paces – the seamsters used the heavy atmosphere and green pitch superbly . . . Arthur Morris and I were still there, but it could scarcely be said we were entirely responsible.'

In the second hour, they settled. Morris swiped a six in Wright's first over, and Bradman cover-drove Coxon for two fours. Suddenly the ground was shrinking in size. In the press box, Fingleton was unhappy with the white circle inside the boundaries making Lord's smaller than it already was. O'Reilly disagreed, but, said Fingleton, 'I think he would have thought differently had he been in the middle as a bowler and saw shots earn boundaries which did not merit them.'

Yardley rang incessant changes. Coxon ran down the wicket, chewing up the 'putty-like' surface for Wright. 'It was soon apparent,' said O'Reilly, 'that [Coxon's] chief asset was likely to be his bulldozer-like effect upon the pitch.' Wright got one to kick off

that spot 'and hit [Bradman] about the part of the anatomy where
it is usual to wear the belt'.

At lunch Australia's 1/82 looked ominous for England, who
might now consider the best bowling conditions behind them.
But three overs into the afternoon they had their man. Bradman,
after two hours of great concentration, clipped Bedser to Hutton
in the leg trap. Fingleton was beginning to think 'that perhaps
O'Reilly was a fifth columnist'.

Notwithstanding the success of his plan, Bedser was still
astonished. 'Although I was bowling in the hope of a catch I could
hardly believe my eyes when it came off, and it seemed to me
amazing at the time that Don should fall three successive times in
the same manner.'

Hassett came out 'with his dryly comical toddle', said Arlott,
'looking smaller and slighter than ever'. Bedser rapped his pads,
encouraging Yardley to avoid repeating his Trent Bridge error and
persist with the old ball.

An intriguing battle ensued, as Arlott saw it. 'Bedser . . . was
now bowling in such a manner that no one watching could doubt
the fact that he is England's best fast-medium bowler. He is so very
powerful that he can bowl easily at a pace likely to compel a grunt
from most bowlers. He is always bowling so completely within
himself that close control comes relatively easily to him. Hassett
played him so gently that the watcher felt power thwarted by
delicacy.' Hassett would make 47 in three hours. England dropped
him three times, further damaging their morale. Morris's bat,
meanwhile, 'seemed all middle, but largely defensive middle . . .
Again and again Morris moved across his wicket to Bedser,
sometimes so far that all three stumps showed clear behind him.'

After his poor early tour, Morris had been even more fretful
than usual the previous night. 'I got very nervous the night before
a Test. I liked a beer or two to settle me down and help me sleep.'
After lunch on that first day, he ground his way back into form.
'I just wasn't batting well. It was true that I was shuffling. It's the

only time I ever thought I'd have done with a coach. I was stepping across, in the habit of covering the ball swinging away. I was on the move, sidewise, when the ball came. I couldn't play back-foot shots. Eventually I just woke up to myself.'

He had some luck, admitting that on 52 he nicked Wright but was given not out. In mid-afternoon he notched his century with a back-foot push off Coxon. 'I just raised my bat. Nobody came up and hugged me. Kids who see this film ask, "Is that all you did?"'

The encomiums that turned his effort from the workmanlike to the fabled would flow from the press box. Arlott said his century 'was a hundred of resource, precision and immense maturity of judgment, confirming, if confirmation were needed, that Arthur Morris at twenty-six was established among the classic batsmen'. Against a difficult diet of outswing bowling, due to the preponderance of right-arm inswingers, Morris was 'titanically safe'. Safer, really.

Fingleton agreed: 'He seemed to be in mental trouble [in Nottingham], but there was not the faintest suggestion of this at Lord's. His century was a century, century all the way . . . from the very first ball bowled to him.'

Bradman viewed Morris's overall improvement with delight:

> Prior to the Lord's Test, Arthur had displayed good form under easy batting conditions, but had been in great difficulties when he encountered a turning wicket or a green-top . . . His batting visibly improved before our eyes. The measure of his superiority became more evident when a great batsman like Miller found the conditions beyond him while, at the same time, Morris was giving a superb display. Only the supreme combination of eyesight and natural genius could have done it. From that day onwards Arthur Morris was a far greater player than before.

Otherwise, the day was England's. Morris was out for 105, slicing Coxon to gully. Then Miller arrived to play the 'most sketchy innings' O'Reilly had seen from him. 'He looked as though he were a tail-ender sent in to act the night watchman . . . After scratching round ingloriously long enough to make people wonder if the tall fellow in the middle really was Keith Miller, he was out leg before to Bedser.'

Having presented arms to the ball, Miller was devastated.

> It is the worst feeling in the world to fail at Lord's. First there comes the long straight walk back to the pavilion, followed by what seems the even longer walk through the appropriately named Long Room. You open the door and walk on rubber. You can hear no sound. Around you are some of the greatest and most distinguished persons in the land. Nobody says a word. In their quiet, dark, conservative suitings they are all looking at you; some sympathetically, some, you feel, gloating at your misery. Young Australians on their first tour are not too keen on playing there for this reason; but Lord's has a habit of growing on you, and as it does your liking for it grows as well. The day you walk through an applauding Long Room at Lord's it seems as if you have had a hallmark stamped on your career.

His solace came from the dressing-room attendant, Jack O'Shea. During the Victory Tests, Miller had told O'Shea he preferred a shower to a bath. O'Shea now showed him 'with a conspiratorial air' to the only shower in the place, 'at the top of the pavilion in a secluded spot'.

Miller's cheap dismissal gave O'Reilly a new reason to fault Bradman. '[Miller's] batting genius was wantonly squandered. His team decided that Miller as a bowler was of more value than Miller as a batsman . . . Miller's dismissal at a most critical part of the game should have been sufficient to prove to Bradman that his policy of bowling the big fellow into the ground was not altogether good captaincy.'

The series would vindicate Bradman's use of Miller, but left a sour taste with those who felt deprived of Miller's batting glories – not least Miller himself.

Edrich, a good friend of Miller's and, as a fellow war pilot, someone who shared Miller's sense of difference from those who had not seen combat, said Miller was far more competitive with Bradman than many realised, and that this was the source of their friction.

> [Miller] made a duck in the Australian first innings in that game, and did not bat in their second innings. I know he did not like it, because he told me so. He has said to me once or twice that too much fast bowling always spoils his batting, and Keith Miller likes to look upon himself as a batsman, not a bowler. Most players are reasonably philosophical about the occasional 'duck', especially when they have Keith's blazing record of big scores, but he happens to be an exception – a nought makes him unhappy.
>
> A . . . Test match is important to anyone; Keith had come here with the reputation (and the opinion) that he, more than any other cricketer, would in this series challenge and probably overtop Bradman in the batting averages for the Tests. There was a background of human and keen batting rivalry between the old champion and the new out in Australia, and each had his own faction.

Although he clearly belonged in the Miller 'faction' – a group that had more members outside than inside the Australian team – Edrich was not, however, unsympathetic to Bradman's aims as team leader.

> A captain has the right, and sometimes has the painful duty for the good of the side, to disregard a player's wishes and bring out one of his abilities – to the ruin of another. It is an

interesting speculation how far this should go; how far, in fact, it can go before the player becomes unmanageable. Keith was very loyal throughout the 1948 tour. If there were occasional moments of rebellion, as at Lord's, they were, so to speak, private to the team, and not allowed to affect match results or cause dissension or faction, or make newspaper controversy.

The next day, one of those 'occasional moments of rebellion' would take place in the open.

Australia were 4/173, a job half-done, as Arlott realised. 'To have got out Barnes, Morris, Bradman and Miller, and then to find yourself bowling at Hassett and Brown was to realise, depressingly, what it meant to bowl against Bradman's 1948 Australians.'

Hassett and Brown put on what O'Reilly called a 'drearisome partnership'. Hassett was dropped by Edrich at slip and nearly pushed Bedser to Yardley at short leg. Luck was running against England. Brown, 0, nicked Wright to Evans but the appeal was turned down. Deep into the last session, Yardley put himself on to bowl. Yardley, said Arlott, 'is not a particularly good bowler, not good enough, at all events, to bowl much more than once a month for Yorkshire. He . . . swings his arm more from a sense of duty than pride in his own powers.'

But he bowled Hassett 'to general surprise and delight', then trapped Brown. Johnson edged Edrich, and 7/258 was a satisfying result for England after losing the toss. It was, for Fingleton, 'England's day without any doubt'. The capacity crowd had stayed till stumps. From the pavilion, Ring had been bemused by the 'strange sight' of 'hundreds of ladies, all lined up, all day' at the single toilet in the outer ground. But they weren't put off. Hundreds exited Lord's only to re-form a queue for the next day.

*

On the Friday, England turned up primed for success. Fingleton said: 'Friday's spectators took their seats early and eagerly, with the expressions of theatre-goers, well-dined, who settle down to watch a play which they know in advance will end happily.'

It didn't take long for the Australians to disappoint them. Tallon reprised his youth with a counter-punching 53, then, said Arlott, 'that now celebrated comedy duo' of Johnston and Toshack produced 'many strokes unknown to the science of the game'. O'Reilly said Johnston played Coxon with such nonchalance 'he could have kept the Yorkshireman out all day with a pick handle'. Rather than getting out as expected, the last pair put on a show. Their runs 'were certainly valuable contributions to the total score but the deadening effect that their batting success had upon the English morale was much more important'.

Arlott's mood descended with the crowd's. His only relief was the manner of the batting. Spectators, 'formerly gaily anticipatory, passed from annoyance to alarm and from alarm to an admiring despair'. From Johnston and Toshack, 'There were fifty laughs and thirty runs to the last wicket partnership.' The extra Australian runs – 92 in seventy minutes on Friday morning – deflated the crowd.

Hutton and Washbrook came out and the Australians limbered up to defend their unexpected 350. Lindwall ran in, three-quarter pace and . . . 'Ouch! – my groin had gone again. After all my bombast in the dressing-room, that was a frightful moment.'

Bradman noticed, with a sinking feeling, but pretended not to. What could he do now? He had Miller, of course.

But no. During Lindwall's opening over, an edge flew near Miller in slips, and as he straightened up after fielding it, he said to Johnson, 'Hell, I think my back's gone again.' Johnson asked if he could bowl. Miller shrugged.

At the end of the over, Bradman threw Miller the ball and said, 'Have a bowl.' Miller was surprised, as he had told Bradman before the innings that he didn't think his back would stand up to a new-ball spell. Miller wrote:

Now, there had been times before when I had had a bad back
and bowled, and maybe [Bradman] thought this was another
of those times. Then again he might have been applying a little
psychology, thinking I would not have the temerity to refuse
because of the huge crowd. Anyway, I simply could not bowl
and I told him so and walked away. I was not playing the prima
donna. I had a bad back and that was all there was to it. But Ian
Johnson . . . inferred that I did play the 'temperamental star'.

Whatever the disputed version between Miller and Johnson, all of
Lord's saw Bradman throw the ball to Miller and Miller throw it
back. According to Miller, Bradman was understanding, saying,
'If you have any doubts at all I'll give the ball to Bill [Johnston].
Don't take a chance.'

It all happened very quickly, said Edrich, who was padded up on
the players' balcony. 'In itself, it was simple, all over in a moment,
and I imagine that the majority of the thousands of people who
actually saw it had no idea of its implications, or that it might have
developed into an affair that could have made trouble for the rest
of the tour.'

Miller later told Edrich he was 'astonished when [Bradman]
threw the ball at me'. Whitington, Miller's friend, who often wrote
what Miller thought, was adamant that Bradman was acting out
of mischief. 'Unfortunately Don was one of those people who
never seemed satisfied as to the genuineness of Keith's injury . . .
A number of people had facetiously described Keith's muscular
problems as "shagger's back".'

Another keen observer from the pavilion was Yardley. 'There
were tales – there are always tales! – of mild dissensions in the
team, and perhaps it could have been true that the opposing
temperaments of the stern Bradman and the exuberant Miller, and
perhaps some others, fizzed now and then in a not-unfriendly way.
What more natural. It never did any harm to their cricket!'

On this occasion, Miller's refusal to bowl might have done

catastrophic harm to Australia's chances in the Lord's Test but for an act of astonishing courage and willpower at the other end of the wicket. What Miller didn't know – but Bradman suspected – was that Lindwall had re-injured his groin in that first over.

'A nagging pain jabbed through my leg every time I ran up to bowl,' Lindwall said, 'but I was determined that none of my colleagues should know of my pain.'

Washbrook was trying to attack, without much success, through the off side. He flashed and nicked Lindwall before lunch. Edrich came out and the Australians thought he also edged Lindwall to Tallon, but the umpire turned down their appeal.

England's day turned calamitous after lunch. Hutton was 'bowled by so peaceful-looking a bowler as [Ian] Johnson after weathering Lindwall', said Arlott, before Edrich and Dollery both let go straight balls from the spearhead. O'Reilly thought Dollery's dismissal 'was perhaps the outstanding example of the season of how much the average English batsman lacks practice against really fast bowling. There was certainly no suggestion of flinching on the part of Dollery. He stood his ground all right and his intentions were excellent. But his bat had not quite attained the zenith of its back swing when the stumps went down.'

Fingleton preferred to allocate more credit to Lindwall: 'He was bowling beautifully, lithe athlete that he is, his loose limbs ambling over the ground until the final four yards, when he gathered himself up and stretched taut every muscle.' Arlott's droll observation was: 'Ray Lindwall is that rare cricketer, the highly intelligent fast bowler.'

Yardley joined Compton. Having started the day thinking of a big lead, the captain was now fighting to avoid following on. As Bradman rested Lindwall, the batsmen had some respite, chipping 87 runs in 100 minutes off Toshack and Johnson. But when the fifty-sixth over came up, Bradman brought Lindwall back and within minutes both Compton and Yardley were out. Miller, in the game even when he was out of it, took two brilliant slips catches and by stumps England were down to their tail, 150 runs behind.

First Morris, now Lindwall: Australia's rising stars of 1948 were asserting themselves. Friday was, said Arlott, 'Lindwall's day. He bowled at great but well-varied speed and at several lengths. He knew where he was putting the ball, but he never allowed the batsman the comfort of automatic bowling: he was working out variations, not only of length and pace, but also on the themes of the outswing and a sharply cut ball which came back off the pitch, in every over. Bradman handled him carefully, never allowing him to bowl otherwise than fresh.'

For an Englishman, the day was miserable. Ted Swanton summed it up: 'A more mortifying day for all but a handful of Australians in the crowd could hardly be imagined.'

On the Saturday morning Lindwall finished off the English innings, bouncing Bedser and bringing a rebuke from Fingleton: 'This was something Larwood never did and I was sorry to see Lindwall so lacking, for the nonce, in a fellow spirit of bowlers.'

England's 215 just averted the follow-on, but they took the field forlornly. Even if they captured the nervous Barnes, what then – Bradman and Morris?

Two nights earlier, after his overwrought failure, Barnes was moping gloomily in his hotel room. 'I started to think about the day's happenings and felt depressed. To take my mind off things, I began to read and about nine o'clock there was a knock at the door.' Von Nida had come to take him out. Barnes rang Alison, who was allowed to stay in London but not in the Piccadilly Hotel, and they went to a nightclub. 'That,' Barnes said, 'was the best thing I could possibly have done.'

His eight-pound bet on making a century still stood for the second innings. When he went out to the wicket, he said to Evans, 'I've never felt so out of form, Godfrey. I hardly know which end of the bat to hold.'

Evans said: 'If ever a man looked to be set for a "pair", he did.' But Barnes survived. As usual, Yardley shuffled his bowlers. Morris popped Laker's first ball back to the bowler, but Laker moved too slowly. The same over, Barnes, 18, went down the wicket. The ball kicked past his pads out of the footmarks, and Evans missed the stumping. Barnes said, 'Thanks, Godfrey, that's the first bit of luck I've had in the last month. I hope I can take advantage of it.'

By lunch Morris and Barnes had racked up 73. Press-box minds wandered from the cricket. Fingleton bemoaned the constant loudspeaker announcements, though it was intriguing to wonder why the Reverend Mr Y. was needed at home at once. Or was it inauthentic? Fingleton recalled how, in Australia, a war correspondent and a doctor had both contrived to have themselves called for by the loudspeaker at cricket matches, in order to advertise their importance.

The excitement inside Lord's faded as the reality of the match and series sank in. Crowds were banned from the field during lunch breaks, ending a prewar tradition of colourful frocks, playful children and zealous curators who were so fast to peg off the pitch area that they sometimes threatened to spike a spectator. The people would be summoned back to their seats by a tolling bell. The bell still tolled, but now it was for England. Stuck in their seats, the public could only reflect on England's worst day of the series. They had other bad days, but none as crucial as that dreadful Friday at Lord's.

Yardley laid a plan, moving Hutton away from short fine leg and creating a gap Morris might aim for. Morris couldn't resist, and, trying to sweep Wright very fine into that gap, dragged the ball onto his leg stump just when, on 62, he looked set to score a second century. That feat was something of a Morris specialty: he was the only cricketer in history to have done it on his first-class debut, and in 1946–47 he'd done it in the Test at Adelaide.

This would not be Morris's day. Bradman's, perhaps? Lord's rose to greet him as a Test match batsman for the last time. Again he started nervously, beaten three times by Bedser's outswinger, offering only a wry smile in response. Arlott wrote: 'For the first few overs of his innings Bradman was a very unhappy man. His methods in the treatment of the elementary off break as bowled by Laker inspired no confidence and achieved only occasional contact.'

Bedser set him up for the leg trap, but Bradman checked his glance and let the ball through. Barnes calmed him with his own aggression, charging down the wicket to Laker, being missed again by Evans but setting a tone that relaxed his captain, who began to unfurl some crashing pull shots.

Five chances were fluffed as the pair batted England out of the match. Barnes, on 96 for ten minutes, then straight-drove Coxon for four. Eyes blazing, he raced down the wicket like a madman, running past the handshake-offering Bradman before remembering to stop.

'I had,' he said, 'avenged myself.'

Now he set out to punish. He hit two sixes off Laker, swiping 21 off an over. Bradman joined in the exhibition-style batting, and another century looked inevitable. Yardley came on with his partnership-breakers. Barnes would say with contempt: 'How [Yardley took wickets] will ever be a mystery to me. The only thing about Yardley's bowling is an odd delivery which is quick and comes over the side of his head. Otherwise, Yardley's bowling is just typical of that negative leg-stump and leg-side theory.'

On 141, Barnes decided to hit the England captain over the rope. The ball sailed towards the crowd until Washbrook, running among the legs and lemonade bottles, took a catch that also saved a six. The ball had been hit so hard he needed to leave the field for medical attention to his finger.

Barnes took his time walking off, nodding to the public and even the bacon-and-eggs brigade. When he walked up through the pavilion and the Long Room he snubbed the handshakes. 'I had my reasons because I knew who had shut the gates at

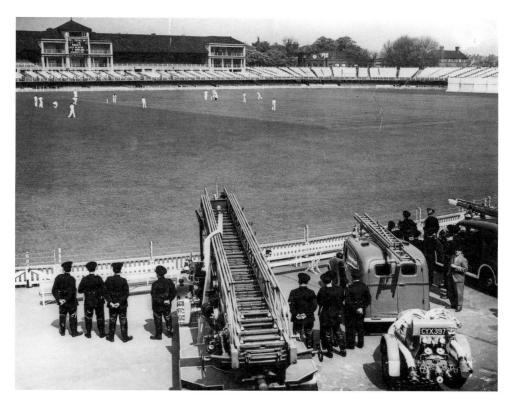

Britain could take it. Even while the country was on the back foot during the war, cricket continued. City Police play the London Fire Service at Lord's in 1940.

Cricket in wartime: players dive to the ground at Lord's in 1944 as a flying bomb lands close by.

The Oval being prepared for use as a prisoner-of-war camp, though it never actually performed this function.

Keith Miller, second from left in the front row, took time out during the war to play for a Royal Australian Air Force (RAAF) team in 1945. Keith Johnson, in the centre of the front row, would be manager of the 1948 Australian team.

Don Bradman was invalided out of the army in 1941 and settled into family life in Adelaide. Here he is in 1942 with his son John.

LEFT Miller wearing his RAAF blazer. His habit of surviving air crashes in the war earned him the nickname 'Gold Nugget', or 'Nugget'.

RIGHT Not wanting to leave his young family was one reason Bradman was reluctant to go on the 1948 tour. Here his wife Jessie is photographed walking their son John to the Adelaide Oval in 1946.

LEFT In 1938, Bradman had fought the Australian board for permission to bring Jessie to England.

RIGHT Bradman and his close confidant Walter Robins, with their wives, on the golf course as Bradman recovered from a foot injury in 1938. As an England selector and Australia's 'liaison officer', Robins's relationship with Bradman would be a complicating aspect of the 1948 tour.

Bradman batting against Worcestershire in the opening match of the tour. After double-centuries on his previous tours, he took it easy and threw his wicket away on 107.

Lindwall's drag, his back foot coming over the bowling crease, is clearly demonstrated in this photo. It took some clever behind-the-scenes work from Bradman to stop his spearhead from being no-balled.

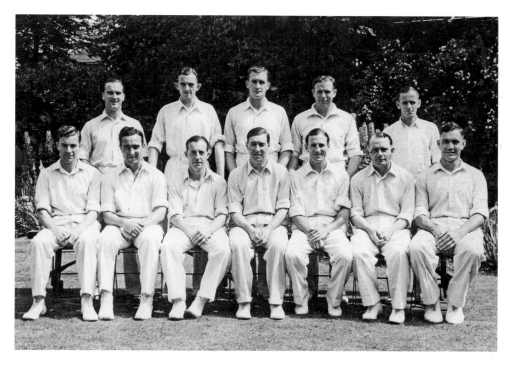

The England team for the 2nd Test at Lord's:
STANDING: T. G. Evans – A. Coxon – J. C. Laker – H. E. Dollery – G. M. Emmett
SEATED: D. V. P. Wright – D. C. S. Compton – W. J. Edrich – N. W. D. Yardley – L. Hutton – C. Washbrook – A. V. Bedser

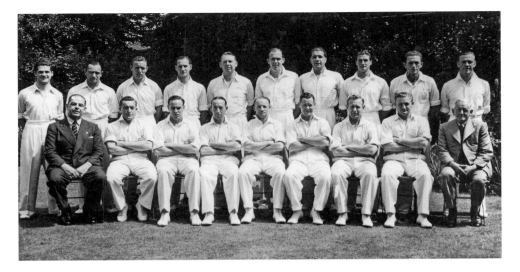

The Australian touring squad, pictured at the 2nd Test:
STANDING: R. N. Harvey – S. G. Barnes – R. R. Lindwall – R. A. Saggers – D. T. Ring –
W. A. Johnston – E. R. B. Toshack – K. R. Miller – D. Tallon – S. J. E. Loxton
SEATED: K. O. E. Johnson (manager) – R. A. Hamence – I. W. G. Johnson – A. L. Hassett –
D. G. Bradman – W. A. Brown – A. R. Morris – C. L. McCool – W. Ferguson (scorer)

Bradman and Yardley inspecting the pitch at Lord's before the 2nd Test. Note the spikes in the danger area!

The 1948 crowds to watch the Australians, such as this one on a sunny day at Lord's, squeezed right up to, and sometimes over, the boundary rope. People were packed in so tightly they coordinated standing up and sitting down to share the view.

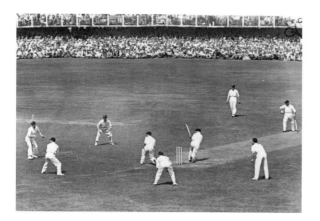

Though thirty-nine, Bradman was still a batting force. Here he hits a boundary off Doug Wright's bowling in the 2nd Test at Lord's.

Dick Pollard, far right, looks apologetic after hitting close-in fieldsman Sid Barnes at Old Trafford in the 3rd Test. Moments later, Barnes would collapse and have to be carried off.

England's domination of the first four days of the 4th Test at Headingley was helped by some sloppy Australian fielding. Here Hassett drops Hutton off Lindwall.

'Nobody knew what to think.' Bradman bowled by Hollies second ball for a duck, 5th Test, The Oval.

The controversial photograph of Bradman, hands in pockets, with King George VI and Queen Elizabeth at Balmoral. Hassett surmised: 'Pocket billiards is not a royal sport.'

Lord's against me just a year before.'

(Typically, Barnes would sell 'the bat that had made the century at Lord's' on more than one occasion over the years. The actual one went to New South Wales' Ken Grieves.)

Hassett, next man in, had been so complacent about Bradman and Barnes that he was dozily watching John Bromwich playing tennis at Wimbledon on television. The Australian's semifinal was reaching its climax when Barnes fell. 'Oh, damn,' Hassett said, 'I've got to go and bat, I'll miss it.'

He walked out to the centre and remarked to the Englishmen that he would be lucky to see the ball, because his eyes were not focused properly after watching television. He missed Yardley's first ball, which made a woody click as it passed through, but Hassett was still so dull-witted he thought he had nicked it and Evans had dropped the catch. He looked down to see the off bail lying on the turf.

Back in the pavilion, Hassett sat back down in front of the television.

'Is it the same game?'

A teammate said: 'It's the same point!'

Hassett shook his head as the laughter broke out. 'You bastards.'

Bedser quipped later: 'It seems to me a practical solution to our many problems against the Australians if we install television sets in all their dressing rooms!'

With a lead of 431, the pressure was off. Arlott said, 'Australia were 296 for 3 wickets – but even 296 for 9 wickets would barely have given England reason for cheerfulness'.

Miller nicked his first ball just short of Bedser at leg slip, and then deposited one into the grandstand. Back at Lord's, his second home, he was keen to do well. He had been socialising with Princess Margaret at the Embassy Club and Kensington Palace, and she gave him her royal standard, the flag given her by the King on her eighteenth birthday. When Hassett saw it in Miller's room he said, 'Seems you've raised your standard in more ways than one.'

Miller would later have it sent to his parents' house in Melbourne to avoid having to explain it to Peggy.

Bradman had set himself for something approaching his 'perfect' 254 at Lord's in 1930, the innings he rated his best of all, technically. But just before stumps, on 89 he snicked the first ball of a Bedser spell and Edrich, in the gloaming, was sharp enough to take it in his outstretched right hand. Bradman was cheered all the way in, his dreams of perfection thwarted by the game, as they would be, more sensationally, six weeks later.

The rest day allowed a visit to Windsor, where the former governor-general of Australia, the Earl of Gowrie, took the cricketers on a tour of the castle before they met the King and Queen in the grounds. They visited Queen Mary, the Queen Mother, at her neighbouring residence, Frogmore House.

Ring, Johnston and Loxton were eager to take photos with their new equipment. As they were leaving, Queen Mary came onto the lawn alone to wave them off. Ring said, 'Do you mind, Ma'am, if I take a shot of you?'

'That's what I'm here for, young man.'

Ring and Johnston got their photos off, but Loxton became flustered. It wasn't the first time he had lost his cool among high-born company. At one luncheon, he leaned back on his chair on a waxed parquet floor: the legs gave way, and the formalities ceased while Loxton picked himself up. Where Loxton was involved, accidents happened – which was what was worrying Johnson now.

'None of them knew much about photography, of course. Bill and Doug had clicked their cameras and put them away. Sam was still mucking around with his focus, with his light. It seemed an eternity! Doug and Bill had walked back and packed their cameras away. We were getting terribly restless with the Queen Mother standing there, and this horrible atmosphere.'

Finally, Loxton boomed: 'Watch the dickie bird!'

Bradman later said, 'Sam, you can't say that to Royalty.'

Loxton replied: 'I tell you what, George, she cracked it for a grin, didn't she?'

On their way back, the Australians were shown around Eton College by the headmaster and his wife. Nearly 500 runs ahead, with Lindwall improving each day, they had every reason to be happy.

Only rain could stop them – and on Monday morning, it teemed. But they got enough batting in for Bradman to declare 596 ahead. Arlott thanked Bradman for not exposing England 'to the possibility of more runs by Johnston and Toshack. Perhaps those worthies themselves protested against such sadistic employent of their specifically light-hearted batting.'

In fact, Bradman had delayed his declaration while the field dried, sparing his bowlers the slippery ball.

Again, Miller did not bowl, and this time the tension between himself and Bradman did not stay buried. After Lindwall's first over, Bradman threw Miller the ball and said, 'Have a bowl.'

Miller said later: 'He was probably hoping I might change my mind, but there was no way I could bowl.'

He said, 'No, I can't, Don,' and tossed the ball back.

Their teammates were astonished. Barnes said Miller 'kicked the ball back to his incredulous captain. I did not catch the comment which went with the action, but I'm assured that Miller curtly advised Bradman to have a go himself. Bradman picked up the ball and – this I did hear – replied: "You'll keep."'

Barnes said Bradman was 'as wild as a battery-stung brumby with his star all-rounder', and believed this incident was the reason Miller would be omitted from the 1949–50 tour to South Africa. Bradman always denied it, but 1948 teammates, including Barnes, 'were never taken in by such protests'. (Miller would join the tour as a late replacement when Johnston was hurt in a car accident.)

At Lord's, the bickering went on throughout the afternoon. In the dressing room later, Fingleton was told that Bradman 'grumbled apropos of Miller not bowling'.

'I don't know what's up with you chaps,' Bradman said. 'I'm 40 and I can do my full day's work in the field.'

To which Miller allegedly replied: 'So would I – if I had fibrositis during the war!'

The silence in the dressing room can be imagined. One of the few occasions when resentment at Bradman's non-participation in the war came to the surface, the exchange was reported by others but was never publicly confirmed by Bradman or Miller.

Out on the field, an English drama was playing out. Between rain showers, Washbrook showed new spirit, taking bouncers on his body rather than hooking. Hutton, however, was cracking. He had batted more often than any other Englishman against the Australians that summer, and had been more consistent than anyone, including Compton. But now, he wafted at Johnston and was put down in slips before scoring. He appeared to be flinching and backing away from Lindwall.

'This exhibition of Hutton's was so bad,' O'Reilly said, 'that it was hard to realize that he was the same man who had put up a world's record score . . . He seemed to have lost all power of concentration and looked like a man being led to the gallows . . . the Hutton of the Lord's Test, 1948, was little more than a masquerader compared with the Hutton who made things hot for us in the previous tour.'

Barnes was right under his nose, ratcheting up the pressure. 'I could see [Hutton] watching me out of the corner of his eye as I took up my fielding position close on the leg-side. I am certain he didn't like to see me so close but there is nothing in the rules to say how close a fieldsman must field, provided, of course, that he doesn't impede a batsman's strokes.'

A more sympathetic spectator, Laurence Kitchin, wondered, watching Hutton face Lindwall, 'what it felt like to advance a bone-grafted forearm along [Lindwall's] line of flight.' A lifelong fan of Hutton's, Kitchin described his batting at Lord's as 'the most mysterious innings I've ever seen him play'.

Hutton's jitters looked even worse in contrast with Washbrook's stoicism. The Lancastrian was 'struggling', Arlott said, 'but seemed to enjoy a grim pleasure in his mountainous task'.

Doug Walters once said, when Mark Taylor was having his notorious run of bad form in 1997, that Taylor's problem was that he was 'batting too long'. Had Hutton been out in the first over, he would have done less damage to his and his team's morale. Instead, a long cringing hour yielded 13 runs before he finally gave Johnson the inevitable slips catch.

Fingleton watched him walk back to a tight-lipped pavilion. 'This was probably Hutton's worst effort in a Test, but I felt sorry for him in trying to sight Lindwall's thunderbolts against the pavilion in this bad light. Hutton returned in cold silence. The chopper was about to fall for him and the silence, presaging it, indicated the general disapproval of Lord's at his showing.'

Hutton's capitulation seemed even worse as Washbrook, reported *Wisden*, was 'receiving blows on the knuckles, hip and elbows'. A.A. Thomson said 'there was hardly a square inch on his body that was not bruised and battered'. Even Edrich, who made just 2 runs, was praised by Arlott for his grit: 'On several occasions [Edrich's] crouch was so low that the bails were to be seen above his head. But, whether he crouched or played, he never moved back from the line of the ball.' Every sign of stoicism from the others highlighted Hutton's disgrace.

Johnson sent Edrich on his way with a fine catch off Johnston, and at 2/52 the rout was on. Toshack replaced Lindwall, and a relieved Washbrook hit his first offering for four. The amiable-looking Toshack, appearing 'almost a collaborator after the hostility of Lindwall', said Arlott, 'mentally rubbed his hands, for his success depends upon batsmen trying to hit him'.

So it panned out. When Washbrook was 37, the ball slipped out of Toshack's hand and arrived as a juicy full-toss dropping outside off stump. Washbrook slashed, but under-edged it.

Harvey, at cover point substituting for Lindwall, recalls clearly what happened. 'Tallon was standing up to the wicket. Toshack bowled a full toss, which was very foreign for him. Washbrook couldn't believe his luck. He shaped up to whack it past me. He went back, got an edge, and Tallon caught it on the full at his boot-tops. I've never seen a catch like it. He was a freak behind the stumps. From Toshack's hand to Tallon's gloves, no pitch was involved. Fantastic catch!'

In Bradman's view it was 'one of the most remarkable catches ever made behind the wicket'.

Tallon did not have a faultless series, but such catches had Bradman rate him 'the greatest wicket-keeper I have ever seen'.

England's four and five batted brightly until stumps. Compton had 'that engaging air of eagerness which he brings to the heaviest of undertakings', said Arlott, while Dollery, 'burly of build, to make the bat in his hands seem like a slight weapon, [had] a walking-stick manner with the bat, which adds to the impression of confidence in his play'. The pair 'seemed like giants to those who clung to hope for England. Here at last men were putting bat to Lindwall as if he were an ordinary bowler.'

Lindwall blamed himself for not getting Dollery cheaply. Bradman, remembering a weakness he had seen in Dollery before the war, suggested a fielding change. Lindwall didn't want it. 'Less than five minutes later,' he said, 'Dollery lifted a chance to exactly the position where Don had recommended a fieldsman should be placed. I moved a man there immediately – but too late. Dollery settled down to a fine innings.'

On the Monday night, there was still a chance for Dollery to be a hero. Realistic hopes, however, ended with the second ball on Tuesday when Compton, 29, drove at a Johnston half-volley. His bat clipped his toe and he edged the ball, which corkscrewed towards Miller at short gully. Miller knocked it into the air and, falling backwards, caught it, 'perhaps the very best slip catch of the whole series,' O'Reilly said, 'a real match-winner'.

As the umpires were unsighted, Compton asked Miller if he caught it. Compton later said, 'Keith's word was good enough for me.'

Dollery batted unflappably for his 37, until he ducked a short one from Lindwall that failed to rise. Lunchtime rain offered England some hope. When the game resumed, the England captain, 'looking, as he always does, rather gentle and apologetic – a very deceptive appearance for a man whom the Australians rate so highly', as Edrich put it, came out to save the situation.

Within minutes Yardley was bowled by Toshack for a duck, putting him on the receiving end of one of England's most famous barrackers, 'Yorkshire Annie'.

'I would never guess publicly at a lady's weight,' said Edrich, 'but I think I may fairly say that there are few more impressive sights than this monumental figure, always in full black, progressing towards her seat before a Lord's match, with ordinary people steaming about in the vicinity.' Her loyalties were, in order, Yorkshire, England and Middlesex. But Yardley's county origins did not save him from her wrath. As he walked off, Yorkshire Annie cried: 'If I'd not hit that for four, I'd have shot myself!'

Yardley was seen to blush.

Toshack was too good for all of the tail except Evans, who batted well enough in Arlott's view 'to make every man turn to his neighbour and say, "If Evans can do it, why can't the others?" If the neighbour did not know, he at least put up some pet theory and found conversational consolation even in adversity.'

By 2.22 p.m. Australia were 2–0 ahead in the series and the Ashes were virtually retained. Toshack took 5/40 and when the last man, Wright, was caught, Fingleton saw 'Miller and Hassett putting more spirit into a rough-and-tumble on this Lord's pitch for stumps as souvenirs than England had put into its batting'.

Though well beaten, the England players still found reason to curse their luck. Fifteen minutes after Wright's wicket fell, heavy rain flooded Lord's. 'That cloud-burst would have ended play for the day,' Evans said, 'but then the match was over, so it is useless talking about "ifs".'

The only respect in which the game was not a crushing disappointment for England was the record attendance. Morris and Barnes had commanded the English bowling, while Lindwall, defying injury, had cowed Hutton, broken the resistance of Edrich and Washbrook, and frightened the tail. Toshack had played the deadly foil.

Some were beginning to theorise that England's inadequacies were due to poor nutrition during the war. Fingleton disagreed, saying England's troubles were 'in the mind. Physically, the Englishmen who played in this game were of a more robust type than the Australians. If we compared the bulk and the strength of the opposing parties, we could not excuse England on this score. The chief trouble was in outlook to the game and technique.'

In Lindwall's 8/131 and the centuries from Morris and Barnes, the main themes clarified themselves at Lord's. Australia had a once-in-a-generation fast bowler. England only had one high-quality seam bowler who could not reduce the full Australian batting strength on his own. O'Reilly said Australia's dominance was now all-round, and he 'could not imagine them losing one game'. After two Test matches, they were beginning to seem invincible.

8

MANCHESTER: THE COUNTER-REACTION

Sam Loxton, having recovered from his early-tour groin strain, was jumping out of his skin. He had expected to be watching the first two Test matches, but the passivity of spectatorship hardly suited the effervescent Victorian.

Loxton was thankful for six-day-a-week cricket. The day after the Lord's Test match, he was hurrying in with the new ball against Surrey at The Oval. He had become a favourite of Arlott, who wrote: 'Sam Loxton is a fabulous person. In the first place he looks like one rough-hewn from flint. Secondly, he could be, in the flesh, that very character from the well-known short story, through whom was passed the entire current of the San Francisco power-station, and who thereupon became immortal and vested with incredible power.'

Lindwall, Johnston, Morris, Barnes and Tallon were rested, and Ian Johnson was considering going home to Melbourne, as he had just received news that his infant son had fallen down stairs. (His wife Lal told him his arrival would be too late either way, so he stayed in England, and his son recovered.)

Bradman was unhappy with the Oval wicket: '[O]ne must allow for the use to which The Oval had been put in war time, but this ridge was obvious to the naked eye and was inevitably dangerous when a reasonably fast bowler was in action. I was thankful we did not play Lindwall – probably the Surrey batsmen were too – for I strongly dislike seeing anyone seriously hurt. Even at Loxton's pace it became a real possibility.'

Loxton didn't care, thrusting with great zest and hitting Surrey's best batsman, Laurie Fishlock, on the head. By contrast, a sulking Miller was in Bradman's bad books after Lord's. The all-rounder went to a concert at the Albert Hall after the Test, and when he staggered back into the Piccadilly at breakfast time, he bumped into his captain, who, later that morning, made him walk from fine leg to fine leg each over. A spectator offered Miller a bicycle. Bradman asked him to bowl, but one over was enough for Miller, who then failed with the bat and dropped two catches.

Centuries from Hassett (his fourth on tour) and Bradman (his sixth) gave Australia an unassailable lead. McCool, his finger recovered, overwhelmed Surrey in the second innings, leaving Australia 122 to win.

As they walked off the ground, Loxton asked Bradman, 'What do I have to do to get a knock in this side?'

'I'll tell you what you can do. You and your little mate go and put the pads on. We need 120. You go out and get them.'

Bradman planned to finish early and see Bromwich in the Wimbledon final against American Ralph Falkenburg. Loxton and Harvey went out and smashed the runs in 20.1 overs. When they came back to the pavilion, Loxton said, 'There was nobody in the room. We wouldn't have been very Invincible if Harv or I had got out!'

Not only were they all gone, but they'd taken the cars.

'What are we going to do now?' Harvey said.

They changed and raced to Oval Tube Station, catching a train to Wimbledon, where their tickets had been left at the gate. At centre court, Loxton sat next to Doug Ring, who said, 'Tell me, Sam. Did we win?'

They had, but the unfortunate Bromwich gave up match points and lost in the fifth set. Bradman watched with Sir Norman and Lady Brookes from beside the Royal Box. Outside cricket, it wasn't a good sporting day for the team: Bradman had been given three strong racecourse tips by the connections of a horse called Bowral Boy, but his teammates were in too much of a hurry to place their bets. All three won. And the tennis was a sad sight. Lindwall, a clubmate of Bromwich's in Sydney, was inconsolable on the train to Bristol for the match starting the following day against Gloucestershire.

Loxton knew he was in with a chance for the third Test starting at Old Trafford in five days' time. Brown, who had split his finger at The Oval, had not enjoyed batting in the middle order. Says Morris: 'Down the order, Brownie was lost, he wasn't scoring quickly enough. He was a lovely player but a bit past it. He said he was sorry he went over – but he did make eight centuries!' Indeed, Brown had been the form batsman in the county matches, racking up five centuries already, but all as an opener. (Over the entire tour, as an opener Brown would score 1300 runs at 65, with eight centuries, and down the order just 148 runs at 29.6, highest score 32.)

If it were a batsman-for-batsman swap that Bradman contemplated, he might have chosen Harvey for Brown. But Miller's fitness and attitude were now a concern, and Lindwall's groin was not yet bankable over a five-day Test. Loxton knew that a good showing at Bristol could see him elevated as an all-rounder.

Gloucestershire were one of the stronger counties, with batsmen George Emmett, Charlie Barnett and Jack Crapp, and spinners Tom Goddard and Sam Cook all pressing for Test selection. Off spinner Goddard, though forty-eight, was a legend in the West Country, and Bradman, who was sitting out the match, told Johnson, 'You'll see a fine spinner in this Goddard. Watch what he does.'

An envious McCool wrote of Goddard: 'It was said of him

that he always bowled a length and that with his hands the size of cartwheels he could spin a ball off a slab of marble. Mind you, he didn't have to wear his fingers out in those days, because they used to treat the Bristol pitch with sand just to whet his appetite!'

Goddard's every ball was greeted from the crowd with, 'Well bowled, Tom', or 'Nice ball, Tom', but his supporters were rudely silenced by Morris.

'Oh yes,' Morris chortles. 'We went to Gloucestershire to play this off spinner who was said to be the best in England. I got a hundred before lunch. Just when I thought, "I'm going to get three hundred here", I hit a full toss back to the bowler.'

Morris's 290, the highest score of the tour, showed how much confidence his Lord's century had given him. From here he would be unstoppable. Goddard got hit in the hand and, Bradman was told, 'seriously questioned one of our players as to whether they had been instructed to hit him out of the firing line. He was disillusioned when told the answer was in the negative and that things were merely taking their natural course.'

Harvey made 95 and Loxton 159. Arlott wrote: 'Three Sam Loxtons in English county cricket would yank up our domestic game by the bootlaces. But while men who comparably combine strength, enthusiasm, fitness and speed are sometimes to be found, one who also possesses so immense an aptitude for cricket appears no more than once in a generation – which is, perhaps, fortunate – for eleven Loxtons would defeat the world – at anything.'

Harvey, meanwhile, had recovered from his miserable spring, when, aside from an unbeaten 76 in the batting-practice end of the Lancashire game, he had only scored 120 runs in seven innings. The absence of sightscreens at most grounds and the uncovered wickets baffled him. A free striker, he too often left an open gate between bat and pad for the finger-spinners to slide through. 'In my first four games I was averaging 7. I was just battling for myself. The conditions were vastly different to Australia's. The wickets had so much grass on them, the ball seamed around, and I wasn't used to this caper.'

He thought the best way to learn would be to go to every match and 'make myself useful'.

> I reckon I'm the only Australian player who's been on a tour that long who's watched every game. Every train and bus, whether I was playing or not, I thought it was the only way to learn the game. I might also have been too shy to look after myself. A big city like London, if they left me there I might get lost. So I went to every game, all around the country. It was a great learning experience even when I had nothing to do. Blokes would bring a crate of beer into the dressing room, and I'd sit in a corner and listen to them. It's amazing how much you can learn.

But when he wanted direct one-on-one help with his form crisis, he didn't know where to go.

'Not a soul gave me any advice,' he says, glinting not with resentment but admiration. Bradman, Hassett, Miller, Barnes, Brown, Morris – such a wealth of know-how and experience, and not one would give the teenager advice. 'They were a great bunch of blokes, but they weren't into helping me. Why should they? We were competing for the same places. It was every man for himself, and everyone wanted to play Test cricket.'

He went to his mate, Loxton. After each disappointment, they would sit in their room analysing each other's batting and talking through solutions. 'I just worked with Sammy, and he worked with me, we did everything together,' Harvey says. 'It was just fending for yourself, which I still think is the best way of doing it.'

But he kept failing. In despair, Harvey says, he tried a bold move.

'I thought, "I can't play this game." Sam was a good mate of Bradman's, so I said, "Sam, can you do me a favour?"

'"What do you want?"

'"Can you go and ask the boss what I'm doing wrong?"'

Loxton went and saw Bradman. 'My little mate's got a problem. He's not scoring any runs, and he wants to know what he's doing wrong.'

Bradman never gave Harvey advice, either then or throughout his sixteen-year Test career, in which Harvey would eventually score more Test runs than any Australian, barring the Don. The answer came back through Loxton. 'You tell your little mate this. I can't tell him how to bat, but if he keeps the ball on the ground he can't get out.'

Harvey took this simple hint and, as the pitches dried, he prospered. He made a century against Sussex, an innings that convinced him he belonged on the tour. 'Sam and I had some very happy conversations that night.' Then, for his fielding, he was chosen as twelfth man in the Test matches and was spoken of as a possible replacement for the struggling Brown. His 95 in Bristol helped Australia to 7/774. The wicket suggested a draw, but Johnson, having learnt from Goddard how not to bowl, put in his best performance of the tour, taking 11/100 in Gloucestershire's two innings and staving off McCool's and Ring's claims to his Test spot.

Meanwhile, Barnes, who, says Morris, 'was having one of his difficult periods', was suffering an emotional letdown after his Lord's exertions. He wandered dreamily in the outfield, ignoring Hassett's attempts to contact him. 'Barnesy was a lovely bloke, a real character,' said Loxton, 'but this day he decided that he'd stay just outside the pavilion, near the sightboard, at third man or fine leg. Whoever bowled the next over, he stayed there. This went on, and nobody was taking much notice. Hassett of course was taking plenty of notice. He brought Ringy off, and Ringy said, "I don't want Siddy there." Hassett said: "What makes you different from the rest of us?"'

Barnes was coming to the end of an all-too-brief, tempestuous international career. He would not last when Hassett became Test captain. 'Bradman understood Barnes better than Hassett did,' Morris says. 'Don knew to treat him gently and got the best out of him, but Lindsay wouldn't put up with it for long.'

Midway through the Bristol game, two of the Gloucestershire batsmen, Crapp and Emmett, learnt that they had been elevated into the third Test.

The left-handed Crapp made an even hundred in the first innings, showing the stubbornness the England selectors were seeking. 'Who but he,' Arlott asked, 'would stolidly have played out the last overs of the day with his score in the nineties and the last man at the other end? And who but he, with the chance of a century on his mind all night, would have completed it so safely, so slowly and so deliberately the next morning?'

Lindwall bowled only twenty-one overs at Bristol, but his brain was active. He sent down just one bouncer at Emmett and learnt what he needed. Emmett, said O'Reilly, 'scrambled it away to fine-leg for a single but he was most uncertain in his method of coping with it. The uncertainty was too blatant to be missed by Lindwall, who wisely refrained from bowling any more balls of that type to Emmett, preferring to let things rest until the Test at Manchester.'

Emmett, in a national sensation, would be chosen to open at Old Trafford. Hutton had been dropped.

The uproar, said Arlott, was immediate. 'Cricketing England and, more especially, non-cricketing England, which had heard or overheard the news, were full of woe and anger.' The most widely heard remedy, he said, was 'Sack the lot.'

Sack the selectors, that is. Robins, Clay, Holmes and Yardley became pariahs. O'Reilly said that Yardley 'must have stolen back quietly to his native county on that Sunday night after England's team had been chosen and two Yorkshiremen, Hutton and Coxon, had been omitted'.

At Bramall Lane that weekend, Surrey captain Errol Holmes was booed – the Yorkshire crowd mistook him for A.J. Holmes, the Test selector. Poor Errol was caught first ball by Hutton in the first innings and bagged a pair in the match. 'It is to [Holmes's] eternal credit,' said his teammate Alec Bedser, 'that nobody was more amused than the victim.'

Pelham Warner's *The Cricketer* magazine, normally a supporter of all selections, voiced its disapproval. Hutton's omission also damaged team morale, Edrich said. '[W]hatever England in general felt about that, the team experienced dismay.'

Hutton heard the news over the radio. The selectors never explained their decision. 'Had they done so it might have softened the blow,' he wrote at the end of his career. 'Privately I held the selectors . . . to be wrong. That was all there was to it. Hard as I searched my mind for an answer, I came up with nothing, and I am still none the wiser.'

He had to take his telephone off its cradle to stop the calls from outraged supporters. 'I had nothing to say,' he said, and went off to Paisley in Scotland to play a match for Yorkshire.

Since the war, Hutton had averaged better than 40 against the Australians – superior to anyone bar Compton. That summer, his two half-centuries for the MCC and his 74 at Trent Bridge had given England hope that he could anchor the top order. He had been jumpy in the darkness at Lord's in the second innings, but were England in a position to drop him for that? It seemed an unaffordable luxury.

Asked who were the best batsmen in the world, Washbrook said: 'Me and Len Hutton.'

What about Bradman, Morris, Hassett and Barnes?

'They only have to face English bowling. Me and Len have to play Aussie bowling.'

Most of the Australian players were incredulous. Morris

thought 'the English selectors were our best friends at times – they did a lot of silly things', while Harvey calls it 'one of the greatest mistakes England has ever made, selection-wise'. O'Reilly talked to the Australians, and found a reaction of 'disbelief which quickly turned to thankfulness tinged with sorrow for the humiliation of a player for whom they had nothing but the highest regard . . . It seemed that the selectors had meted out cautionary punishment for Hutton's naughtiness at Lord's; that some feeling of hot-headed vindictiveness had prevailed where cool-tempered common sense was desperately required.'

English and Australian commentators searched for reasons. Surely he wasn't dropped on the basis of one innings?

Arlott saw Hutton's dropping as a culmination of a deliberate Australian campaign:

> Hutton is so good a batsman and so thoughtful, knowledgeable and conscientious a cricketer that the situation inevitably caused him considerable mental anxiety which was reflected in his play, and which must certainly have affected to some degree the confidence of his team-mates, all of whom hold him in considerable respect. This was certainly the result that the Australians, who are realists in their cricket strategy, must have desired. It was well known that the English batsman they most feared was Hutton. Their fast bowlers had worked, on every conceivable occasion, to shatter Hutton's confidence, and they had succeeded.

There was also a knock-on effect. Hutton's 'manifest dislike of the short rising ball was likely not only to lose him his wicket, but also to disturb the morale of the batsmen who followed him'.

'That arm must surely be in the back of his mind,' said a sympathetic Fingleton. 'He had two operations on it. It is noticeably shorter than the other, has had forty-five stitches in it and carries pieces of grafted bone from Hutton's legs.'

It might have been true, as Barnes said, that Hutton was 'a dismal Desmond in his own dressing-room'. But that did not stop the question being asked: what were the selectors up to?

Yardley offered an explanation in his 1950 autobiography:

It was felt by the Selectors that Len, especially in the second innings at Lord's, had shown a fatal tendency to flash at rising balls outside the off stump. The Australian bowlers knew this, and 'fed' Len such balls. Now the task of an England Number 1 is to lay the foundation of a big score by wearing down the opening shock attack, however much patience this may require. On his performances in figures, the Selectors were not justified in dropping Hutton; but in the light of his weakness against Australian bowlers captained by that great tactician, Bradman, they were. They took the bold course, knowing what a storm of adverse criticism would meet their action, and Len was dropped.

Interesting, that use of 'they'. Yardley was attempting to hide behind selection-room confidentiality, possibly to deflect criticism from his own role. As a Yorkshireman, he knew he would not soon be forgiven. But later in his autobiography, he was clear on the point that he got the teams he wanted: 'The attitude of the Selectors to me was grand. Although all most outspoken, and fully prepared to give constructive criticism, their view was, "You're the chap who has to lead these fellows on the field; within reason, you should have who you want." That does not mean to say that I personally selected the teams. But a casting vote was often left with me.'

Outside the England selection panel the only person, intriguingly, who continued supporting Hutton's omission was Robins's mate, Donald George Bradman.

Bradman was spending a lot of time with Robins in that first week of July. While the Australians played in Bristol, Bradman was staying with Robins and his family in Berkshire. Bradman and Robins ate at the Hind's Head Hotel in Bray. Bradman ordered duck. (The Hind's Head is next to the building that would eventually house Heston Blumenthal's The Fat Duck restaurant.) Over the next few days, Robins, with his fellow selectors, dropped England's premier batsman, the one Bradman feared most.

'People assumed that the Selectors had dropped him as a disciplinary measure following his display at Lord's when in many quarters his batting against our fast bowling had been severely criticized,' Bradman said.

> Are Selectors entitled to drop a player even though they believe he is good enough to play? My answer is unhesitatingly yes . . . If Hutton was not opening the English innings in a manner calculated to inspire confidence in the less gifted batsmen who were to follow, he could conceivably have been upsetting their morale. Numbers 5, 6 and 7 do certainly react quickly to the way numbers 1, 2 and 3 handle the attack.

Which poses the question: was Bradman acting, sub rosa, as a fifth selector? The amount of time he was spending with Robins, when Robins was part of a panel deciding Hutton's future, is suggestive. Was the Australian captain not only attacking Hutton on the pitch but, via Robins, in the selection room?

Fingleton thought there was something in it. 'The Australians have long had a reputation in England for trying to force inferior people into Tests, to the advantage of the Australians, and no doubt Robins thought Bradman was up to an alleged Australian trick.'

Harvey has few doubts.

> I believe Bradman would have tried to influence Robins. When you're playing an Ashes series, psychology comes into it. If a bloke looks out of form, you can try what you can to get rid of him. Bradman, Robins, Allen and [Kent captain] Brian

Valentine were all very close friends and he spent a lot of time with them during the '48 tour. I can imagine Bradman voicing doubts about Hutton. I wasn't privy to it, but I wouldn't be at all surprised.

Bradman and Robins were silent on the matter. Morris, with a wink, says: 'I wouldn't put it past Don. Maybe he was putting ideas in their heads.'

Both teams checked into the Midland Hotel in Manchester. The little-known Crapp arrived after Bedser. Supposedly, the receptionist said: 'Bed, sir?'

'No – Crapp!'

'Second door on the right, then, sir.'

The Australians told their counterparts how surprised they were not only about Hutton's omission, but also Doug Wright's. Morris says Wright 'was their finest spinner, very awkward, and they dropped him. He could do you with his bounce, beat you and the ball would go over the stumps. He bowled fast wrist-spinners, so it was difficult to control, but when he got it right he could really bowl.' McCool said Wright was 'an enigma . . . He could bowl anybody out. Anybody. He could also fail to bowl them out, missing bat, stumps and wicket-keeper with a consistency of misfortune that was downright cruel . . . On his day Doug Wright was just plain, plum magnificent. He was also unreliable, erratic and terribly expensive on occasions. But then you seldom get genius without the wayward streak, too.'

Wright's omission was also seen as an effect of Bradman's mind games. He, of course, would not play his leg spinners, McCool and Ring, preferring Johnson as a defensive option exploiting the 55-over new-ball rule. England's selectors were now following his example. It was as if he could control them. In the fourth Test at Leeds, the absence of Wright would prove decisive in Australia's favour.

McCool was trying to make the best of a bad lot. In the Australians' rooms in the Midland, he conspired with Lindwall and Miller to play a prank on his roommate and fellow Queenslander, Tallon. The leg spinner was fascinated by the wicketkeeper's habit of never unpacking. 'He was the only man I ever met who literally lived out of a case on tour. He rarely unpacked when we arrived at a new hotel, and if he wanted a clean shirt he simply rummaged about in his case until he found one, then stuffed the dirty one back in.'

McCool discovered a hatch in the wardrobe connecting their room to Miller and Lindwall's. The three decided to do a job on 'Deafy'. (Tallon got his nickname in a county game when, unusually, he was the only Australian not to appeal for a snicked catch. Hamence said, 'What's the matter with you these days? You must be deaf as well as dumb.')

Tallon, as usual, dumped his bags on the floor. The fast bowlers came in and goaded him into unpacking.

> Slowly he shook out his dress suit, placed it on a hanger, walked over to the wardrobe and hung it on the rail. While we all talked loudly and cheerfully, Lindwall nipped down the corridor into his own room and grabbed the suit through the hatch. Again Tallon advanced on the wardrobe, again he hung up a suit. It was when he went there for the third time that he twigged something was wrong . . . There's never been such an expression as there was on 'Deafy''s face when he peered into that wardrobe and realised that the suits he had hung there half a minute before had all disappeared. Miller and Lindwall were in such a state I thought we might be without a fast attack for the Test match.

Lancashire had been a defiant powerhouse of English county cricket since the days of its great amateur–professional opening pairing, 'Monkey' Hornby and Dick Barlow. Hornby was the son of an immensely wealthy cotton-mill owner; he led England in rugby and cricket and played football for Blackburn Rovers. Barlow, the son of an ironworker, played cricket for a living. They would enter by different gates and only meet in the middle, and if they became confused running between wickets, Barlow was expected to sacrifice himself. In return, Hornby would pay Barlow a guinea.

Lancastrian cricketers also had a reputation for cussed independence rivalled only by Yorkshiremen. Hornby, who was England captain in the most famous Test match of all, the 1882 'Ashes' match, boycotted Tests when he was not allowed to select his fastest bowler, Arthur Mold, widely believed to be a chucker. He was succeeded, in spirit, by the imperious Archie MacLaren, the great amateur opener of the Golden Age. MacLaren was in many ways the classic gentleman cricketer, haughty and autocratic, but he also saw himself as an outsider in the south. A poorly paid schoolteacher, he had to borrow money to keep up his subscription to the MCC, where he said he felt he would be given 'six of the best if I walked in the wrong door'. Like Hornby, MacLaren made his most famous alliance with a professional, Sydney Francis Barnes, the greatest bowler England has ever produced and the crankiest. Barnes preferred to play for better pay in the Lancashire and Staffordshire leagues rather than make himself available for county and Test matches. When he did, belatedly, get his chance for England, under MacLaren's influence, Barnes destroyed Australia and South Africa on both sides of the world.

Old Trafford, then, was another outpost of a very strident parochialism. Manchester's weather also made the place different: no Test match had been completed there since 1905. This, Bradman's fiftieth Test match, would take place on the one ground where he was, in his own words, 'notoriously unsuccessful'.

It was another venue still bearing wartime scars. During the conflict, the groundsman, Harry Martin, had to wheel his barrow after air raids to pick up hundreds of unexploded incendiary bombs. The stands and field had been damaged, but the Mancunian spirit was undimmed. Two southerners arrived on the first morning, laid their hats on seats as they would at Lord's, and took a walk. When they came back, two locals were in their seats with the answer: 'It's booms, naat 'ats, whaat keep seats oop 'ere.'

The day was ideal 'for football or spinning cotton', as O'Reilly put it, and the pitch so green that Hammond said he'd have sent an opponent in, but when Yardley won the toss he batted. Bradman would have done the same: '[W]hen the wicket rolled out slow and easy on a cold and cloudy day, I visualized the possible realization of my worst fears.'

Because Australia only needed a draw to retain the Ashes, Edrich said, 'from the start there was a desperate mood about [England's batting]; nothing less than a win would be any use to us.'

Washbrook, the local hero, knew he was on 'my last chance' after Hutton's omission. He was moved 'minutely, but significantly, from No. 2 to No. 1', said Arlott, as Emmett appeared 'overawed'. On the first ball of the match, the pair narrowly avoided running each other out. Never had a Yorkshireman received such sympathy in Manchester as the absent Hutton that day.

Bradman switched Lindwall and Johnston after one over each, due to the gusting wind. Miller couldn't, or wouldn't, bowl, so Bradman gave the ball to his newest paceman. Loxton, who would have been excited to walk onto the field to carry the drinks, was bubbling over. Arlott, now one of his greatest fans, was warmly supportive: 'Loxton is a fast-medium bowler . . . of no great subtlety, but he is always endeavouring to bowl the fastest ball ever bowled.' As a batsman 'he is always trying to hit a cricket ball farther than a cricket ball was ever hit before.'

Flanagan saw a serious dedication underlying the somewhat madcap exterior. 'He placed his success as a cricketer above all else and not infrequently absented himself from parties and other celebrations in order to safeguard his physical fitness by maintaining his rule of "early" nights.'

Loxton started with three long hops outside leg to Emmett, who obeyed orders not to hook or pull. Arlott soon changed his view on Emmett, saying he was 'perfectly self-possessed in his first Test innings. The wicket, even as Lindwall worked up to pace, remained as amiable as Denis Compton.'

Bill Johnston was also amiable, but deceptively. At 22, he bowled his signature floater, yorking a confused Washbrook. The crowd's silence took Bradman back to his golden duck in Melbourne in his first innings of the Bodyline series.

Edrich, the missing link for England in the first two Tests, had just scored a century for Middlesex. 'Everyone expected to see a reformed Edrich,' O'Reilly said, but he 'started as though he had not had a bat in his hand since [1946–47]'. He swung and missed outside off stump and broke his duck with a streaky four through slips.

The cagey Lindwall decided Emmett had been in long enough. He had bowled him one bouncer at Bristol. He now bowled him one at Manchester. Emmett ducked, but his bat stayed horizontal above his arms, for which he was widely derided, but McCool thought he did well just to make contact.

'When "Lindy" talks about the most dangerous ball he ever bowled, he invariably mentions the one he let Emmett have. It was a flier, only a shade short of a length, and it flew at Emmett's face. Even at 120 yards away on the balcony my blood ran cold. Nobody likes to see anybody brained, not even in a Test match! I rate it a major achievement that Emmett got his bat up in time to protect himself.'

Barnes pocketed the simple catch and Arlott said, 'Men sighed and cursed their optimism and resigned themselves to things being as bad as ever.'

From that moment it was a certainty that Hutton would be back for Leeds. O'Reilly 'could not help singing a hymn of hate against the selectors, who in dropping Hutton had bunged in a man who had not had any previous experience of the Australian opening attack. It was a terrific gamble and it failed miserably.'

On the hour, Lindwall hit Compton's elbow. Then he bowled a long-hop – not a bouncer – which umpire Davies called no-ball. Compton, distracted by the call and trying to smash the ball to the boundary, top-edged his hook into his face. The ball was travelling so fast it didn't bounce until it was halfway to the rope.

Lindwall was heckled, but film footage and Compton's testimony show the ball was only waist-high. Nonetheless, Yardley again found an opportunity to accuse the Australians of hypocrisy: 'I wondered what an Australian crowd would have said if it had been Bradman – or what Bradman would have said.'

With Compton retiring hurt, Jack Crapp came out. Crapp was not the typical Test debutant. He was hard, phlegmatic, and confident after his Bristol hundred. '[P]lacidly as a man starting a day's work in the fields, came Jack Crapp,' said Arlott. 'Crapp contemplated the approaching Lindwall with an air as of one with a straw in his mouth.'

Crapp and Edrich batted for survival. Toshack started his spell with five maidens, and the innocuous Johnson conceded seven runs off his first ten overs. O'Reilly was irritated, saying Edrich's play 'resembled patball more than it did cricket', but his beaten-down English colleague Arlott saw things differently. 'Here, at last, was a fighting quality akin to that of the Australians. I believe that the Australians must have sensed the antagonism of the batting and that they reacted in taut sympathy – there was less than the usual amount of banter, neither Edrich nor Crapp was inclined to conversation or any distraction from their concentrated resistance. The bowling and fielding was tight as a vice.'

After lunch, the batsmen attacked Johnson, Crapp lifting him over the sightscreen. Arlott observed: 'A man dallying on his way back from lunch dropped his glass at the sight: Crapp, for his part, stood motionless with the air of a boy pretending he hadn't broken a window.'

The fifty-five overs of the first ball yielded just 87 runs. Lindwall returned with a second ball, but Crapp continued bunting him around without hurry. Lindwall got a lifter to strike Edrich's hand, and it took a full ball to end Crapp's vigil. The left-hander meant to leave one outside off stump, but, Arlott reported, 'in the last yard before pitching it curved in like a boomerang – more sharply than I have ever seen a ball swing before from a bowler of such pace.' Bowled for 37, Crapp left, 'quietly disappointed in himself, and, indeed, he had given the impression of knowing precisely what to do with every ball he received up to Lindwall's masterpiece – a superb full ball of pace, length and swing'.

Compton, his eyebrow patched over two stitches, wanted to go back in, but Yardley told him to rest, in hope that the Edrich–Crapp resistance would obviate the need for Compton until the next day. But Dollery missed a Johnston yorker, and Edrich, having 'lost everything but the will to hold on', said Fingleton, was out pulling his bat away from another Lindwall scorcher. In three hours he had scored 32. Denzil Batchelor wrote, rather unkindly: 'Perhaps the difference between Barnes and Edrich is the difference between Australian youth, totally self-confident, brimful of belief in the future, and the Englishman with corrugated brow, who dares nourish no hopes beyond the sneaking ambition to cope with next year's income-tax demand.' It might have been a projection of Austerity Britain onto the tough little war hero's face.

Compton came back at 5/119. Miller cried: 'You're plastered!'

Compton retorted: 'You will be, if you bowl.'

Yardley chipped Johnson limply to midwicket. O'Reilly, simmering all day, had had enough. Compton, he said, 'was showing every sign of making a ding-dong fight of it. It behoved Yardley to take things easy with Toshack whom he could have continued to play safely without scoring. But the urge to lift the lefthander over his tightly packed on-side field proved too much for Yardley's powers of concentration and he paid a penalty which amounted to a match-losing one for England.'

Not yet. Compton and Evans sparked up for 75 at a run a minute. Evans was out late, but where there was Compton, there was hope. The English might have been all out but for two misses from Tallon, whose hands were feeling the effects of two months of taking Lindwall. His second fumbled catch was off the last ball of the day, but observers had seen the wicketkeeper flinching throughout. Tallon would develop a style of taking everything with his fingers pointing downwards rather than towards the flight of the ball, to save his fingers from injury, a technique that would be almost universally adopted in later years.

It is also possible, as Phil Derriman speculates in his biography of Tallon, that the wicketkeeper was carrying an unseen handicap. Tallon's off days were explained by one teammate: 'It's pretty hard to keep well when you're suffering from a hangover.' He suffered from stomach ulcers as well, says Derriman, which may have affected his keeping.

Seven for 231 was another day that was neither as good nor as bad as it could have been for England, and, Arlott said, 'Compton was there against the morrow'.

Bedser, too! In the Midland Hotel, the BBC's Rex Alston ran into the big bowler.

'How long are you going to stay there tomorrow?'

'I'll stay,' Bedser joked, 'as long as there is someone to stay with me.'

In eleven days of Test cricket, England had so far been unable to turn the momentum of a match. They had stalled Australia for long periods in Nottingham, and worried them on the first day at Lord's, but had not yet been able to transform an advantage into a result.

Day two at Manchester, 9 July, would change all that: a day of 'epic cricket for England'. Arlott's suffering was arrested, first by Compton and Bedser, and later by Pollard.

Beneath clouds as dark as his eye, Compton marched to his eighth century in ten Tests against Australia. As on Thursday, the visitors' sloppiness helped, Tallon again putting Compton down. Subduing his aggressive instincts but not his natural grace, Compton played what Bradman called 'a class innings of enormous value. It was all the more commendable following his injury.'

Farming the strike from Bedser, Compton outwitted Bradman and the bowlers. No fieldsman was within seventy metres of the bat, but he still punched fours. When Bedser couldn't avoid the strike, he was solidity itself, with a touch of luck. In one over Toshack, after beating Bedser with five balls, shook his head sadly.

Rain again had the players on and off. During delays, Miller played poker in England's room with Edrich, Evans and Compton. At one point, when a large pot had built up, Hassett looked in and told Miller the Australians were going back onto the field.

'Go on without me,' Miller said. 'I'll follow you out.' He won the pot and raced out, coins jingling in his pockets. He turned back to the England players and shouted, 'Hey, boys, I've got it all, all your money!'

Bradman shared none of his levity as the Compton–Bedser stand lasted into afternoon. Even the wildlife was turning against the Australians: a dog described by Fingleton as 'the dirtiest little cur in Manchester' held up play. Loxton tried to tackle it, and Bradman tried to blind it with his cap, but it outran everyone except the police.

It took an element of the bizarre to break up a stand that seemed destined to run all day. After hitting two fours off Lindwall and one off Johnston, Compton pushed the ball between the two cover fieldsmen, Loxton and Bradman.

The batsmen ran one, and then, as Bradman and Loxton both overran the ball and engaged in what O'Reilly dubbed a 'Gilbertian tussle' for the ball, Compton called for a second. Bedser saw what was about to happen. As he ran, he shouted at Compton: 'You've done me, you bloody fool!'

'I recovered,' said Loxton, 'and got it to Tallon. Bedser was out by a fair way. It wasn't a stunt. It was one of those run-outs on a bad bit of fielding, which do happen, as we all know.'

Bradman said Loxton 'did some stupendous things to get run-outs. I have never seen anyone who had such a powerful throw when off balance.'

For the English pair, it was a horrible lapse in concentration after so much endurance. Bedser was, in O'Reilly's estimation, 'still far enough out of his crease to require the services of a taxi to make the event interesting'.

Bedser traipsed to the pavilion. His teammates jibed, calling him 'baby elephant' and 'heavy-footed fairy'. When he got into the shower, Edrich yelled at him to get his bowling boots on, a leg-pull that didn't brighten Bedser's mood.

Humbled by Australia's aggressive gamesmanship so far, now England literally struck back. Even as the tide had turned England's way, Barnes held his position under the batsmen's eye. His safety depended on the accuracy of the bowling and the timidity of England's batting. During the previous Test, O'Reilly had written that a batsman 'has one really convincing method of persuading a man to get back to greater distance . . . The suggestion that Barnes was too close was a feather in the fieldsman's cap and a tribute to the accuracy of the Australian bowling.' But, he added, 'I would not like to go there for any type of bowling, [and] wild horses could not drag me there for a slow off spinner.'

It had gone on for ten weeks now, and Barnes was still prepared to back his bowlers. In his account of what happened next, he said:

> I happened to overhear Denis tell Dick Pollard . . . to keep his end up and leave the scoring to him. I laughed at this. Denis is not a very secretive person and I had no intention of overhearing him but his whispers were loudly spoken . . . 'Now, Dick,' said Denis, 'leave it all to me. Don't you try to score at all. I want you to keep your end up and I will go for

the bowling.' . . . heartened by Denis's orders, I went up close
to Pollard. I should never have done it and deserved all I got.
A fieldsman shouldn't go up close to a tail-end batsman; and
anybody who does go close for an off-break bowler, and Ian
Johnson was bowling at the time, is just looking for trouble. I
got as much trouble as I wanted.

Compton said that as Pollard took strike, he 'glanced at [Barnes]
with an expression that seemed to show surprise and wonderment
that anyone should stand so close when he was at the wicket'.

'Dick Pollard is a beefy chap who rolls his sleeves high,' Barnes
recollected, 'and when Johnson tossed up what I later learnt was a
"donkey-drop", Dick forgot all about his instructions from Denis
to play doggo and opened his shoulders.'

> I never saw the ball from the bat. All I knew was that I had
> received a terrific blow over the ribs on my left side. I suppose I
> was lucky it didn't kill me as some are killed from such a blow
> near the heart when playing cricket. My legs buckled under me
> and I collapsed. My first thought as I was hauled to my feet was
> that I had gone blind in the left eye. My whole left side seemed
> to be paralysed and I couldn't see from the eye at all.

Bradman said Barnes was about eight yards from the bat, though
it is likely he was closer. The ball, clubbed hard enough to have
cleared the boundary, hit Barnes so squarely it did not glance off
his body but dropped at his feet. Edrich was horrified: '[I]t was a
bit of good fortune that he was not killed, as he would have been if
the ball had landed two inches to the left and a trifle higher.'

Some in the crowd cheered, though it is unlikely they – like
radio commentator Rex Alston, who laughed, thinking it was
more of Barnes's tomfoolery – realised how badly he was hurt until
four policemen came onto the ground to carry him off. When
Pollard saw what he had done, he became visibly upset.

Escorting Barnes off, also anxious, was Bradman. Here was what many thought he and Barnes deserved. They had pushed the rules too far. When Barnes had recovered, Bradman would maintain his self-vindication: 'Here was the greatest short-leg fieldsman in the world badly injured because he was capable of doing what nobody else could do.' But his face, as he walked Barnes off, was wreathed in self-reproach. Had Bradman taken his will to win to the point where he had breached his duty of care to his fieldsman? Scorer Bill Ferguson could have been speaking for Bradman when he said: 'I am thankful that Sid was carried to the hospital, and not to the mortuary . . . as he easily could have been.'

Yardley was in no doubt that Bradman was feeling culpable: 'The Australians all admitted that they knew the day must come when this would happen. The showman had at last suffered for his own bravado and his captain's will to win.'

In the press box, O'Reilly – a consummate gamesman himself – immediately grasped the consequences. Barnes's presence, up to then, had kidded batsmen into thinking Johnson was more dangerous than he was. The injury to Barnes 'robbed Australia of their opening batsman and also reduced the wicket-taking capacity of Johnson for the rest of the tour'.

The Invincibles were not quite the unified team that has sometimes been portrayed. The out-of-sorts Miller saw the incident through independent and suspicious eyes. 'I do not know to this day how badly hurt he was. Sid was a great actor. A lot of our players were dubious about the extent of his injury. I thought that he was not too badly hurt. It was said by the boys who carried him off the field that he crossed his legs to be more comfortable!'

Yet Morris, Barnes's roommate and opening partner, was convinced. 'Later, I said to Siddy, "Why didn't you catch it?" He said it would have killed an ordinary man, and he might have been right.'

Pollard was soon out, replaced by the literary Young, who quipped to Compton: 'Doctor Livingstone, I presume?'

Compton replied: 'No, don't worry. Just play up the line.'

Misunderstood and under-equipped, Young was soon out, leaving Compton unbeaten on 145. Edrich said Compton 'had to be told after the innings why everyone was laughing'.

His heroic innings, over five-and-a-half hours, against some fiery bowling from Lindwall and Loxton and the probing swing of Johnston and Toshack, embodied the era of 'Britain Can Take It'. At Euston Station in London, a Brylcreem billboard with Compton's face now had a piece of newspaper glued above his eye to represent his sticking plaster.

Having had three opening batsmen at Trent Bridge and Lord's, Bradman suddenly had one. Rather than risk Hassett, the natural choice, Bradman asked Johnson to open. The Old Trafford members, still stirred up by Lindwall's pace, heckled Johnson and Morris as they walked out. Unsettled, Johnson edged Bedser, bringing Bradman in with 3 runs on the board.

Bradman started more certainly than at Lord's. He had a high regard for the local hero Pollard, the pink-faced redhead known in Manchester as the 'Chain Horse'. Fingleton loved him: 'He is, and looks, the perfect and most honest tradesman imaginable. He gives a huge day's work. He never falters in his job and there are, with him, no middle of the pitch tantrums. If he has misfortune – and he has more than his fair amount of this – he turns side-on to the batsman, faces cover, puts his hands on his hips, whistles and then bursts out laughing.' Off the field Pollard also played piano 'splendidly'.

A few minutes later, Pollard forced Bradman back and hit him square on the pads. The umpire's finger went up and so did thousands of cloth caps. Everybody, Fingleton said, 'shouted, laughed and talked at once. What bedlam it was, and in the midst of it Bradman, the centre of it, walked out very slowly. What a tribute to a cricketer that his dismissal should cause such a scene.'

Rosenwater wrote that 'the roar might have greeted the winning of the Ashes by England. (In the absence of that unlikely miracle, the dismissal of Bradman for 7 by a Westhoughton-born bowler was an acceptable substitute.)'

Bradman had, perhaps, been too clever by half in his conversations with Robins, having encouraged not only the omission of Hutton but also the selection of Pollard.

Pollard bowled seventeen overs unchanged, amazing Arlott. 'Pollard, with his long, padding, flat-foot run, seemed to bowl steadily faster and faster. His stamina is immense: apart from growing even redder in the face, he shows little sign of the long bowling spell. He, to a greater extent than Bedser, could compel the hasty stroke even from Hassett, that master of timing in defence.'

Hassett took on the left-arm orthodox Young, but mistimed and was caught at cover. By stumps Australia were 3/126, trailing by 237, and the next morning, even though Miller was looking for boundaries, Fingleton said he had 'rarely seen runs look more difficult'. A big crowd caused the gates to be closed at nine. Manchester broke out in sunshine for the occasion.

Loxton, ready to bat in his first Test match in England, was padded up on Bradman's instructions. The captain came into the dressing room and asked: 'Anybody seen Siddy?'

One of the players said Barnes had been in the nets. Bradman bustled out.

None of the players expected Barnes to be anywhere but the Manchester Royal Infirmary. The previous night, he said, he received 'flowers, chocolates, home-made cakes and all manner of presents . . . I never knew I was so popular.' Bedser visited him to see if he was all right. In the morning he came to Old Trafford and tried to bat in the nets, but gave up in distress. Fingleton 'saw his ribs and they were all colours'.

Nine runs into the morning's play, Miller, worried by the coming new ball, was lbw to Pollard. Loxton stood up to leave the dressing room, but Barnes appeared, ready to bat.

'What have you got the pads on for?' Barnes asked.

'I'm next.'

'No you're not, I'm next.'

'Braddles said I'm next.'

Barnes pushed Loxton back into his seat and walked out with his gloves and bat. Bradman came rushing back into the dressing room.

'What are you doing here?' he asked Loxton, who told him what Barnes had done.

They looked out to the centre. Barnes was shaking Pollard's hand as a point of honour.

'Then,' Loxton said, 'Arthur got out [for 51], and I'm in. I'm facing Bedser, who I've never faced before. They're going everywhere, off the seam and in the air. Barnes was on one. I pushed one into the covers. I'm halfway up the wicket, and he's looking the other way. I have to race back. At the end of the over, I walked up and said, "Listen to me. This isn't on. When I call you, you make sure you run. There'll be a run on. If you don't, we'll both be at one end."

'So the next over from Bedser, I pushed one into the covers and he ran. Next thing he's being carried off for the second time in the match.'

Again there were those who suspected Barnes of play-acting as he collapsed on the pitch holding his ribs. A photograph showed Evans laughing heartily. 'I knew Sid was a good actor and I'm afraid I wasn't convinced that he was not acting on that occasion.'

Barnes went back to the Manchester Royal Infirmary for the rest of the weekend.

This time there was no miraculous Australian fightback. England grew confident to the point of recklessness. They had been taking punishment all summer, and now, when Lindwall came in, Edrich said to Evans, 'Stand well back this over, Godfrey. I'm going to slip in a few really fast ones.'

Edrich bowled Lindwall 'a couple of absolute scorchers with all I had in them. We were willing to admit the big gun–peashooter allegory for the time being, but we wanted them to know that peashooters can get tough.'

Edrich's view was that, even though he was nowhere near as fast as Lindwall and Miller, it was worth a crack. 'In cricket, as in life, what ye sow, so shall ye reap – so long as there are any sowers about. England has been short of sowers of that sort; I don't really qualify.'

But he did please his selector. 'I looked up and saw Walter Robins, my Middlesex skipper, literally and actually dancing with joy on the pavilion balcony and signing to me, for all he was worth, to carry on! I dare say he felt – as we all felt – that the tide was about due for a small turn!'

Edrich ran in again to Lindwall, bounced him again, and hit him on the wrist. Edrich walked up the pitch to rub it and ask if it was all right. Lindwall laughed: 'You can't get away with this, you know, Bill. Don't forget, I'll be bowling on this wicket next innings.' Edrich grinned, went back and bowled another bouncer.

Edrich thought, 'That's enough to teach him to be sensible; now he knows what he's made us feel.'

But things didn't work out quite like that. I noticed – we all noticed – that the atmosphere on the pitch had become electrical. Everyone was suddenly tense. Lindwall himself, judging by the way he played and looked, had never had to face a bouncer before, though he had bowled enough of them at almost every English batsman of post-war fame. He did not like being at the batting end. When my over finished, he gave the 'thumbs up' sign to the pavilion. An Australian who was there later commented: 'I made a mental note of what Edrich was preparing for himself in the second innings.' That seems a bit silly. In fact, the whole Australian attitude over these bouncers seems to us to have been that they had a divine right to send the ball into our faces whenever they chose or the position of the game demanded it, but that it was black and mortal sin if we did so to them, only to be expiated in blood.

> The English view was – what's sauce for the goose is sauce for
> the emu. Why not? We sent no cables to the Australian Board
> of Control . . . Two bouncers in a Test match is not a lot to
> face. We had more than that.

Edrich's reference to Bodyline, when Australia had sent plaintive
cables to Lord's, gets to the heart of the matter. The players knew
that the violent edge to the 1948 series was all about the Australians'
desire to settle a fifteen-year-old score. The fact that Bradman was
the only surviving player from Bodyline, the only man on the field
who held a personal grudge, underscores his central role in the
execution of Australia's vendetta.

Battered by Edrich, Lindwall had given the thumbs up – or
the green light – to his best mate in the pavilion. All of a sudden,
Miller's back was feeling better.

'There was real drama in the air,' Flanagan said, 'when England
began the second innings. Australia was being definitely challenged.
Defeat was threatening and it was good to see our players roused
out of their usual complacency, and fighting for victory. Lindwall's
deliveries came down like thunderbolts. He was stirred by the
challenge and nervy with excitement.'

Washbrook got off the mark on Lindwall's second ball. To the
next, Emmett pushed away from his body and Tallon leaped for a
one-handed catch.

It was on. Edrich walked to the middle.

The previous evening, after his bouncer attack, Edrich had
enjoyed a beer with Lindwall, Miller and Compton. Lindwall, he
noticed, 'was continually massaging his wrist'.

'The next day when I went into bat I rated a bumper barrage
from Ray as a certainty. It did not materialise . . . but his soulmate, Miller, made up for it. He was more hostile than ever.'

O'Reilly described the tension:

Edrich must have expected some retaliatory measures from Lindwall, for he wasted no time whatever in crouching low to let the first round of the broadside pass high over his head. He could have had no idea, however, that it was to be a double-barrelled affair; his surprise was shared by many spectators when Bradman threw the ball to his other fast bowler, Miller, who had been on the injured list for some time. Miller's few overs were bowled at his fastest pace and were interspersed with frequent bouncers.

Miller's back was somehow fine again. Washbrook said it was 'to our astonishment' that Miller was bowling at all, let alone with such fire. He unleashed 'the fastest and most fiery attack I have played against. Nothing we experienced in Australia compared with this. There, we had received an occasional short-pitched ball. Now we were getting them consistently. The ball was continually flying around our heads.'

The toughest English batsmen, Washbrook, Compton and Edrich, enjoyed the fight with the Australian fast bowlers. They respected each other as men, having taken part in the war, and deepened their friendship with drinks and games of cards off the field. The Englishmen's attitude towards Bradman, however, was completely different. Washbrook said:

Judge my amazement when after one particularly hectic over, Don came up to me as he crossed the wicket and apologised! His words were, 'I hope you don't think this is my wish, Cyril. It isn't. I don't mind an occasional bouncer but I don't agree with using them consistently.' My reply to this was, 'It's all right, Don. I'm not worried about it. Carry on . . .' You may wonder why Don, as Australia's captain, did not take off his bowlers or at least order them to stop pitching short repeatedly. I'm afraid I just don't know.

But he was prepared to speculate. While winning comfortably, Bradman restrained his pacemen. Once under threat, in Nottingham and now in Manchester, he dropped his scruples. '[W]e had to remember that this was the first time in a post-war Test that the Australians had been in trouble,' Washbrook said. 'Their intentions to hit back with all possible means in their power could not be doubted.'

Then umpire Dai Davies no-balled Lindwall for his drag.

'Let's get on with the game,' Lindwall growled. The atmosphere was now even more charged than in Nottingham. At the end of the over Davies threw Lindwall's sweater at him. It fell on the ground. Lindwall remonstrated, and the umpire fobbed him off.

Bradman told Lindwall to settle down and the bowler shook his head in disagreement. Passions rising, Washbrook decided it was time to bring out his hook shot. It was always a mistake, but, as Arlott said, Washbrook 'recalled that this was Old Trafford and that he was Washbrook'.

He top-edged Lindwall straight to fine leg, where the ever-safe Hassett was stationed. Hassett juggled the ball once, twice, and dropped it. His subsequent 'gestures of self-reproach', said Arlott, 'were not entirely humorous in conception'.

The barrage went on. A Lindwall bouncer nearly hit Washbrook in the face. Edrich followed Washbrook by hooking the bouncers off his nose. The brave right-hander explained his hook: 'The best way is to let it come on here,' pointing to a spot between his eyes. 'Then you've got to hit it. The hook's safe enough as long as you remember that the ball never hurts as much as you think it's going to.'

He still had a wound on his temple from being hit by the late Ken Farnes in 1938, in the fastest spell he ever faced. Lindwall and Miller held him in the highest regard. Lindwall said: 'If I were asked to pick a side from post-war cricketers Bill Edrich would be among my first choices. He is a great fighter at all times, never better than in a crisis.' Miller called him 'a deadly hooker' – which he would not have said about any other Englishman that year.

Fingleton thought the bouncers were now 'grossly overdone'. Miller hit Edrich in the elbow. Bradman spoke to Miller and next over there were no bouncers.

England were on top. They had withstood the blitz. Their batting, Washbrook said, 'proved that the Australians were far from invincible, and that their fast bowling could be mastered'. But as so often was the case, change and relaxation brought the breakthrough. The stand was 124 when Washbrook played the new bowler, Toshack, towards Morris in the covers. The batsmen changed their minds, got stuck, and Morris threw down the stumps.

Edrich, 53, had been so close to redeeming his sorry series. He thought Miller and Lindwall 'overdid their ration' of bouncers, but reserved his bitterness for Bradman, not the bowlers. It is worth noting that whatever rancour there was on the field, its form of expression did not flow over to verbal abuse. Hutton said, 'I cannot recall a harsh or heated word being exchanged between us. They were hard, mighty hard, but they were totally fair and never tried to umpire me out.'

It is in this respect (if only in this respect) that Test cricket of 1948 may be seen as a gentler sport than in later times. Whatever they felt, players strived to maintain a friendly face. The tenor of the time was to maintain public composure, and the Englishmen saw themselves as proving their moral superiority over Australians by not complaining about the bouncers. Yardley said, 'We did not always like the bumping ball, and it was used to excess at times under conditions that would have brought very violent protests from Bradman if things had been reversed; but there was nothing against the Laws of Cricket in any shade or degree, and English cricketers are not men to squeal under an occasional blow on head or body which they are too slow to avoid.' There was no mistaking the resentment Yardley and his men felt towards Bradman, but their conception of English honour was to offer a smile and a handshake and leave the antagonism on the field.

*

Waiting for Compton, the Australians played their usual fielding games. Hassett borrowed a helmet from a bobby, as if that was what he needed to take a catch, but he was biting his lips and blinking back his embarrassment even as he took a bow to the laughing crowd.

Compton came in, and was brilliantly caught at slip by Miller off Toshack. 'The novel experience [of coming in with runs on the board] was too much for Denis,' said O'Reilly.

Having gained an advantage, were England going to secure or squander it? Lindwall came back and Washbrook couldn't help himself now. He was in; this time he would master the bouncer. The previous day, booksellers in the ground had been trying without success to market a booklet about Washbrook. Now, Fingleton said, it was 'selling like Test tickets'.

Full of confidence, Washbrook hooked – and top-edged. The ball sailed once more to the bucket-like hands of Hassett.

'Catch this one,' Lindwall said flatly.

The little gunner's eye was out again. He dropped it. 'We were laughing,' Morris remembers, 'but it didn't amuse Lindwall.'

The miss loomed as a turning point that could let England back into the Ashes battle. It also confirmed in Washbrook's mind that, after two difficult Test matches, he was back to his old self. 'Had Hassett held that catch, Washbrook would have been in direst disgrace,' said Fingleton, 'but at this time he was almost equalling Pollard as the country's hero.'

After Hassett's second miss, a small boy called out, 'Give 'im the money, Barney!'

Suspicions began to circulate. So shocking were Hassett's lapses, Bradman heard later that 'a prominent Lancastrian refused to attend the rest of the match because he believed Hassett had dropped the catches on purpose. He claimed they were too easy to miss and Australia were playing "dead" for the sake of the gate. If only he knew the chagrin felt by our whole team as they saw those catches dropped. Test Matches are not rigged. Thank goodness cricket is above suspicion in that regard. The game is too complex – events cannot be ordered even if so willed and the public need never doubt the genuineness of a match.' Another difference between 1948 and the present day!

Crapp, nearly bowled before he had scored, helped Washbrook put on 49 by stumps to take the lead to 316. Washbrook and Davies sent drinks to, respectively, Hassett and Lindwall. It was an evening for English magnanimity. Australia, Fingleton thought, 'by no means looked a good side let alone a great side'. Bradman said, '[W]e finished the day in a bad position and had much to reflect upon over the weekend.'

Better a general be lucky than good, Napoleon said, and the team that is both good and lucky will be invincible. To make up for the disparity in the sides' bowling attacks, England needed luck. Whenever it intervened, however, it seemed to go Australia's way.

On 11 July the England players were grouped in the Midland, watching their hopes go down with the barometer. On the Australian side, Bradman was in a curt mood, as recorded by this exchange with the gossip writer of the *Manchester Evening News*:

'After five embarrassing minutes in his company I am compelled to the opinion that while Mr Bradman may be the greatest cricketer in the world he is hardly one of the most tactful.'

Bradman's apparent crime was to stay in his room, 'like Achilles of old', while boys waited in the foyer with their autograph books. When he came down to answer to the writer's questions, Bradman was 'completely off-hand and, after rebuffing me, he stalked out and drove away, ignoring also the worshipping small boys'.

Bradman's discourtesy was rare, but he was preoccupied: Australia were too far behind to win the match. This was the ground where he had never succeeded. But his hopes were answered, Fingleton wrote, by 'familiar Manchester sounds – the clippety-clop of horses' hooves along the cobbled streets and the sound of rain'.

Players, officials and 21 000 spectators went to Old Trafford on the Monday. The rain kept falling. Most of the crowd were uncovered. In the Australian dressing room, Loxton kept looking out the back window to urge on the clouds and tell his teammates, 'No need to worry, she's coming from Burnley.'

Arlott gave voice to England's despair: 'On Monday it rained: it rained: it rained. England had fought to a winning position, and now we stood by and watched it all washed away.'

Not a ball was bowled, nor a penny refunded. No free tickets were handed out for day five. London columnists sharpened their pencils for a campaign to strip Manchester of its Test match. Moist air was better for the cotton looms than for cricket.

The lost day gave Australia an even-money chance of a draw. On the Tuesday, more rain delayed a start. Fingleton was tickled to see the contrast between Yardley and Bradman when they inspected the pitch during breaks: 'Yardley was in flannels; Bradman, overcoated and muffled to the ears, looked as if he were contemplating a trip to the Australian Antarctic expedition at Heard Island. The condition of the pitch, to captains, is nearly always dictated by the state of the game and it was obvious the captains would disagree.'

At 2.15 p.m., they resumed. Australia would be given sixty-nine overs to survive.

The denizens of the press box probably let their disappointment distort their view of what followed. Arlott said the rain only 'stopped to allow a mockery of a match to take place'. O'Reilly said the ball was too wet and the pitch too greasy for England's bowlers to have any chance. Fingleton thought the Australian batsmen exaggerated the difficulty of the bowling when they didn't want Yardley to make a change.

The batsmen's view was quite different. Bedser took the new

ball and Johnson was terror-struck to see it bending and cutting. Morris blocked each ball. At the end of the over, Morris said: 'It's doing a bit. We'd better stick around or Alec will run through us.'

Johnson agreed. 'Okay, but if we have to do that, you keep Alec. I'd have no hope against him the way he's bowling.'

This was a real challenge for Morris, who, teammates such as McCool thought, had needed Barnes's protection from Bedser while the ball was swinging. Without Barnes to counter the movement with his brand of 'French cricket', Morris had to take full responsibility.

For the forty-five minutes of his innings, Johnson did not face a ball from Bedser. He wrote:

From my end, I saw from Bedser possibly the finest exhibition of fast-medium seam bowling I have ever experienced. Or rather, I did not actually experience it. I held a watching brief. Alec dipped the ball in the heavy atmosphere and cut it back at varying heights off the deceptive pitch. For the whole forty-five minutes I batted, I merely had to watch Bedser. Morris 'took him' the whole time, and not one ball missed the middle of the bat. It was superb cricket; magnificent bowling checked only by superlative batting; a contest guaranteed to satisfy any cricket connoisseur.

On 6, Johnson nicked Young to Crapp at slip. Bradman then took twenty-eight minutes to get off the mark, the longest in his Test career. The greatest batsman of all needed Morris's protection.

Johnson recalled that 'the players in our dressing-room were hoping that Morris would continue to deal with the "Big Fella" and keep even the mighty Bradman away from him until he had settled down. Morris did so, and not until Alec had bowled something like the sixteenth or seventeenth over was he able to attack anything other than Morris's defiant bat.' In a period of 100 minutes, the batsmen did not change ends.

'We were not interested in scoring runs,' Morris says. 'We just had to defend. If we'd had to play the previous day, we'd have been in great trouble.

'I took Bedser every ball, even when Don came in. He had Pollard. We were both just playing back. We only wanted to hold our wickets and it wasn't easy. It wasn't a real turner, but the ball was jumping about. Yardley didn't drop the field to let me take a single. He kept the catchers in.'

More rain interruptions made things harder for the bowlers, as Bedser recalled: '[T]he wicket by then was just a mud heap, making it very difficult to run up properly. In fact, when I started to bowl the water came over the soles of my boots.'

Bradman stonewalled, to the crowd's heckling. When a spectator told Bradman to give his bat to Compton, O'Reilly said, 'I heartily agreed.'

O'Reilly's passionate nature got the better of him:

> If [Bradman] had the thought at the back of his mind that he was for the first time in his career playing a valuable innings on a sticky wicket then he was fooling himself. The wicket was a batsman's paradise . . . [Bradman should have] made admission as to the wicket's favourable nature by giving the crowd who had sat through rain and cold for days something decent to look at, instead of pretending to himself that the wicket was difficult and that Australia must not take the slightest little risk. This unwillingness to take a risk or to accept the challenging call of some particular phase of the game is one of the greatest flaws in Bradman's captaincy. Strange that one who takes risk after risk as he bats and to whom the challenge from the bowler is meat and drink should completely discard these tendencies when he takes charge of the destinies of a team.

While O'Reilly's general point about Bradman's captaincy has some merit, it was misguided on this afternoon. Fingleton was equally wrong, saying Bradman's 'exaggerated patting' of the pitch suggested 'it was a nasty business' but 'not a single ball flew'. He thought Bradman was trying to con Yardley.

Morris says this couldn't have been more incorrect: 'I was a bit annoyed with Fingo. The ball was popping off the wicket, and moving both ways, digging divots out of the pitch. And Fingo said there was nothing wrong with it! He wasn't out there.'

After blocking for the best part of three hours, Bradman and Morris were allowed off. Two–nil up with two games to play, Australia officially retained the Ashes at 5.47 p.m.

9

LEEDS:
THE GREATEST TEST

How good were they? 'Invincibility' in a sporting team is more an idea than an empirical fact. It rests in that team's capacity to redeem hopeless situations; to win from any position, however dire; to be in front in the last stride at the finish line, regardless of what transpired earlier in the contest. Above all, invincibility is an idea that resides in the contestants themselves, on both sides. It comes from the moment the winner reaches the belief that he can never lose, and the loser decides that he can never win.

For the 1948 team, that moment came in Leeds, the Headingley Test match that shimmers as the greatest of that year and one of the greatest of all.

In Bradman's view, the tour was always a staged campaign, with three steps. First, retain the Ashes. Second, win the Test series. And third, if possible, go through the tour unbeaten. It was while waging all three campaigns concurrently that Australia was most vulnerable. When the first two had been attained, the touring group could grow stronger to the point of irresistibility; but this might also be the time when, with their main objectives behind them, they could grow complacent or stale.´

As a trophy and symbol, 'the Ashes' was still growing in

impact. Although the foundation of the Ashes story went back to 1882, when Reginald Brooks's mock obituary of English cricket in the *Sporting Times* talked about its 'ashes' being taken back to Australia, and then in 1882–83, when some young Australian women presented a pouch of ashes to England's captain Ivo Bligh, it was not for another twenty years that the Ashes were seen as the prize in Anglo–Australian contests. In the 1880s and most of the 1890s, England dominated Australia. Only after Joe Darling's great team of the Golden Age – the team of Hill, Trumper and Noble – won four successive series between 1897–98 and 1902 did the MCC start to take the contest seriously enough to send its own team to Australia rather than leaving the job to private promoters. In 1903–04, Pelham Warner took the first MCC team in search of 'those Ashes'.

Between the wars, Anglo–Australian Test cricket reached a high point during which its prestige as a national contest superseded earlier conceptions of 'entrepreneurial' tours. The rise of Bradman added to the glow, and even though South Africa, the West Indies, New Zealand and India entered the Test cricket club, sometimes defeating the old powers, their arrival only enhanced the status of the Ashes. In the 1950s that would change, as a West Indian team became arguably the world's best and the game would have to acknowledge a more global presence. But in 1948, the Ashes were still in their full brilliance. Australia had now held them since 1934.

At Old Trafford, the Australians had made sure, albeit unconvincingly, of keeping the urn. They should have, and without rain probably would have, lost that Test match. But they didn't, and Bradman was very keen to redirect his men forwards, to Leeds, where a win or draw would seal a series win. Then they could start thinking about comparisons with the benchmark Australian teams of 1902 and 1921.

With the Ashes retained, some relaxation was inevitable. Hassett joined O'Reilly and Fingleton on a visit to Ireland, where, said Johnson, they 'drank copious pints of Guinness and, after three days, had a brogue that even the locals could not understand'.

The team went to London to play Middlesex at Lord's and attend more black-tie dinners. After one such occasion outside London, Miller, Hassett, Johnson and Johnston were driving back to the Piccadilly. At Hassett's request they pulled up at a two-storey mansion in a country estate.

'Who lives here?' Miller asked.

Hassett pressed the bell. A window opened upstairs, and the owner called out, 'What the hell are you doing?'

'Just thought we'd pop in,' Hassett said.

'Are you Lindsay Hassett?'

'Indeed I am.'

'Good God! That's Miller! Wait there.'

As the owner ran down, Miller asked Hassett: 'Do you know him?'

'Never seen the old boy before in my life.'

The nobleman entertained them until late, and would dine out on the story for years.

But there was still a cricket match to be played, against the champion county at that, and Bradman would not loosen his grip. Arthur James, the masseur, later revealed that Bradman asked him to stay up late at the Piccadilly and note the arrival time of each player after a night out. On the morning of 17 July, Bradman ran into a dusty Miller and Lindwall. Miller had a cricketing rationale for his dishevelled state.

> If I have had a night without a few beers I cannot sleep a wink.
> A drink or two of ale relaxes me physically and mentally. I hit
> the pillow and can go off in a trice. I'm out for eight, nine or
> ten hours. Next thing I know is the telephone ringing in the
> morning – almost sure to be someone trying to scrounge a Test
> ticket! . . . Ray Lindwall agreed with me that beer and a long
> sleep were the best of all relaxations. They were the two things
> which allowed us to keep going for long spells.

Socially, the pace bowlers were almost as inseparable as Loxton and Harvey. As roommates, they shared ties, shirts, socks and suits and split their hotel bills fifty-fifty, Lindwall said. 'Being rather casual in leaving money on dressing-tables and in drawers, we never know or care whether the shillings and pence we pick up hurriedly belong to one or the other. We reckon that in the long run everything evens out.'

The more time they spent together, the more their lifestyles harmonised. They loved a game of golf, and claimed to try to end county matches early so they would have time for a round. Domestically, they were the perfect couple. 'Frequently Keith Miller and I ordered breakfast in bed at ten o'clock,' Lindwall said.

> Then we bathed, dressed and were at the ground as early as many of the home players. Hotel life, it must be remembered, is entirely different from living at home. There are no coals to fetch, fires to light, shoes to clean. When a man takes breakfast in bed at ten and starts work at half past eleven he is not faced with the same necessity for an early bedtime. In any case, no two individuals require the same amount of sleep. If I have seven hours I am thoroughly ready for another day.

Miller, for his part, hated to arrive at a ground more than a quarter of an hour before play started. 'I like to get changed, go straight on to the field and start playing. Some fellows arrive at the ground an hour or more before the start. They practise, dawdle about the dressing-room, fidget, think, think some more, and then, when the time comes for them to go out to the middle they are nervous wrecks. The art of relaxation means a great deal.'

But this time, they might have relaxed a little too much. Lindwall asked if he could have the Middlesex game off, but Bradman shook his head and said, 'Open up and we'll see how you go.'

On a warm day, Lindwall bowled sixteen ineffective overs.

During one break, he lay on the grass. Bradman dropped the ball at his feet.

'Have a nice time last night, Ray?'

Middlesex made 203, Compton top-scoring with 62 and Loxton taking 3/33. Young John Dewes tried to improve his record against the Australians, but failed.

> I was described as stubborn and stocky – and I was. My job was to stay in until lunch and not worry too much about how many runs I scored. We had Compton and Edrich, who would hit it around, so I had to take the shine off the new ball for them.
>
> You had to be very careful, though, because Compton was apt to take runs when there wasn't one. We all liked to get a run off the last ball of an over and keep the strike. I'd shout, 'One, three or five!' But Denis also wanted the strike, and even though I was young I had to say, 'No, Denis!' I was known as being extremely quick between the wickets. I hated being run out. But Denis, you didn't know what he was doing.

Earlier in the tour, Loxton had been disappointed to be left out of the MCC match at Lord's. But by mid July, Loxton was a first-choice all-rounder and eager as ever. His and Morris's centuries underpinned Australia's batting. When Loxton got out for 123, 'I walked up through the Long Room and up the stairs and the first bloke I saw in the dressing room was [Bradman]. He shook my hand and said, "Well played, Sammy. Aren't you pleased now that you didn't play against the MCC?"'

During the tea break on the second day, the players were to be introduced to the King and Queen. Barnes, just out of hospital, asked the MCC president, the Earl of Gowrie, for permission to film the encounter. He had a plan to shoot, edit and market a documentary film about the tour. Gowrie readily agreed – he had also given Barnes permission to film the Royals during the team's visit to Windsor – and when the players were presented to the King, Barnes stepped out of the line and recorded the event. Members of the MCC staff rushed forward to stop him, not because it would inconvenience the King and Queen, but because the BBC had exclusive filming rights. Brushing them off, Barnes answered that he had Gowrie's permission. But he was not entirely candid about his intention to use the footage commercially, and two years later, when Australian cricket authorities chose to drum Barnes out of the game, they used this and other peccadillos from the 1948 tour in their case against him.

On the third day, a better-rested Lindwall polished off the Londoners' top order, dismissing Test batsmen Edrich and George Mann and felling Jack Robertson with a ball in the jaw. As the boos and angry comments rang out, Robertson said, 'Don't take any notice of those people. It was entirely my own fault.'

The only home player to impress was Dewes, whose patient 51, out of 135, marked him down as the kind of newblood England might pick if they felt they had nothing more to lose.

Dewes had idolised Lancashire's Eddie Paynter, a left-hander, in the 1930s. 'I'd go to Old Trafford in the hope of seeing him batting,' Dewes says. 'I was not actually left-handed. But when I played cricket in the garden with my father, and I said, "I don't know which way to bat," my father said, "You should bat left-handed, because England needs a left-handed opener." I was six at the time!'

After the Test match at Old Trafford, England were not yet desperate enough to call on the young man. A series could still be saved. Hutton scored a century in the Gentlemen–Players game, making his recall for the fourth Test at Headingley inevitable. Said O'Reilly, 'the selectors had plenty of time to stew over the utter nonsense they had perpetrated; and Hutton was returned almost with a fanfare of trumpets.' Perhaps, he added, the selectors 'did not relish the idea of appearing at Headingley if Hutton were not included'.

Hutton's biographer Laurence Kitchin put it more simply: '[N]obody, except Australian bowlers, liked the look of an England team without Hutton.'

It was now commonly, if retrospectively, agreed that Hutton's omission had been a rap over the knuckles for his display at Lord's, all part of a master plan to sharpen him up. Lancashire's captain, Ken Cranston, was brought in for Dollery – 'another indication that the selectors were again hankering after the non-existent Test all-rounder', said Arlott – and Laker came back. In most opinions, this was the best England selection of the summer. It had only one obvious weakness: the absence of a leg spinner, such as Wright, who might be able to exploit a wearing pitch on the last day.

On 21 July the teams travelled to Leeds. Fingleton noted a new mood on the train: '[T]he Englishmen were not present as if they had an apology in their pockets. They met the Australians on level terms.' Manchester had revealed 'that Bradman's team was not quite the unbeatable one many had at first imagined it to be'.

The Australians were put up at what Flanagan called the 'palatial Queen's Hotel' with 'a fleet of Rolls-Royces' as transport through the slums and garden suburbs from central Leeds to Headingley. On match morning, Harvey was sitting in the hotel's restaurant eating what he estimated was his 'five hundredth kipper of the tour'.

'I'd been twelfth man for the first three Test matches and looked like being twelfth man for all five. But you know, I was having the time of my life. I didn't mind.'

Harvey expected Brown to come back in for the injured opener Barnes. Suddenly Bradman sat beside him.

'You're playing today.'

Harvey smiles at the memory. 'That was all he said. I pushed my kipper aside and the butterflies took their place!'

With Saggers replacing Tallon – whose fingers were wrecks

after Old Trafford – bringing in the teenager was a bold move by Bradman. Brown, the champion opener of the 1930s, had been the outstanding batsman of the non-Test games, with four centuries and a double-century. Harvey had shown flashes of form but not Brown's reliability. Elevating Harvey would also force Hassett to play as Morris's makeshift opening partner. Yet Bradman was able to cast his pragmatism aside and yield to his imagination. The boy would play.

The Englishmen, meanwhile, were newly confident after dominating the match at Old Trafford. Yardley told his squad of thirteen he would delay naming his XI until match morning. Jack Young, who had two sisters coming up from London to watch, asked Yardley if he should call them to cancel their train tickets. Yardley said no; Young was a virtual certainty. The spinner phoned his sisters to tell them to come.

On match morning, Young was buttoning up his cricket shirt when Yardley walked up to him and said, 'Sorry, Jack, if I put you wrong, but we've altered our plans this morning and you won't be playing after all.' Yardley's decision, not to mention upsetting for Young and his sisters, would be crucial.

While Yorkshire turned on the style for the cricketers, spectators at Headingley suffered worse, if possible, than elsewhere. Some slept on pavements to beat the morning queues, but when a pair put up a tent, the police made them tear it down. After standing in queues since dark, thousands were turned away from a ground that could fit 35 000. If they got in, they had to sit on wooden forms or stand on the grassy slopes. An overflow of spectators onto the field shrank the already small playing surface. Only one small stand, and the members' pavilion, had roofs. Flanagan described the facilities as 'deplorable'. The catering was 'a positive disgrace' and the toilets were 'disgusting in the extreme with women and men . . . obliged to queue up in parallel lines in full view of people in the stands'.

Before play came a public address warning about a gang of pickpockets. Morris said to Edrich: 'What about your catering departments? They've got all our money and valuables already!'

Leeds had turned out in such numbers, and put up with such discomfort, to see an England fightback, to see Hutton's return, and to see Bradman for the last time. It was here that he had scored 334 in 1930, 304 in 1934, and 103, arguably the best innings of the lot, against Verity and Farnes on a sticky in 1938. If Bradman had a spiritual home outside Australia, it was surely Headingley, in a county whose cricketing characteristics so resembled his own.

The wicket, said O'Reilly, was 'so green that it was difficult to decide where the out-field ended and the pitch began'. After a net, Washbrook and Hutton went out to ask the groundsman what he thought. 'Well,' he said, 'I don't think anybody will get hurt on this.' Not to be fooled on his home ground, Yardley decided to bat.

The cheers for Hutton were a rebuke to his captain. Fingleton said 'the reception given Len Hutton by this densely packed crowd was worth the trip to Leeds alone. Intensely loyal are the Yorkshire people, and the roar of delight as Hutton scored a single in Lindwall's first over was thrilling.'

Hutton greeted Miller with a 'sizzling' off drive, and the partnership seemed ready to resume normal service. Yet the crowd, said Arlott, 'was quiet and watchful, hardly daring but to fear disaster, for never in the series had England's first wicket outlasted the spell of the opening bowlers'.

It did this time. An out-of-touch Miller was replaced after two overs, and Johnston and Toshack soon showed the effects of the work Bradman had given them. Lindwall tried hard without getting much life from the wicket. Hutton and Washbrook 'settled down to business as though they had finally decided to make the Australian attack pay for all past humiliations', said O'Reilly.

Loxton, just the type of ebulllient reinforcement Bradman needed at this point, forced the only mistake before lunch, but Hutton's fend to leg found Hassett deeper than the Barnes position. The vice-captain dropped another chance, and Loxton was left waiting for his first Test wicket.

Barnes's absence removed one of Australia's psychological weapons. Edrich had been told, probably by Miller, that the team had rebelled against Bradman.

It was noticeable that Bradman put nobody fielding close in, after the Barnes incident. I have been told that there was a council of war in the Australian hotel, and it was pointed out to the skipper that suicide tactics were not popular with the team. Bradman, a merciless commander, always had a reputation for making his fieldsmen do just as he wished. Whether they liked it, or whether the bowlers liked it, did not seem to matter to himself if he felt tactics demanded his way of doing things . . . But after Barnes was hit, a peaceful revolution was successfully accomplished.

Bradman, injecting energy where there was no menace, changed his fields regularly and placed more catchers than usual on the off side, tempting Hutton and Washbrook to play across the line, but this time they were disciplined and focused. Washbrook put away his hook shot, against his better judgement. 'I have sometimes got out, trying to punish a bad ball. A shocking stroke, says the critic. Not necessarily. If that stroke has brought me 500 runs in a season, I must accept the odd times when it gets me out.' It was a measure of England's desperation to win this Test that Washbrook was prepared to shelve his principles.

Lunch was taken at a welcome 0/88, Hutton and Washbrook closing on half-centuries, 'their batting growing', said a now excited Arlott, 'like the work of experienced gardeners, from the nursed seedlings of defence towards the full growth of stroke-play'.

After eating, they attacked, hitting Lindwall for five fours in six overs. Arlott said that 'one cover-drive from Hutton was a stroke

to stir the romantic cricketer to extravagance. As Hutton overtook
Washbrook, he was himself again – a great batsman.' The century
stand came up in 131 minutes, 'behind the clock, but they were
ahead of expectation – even abreast of hope'.

On the Australian side, Bradman looked pensively at the
ground as his bowlers delivered a diet of full-tosses. Miller,
Johnston and Toshack were at the end of their tether. Johnson was
bowling restrictively to a wheel field, which Bradman was forced
to copy from Yardley. Loxton offered zest, but too much rested
on Lindwall, who could not, for once, break through. Bradman
had to be watchful, above all, of demanding too much of his
spearhead, lest he end up with four crocks. The bowling overall,
said Fingleton, was 'atrociously bad'. Moreover, without Tallon's
vocal presence the team was lacking spark. Lindwall had an lbw
shout against Washbrook, but Saggers, an honest and judicious
appealer, left the bowler to do it on his own.

The better Hutton batted, even his supporters, such as
Thomson, wondered if dropping him might have proven a good
idea. 'There were, as we say, riot squads out in the West Riding, but
it is just possible that the selectors were not so demented as their
critics thought them. If ever there was a man capable of staging a
magnificent come-back, it was Leonard Hutton, and to see him
joined with Washbrook in a perfect partnership of 164 was a sight
that English eyes badly needed.'

A second new ball didn't deter them. Miller tried to think his way
through the problem, but couldn't find an answer. Hutton drove
Lindwall through extra cover, the bright red seed scooting into the
crowd. Then Hutton played forward, defensively, and somehow
missed it. He was out for 81. The partnership, as Arlott extolled
it, 'was more than the vindication of Washbrook and Hutton, it
was the symbol of an English professional cricketer holding his
place as the practitioner of an enduring and still vital craft'. Arlott
had a true love of the tradition of professional cricket in England,
and longed for its vindication. 'On a sane and economic level no

argument can be adduced for a man becoming a county cricketer,' he wrote. 'He is valuable to the student of social history only as an example of the incurable romantic – but it is difficult indeed to deny him sympathy, perhaps even envy.'

Washbrook, after four chanceless hours, coolly efficient in his sweater, registered his century 'with the certainty and smoothness of an express train . . . and then laid out the delights of stroke play. He hit a four past mid-on with the walking-stick ease and the perfect timing of a Frank Woolley. Edrich hit the loose ball as if he hated it.'

After rediscovering his form at Old Trafford, Edrich batted vengefully. But England were, at bottom, a traumatised team, and in a final hour when Australia's bowlers were utterly flattened, Washbrook and Edrich closed down and batted for stumps. Unfamiliar with dominance, England batted as if worried. The tense, grey old country could not bring itself to press forward optimistically.

'I thought England made a tactical error by not forcing the pace towards the end,' Bradman said. 'We were tired and here was a golden opportunity, but England seemed more anxious to preserve wickets than get runs.'

In this strange vein, Washbrook aimed a jittery push at Johnston and edged to Lindwall at slip. His was a grand 143 but, like Hutton's 81, somewhat let Australia off the hook. Bedser came out to face four balls, 'massively and amiably to the wicket as the most solid of night-watchmen', as Arlott saw it, 'and the day's score went out to bring a minor but definite warmth to the stomachs of men who, day by day, found little of cheer in their newspapers.'

England were 2/268, a result Bradman viewed as passable. Fingleton, however, had seen 'Australia's poorest day in attack in post-war history', and O'Reilly went to town: 'From the first few desultory overs of the day the Australian attack functioned without object – hopelessly and meaninglessly . . . Some of the so-called attack was so blatantly inaccurate both in direction and length that the spectator who thought from the standard shown that another monotonously uninteresting county match was in progress might well have been excused.' The Australians, he felt, started the day with 'a pronounced air of levity' but the 'smiles left their faces as the day wore on'.

Bradman differed strenuously. He thought that 'by general consent Leeds has never seen a finer day's fielding'. He remembered days of heavy England scoring against O'Reilly in 1934 and 1938. 'I do know that O'Reilly in those days quickly reacted to criticism in the press, and gave full play to his very eloquent vocal chords in explaining what he thought of the wickets he had to bowl on.' He resented O'Reilly's 'carping criticism every time the bat assumes the ascendancy', at a time when 'Players look for helpful guidance in his comments'.

Since Old Trafford, the series had been drifting towards England, and the cracks between Australia's players and reporters began to open. Not without justification, the Australian players sensed that O'Reilly, a pressman first and a patriot second, was barracking for a contest. Provocatively, he wrote: 'There were many smiling English faces to greet the Australians as they returned to their fashionable hotel that night for dinner.' His, too.

Leaden skies on Friday, 23 July invoked memories of Manchester. On top again, England found reason to fret. When Edrich and Bedser resumed, Fingleton saw their batting as 'more in keeping with the funeral of a notable national figure than a cricket game'. In their dressing room, he observed, the English 'were looking at the sky more than the play . . . I pondered then, too, on the difference between the Australian and English dressing-rooms during a Test. Our Test room is sacrosanct – players only, which is as it should be because a Test skipper and his men have enough worries without intruders. The English room, on the other hand, often seemed to be the centre of a levee, an at-home or a garden party.'

Just 22 runs were scored in the first hour. When Johnston bowled the new ball to Bedser, 'the first three I hardly saw and waved my bat hopefully'. Bedser said the poor light was 'made worse by the fact that there are no sightscreens at either end at Headingley and you are looking into a black stand at one end and some tall poplar trees at the other. Anyone who has played the game of cricket must know how dark these trees can look when the light is dull.'

After drinks, as the skies lifted, Bedser decided he could 'swindle' a few more runs out of the bowlers, and opened up on Toshack and Johnson. Lindwall, having conceded 57 runs from thirty-one overs in four sessions, was being used as a stock bowler, trying, Arlott said, 'furiously hard with arm and cricketing brain to take a wicket, but he had no weapon to overcome the pacifism of the wicket'. Toshack 'wheeled his arm and dropped a pin-pricking length on the leg-stump, swinging in a little, sometimes tending to straighten off the pitch, sometimes not. He called a tune in very slow time, and Edrich and Bedser, harmonizing with his accuracy and his meticulously placed field, played that tune.'

Nothing was happening for Bradman. He attacked with the third new ball to no effect, then defended again. O'Reilly decried his 'deplorable' fields. 'They ruin the game as a spectacle and reduce otherwise assertive bowlers into characterless pieces of political machinery.' Bradman set Johnson's field so deep 'that the bowler himself must have longed for a sheepdog or two to yard-up the short singles which were to be had for the taking'.

Without resorting to quite the same lengths, Bradman was playing the same game as Yardley's at Nottingham. Just as Bradman and Hassett had kept their heads there, so did Edrich and Bedser here. Miller bowled some harmless off spin, and Edrich, said O'Reilly, 'was in complete control of the bowling and appeared to be capable of dealing drastically with every member of the attack except Lindwall, who seemed to have the drop on him during every one of their duels'.

Notwithstanding his poor form early in the series, Edrich held the Australians' respect. McCool said, 'when you think of guts you automatically think of . . . Edrich. I have never seen any Englishman play cricket so 100 per cent as he did. When he was batting you thought you'd need to dynamite him out. He bowled as if he were trying to blast a hole in the sightscreen (and he wasn't a big fellow), and even when he ran after a ball you thought he was going to blow a boiler.'

Britain had been taking it all summer, but now they were dishing it out. O'Reilly 'had become bored with the monotonous flow of easy Australian victories. I wanted to see how our team would react when the acid test was placed upon them.' Lindwall 'kept slogging away, tirelessly retaining his pace and enthusiasm long after the other members of the attack had lost all signs of hostility'. Bradman's heavy use of him was 'a tremendously dangerous strain upon a bowler of such speed' and reminded O'Reilly of the way Jardine overused Larwood in the fifth Test in 1932–33. Nobody missed the significance of a Bodyline veteran comparing Bradman's captaincy with that of his archenemy.

After taking lunch at 2/360, Edrich stepped up the pace, steaming through the nineties with a six off Johnson and a boundary off Morris's Chinaman. But at 423, Bedser, on 79 and possibly distracted by thoughts of three figures, chipped Johnson down the wicket. Bedser wrote: 'Every cricketer plays his strokes over again in his armchair before the roaring winter's fire, and as I write these words in our home in Woking I can picture myself hitting Ian's ball into the stand and perhaps going on to make a century.'

When he saw Compton coming out to take his place, however, Bedser thought England would make 600. But three runs later Edrich, 111, lifted Johnson to Morris at mid-on. Compton, the hero of so many rearguard actions, was less stable as a front-runner – he played the worst Test innings O'Reilly had seen of him, 'and was finally lucky to get out before he did any further damage to the remarkable reputation he has built up for himself'.

After clawing their way to 2/423, England surrendered their last eight wickets for 73. Fingleton thought they 'did not know how to handle' the idea of being so far ahead in the game. 'They had wickets to spare and wanted runs quickly but didn't quite know how to go about it.'

The chief tail-snipper was Loxton, who took his first three Test wickets and, said Arlott, 'rolled up the remainder of the English innings like a shutter'.

His first wicket was Cranston, bowled for 10. Fingleton saw Loxton 'turn himself inside out in ecstasies. He is a tearaway bowler, halting at the moment just before delivery, but he certainly has spirit. Had chances been taken, he would have had his first Test wicket long before this, so his exuberance can be understood.'

Bradman expressed his love of Loxton's cricketing attitude: 'I can still picture Sam Loxton after a lengthy bowling spell chasing a ball down-hill to the boundary with such energy that he could not stop at the crowd and nearly caused several casualties. His clear expression of disgust at the failure of his hopeless chase, indicated by the well-known method of throwing his cap on the ground, greatly amused the spectators.'

There was another comical moment when, on Pollard's arrival, Hassett made a big show of cowering at short leg. But nothing could sugarcoat another lost opportunity for England. O'Reilly called England's collapse 'a disgustingly bad show'. Washbrook and Hutton should have been 'furiously angry' with the middle order. Bedser 'was perfectly entitled, I believe, to lay about him in the dressing-room with a heavy hand or heavier boot'.

England's 496 began to look better, however, when Morris was caught for 6. A human tunnel formed for Bradman. Nowhere were the crowd as intimately involved with the game as at Headingley, and they had been forming such tunnels for him since 1930. At the wicket he raised his cap, then waved his bat. It 'certainly raised a lump in my throat', he said. He started with great intent, clipping his first ball almost to the boundary and speeding to 31 not out by stumps. He had a perfect record here to maintain.

Like all the great players, Bradman aroused the strongest passions. While there were many in and around the England team who despised the way he had conducted this tour, large sections of the general public adored him. The hero only had feet of clay to those who saw him close-up. From a distance, Bradman was seen as what he was: a once-in-a-lifetime phenomenon. A few days later, he would open a fan letter that had been written that Friday night:

> My friends and I gambled on our English weather, three doubtful cycles and the fortune of the road, and cycled to Leeds to see the second day of the Test. My friend broke a gear on the way back, I broke a mudguard and we both had to push our exhausted friend back over the moors, but it was well worth it.
> Yours very sincerely
> From one hopeful cricketer,
> One not so hopeful,
> And
> One who cannot play at all.

The third day was, said Fingleton, 'as perfect a day's cricket as a man would ever wish to see'.

After overnight rain, the morning was sultry and the wicket dicey. An early ball from Bedser gave Bradman 'a nasty crack in a place which, had I been a boxer, would have enabled me to claim a foul'. O'Reilly said Bradman 'writhed in pain for some time and when he resumed his innings after the blow he appeared to be quite pale'.

At the other end, Pollard 'turned from the pink of healthy effort to the scarlet of joy' when he clipped Hassett's outside edge, the slips catch being taken by a nonchalant Crapp. Arlott said of him: 'He stood at slip, next to . . . Evans, through three Tests, and Evans is certain that Jack voluntarily spoke to him on at least one occasion – his impression is that it was during the Leeds Test.'

Bradman looked like the impregnable commander of Headingley. He gave the incoming Miller a serious talk, to which the all-rounder responded by crashing his first ball for three.

Pollard ran in to bowl to Bradman. The way Bradman recalled the ball, it 'pitched on my middle stump, and turned slightly from leg and kept very low to knock my off-stump clean out of the ground'.

Miller thought the description was exaggerated. He said it was the first time he had seen Bradman bowled by a ball that did nothing, either in the air or off the pitch. O'Reilly, too, saw not bowling genius but batting weakness: Bradman 'flinched noticeably', afraid of being hit again.

The cheering, Arlott said, 'rolled like thunder, and Pollard's face was the roundest, happiest, rosiest sight seen in Yorkshire since the previous evening's sunset'. Fingleton saw 'almost indescribable scenes of bedlam as Bradman walked slowly and thoughtfully back'.

The great man's Headingley finale had fizzled. More to the point, Australia were 3/68. The deficit was 428 and the trio with the best prospect of erasing it were gone. Bradman crossed paths with Harvey, the boy. 'A silent prayer from me went with him,' Bradman said. 'Surely it was asking too much of him to succeed where we had failed. There wasn't a man in that vast audience prepared for what followed.'

Early in the tour, Harvey had been looking enviously at the well-equipped senior players. He had his old Crockett bat borrowed from the Fitzroy Club kit, but the big names were sponsored, with free bats on tap. Hassett was with Stuart Surridge, Miller with Gray-Nicolls, but Harvey 'had nothing'.

'Don was sponsored by Slazenger, and he was obviously very good to them. So they said they'd give all of us unsponsored players two bats each. From there on, I used one, and kept the other in reserve. I thought, "If I ever get into the Test side, which I can't see happening, I'll take this one out."'

Now, capless, quickstepping, Harvey entered the arena with the brand-new bat under his arm. 'I'd made my promise, and took this brand-spanking-new bat out. It hadn't even hit a practice ball.' He felt few nerves, having been spared the long anxious wait for his turn. Indeed, he'd had to rush: having started to pad up when Hassett was out, Harvey only had one pad, his right, buckled 'when an unearthly roar shook the air'.

'I've never been one to hurry too much with padding up,' Harvey says, 'being able to rely on the two fellows out there. I looked out the window and saw Bradman's off stump on the ground.'

Loxton rushed in and said, 'Hurry up, Braddles is out.' Loxton fumbled with his own pads – not a sign of automatic confidence in the youngster – while Harvey calmly finished his preparation.

Flanagan was most impressed by his demeanour once he reached the middle: '[H]is head moving from side to side as he surveyed the field, Harvey seemed to give pause to the general belief that he was in any way intimidated. There was a jauntiness, an air of indifference, perhaps of confidence, in the very approach of this lad to the colossal test confronting him.'

Bradman unpadded and watched from the pavilion, knowing that his hopes of an undefeated tour rested, for this moment, on Harvey. Miller's form had been too inconsistent to warrant full confidence. Aside from his lionhearted bowling at Nottingham and some vital slips catching, he had been mostly dormant in the big matches.

Fingleton watched the boy. 'I don't think Neil Harvey, capless, so diminutive that every mother's heart on the ground warmed to him, gave the situation more than a second's thought as he emerged, quizzically, from the end of the human tunnel and looked about as if wondering what the fuss was all about'. He walked 'boldly and composedly into the crisis as if [he had] been dealing with them for decades'.

The senior partner for their state team, Miller walked down the pitch to give advice. To his surprise, the boy said: 'What's going on here, eh? Let's get into them!'

Harvey doesn't remember saying that, but he does remember Miller's level response: 'You get up that end, get yourself settled in, I'll take over the bowling for a while.'

'That,' Harvey says, 'was good enough for me. I couldn't get up there quick enough.'

Harvey got off the mark with a cut behind point. Laker threatened him with one that popped over bat and stumps. Then Miller took over, 'like an older brother protecting his young one from a bully', and off-drove Laker for four. Deceived by the next, a faster fuller ball, Miller jammed down on it and laughed with the crowd. He smashed the next straight and low nearly for six, scattering the boys around the perimeter.

'Two balls went rising over my head on the way to clearing the boundary,' Harvey says. 'Keith was great to bat with. The way he was going, I thought, "Gee, this can't be such a tough game after all."'

These strokes started a partnership of which Fingleton said: 'I don't think I have known a more enjoyable hour of cricket'. Miller turned it on, batting, Arlott said, 'like an emperor'. He 'looked greater than the ordinary common sense of batting in an innings of which every stroke would have been memorable but that each ousted its predecessor from the appreciation. Miller's was not merely a great innings, but I cannot believe it possible for a cricket brain to conceive of any innings which could be greater.'

Miller, said Fingleton, then 'hit Laker as high as any bowler, surely, has ever been hit. Out on the long-off boundary, Hutton, eyes on the ball, edged back and back, but the ball cleared his head by yards and fell into the crowd. This time somebody was hit.'

Ambulance officers led away a blonde in a green dress.

What staggered observers, and rattled the English players, was the two Victorians' absolute carefree confidence in circumstances that threatened disaster. At times in the previous two days, English batsmen had had the Australians on the floor, but turned timid. Now, in the worst situation, Miller and Harvey were batting as if for a declaration. 'They laid about them with such joyful abandon,' said O'Reilly, 'that it would have been difficult, if not absolutely impossible, to gather from their methods of going about it that they were actually retrieving a tremendously difficult situation'.

This was the zenith of the summer, the expression of a young animating spirit. Miller and Harvey were not major players in the tour, not in the way of Morris, Bradman, Johnston and Lindwall, but they breathed life into the cricket, promising brightness for years to come. That those years would not pan out so well for Australia only made this session at Headingley shine all the more in memory and myth.

While Miller's counterattack might have been true to type, it was Harvey's refusal to play second fiddle that shook the English and, said Flanagan, 'raised the first breath of suspicion, the first betrayal of a doubt, that Australia might not collapse, might fight back yet. And within an hour this doubt, this suspicion became resolved almost into reality.'

Arlott's patriotic sentiment was suspended. 'Harvey settled in the warmth of Miller's innings . . . Had Miller not batted, Harvey's innings would take all the superlatives . . . Here, before our very eyes, two of the greatest innings of all Test cricket were being played. He would have been a poor cricketer who could allow partisan feeling to mar his delight in such greatness.'

Yardley brought himself on and Miller spreadeagled the field. Yardley turned to leg theory. On 58, Miller tried to hit him 'out of the ground, possibly out of the county', said Fingleton.

He overbalanced, and in falling somehow or other just tipped the ball, which tipped Evans on his cranium, and, diving from short fine leg, like a Rugby international going for the line with the score 13-all and the final whistle blowing, Edrich caught the ball on the tips of his fingers and Miller was out. What a sensational piece of work this was! Judging by their demented behaviour it looked as if some of the spectators should go outside and pay their admittance money again. They were certainly enjoying themselves.

It took the extraordinary to end the extraordinary. Edrich's catch was the most acrobatic of the year. Miller made a thespian exit, tossing his hair, plucking at his shirt, raising his bat as he walked down the human tunnel with a police escort. His batting 'will remain in mind', said Arlott, 'if every other innings I have ever seen is forgotten'.

Miller walked off Headingley and did not see what followed, as he was soon on the adjoining rugby league ground instructing several hundred spectators in how to drop-kick, still wearing his cricket boots and flannels.

Miller's exit was expected to calm things down for England. The damage had been contained, and Australia were still more than 300 behind. England could zero in on the inexperienced Harvey and Loxton and regain control.

But Harvey wasn't finished. Harvey had barely started.

'Sam says that when he came out, I said, "They can't bowl, Sammy." Whether I said that or not I don't know. That's what he says I said.'

When Loxton arrived at the wicket, Evans said, as usual: 'Afternoon, Sam. How are you?'

Not so well, initially. Loxton was in some bother against Bedser, beginning, said Arlott, 'with a few gangling strokes not good enough to obtain fatal contact outside the off-stump. He soon discovered, however, that the honest Loxton manner would pay its dividends, and then he was happy.'

Harvey twice struck Cranston to the leg-side boundary, and Bradman was thrilled by his cutting. O'Reilly was rather more frightened by Harvey's risk-taking: 'I found myself wishing that I could call out and ask him to forget about the square cut until after he had passed the 100.'

At lunch Australia were 4/204, a scarcely believable 138-run session. The loss of Hassett and Bradman in the first half-hour seemed an age ago.

The new ball came after the break, and Loxton found its pace and hardness to his liking. He spanked Pollard for several fours, then a six.

'It wouldn't have been a six at Melbourne,' Evans said.

Mock indignant, Loxton replied: 'We are not in Melbourne and I was easing up on the shot.'

He wasn't in Melbourne, but he and his little mate were having the time of their lives. All the meals, all the sightseeing and travelling and rooming and practising, all the disappointment of being outside the Test team – and here they were, given their chance, taking it. 'It was pretty tense, I tell you, but it got easier,' said Loxton. 'We'd batted so much together, we understood what each other was doing.'

Harvey only slowed down when he reached his nineties. On 99, he was becalmed for three or four overs. Alan McGilvray said on ABC Radio: 'Don't worry, Mr and Mrs Harvey, he'll get them.'

Finally he off-drove Laker, bringing up his century in 177 minutes. He and Loxton ran the single, and Loxton, so keen to get back to shake his mate's hand, almost got himself run out as the English thought he was attempting a second.

'That was the proudest moment of the tour for me,' said Loxton, 'to be batting with him when he achieved such success.'

'I can still feel Laker pat me on the shoulder,' Harvey says. 'I felt like I'd won the lottery.'

Flanagan took out his binoculars and watched the English

fieldsmen. He noticed that all of them 'eyed the boyish Harvey with a contemplation with which men behold an idol'.

It was the spirit, as much as the substance, of Harvey's innings that had had a cleansing effect on the game. O'Reilly was more excited by an innings than by anything he had seen since Stan McCabe's fabled 232 at Nottingham in 1938. '[Harvey's] delightful innings will always remain to me as the very mirror of truth in the batting art.'

In that session, Harvey had embodied his country's youth. England were choosing grizzled veterans and playing the game with taut grimness. And here came a teenager from Melbourne, in his first Ashes Test, at 3/68, who tore them apart as if slogging his brothers on the cobblestones of Argyle Street.

The hundred up, Harvey lost his composure. 'I went berserk. I was young and stupid, and proceeded to hit Laker for three fours in a row, mainly over midwicket. I was bowled trying to hit a fourth one.'

Fingleton thought he was 'out to his worst stroke. Indeed, he will never play one worse in all his career. He played a rank, cross-bat sweep to a well-pitched ball [from Laker] and was clean-bowled.'

Fingleton saw Bradman on the neighbouring balcony. For all his delight in Harvey's achievement, Australia were still 202 runs in arrears. Had Harvey, like Hutton on Thursday, let the bowlers off the hook? Fingleton, reading Bradman's mind, saw fresh anxiety.

> Just across on the balcony I saw Bradman throw back his head, clutch it as if in agony, and then walk into the dressing-room. At such a time and at such a score, Bradman would never have played such a stroke. It showed that Harvey was perfectly satisfied with making just the century. Bradman's gesture showed that he thought Harvey should have gone on and on, but I saw something in the lad to admire in the manner of his dismissal. He had done a grand job under difficult circumstances and was, no doubt, soon forgiven this indiscretion. Such was

his general demeanour that one would have thought he was playing in his twentieth Test against England, not his first.

O'Reilly 'could not resist a sympathetic thought for the boy who had thrilled a large crowd of people but who was on the return journey to the pavilion to find the spontaneous delight of his teammates at his success to be tempered by the keen disappointment of his captain in losing such a valuable wicket in so reckless a manner with the game still in a critical position'.

Harvey recalls that Bradman said he'd have liked to be with him in the middle 'to curb my youthful exuberance. I wish he was too. You couldn't send messages out in those days, and Sam wasn't going to pull me back. But more or less giving my wicket away was not the thing to do. We were still 200 runs behind, and it wasn't the time to do stupid things. Still, I did it. I didn't get a roast from the captain. He said, "Well played," and saved his thoughts for later.'

Bradman might have been disappointed, but two years later, in his autobiography, the ultimate result of the Leeds Test match had erased any mixture of feelings. He said Harvey's dismissal 'was a natural end to one of the greatest innings any batsman, old or young, has ever played'.

Harvey would carry the memories forever – with a little help. Eight years later, when he failed twice at Lord's during a very different tour of England, an old lady came up to him and said, 'Never mind about this match. You are a beautiful cricketer. I saw your first innings in a Test match in this country at Leeds in 1948, and anyone who can bat in such a lovely way must be a great batsman.'

And in 1961, when Harvey was part of an Australian cricket renaissance under Richie Benaud, a man in Leeds handed him all the clippings he'd kept of Harvey from that Test in 1948.

For now, he also had a new bat sponsorship.

'Stuart Surridge came up and said, "Well played today, we'd like you to use our gear from now on." We shook hands, and from that day onwards I had Stuart Surridge bats, pads, gloves and box, for the rest of my career. I was fully equipped!'

Harvey never used the Slazenger bat from Leeds again.

It sat in a cupboard in my back room for years. The grip perished. When Sammy Loxton, Bradman and I were Australian selectors [in the early 1970s], Sam was going to Adelaide while I stayed in Sydney. The day before he left, we had dinner. After dinner, he said, 'Where's that bat of yours? I want to have a look at it.'

'What for?'

'Just get it out.'

I showed it to him, and he said, 'Have you got any brown paper?'

'What for?'

'Mind your own business, just get some brown paper.'

'What for?'

'Mind your own business, I'm taking it to Adelaide.'

I got the paper, and wrapped it up.

'I won't lose it,' he said, and I had to trust him. We'd been mates for years.

He took it to Adelaide, and the first morning of the Test match he sat next to Bradman and took it out and said, 'It's the kid's bat from Leeds, can you put something on the back for him?'

Without a word, Bradman took out his fountain pen and wrote: 'This bat is a symbol of a great innings by my friend Neil Harvey in Australia's greatest ever Test victory, Leeds 1948. Don Bradman.' It's as clear today as the day he wrote it.

Just as Miller had handed over to Harvey, now Harvey handed over to Loxton. The Australians were batting like a relay team. The pitch was calm, and O'Reilly sensed that England were regretting

the absence of Wright or another leg spinner such as Warwickshire's
Eric Hollies.

Loxton set out on a campaign of destruction, raising his 50
with a six off Cranston, 'such a glorious hit that all the fieldsmen
spontaneously applauded', said Fingleton, who had grown to
admire Loxton greatly. 'Nobody, in my experience, has brought
more actual and visual enjoyment to the game than Loxton.'

Bradman, watching from the pavilion with Robins – Australian
captain watching with England selector – soon lost his fear that
Harvey's dismissal would presage a collapse. Cranston overpitched
and Loxton drove the ball so high that Neville Cardus cricked his
neck watching it rise. Bradman said it was 'the most glorious six
I ever saw hit'. Bradman never forgot the expression on Robins's
face, 'a look of incredulity – could this be true in a Test Match
where a side was fighting to save defeat?'

Loxton hit five sixes, some landing 'so far back into the crowd
that it was almost a shilling ride in a London taxi to bring them
back', O'Reilly said.

On 93, Loxton attempted to hit Yardley for what Morris calls
'a seven'. He was bowled. 'It would be difficult,' said O'Reilly, 'to
describe the look of blank amazement on Loxton's face when the
full purport of the noise he heard behind him seeped in.'

Fingleton was equally stunned: 'I never remember seeing a man
in the nineties in a Test playing such a stroke before.'

Loxton, on a high, didn't care about missing the century. 'I'd
enjoyed myself too much. Braddles probably said he'd kick my
bum for getting out. But he didn't say anything to me.'

Instead, the first to speak in the dressing room was the former
and future Australian prime minister, Robert Menzies.

'Rather a rash shot, Loxton.'

Loxton replied: 'Well boss, I suppose you've made a few bloody
mistakes in your own time too.'

Those three innings – Miller's, Harvey's and Loxton's – had
carried Australia within sight of parity. Bradman felt that the

shock of Loxton's assault damaged England's confidence most. 'Nobody can ever quite assess the value of that innings. It simply demoralized the bowlers who would not have expected such treatment in a village green charity match.'

But there was still work for the tail in the last session. Johnson and Saggers failed, but Lindwall shared solid partnerships with Johnston and Toshack. When Saggers was out, Australia were eight down and 141 behind. Bradman told Johnston to lunge forward and block every ball, and he played, said Arlott, as 'his usual acrobatic and astounding batting self'. Johnston and Lindwall added 48, assisted by Yardley keeping himself on for an hour and allowing Lindwall to farm the strike.

The day's play was completed in high comedy. When Johnston was caught by Edrich off Bedser, he didn't leave the field.

'This fellow Johnston is a great humourist,' said Bradman, 'and as he walked about out there, waving his arms and bat, and talking to umpires and fieldsmen, the populace got the impression he was disputing the fact of being out. Some of the people had even begun to become vocal . . . Meanwhile we had spent a couple of minutes roaring with laughter.'

Toshack, the last batsman, was lame after his thirty-five overs. His knee had troubled him since Worcester and he had been bowling lengthy spells in pain. Johnston's hijinx continued as he struggled to interpret the rules and etiquette, not to mention the main purpose, of a runner. O'Reilly said: 'Johnston himself was never quite sure where he had to stand and I am quite sure that I have never seen a man cover so much ground as he did whenever he was called upon to run a brace. The territory he covered in taking two runs resembled the effort required of a baseballer in scoring a home run.'

By stumps Australia were 9/457, Lindwall 76, Toshack 12, after the best day of the summer, on which eight wickets had fallen for nearly 400 runs and the Test match had taken several switchbacks. Now it was more or less even. England had lost the initiative again.

*

Monday, 26 July was a local holiday, the beginning of Wakes Week. Fingleton said 'it seemed that all employed in the heavy woollens industry were outside the ground, trying to get in'. The playing area shrank even further.

Even though the innings was over within minutes, Australia's 458 was 'a national calamity', O'Reilly thought, for England. With the pitch wearing, a certain England victory had come back to even money.

But this was a more resilient England and a spent Australian bowling attack. By lunch, Hutton and Washbrook were again on the spree, batting, said O'Reilly, 'as if they had made up their minds that the game was as good as won'.

Bradman, correspondingly, tried to slow things down, stopping the game for eight minutes to urge the umpires to pull the crowd back to the line. A child ran on to seek autographs; Fingleton said 'the game was getting out of hand'. It was, literally, for Bradman too, when he dropped a running catch off Washbrook.

After lunch, Hutton and Washbrook passed a little-known world record, becoming the first Test openers to register two century partnerships in a match for the second time (the first had been in Adelaide seventeen months earlier).

On 65, Washbrook chose to hook Johnston. Again, the extraordinary intervened. Fingleton watched from the press box as 'out on the boundary Harvey sprinted like an Olympian, stooped on the run to catch the ball at his toes, tossed himself up a little catch, caught it again and, while on the run, drop-kicked the ball the rest of the way in to wicket-keeper Saggers. This was the catch of the season – or, indeed, would have been had Harvey not turned on several magnificent aerial performances down at The Oval in London earlier in the tour.'

Harvey, who would become one of the greatest fielders of all time, is more modest: 'You remember the good ones, not the ones you dropped!'

Hutton spooned a catch to Bradman at mid-off, but England weren't capitulating. Bradman again used Lindwall as a stock bowler, without a slip. Compton grew impatient, slapping his legs with his bat. Lindwall stumbled in the footholes and went around the wicket but was warned by umpire Baldwin for running on the pitch. Nettled, Lindwall bounced Compton, who hooked him for four.

O'Reilly thought Australia could have thanked the umpire, as, if Lindwall had kept bowling round the wicket, 'he would have done sufficient damage to ensure an English victory. The pitch was capable of giving enough help to the English bowlers without Lindwall ploughing it up for them.'

The second new ball, England's undoing all summer, did not endanger Edrich and Compton now. Batting with what Arlott called 'something approaching hilarity', Compton cut Lindwall 'so late that his stroke was within a sparrow's blink of being posthumous'. After tea they piled on 153 runs. Edrich was 'almost frightening, his feet take him on savage tip-toe to the ball, and his whole body is contorted with the violence of the blow he strikes'.

He made 54, Compton 66, and England extended their lead to exactly 400 with Evans on a brisk unbeaten 47. '[Bradman] found it very difficult to set a field for my batting because no one, not even me, was ever quite certain where my shots were going.'

'It had been a good day's cricket,' Arlott concluded, 'not, perhaps, achieving the heights of Australia's innings of Saturday, but adding up, with the three preceding days, to a magnificent Test match – an even matching with brilliance from players on both sides, constant fluctuations and steadily good cricket.' This was what the crowds had returned for, the first really even contest since those long-ago 1930s.

*

The Australians arrived at Headingley the next morning expecting to lose. 'You'd been to bed,' Loxton says, 'had a bit of sleep if you were lucky, and woke up to the news that England would win. Even Bradman thought England would win.'

Yardley, whose wife was in labour, decided to bat on for two overs and ask for the heavy roller to perform what O'Reilly called 'the nefarious work' of breaking up the pitch.

The English captain would receive much criticism for batting those extra two overs and getting a second use of the roller – one before play, one between innings. Bradman said he had never met one groundsman 'who thought the use of the heavy roller would break up the pitch . . . No doubt writers will go on writing about the heavy roller being used to break up the pitch and about the innermost thoughts of Test captains, but if ever a Test wicket is damaged by a heavy roller I would like to be called post-haste to see the damage. It will be a novel sight for me.'

The target was 404 in 344 minutes. Yardley said: 'I was giving them a chance. I wanted to do so. A side going for runs is often easier to dismiss than one playing for a draw. In cricket you seldom get unless you give, and, though I could have held on while we collected a few score more runs, it was certain that if I did so the Australians could play out a draw if they wished. I wanted to win.'

Bradman made a short dressing-room speech, saying, 'Come on boys, we can win this match, we can do it.' Johnson said the captain's optimism 'changed the whole thinking' of the side, but privately Bradman, knowing a Test match hadn't been won against a declaration in seventy years, remained pessimistic, telling Ferguson to arrange for the team bus to come to Headingley between lunch and tea. The previous night, he had written in his diary: 'We are set 400 to win and I fear we may be defeated.'

In seventy-two years of Test cricket, no side had ever scored more than 350 to win in a fourth innings. Certainly, after four days of sunshine and heavy-duty cricket, the Headingley wicket was going to test the batsmen's survival skills. 'Even the most optimistic Australian present at the ground,' said O'Reilly, 'did not believe that Australia had the "Bolter's Chance" of winning the game.'

Morris, who walked out with Hassett to start the chase, recalls that as the 'papers had been saying we would be all out by lunch, it gave us a lot of determination to prove them wrong'.

Bedser bowled three overs, Morris chipping one ball just wide of Cranston at mid-on. Laker came on, Yardley's first big move. The turn was evident but slow. Laker conceded 13 runs off his first over, but only 2 off his next six.

Morris and Hassett went cautiously, scoring 32 runs in forty-five minutes. Hassett overbalanced to Laker, but Evans missed the leg-side stumping. When Laker spun one past Morris, a wrily grinning Hassett gestured to the pavilion that the ball was turning a foot.

During this tense stand, Tallon and Miller, inveterate gamblers, started their customary game of two-up. The tink of the coin on the concrete floor annoyed Bradman, who snapped, 'Give it a break.' They laid down a blanket and kept playing.

Compton came on, betraying England's need for a wrist-spinner. Compton was a competent hobbyist at the Chinaman's art. Morris hit him for two fours. O'Reilly said Compton 'appears to me as one who should try to make himself more savage than he is when he bowls. He certainly has the ability to spin the ball quite a lot but he does it almost in an apologetic manner instead of letting them go as though he intended to dispose of the whole team in double-quick time.'

In Compton's next over, Morris, 32, advanced and missed, but the ball struck Evans in the chest and Morris regained his ground. The batsmen, perhaps unsurprisingly, would contend that the missed chances that day, of which there would be seven, were all difficult. Bradman said, 'the wicket-keeper was never born' who could have stumped Morris off Compton: 'A vicious yorker which pitched in the rough outside the off stump spinning away with

Morris obscuring the keeper's view by hitting over it.'

But Evans recalled the miss in excruciating detail.

> I remember thinking to myself, no one could miss that, and I
> took my eye off the ball and glanced, automatically I suppose,
> towards square leg where the [previous shot] had gone. Arthur
> went forward again, out of his ground, but he missed it. He hit
> over the top of it, and the ball landed almost in his block and
> came through to me outside the off-stump for what should
> have been an easy stumping; but I had taken my eye off it,
> couldn't pick it up quickly enough, and missed the stumping
> and felt extraordinarily angry with myself.

Two runs later, at 0/57, Hassett poked Compton down the wicket
and was caught, left-handed, by the bowler.

Now came Bradman. At Scarborough a few weeks later,
receiving life membership of the Yorkshire County Cricket Club,
Bradman would say the reception as he went in to bat on the last
day at Headingley was 'the greatest I have ever received from any
public anywhere in the world'. The noise went into a lull as he
arrived at the end of the human tunnel, and then, when he got to
the wicket, started up again.

The master tried unsuccessfully to sweep his emotions away.
'My thoughts weren't altogether clear. We wanted to win. We
didn't want to lose. What should I do?'

Bradman hadn't had a good series by his admittedly incomparable
standards. The gritty Nottingham century had preceded his run
of dismissals to Bedser's leg trap, disappointments at Lord's, then
failure at Manchester and in the first innings at Leeds. Now he
focused from the start, beginning with a freedom lacking in the
earlier Tests, nibbling a single off Compton to get off the mark
before dancing forward and driving Laker to the long-off boundary.
In six minutes, he was 12. Fingleton said:

Then came a most incredible over from Compton. This is worthy of close description because I think it ranks as Bradman's most uncomfortable over in his whole Test career. Bradman failed, first of all, to detect a bosie. He snicked it very luckily past Crapp at first slip for four, an accident of a stroke. Up came another slip and Bradman glanced Compton for four. Next ball he failed to pick Compton's bosie again, played for an off-break, snicked it as it went the other way and was missed by Crapp, yes, Crapp, in the slips. The last ball of the over beat Bradman again completely and rapped him on the pads. Phew! What an over of excitement this was!

Evans could not believe what he was seeing. 'I raised my hands in horror as the ball just skimmed over the top of off-stump.' In the Australian dressing room, Miller had seen enough. He rose from his two-up game and began packing his bags for the trip to Derby.

Bradman said he was struggling to see the ball against a background that resembled a draughts board. 'It was a hot and sunny day and all the time we had difficulty seeing the ball for the spectators had discarded their coats, leaving a motley array of white and coloured shirts in the sun.'

The pitch, also, while not breaking up, was turning considerably. 'Don't take any notice of those who say the wicket was still good. Jim Laker bowled me more than one ball which pitched well outside the off stump and clearly passed outside leg stump.'

The wicket was, in fact, tailor-made for a specialist wrist-spinner. But England had none. Fingleton said they would now gladly give up one of their last-remaining colonies for a leg spinner. Yardley, with oodles of runs to play with, made his gamble. He gave the ball to Hutton.

By nobody's estimation was Hutton a reliable or even good leg-spin bowler. In the 1946–47 series, he had bowled three overs. For Yorkshire in 1947, he took four wickets for 176 in novelty spells spread over the season. In 1948, he had bowled just twenty-two overs. As Arlott said, 'Hutton was Yardley's gamble for a win – he had to gamble.' But the gamble was not a calculated one, rather an admission of desperation.

Morris and Bradman seized their chance. Just before the lunch break, Morris destroyed Hutton, turning five balls into full-tosses and smacking them to the boundary. Bradman hit another two. Morris got back on strike. 'Don was kind enough to share him a little,' Morris says.

By lunch, Arlott said, 'The Yorkshire crowd's cold unhappiness could be felt.'

Away from Headingley, A.A. Thomson was one of millions of distraught English radio listeners: 'I remember listening to those martyred overs on a radio set, smuggled into my office, and I sweated for Hutton as I am sure he never sweated for himself . . . There was an awful sense of miniature tragedy about the thing and when Hutton at last was taken off, the match seemed irretrievably lost.'

Yardley recounted his decision to bowl Hutton, in his autobiography, with self-vindication. 'I did not want a draw, I wanted a victory, so I experimented with the bowling, some of which was expensive; but if it had come off and wickets had fallen I should have been praised for what I did. In cricket and in war, only victory excuses the captain who takes chances. Bradman lifted a ball only just short of mid-on, off Hutton; we very nearly had him.' Indeed, from the captain's point of view, it is always the possible as well as the actual outcomes of a decision that should be taken into evidence, the thinking as much as the result, rather like a maths teacher will mark a pupil's workings and internal logic as well as the final answer. But in cricket, the thinking is always forgotten after the scoreboard delivers its cruel verdict.

The match wasn't decided yet, but the Australians were catching up to the clock. By lunch they were 1/121, instead, Washbrook said, 'of about 80 for three or four, as would probably have been the case if we had possessed regular slow bowlers'. Bedser was disconsolate. 'I ate the unhappiest lunch of my career.'

After the break Compton replaced Hutton, but he had lost his pre-lunch magic – mainly because he had to bowl almost exclusively to Morris, who took 37 runs off him while Bradman scored 3. Fingleton said it was Morris's luck to enjoy the 'choice offerings' as Compton lost his length, but it was part of a deliberate plan, as Morris remembers:

> We got in front of the clock when I went after Compton. And he was also the main bloke we were worried about. Don wasn't picking Compton's wrong'un, and wasn't playing him well. Jack Crapp dropped a very hard chance, and Don kept playing and missing. So it was my intention to protect Don and hit Compton out of the attack. I took every risk against Compton. If he pitched it up, I left my crease. If he dropped short, I really went after him. Fingo said Don was unlucky not to get the strike after lunch. It was unfair of Fingo to say that. Swanton wrote that if Yardley had kept Compton on, England would have won. I thought if he'd kept him on, we'd have won an hour earlier. I had him by the throat.

Compton lost all confidence under the pressure of Morris's assault. Within half an hour of lunch, Yardley had taken the part-timer off and the batsmen were able to settle into a routine of accumulation against the seamers and Laker.

Bradman's 50 came up in an hour. On 59 he skewed a drive off Cranston, but Yardley dropped it at point. If England's lack of a leg spinner cost them, their missed catches and stumpings were catastrophic. Fingleton thought that if they'd taken their chances before lunch they'd have won by tea. Evans, having the worst day of his career, missed stumping Bradman off Laker, then Laker put down Morris at square leg, and Evans again missed stumping Bradman off Laker. 'I missed the Don – WHAT AGAIN? – off Laker, a well pitched up off spinner, and it shot over my left shoulder for four byes. At that stage, I heard afterwards, there were absolute panic stations in the Australian dressing-rooms with four batsmen padded up and waiting to go in, and all of them thinking they were going to lose the game. If I had got that stumping I think they would have lost the game.'

But England, O'Reilly said, were now 'completely demoralised'. Eight chances were missed in all. 'None of the chances was absolutely easy,' said Arlott, 'but none of them would have been called remarkable if taken. They should have been accepted by Test cricketers; since they were not, the side which missed them deserved to lose.'

Colin McCool didn't rate Evans the best keeper in England. Evans 'snatched, and that's unforgivable in a wicket-keeper. I can't forget the nightmare day Evans had against us at Leeds in 1948. He made just about every error in the book and Australia won a match they should have lost.' Evans put down his failures to complacency. 'I am afraid we all took our task too lightly. We were all so delighted at being on top before the Australians batted, that we never really got down to solid concentration.'

By mid-afternoon the English were beyond despondency as the horrible truth dawned on them. Even this far out they felt like spectators, unable to influence the game. They were going to *lose*. Yardley took the new ball, but Bedser and Pollard found no life in the wicket. At 3.10 p.m. the 200 came up; Australia were halfway. By 4 p.m. Australia were 250 and seeing the light at the end of the tunnel. Morris and Bradman passed their centuries, toting up the runs, said Arlott, 'like well-planned trains to their time-runs schedule'.

England caught a late ray of hope in Bradman's failing fitness: after hooking Cranston for four, he clutched his side painfully, feeling a 'stabbing pain'. Soon a kind Pollard was giving him a massage. Bradman was worried he had torn his rib cartilage again.

'He asked me to take over,' Morris says. 'If we were going to run twos, we'd take ones. Then after fifteen or twenty minutes he was all right. It was just a spasm. He never thought of getting a runner.'

The spasm passed, but not the need for runs. At tea, Australia needed 112 in 105 minutes: in ordinary circumstances a tall order, particularly if wickets fell. But Bradman and Morris kept chugging along, and as they neared their target the tension ebbed out of the match. By five o'clock, 'the great match of the first four days had spluttered out,' said Arlott, though when Morris was finally out, and Miller soon followed, there seemed a moment of possibility. Cranston, who dismissed Miller, would later criticise Yardley's over-emphasis on spin: 'Of the 114 overs bowled in Australia's innings, I bowled only seven – for the wicket of Keith Miller! Perhaps a little more seam and a little less spin might have saved the day.'

In the Australian changing room, Lindwall told everyone they couldn't move, even to go to the toilet.

But there was no risk. The win came at 6.15 p.m., with fifteen minutes to spare. Bradman was unable to score the winning runs off Pollard. It was reported that he blocked Pollard to allow Harvey to score them, but Harvey does not believe it. Harvey duly clipped Cranston off his toes for four. Bradman ran past him and called, 'Come on, son, let's get out of here!' Harvey snatched a stump and sprinted off after him.

As it turned out, Harvey says, 'It was my fault he didn't average a hundred in Tests! I hit the four. If he'd done that, he'd have got the hundred average whatever happened at The Oval. I'll take the blame – it was my fault!'

Bradman, 173 not out, had scored his 6996th, and last, Test match run.

The immediate post-mortems focused on England's poor team balance and fielding, what Fingleton called their 'wretched cricket on the last day'.

'Had the selectors given Yardley one leg-spin bowler to use on that fifth day I honestly believe that the game would have been over before the tea adjournment and that England would have won well,' O'Reilly said. Instead it was 'one of the gloomiest days in English cricket history' and the win was 'more hollow perhaps than comfortable . . . If ever a game was tossed in the air this was it.'

Bradman said, humbly, that if England had had a spinner like Wardle or Hollies, 'we would not have made 250'.

Evans took full responsibility but still saw room for hope. 'We could tell ourselves at last that the Australians were not invincible, if only we would take our chances. Sooner or later we knew we could beat them.'

England's misery was also tempered by an acknowledgement of the greatness of the batting. Edrich, who usually played the role of antagonist, said: 'I have seldom admired the Australians more than I did on that last day.' Bradman doubted 'if a more valuable innings was ever played' than Morris's 182.

Denzil Batchelor wrote that Bradman 'earned the better part of his knighthood on that day'. The scorer Ferguson heaped most praise on Bradman's winning attitude. 'Bradman provided the perfect answer to all those depressing theorists who insist that the only way to safeguard your wicket is to sit on the handle of the bat. Australia's tremendous orgy of run-getting cost a mere three wickets. There is a moral in that somewhere!'

Bradman was not only a cricket captain and batsman but, as Rosenwater put it, 'manipulator of fate'. Invincibility had become a state of mind, dictated by the Australian captain.

Jim Laker would be dropped after that day, his career stalled. He would re-emerge as a great off spinner half a decade later. But he would never forget bowling to Bradman at Headingley.

'Don Bradman was the only batsman I have known to give me an inferiority complex . . . As I ran up to bowl, Bradman seemed to know what I was going to bowl, to know where the ball was going to pitch, and to know how many runs he was going to score. That was exactly the uncanny impression he gave.'

Headingley was the zenith of the 1948 summer. England had finally come to terms with a tiring Australian bowling attack, and led the match for four days before batting of unsurpassed adventure and skill beat them. Most of the Australian cricketers would never play in a greater victory.

10

THE OVAL: 99.94

On a six-day-a-week cricket tour, there was no time to pause and reflect, least of all for Bradman, who now entered a period of nervous agitation. He was never a relaxer. The Ashes and series had been won, so his men might feel like celebrating, particularly after the miracle of Headingley. But to the unrelenting captain, celebration meant danger. His 1938 team had also been undefeated until now, and the tour had ended in defeat. Armstrong's 1921 team had sustained their competitive tension until the last week. Bradman was now competing with history, an opponent that would not show the same weaknesses as Yardley's men.

The busy schedule helped keep his team focused. Four hours from Leeds, a fixture against Derbyshire was starting the next day. The players were taken directly to the Leeds train station, where a boy with an autograph book showed the durability of Yorkshire parochialism. Scanning the Australian faces, he shook his head and said: 'I don't want thee. I'm looking for Len Hutton.'

Morris and Johnson, given the next match off, took a train to London where they attended the Olympic Games at Wembley. As for the others, any commemoration of what they had done would have to wait. Bradman said, 'Probably [the public] envisaged a wild celebration or at least a celebration of some sort plus some relaxation. How far they would be from the truth.' On the train, the cricketers had a cold hamper meal and soft drinks. On a hot, humid night, the train was delayed and they did not arrive until after 11 p.m. at their hotel in Derby, where they had a quick meal. 'We must have drunk quarts of tea, and by the time our trunks had arrived and been placed in the rooms it couldn't have been far short of midnight. Not such an exciting evening as the world at large probably imagined!'

Australian cricketers had never classified themselves as 'professionals' in England – they were paid for their cricket while enjoying the prerogatives and treatment of amateurs. Yet there was never any doubt that they worked full-time. The next morning, Bradman was up early to win a toss and bat against Derbyshire in front of another record crowd of 17000. Record attendances had become routine: 133000 in Manchester, 158000 in Leeds. For all the controversies Bradman roused, there was no doubting his pulling power.

Brown, 140, made his customary century when filling in as opener, while Bradman, Miller and Loxton continued their Headingley form with half-centuries. Brown's careful accumulation did not please the locals: Simmo, the souvenir booklet seller, said people were telling him, 'We'll not buy book if photo of yon so-and-so is in it'.

Derbyshire, the county championship leaders, were resting their fastest bowlers Fred Pope and Bill Copson. Instead Bradman was bowled for 62 by 'a somewhat elderly insurance manager named Gothard, grey-haired and bespectacled', according to Fingleton, who took five wickets in the season outside this game. It was the only time on tour Bradman was dismissed by his opposing captain, and ensured that Derbyshire would be one of the rare counties against whom he never scored a hundred.

Barnes, ever eager to get back into the fray, batted but retired hurt. As he lay groaning on the massage table and a local official came in asking the team to sign a bat. Miller observed:

> Suddenly Sid's eyes opened. He looked over and saw the man
> standing there with a brand-new blade. Quick as a flash he was
> off the table and rooting in his bag. 'I can save you waiting
> while the chaps sign their names. I've got a bat with all the
> England as well as the Australian players' signatures,' he said.
> He took out a much cheaper bat and handed it over. The
> official thanked him profusely. Sid took the new bat of first-
> class quality, put it in his bag and climbed back on to the table.

Miller's mate Compton shared his scepticism, even dislike, for
Barnes. 'I was not greatly attracted to [Barnes] – for one thing, it
always seemed to me that Barnes was always too much concerned
about how Sidney Barnes was getting along, and too little about
anyone else . . . he appeared to be a man with a chip on at least
one shoulder.'

Compton also detected that Barnes and Bradman were drifting
apart. During the Leeds Test, Compton said, he had been sitting
with Barnes at lunch.

> Perhaps understandably he seemed a bit unhappy about [not
> playing], maybe even disgruntled. We had, I think, been
> talking about Bradman, and Barnes turned to me and said,
> 'Mr Bradman, he gets all the publicity, let him get all the
> bloody runs.' There was an Australian astringency about the
> comment which was refreshing in a way, even if it was not
> entirely justifiable. Its content revealed as much about Barnes
> as it did about Bradman.

During the Derbyshire game, Bradman's men finally celebrated
with a champagne party, captain and manager paying for the drinks
rather than asking the players to dip into their meagre expenses

allowance. Loxton had fond memories of Bradman unwinding that night: 'Braddles loved a drink, don't worry about that. You couldn't get him into a pub or a bar. His chest would be where his back is. He didn't mind people having a drink, because he loved to drink himself. But he was a wine drinker, he didn't drink beer.'

Australia overwhelmed Derbyshire, not without some champagne-induced rustiness, Johnston taking a catch in one hand that he intended to go into the other. Still there was no rest: a Friday-night train trip to Swansea via London meant they would arrive just before dawn on Saturday for a match against Glamorgan, on their way to winning their first county championship that season. Allan Watkins said their success was based on 'fair fielding, bad batting and never winning the toss'. Perhaps more fairly, Thomson said, 'the fielding was superb, the captaincy was shrewdly forceful and the batting was not strong enough to waste too much of the time that should have been spent in bowling the other side out.'

The Welsh, seeing themselves as a country rather than a county, were disappointed that Bradman chose to stay in London. But there were limits to even Bradman's will to personally ensure victory. Arlott sympathised, for 'when Bradman rests for one match of an arduous tour of England, the local spectators are hurt and they adduce fifty "good" reasons why Bradman ought to have played. If he moves himself down in the batting order he "insults our players". If he throws his wicket away, he has robbed ten thousand people of the conversational gambit, "When I saw Bradman make his hundred at − " . . . It is all so futile, so bad for cricket, so bad for Bradman.' This constant pressure was wearing on all the Australians; it was a central reason why many of them said 1948 was not their most enjoyable tour. They were not (apart, perhaps, from Miller and Barnes) jealous of the attention Bradman received, but felt that his presence always added another layer of the sometimes claustrophobic observation under which an Australian team travels. Years later, in 2003–04, when Steve Waugh took his 'farewell summer' of Australia, his teammates remarked on the same discomfort. Their personal feelings towards him were not ungenerous, but the extra pressure was something they could have done without. Every man saw himself as a Test cricketer, not just a member of a supporting cast.

When Glamorgan made 197 on a cold day before a massive Saturday crowd, the Australians were playing their seventh straight day of cricket, including the nerve-jangling last two days at Headingley. Setting aside their other achievements, Ashes tourists were ironmen of cricket.

They might have been vulnerable at Swansea, against the surprise spin of J.C. Clay, the fifty-year-old England selector, who would head the county bowling averages that year with forty-one wickets at 14 apiece. Then Hassett and particularly Miller got hold of him, Miller blasting 84 before getting out, as Fingleton said, 'trying to hit Clay back into England'. A storm ended any chance of a result.

With the Test series won, there was a thaw in relations between team and press. Hassett invited O'Reilly and Fingleton on the team bus from Swansea to Birmingham, and the pressmen joined in the team songs, Fingleton said, 'quite like old times'.

They were off the bus again by the time Bradman rejoined the team. Warwickshire, another county with some hopes of toppling Australia, boasted a middle order including Test discard Dollery, New Zealand star Martin Donnelly and India's Hafeez Kardar. Seamer Tom Pritchard headlined the bowling, but the most attention-grabbing prospect was the front-of-the-hand leg-break bowler Eric Hollies.

The blond Hollies, thirty-six, was one of the game's nonconformists. In 1946 he had taken ten wickets in an innings against Nottinghamshire, but he had not played a Test between 1935 and 1947. He didn't like to travel; when he first went to Yorkshire, he was amazed by the language they spoke. Fingleton was told that Hollies 'dislikes Test cricket', and even if England picked him, he would have to be talked into playing. In late 1948, Hollies would decline an invitation to tour South Africa.

Back in 1938, Warwickshire, whose finances were poor, tried to obtain insurance against Bradman not playing. No insurer would cover them against the risk. Rosenwater wrote: 'They happened to save themselves the cost of a premium, but it was just as well that Hollies, on his first meeting with the great man, did not choose to bowl him second ball!'

Now, ten years later, the crowd trying to get into Edgbaston was so large that local youths, banned from entry unless they were with their parents, arranged instant 'adoptions' outside the gates.

Lindwall, Johnston, Johnson and Loxton accounted for Warwickshire's strong-looking batting line-up for 138, making defeat unlikely, but then Hollies dismissed Brown and Morris, and, with a wrong'un, bowled Bradman for 31. Fingleton 'thought the ground would explode. Not even Bradman has known such youthful adulation.'

Next ball, Hollies bowled Harvey, who, said O'Reilly, 'was beaten so completely that he waited for the umpire to give a decision on the manner of his exit . . . I felt sure that Harvey was not quite certain whether Hollies had pitched a cricket ball or a handful of confetti at him.'

With Hassett's wicket for 65, Hollies had the entire Australian top five. He followed up with Lindwall, Saggers and Johnston to capture 8/107. *Wisden* said his bowling surpassed 'anything done by an English bowler in an innings throughout the tour'. Where, then, had Hollies been when England needed him at Headingley? Hindsight, as always, had greater clarity. The Test selectors had been unimpressed by his reluctance to play for England, and his three international appearances against South Africa the previous summer yielded a modest 9/331. Wright was by far the more accomplished leg spinner. And yet, the week of the Headingley Test match, when Len Hutton was the best England could do for a leg spinner, Hollies was taking ten wickets for 139 against Glamorgan. O'Reilly, though biased on the subject of leg spinners, was right. England's selectors, by overlooking both Hollies and Wright, had squandered the chance of winning the Test match.

Australia's own forgotten leg spinner, McCool, ensured victory with four second-innings wickets. Bradman had a brief bat in Australia's chase for 41 runs, to take another look at Hollies. The bowler, astutely, sheathed his wrong'un. Hollies told Dollery, 'I know I can bowl him with it, and I'll give it to him second ball at The Oval.' Warwickshire captain Ron Maudsley confirmed this story as the only time a bowler had nominated how, and with which ball, he would dismiss Bradman.

A day later it was up to Old Trafford for the return match with Lancashire, Cyril Washbrook's benefit. Bradman struggled on a wicket he felt was playing 'in a most peculiar manner' due to its being covered, a step taken to ensure three days' play for Washbrook's sake. While Bradman was scratching his way to 28, Lindwall saw a bookseller hawking Bradman's *How to Play Cricket*. A two-shilling piece was thrown to the seller, and 'as he bent to pick it up, a typically Lancastrian voice called out: "Go and give 'im one 'isel'. He couldn't 'ave read it!"'

Lindwall and Miller cut loose, Washbrook the only Lancastrian to resist. Washbrook secretly asked Lindwall to bounce Bill Roberts, a bunny. Lindwall gave Roberts three, one 'whizz[ing] only an inch or so past Bill's nose', Lindwall recalled. 'Bill, visibly shaken, turned to Sid Barnes, fielding at short leg, and in a hoarse whisper, enquired, "How many left, Sid?"

'"Three," replied Sid.

'"Three too blooming many for my liking," grunted the batsman – only he didn't say "blooming".'

Leading by 191 on the first innings, Bradman showed much-appreciated sportsmanship by batting into the Tuesday, rather than asking Lancashire to follow on, thereby ensuring a much higher gate for Washbrook. The game was not, however, a charity affair,

Washbrook later said. 'They can make friendly gestures, such as they did to me when they did not ask us to follow on but, once our second innings started, the gloves were off. They were keyed up to win the match.'

Bradman and Barnes, putting on 161 in the second innings, were at each other again over strike hogging. At one point Barnes turned his back on his captain, refusing a run. Bradman rebuked him down the pitch. Barnes made as if to walk off, and said to his captain, 'Here, you come and have it all. I'll have none.'

Bradman ended up with 133 not out, his career highest at the one English ground that had denied him a Test century. Fingleton could not help admiring his hunger. In 'his 120s he scuttled as hard to run a three as a tyro would in running a three to make his first century in any type of game. That was typical of Bradman. He never lost his zest for runs, even in his fortieth year.' Lancashire showed its gratitude for his commitment to the game, and to Washbrook's benefit, by making Bradman a life member.

By the time he declared, he had left Lancashire fifty-seven overs to make 457 runs. He was prepared to help Washbrook's bank account – which grew by £4270 thanks to the 50 000 who attended over three days – but would go no further in risking his team's clean sheet.

A benefit match? Not for the 1948 Australians. Lindwall, tearing in, crushed Washbrook's right thumb and put him out of the fifth Test. Jack Ikin, Bradman's would-be 'catcher' in Brisbane in 1946, got to 99 against Lindwall's second-innings blast. Tallon, standing further back than usual, 'wrung his hands every time he stopped one', Bradman said. 'A catch went to a slip fieldsman who was almost halfway to the fence, and it just simply crashed through his hands and went to the boundary. My thoughts went to Eddie Gilbert in Queensland in 1932 and Larwood's bowling the same season. Dick Pollard never saw the ball which bowled him.'

At the end of the day, when Lancashire looked like saving the draw and Ikin was on 99, Bradman took a second new ball.

Miller refused to bowl, saying Bradman should let Ikin make his hundred. Lindwall walked up and asked Bradman for the ball. He sprinted in and bowled Ikin, who later told teammates he 'didn't appreciate' what Lindwall and Bradman had done.

Lindwall disagreed, writing, 'No batsman worth his salt likes to feel that the bowler has given him easy runs. The most enjoyable century is that which has been fought for from first ball to last. I am sure John Ikin would have quickly silenced anybody accusing me of unsportsmanship.'

The toughness of the 1948 tourists, again, contrasted with what might have been expected in a country still echoing with shell-blasts. O'Reilly, remembering that Bradman in 1938 had given Middlesex a second innings 'when there was no other reason than his thoughtfulness for [Bill] Edrich' wanting to get his thousandth run, said 'Bradman was a much tougher captain in 1948, however. Probably it was because he had the responsibility of showing a large number of fledglings in his team the real atmosphere of international cricket.' O'Reilly might have contradicted Bradman on many issues, but not this hardness. Whenever there was a debate over whether Bradman was too uncompromising in his desire to win, O'Reilly was on his side.

It was during this period that Fingleton visited Harold Larwood in his confectionery store in Blackpool. Larwood was wary of Fingleton as a newspaperman, but, with George Duckworth smoothing the way, they sat and talked about Bodyline. Larwood confirmed that the Englishmen thought Fingleton was the Adelaide leaker; Pelham Warner, their manager, had promised his bowlers a pound if they could bowl Fingleton out. Larwood had done it and received his pound. Now, he said to Fingleton: 'Here's a pound note. Let's all go and have a drink and we will say it is on Sir Pelham.'

The scapegoat for Bodyline, Larwood had not played another

Test. An Australian might have felt a sense of obligation. Bradman
didn't, but Fingleton later helped the great paceman emigrate to
Australia, and arranged his accommodation in Sydney. Through
Fingleton, Australia's Prime Minister, Ben Chifley, secretly paid
half of Larwood's rent in a converted hotel in Kingsford.

Larwood would write to Fingleton: 'Had you not come into my
shop [in 1948] . . . I would never have come to Australia. Coming
to Australia is the best thing I have done in my life.'

The final build-up for the Oval Test was hardly ideal; the demands
placed on a touring team became overwhelming. Toshack's knee
finally gave way in Manchester. His tour was over, after 502 overs
and fifty wickets as Bradman's stopgap with the old ball. Toshack
sent the Australian Board a cable asking if he could have his knee
operation in England so he could recover on the boat journey
home. The return cable's first question was 'How much will it
cost?' Some of the players, reading the cable in the Oval dressing
room, hooted in derision.

Rumours of a knighthood for Bradman came up. He rested
in London while the team travelled to Sunderland, where their
two-day match against Durham was mostly washed out. Their trip
back south was delayed by flooded crossings and disabled bridges.
It was pouring throughout England, the beginning of summer's
end. The Oval was inundated, its wicket reduced to stodge. For
his final Test match, Bradman would not be getting the kind of
Kennington road he was used to.

Five batsmen scored ducks on Saturday, 14 August at Kennington
Oval. Only the last is remembered, but the other four were as
noteworthy for the psychological edge – an aura of invincibility
– that they would leave with Australia for another five years in
Ashes cricket.

For the rain-sodden wicket, Bradman strengthened his batting line-up, reinstating the fit-again Barnes in place of Johnson. In something of a risk, with Toshack also gone, Bradman called up a leg spinner, Ring, for his first Test, meaning McCool and Hamence would be the only Invincibles not to play in the series. Ring would be Australia's fifteenth Test player that summer. England were about to choose their twenty-second. There was another push for Robins to replace Yardley as captain. 'I can admit, now,' Yardley wrote in 1950, 'that before the side for the Oval was chosen I offered to stand down. I thought that a change of captaincy might bring England luck . . . But the Selection Committee firmly overruled me. They wanted me to see the series through. I may add that I happened to know, at the time, that Robins had no desire to return to the rough-and-tumble of Test cricket.'

The anachronism of an amateur captain was on its last legs. The truth was that neither Yardley nor Robins, now forty-two, was Test standard. Nor was Allen, at forty-five, in the West Indies. And nor would be Yardley's Ashes successor, Freddie Brown, who would turn forty during the 1950–51 series he led in Australia. England was still playing Australia with one hand tied behind its back. It was not until Hutton's appointment as captain in 1952 that the MCC would catch on.

Robins, of course, had no intention of coming in to face Lindwall and Miller on a damp Oval pitch. But he took pride in instituting a long-called-for 'youth policy', bringing in 21-year-old Dewes, to open in Washbrook's place, and the energetic if under-accomplished 26-year-old Glamorgan all-rounder Watkins, to replace Cranston. 'To say that [Watkins'] inclusion caused surprise would be one way of understating the public reaction,' O'Reilly said. Some good hooks off Miller's bouncers at Swansea seemed to have been 'his ticket to Kennington Oval'. Watkins said: 'I nearly fell through the floor when I heard. It was Wilf [Wooller] who told me. Then we heard it over the wireless – there was no television – and Molly [his wife] couldn't believe it. I knew, but I didn't say much about it. I said, "I think I might be playing."'

Nor could he believe that he'd be opening the bowling: 'Why I came to be an opening bowler, I haven't a clue. I wasn't an opening bowler for Glamorgan.' In 1947 he hadn't bowled once for Glamorgan, though in 1948, he was achieving some success imitating Toshack's tight medium-pacers.

Young and Laker continued their selection merry-go-round, and Hollies came in for the unlucky Pollard. With Hollies, as always, it was no sure thing he would turn up. Leslie Duckworth wrote in his history of the Warwickshire County Cricket Club: 'When the invitation to Hollies to play arrived he told Leslie Deakins he would rather play for Warwickshire. The [Ashes] rubber had already been decided and it would have meant that he would have missed two county games when he could ill be spared. It was the Warwickshire Committee who persuaded their "home boy" to play; if they had not succeeded cricket history would almost certainly have been different.'

At The Oval, the England dressing room was now a place of silent misery. 'I remember a team meeting to get our pecker up, but didn't take much in,' Dewes says. 'Yardley was a nice chap but not a great leader.'

For this Test, they reverted to the prewar custom of only arriving from their county games on match eve. There was no team dinner. On the Friday night, the debutant Watkins stayed with his sister Millie at Hither Green. He travelled by bus to The Oval on Saturday morning. 'I didn't know any of the team really,' he said. 'I felt a bit lonely. And coming from a side of Welshmen, you know how noisy they can be. With Glamorgan there was a lot of back chat and pulling your leg, and suddenly I was in a team that were all individuals. It was sort of quiet and a bit dignified really.'

He didn't feel he belonged in the England dressing room. Depressed by their inability to convert winning positions at Manchester and Leeds, the England players had retreated into their shells, and couldn't have been in a worse mental state for the Oval Test.

If The Oval had character, it was the brutalist mid-century kind that saw a rugged beauty in the gasometers and blocks of flats overlooking the ground. Miller hated the place:

> If Lord's has atmosphere plus, then the Oval has it minus! . . .
> I am conscious all the time of people glancing out of their living-room windows while they are having their midday meal or afternoon tea, of buses, and until recently of trams grinding along Harleyford Road. Out of the corner of my eye I catch the giant cranes at the docks in the background moving to grapple with their tasks, or I find myself waiting for the factory chimney behind the Vauxhall Stand to start belching clouds of black smoke. To me the Oval seems like a splash of emerald imprisoned by the signs and sounds of commerce and everyday working life.

Of more immediate concern was the wicket, which could not at first be seen because it was covered by tarpaulins. Bradman and Yardley went out for its unveiling and found it soaked but firm. As at Nottingham, Bradman was glad to lose the toss. He would have sent England in to bat, but 'did not envy Yardley having to make the decision'. The pitch might be wet enough to hamper the bowlers more than the batsmen, Yardley thought, and it bucked all convention to bowl first at The Oval. Barnes said: 'We gave three cheers in the dressing-room . . . [Yardley's] decision to bat presented us with this Test.'

For the first time in the Tests, Lindwall and Miller would be fit, fast and fresh together. On the dubious-looking pitch, they promised mayhem. *Wisden* said: 'The sodden state of the pitch, with sawdust covering large patches of turf nearby, made one doubt its fitness for cricket.'

When Dewes walked out with Hutton, Loxton shook the

debutant's hand. O'Reilly, as ruthless as Bradman, ranted: 'It may be perhaps a nice friendly gesture but I prefer to see those things happen in the dressing-room. It is not a habit to be encouraged.'

Loxton was appalled that O'Reilly criticised him.

> There was a school of etiquette. It was a happy game. Godfrey Evans always welcomed you to the crease. [And Loxton had, in 1946–47, scored 132 and 252 not out with a bat he had borrowed from the English keeper.] I shook hands with John Dewes at the Oval. O'Reilly criticised me for that in his book. I never really fancied O'Reilly. I can't remember the incident well. But Dewes was a young player, he'd broken into the side, and I hadn't seen him since his selection. When he walked out, I said, 'Well done, son, congratulations, good luck.' What's wrong with that?

Dewes has no recollection of Loxton's gesture. 'I was very nervous. I was playing for my country, and Lindwall and Miller were such a different experience. I had my towel stuffed down my right side. I wasn't really seeing or hearing anything that was happening around me.'

After meeting the Australians in a Victory Test and two first-class games, Dewes was aware that this, real Test cricket, was entirely different. 'It was high pressure – the Australians had been a colony until recently and were determined to teach us bloody Poms a lesson. The chip on the shoulder was much bigger then.'

Barnes made his return to short leg, where, Lindwall said, he was 'a source of inspiration to all the bowlers, to me in particular'.

Off Lindwall's second ball, Hutton took a single that Loxton's wild return nearly turned into a five. It put Dewes on strike. The young left-hander was, O'Reilly observed, 'particularly nervous'.

> He found it hard to stand still and I felt certain that Hutton would need to nurse him very, very carefully to get him over

the early stages of his ordeal . . . [Dewes] had scored a few runs in rather elementary style against the Australians . . . but he could not have been seriously considered to have been ready for Test cricket . . . I think the selectors have done this young man a great injury in throwing him into Test action long before he was ready for the ordeal. Only those who have experienced the terrifying experience of making the first appearance in a Test between England and Australia can understand the enormous strain . . . It was tantamount to asking a young first-year medical student to carry out an intricate operation with a butcher's knife.

Dewes got his first Test run off Lindwall, but, as Fingleton pointed out, the trouble was at the other end: 'if Dewes has feverish dreams about cricket (and what Test cricketer doesn't?) Miller must always figure in them'. Since 1945 Dewes had been a bit of a bunny for the big Victorian. Second ball, Miller bowled a perfect outswinger, or inswinger to the left-hander, and put Dewes's short agony to an end. His forgiving captain (and self-forgiving selector?), Yardley, said: 'Anyone might have failed in that way at that stage of development.'

Edrich hooked Johnston to a diving Hassett at square leg, and England were 2/10. Compton might have been out immediately, but, after having his bat knocked out of his hands and being stranded at the same end as Hutton, he was reprieved by the fieldsman, Hassett, in an act of sportsmanship that went part-way to redeeming some of the bloodier encounters of the summer. 'This was a pleasant gesture on a Test field,' Fingleton said, 'and Hassett was warmly applauded.'

Not by the man sitting beside Fingleton, he wasn't. Hassett got a cheer which, O'Reilly said, 'I am sure he did not deserve. That type of sportsmanship is quite all right in its place, but a Test match field can hardly be chosen as the place to give quarter where quarter is not deserved . . . Hassett is a valued personal friend of mine but I took a sour view of his action in this incident and wasted no time in telling him about it later on.'

Wickets continued to fall, and Bradman had 'one of those dream days for a fielding skipper'. One of his players, at least, thought he took the idea of his personal magic too far when Compton hooked a Lindwall bouncer straight to Morris. Miller said:

> Ray bowled a bumper, Denis played a magnificent hook shot, getting right on top of the ball, but Arthur Morris, fielding at short square leg, held a wonder catch inches from the ground. This was cricket at its greatest. We were all jubilant. Bradman rushed up to Morris and said, 'Well caught, Arthur. You know why I put you there now. I remember he played that shot in 1938.' I thought that was carrying egotistical captaincy too far!

Morris recalls that Bradman did move him finer prior to the catch, and believed he did have 'a memory like an elephant' – though it may be asked why, if Bradman knew the secret to getting Compton out, he had waited more than 500 runs into the series. Morris recalls another limit to Bradman's memory: 'Years later, he even bet me money that this catch had happened at Lord's, not The Oval. He was wrong, of course, and he paid me. When I got the cheque, Bill O'Reilly told me to frame it.'

Bradman also went out of his way, later, to inform Compton that he had fallen victim to a set plan. Compton's biographer, Tim Heald, questioned whether Bradman needed to rub it in, and indeed whether it was true. 'Who knows? Sometimes these things are true and sometimes false. Whether or not it was as carefully planned as he made out, it sounds entirely in character for the Don to talk to Denis in this manner. Bradman was a total cricketer. And ruthless with it. To have explained the ploy to the unsuccessful Compton was a typical example of Bradman gamesmanship.'

Miller simply ridiculed Bradman's claim to genius: 'This was a little too much. We thought Don was stretching his imagination rather too far, so we all burst out laughing and told him so.'

Just before lunch, Crapp nicked Miller, and after the break Lindwall took five wickets in eight overs in what Bradman called the best spell of fast bowling he ever saw in Tests. A young boy watching from the terrace under the gasometers, Laurence Kitchin, was besotted:

> [T]he centre of gravity of this Test match had shifted to Lindwall . . . this emphasis on Lindwall was so strong that the alternate overs when he wasn't bowling passed as uneventfully as the sliding, intermittent trains. Tension was re-applied every time he took off the second sweater he was careful to wear between overs . . . His care to keep warm between overs, his conscientious limbering exercises and the slow, thoughtful walk back to his mark, all helped to underline Lindwall's menace. This was a great fast bowler, adding controlled and disguised variations to the threat of mere speed; and in addition, he had the incentive of revenge for Australia's catastrophic defeat on the same ground in 1938. When he turned and began his long, gradually accelerating run, the uncomfortable silence of the crowd was so complete that we seemed to hear the beat of his footsteps from the terraces.

Lindwall bowled Yardley, and then came Watkins, feeling out of his element. He missed a hook off Lindwall, taking the ball hard on his shoulder, and was promptly lbw to Johnston. Watkins walked into the dressing room and sat down. The only person present was the former Test wicketkeeper Herbert Strudwick.

'Christ, Allan, what the hell's happened to you? Look at your shoulder.'

Watkins' shoulder was a mass of bruising. He feared that he would be unable to bowl.

He would find out soon enough. Lindwall bowled Evans, Bedser and Young with the addition of two runs. 'It was harrowing sitting in the dressing room and seeing batsman after batsman return with a long face,' Bedser said. 'I hope this was England's rock-bottom performance.'

The Australians bubbled in the field. *Wisden* observed that they were much more effervescent and hostile with Barnes back at short leg. Between wickets, they still kept themselves active and intimidating with their fielding and catching games.

Throughout it all, practising the theory that the best place from which to play a great fast bowler is the non-striker's end, Hutton went on as only Hutton could. The man who had been dropped was England's colossus, his impeccable technique proving a gold standard in the circumstances. Only one ball beat his bat. Cardus watched him go about his work 'in splendid isolation, an innings of noble loneliness withstanding one of the finest pieces of fast bowling of our times'. Thomson likened him to 'the fearless leader of a garrison being bombed and shelled out of existence'. Kitchin said Hutton's 'survival became dramatic, like that of some intrinsically commonplace building in a devastated area'. Hubert Doggart, who was also in the crowd, says, 'I would like to have seen Hutton bat before his arm was shortened. I once fielded when he made 175 at Hove. He was wonderful at letting the ball come to him and playing late. At The Oval, because of his mastery of technique, he coped with the wicket.'

Others disagreed on the merits of his batting. When the score was 9/48, Hutton drove Lindwall high and straight down the ground for the only four of the innings. Bradman, whose respect for his most challenging rivals was grudging, criticised Hutton for not taking the initiative. 'Sometimes desperate measures are necessary to combat a desperate situation and, after the early disasters, to whom could they look but Hutton? He hit only one boundary in 130 minutes – his last scoring shot.'

It is difficult to imagine what else Hutton might have done. He scored 30 out of a total of 52, and was unlucky in the extreme to get out. Lindwall bowled an inswinger that Hutton leg-glanced.

He might, Bradman said, 'reasonably have looked for a boundary. Instead he saw Tallon move across with uncanny anticipation, scoop the ball in his outstretched left glove as it sped towards earth, turning a somersault but serenely holding the ball aloft. No greater catch has been seen behind the wickets.'

All out in two hours and ten minutes; it was hard for anyone to know what to say. The Australians, most of them more appreciatively than Bradman, applauded Hutton to the pavilion. Kitchin said: 'False modesty was not a characteristic of their team on that tour, and they weren't in the habit of paying empty compliments. They were showing their appreciation of a small slice of cricketing stubbornness, cut after their own pattern.' There was also, after the bitterness of the Nottingham and Manchester Tests, a clear desire among the rank and file to put the mongrel in its kennel and play out the series as gracious winners.

Walter Robins, playing that day against Kent in Dover, never felt so ill as when he heard the scores coming through. Brian Valentine, Kent's captain, sent a telegram to A.J. Holmes at The Oval: 'Robins has shot himself.'

As so often, the moment a new team walked out to bat, the wicket's behaviour changed from Hyde to Jekyll. 'If anyone retained any suspicion that there was life in the wicket,' said Arlott, 'Barnes and Morris at once removed it.'

England's attack was immediately weakened by Watkins' shoulder injury, which he tried unsuccessfully to bowl through. 'What do you think the bloody skipper did? He only gave me the new ball to bowl!'

The Australian openers rattled up 117 amid what Fingleton called 'a feeling of intense gloom'. Watkins, his 'arm falling off', left the field for treatment. 'His bowling was not successful in terms of wickets,' said Arlott, 'but it was amazing as a physical achievement in that he succeeded in bringing his arm over at all' when 'the merest touch on his bruised shoulder rendered him helpless with pain.'

He was back on the field just before six o'clock when Barnes, 61, advanced on Hollies but was beaten by a perfect leg break.

The stage was set – but for what? England's score and the Barnes–Morris stand had already made it almost certain that Australia, and Bradman, would only bat once in the match. This was it.

All along, Bradman was nodding to the game's history by playing his last Test matches in England. This was where players believed a more authentic version of Test cricket had taken place since 1880. The early Australian teams had striven to prove themselves 'at home'; they did not see the Antipodes as their motherland. The two greatest Australian cricketers of those days, Fred Spofforth and Billy Murdoch, had made their names on English turf and then, becoming wealthy through marriage, had settled 'at home' as English gentlemen. To succeed in England, and then live there, had been the ultimate ambition for an Australian.

Times had changed since then, and were about to move very fast away from the idea of Britain as 'home', but Bradman belonged to a generation that still saw English fields as centre stage. He had played his most fabled innings there, ever since his unparalleled 1930 series, when he set a world record that still stands. His feats in Australia were prodigious, but in England they had an air of legend. England was still where a cricketer such as Bradman felt most valued.

As Barnes walked off, Fingleton observed 'a lithe, athletic figure [walk] down the steps, and he fingered his cap to the applause as he made his way to the middle, his trunk slightly bent forward of his legs'. Hundreds of people had 'queued all night. They had slept on wet pavements so that they could see . . . the final appearance of Bradman, and his reception could not have been bettered.' O'Reilly said 'the din must have been audible across the river in Whitehall'. It outdid even Headingley. Ferguson, in the scorers' box, heard what he called 'the most thunderous applause I have ever heard at a cricket ground'. That was saying something: Fergie had toured since 1909.

The crowd was already singing 'For He's a Jolly Good Fellow'. For the common Englishman, the little Australian was more than a batsman; he was a historical event that they were thrilled and proud to witness. Bradman incited the most criticism in England, but also the most admiration. This duality of feeling, a love for the tormentor, has characterised crowds around the cricket world: the brutal West Indian teams in the 1980s and Australians of the 2000s were most popular in the countries where they humiliated their hosts. Fingleton admired the English public's enthusiasm, even when it bordered on the masochistic: 'Though he had flayed them over the years with his bat, England's cricketing representatives still wanted more of Bradman. Like London during the blitz, they could take it! But what a stir there would have been in 1934 had Woodfull, landing at Tilbury with his team, expressed the hope that Larwood would play against his side!'

As Bradman reached the middle, Yardley said to his team, 'We'll give him three cheers when he gets on the square.' To Hollies he added, 'But that's all we'll give him – then bowl him out.'

There was little awareness among the players that Bradman needed four runs to take his Test run-scoring tally to 7000. As he had been dismissed sixty-nine times before, such an aggregate would take his average, over the twenty years since his Test debut, past 100. Bedser said that, had he known, he would have bowled Bradman a full toss to let him hit the requisite four. But, says Harvey, 'Statistics weren't in the dictionary. Nobody was saying Bradman needed four runs to average a hundred. Commentators, press – nobody was talking about it.' Were the match played today, scarcely a human alive in England would not know that the batsman needed four. Not in 1948.

All the Australians wanted was a fitting sign-off at one of his more prolific grounds, but also the one that had, in 1938, given him the lowest point of his captaincy. Barnes, without unpadding, picked up his movie camera and stood on the balcony to capture the moment.

Before the tour, Cardus had written: 'A duck by Bradman is against nature; a duck by Bradman will next season be as momentous news as ever, and as taxing to the credulity.'

But Bradman had made a duck at Nottingham, and started shakily in every Test except Headingley. Ducks seemed just that bit more possible. As many observers had pointed out, one of the differences between the postwar and prewar Bradman was his vulnerability in his early overs.

Morris, at the other end of the wicket, did not speak to Bradman. 'I was surprised he came out. We were so far ahead and I thought he might have sent a nightwatchman. But he made the decision and there it was. I didn't know whether to join in the three cheers or not. In the end, I just stood there alone at the other end.'

Watkins was moved to forward short leg.

Yardley said, 'Right, Allan, as close as you like to get.'

'How close is that, skipper?'

'See the whites of his eyes.'

Dewes was deeper on the on side. There had been talk, he says, that 'Hollies had played against Bradman for Warwickshire and realised that Bradman didn't recognise his googly.'

As Yardley shook his hand and he looked at the wicket, Bradman felt that 'the reception had stirred my emotions very deeply and made me anxious – a dangerous state of mind for any batsman to be in.' He walked a few paces down the wicket, bent and banged down an uneven spot, pocked by the Australian attack earlier in the day and now dried, with the back of his bat. Hollies bowled a leg break and Bradman played it off the back foot, 'though not sure I really saw it'.

Hollies, who had told his Warwickshire captain that he would bowl Bradman with a googly second ball, came in again. This time Bradman stretched forward to try to smother it. The ball,

Bradman said, 'was a perfect length googly which deceived me. I just touched it with the inside edge of the bat'.

Evans, behind the wicket, wrote: 'I could see it was his googly: Eric's googly was always a little obvious. Equally, I could see that the Don hadn't seen it, I don't know why, and as he pushed forward just outside the off stump, with the spin as he thought, I could see he was going to be out, and the ball found the gap, came through and took the middle of the off stump.'

Watkins, in close, said Bradman 'had the shock of his life when it bowled him! He looked down very quickly to see what the hell had happened.'

The ball kicked the off bail out of its groove. The leg bail popped out in sympathy. Morris felt numb. 'It was extraordinary, the silence. I thought, "That's pretty odd." It was such an anticlimax, after all the build-up.'

Dewes recalls: 'We didn't all rush in together. It was just, "Oh, he's out."'

In the dressing room, Ring said, 'You could have heard a pin drop.' Fingleton called the moment 'one of the strangest experiences I have ever known at a cricket ground'.

Swanton, in the press box, observed Fingleton and O'Reilly burst into laughter. Loxton, who heard that story, said bitterly, 'It's all very sad.' But if they did laugh, it was more likely at the cruel irony of the cricket gods than in mockery of Bradman. Sometimes laughter is the instinctive response. Bradman, however, also heard the story and believed his press box nemeses had laughed out of spite. He told his biographer Charles Williams that O'Reilly's laughter exposed 'the disloyalty I had to endure during my early years as Australian captain, a disloyalty based purely on jealousy and religion'. He said Fingleton 'was the ring leader. He conducted a vendetta against me all his life and it was most distasteful because he was a prolific writer of books and articles. Conversely, with these fellows out of the way the loyalty of my 1948 side was a big joy and made a big contribution to the outstanding success of that tour.'

In the moment of his failure, Bradman was all bemused equanimity. He was cheered to the pavilion. Hollies said to Jack Young, 'Best f-ing ball I've bowled all season, and they're clapping him!' That night, Hollies phoned Dollery and said, 'He never saw it, Tom.' The Melbourne *Herald*'s cartoon next day portrayed Hollies as 'the prickly fellow who put the "o" in Don!'

On his way through the pavilion, Bradman was accosted by Field Marshal Montgomery, who said, 'Sit down, Bradman, and I'll tell you where you went wrong.' Bradman managed to deflect him and kept on walking.

When he returned to the dressing room and unpadded, all he could say at first was, 'Fancy doing a thing like that!'

His teammates kept their distance. Harvey says, 'We weren't game to even say sorry. He came in, sat down, took his pads off. It was one of those sad endings. It would really have been something to average a hundred in Test cricket.'

Then Barnes, the anti-sentimentalist, came into the room and wisecracked: 'Got your whole innings on film, skipper.' Bradman laughed. Hamence, Bradman's young South Australian acolyte, said, 'Bad luck, Braddles.' Bradman replied: 'No, Ronnie, it's just one of those things.'

Johnson approached him and said, 'The reception must have upset you.'

'No,' Bradman said, 'it didn't upset me. I got two balls that would have beaten me even if I was on 100.'

Johnson thought that 'was the most generous thing I'd heard anyone say after being dismissed like that'.

The story that Bradman's vision was blurred by a tear was a product of romance. Arlott was the first to speculate on such a thing, embroidering his live commentary for the BBC: 'Bradman, bowled Hollies, nought. And – what do you say under those circumstances? I wonder if you see a ball very clearly in your last Test in England on a ground where you've played some of the biggest cricket of your life, and where the opposing team have just stood around you and the crowd has clapped you all the way to the wicket. I wonder if you really see the ball at all.'

Hollies wrote that Bradman must have had tears in his eyes, but only as a joke. Fifty years after the event, Watkins, the nearest witness, said: 'I can tell you he was dry-eyed.'

Evans wrote: 'I didn't see any tears, and I was standing behind the stumps, right up close. All I could see was the usual determination to make 100 and then 200 and then 400 maybe. Unyielding determination was the Don's great characteristic and I was glad to see it there even at that final moment.'

Harvey sees it differently – not that Bradman had a tear in his eye, but that his concentration had to be obscured by emotion.

> I think he must have been emotionally involved. He said he wasn't, but if you're playing your last Test match ever, against the enemy, the English boys circle around you, take their caps off, give three cheers, the Oval crowd doing the same – it's got to affect you somehow. If it had been me, I'd have had tears running down my face. He said it didn't affect him, but I don't quite believe that.

The other unresolved question about that ball is whether Bradman inside-edged it. Barnes's film footage shows Bradman overbalancing as he plays half-forward, but is inconclusive on whether he hit it. Bradman maintained that he edged it, but that could have been the typical Bradman, never quite prepared to discount an element of luck in a bowler's success over him. And Hollies' would be one success that Bradman could not avenge. Morris didn't see Bradman hit it: 'I didn't know that he edged it,' he smiles. 'But Don said he did.'

Evans reflected: 'What is a nought in such a fabulous career, even such a nought at such a time?'

Not all of the English were disappointed. Dewes says he

'cheered' when Bradman was out. There was still a match to win, however unlikely England's chances.

Bradman's failure at The Oval served, according to a leader in *The Times*, 'only to remind spectators that he was a miracle of flesh and blood and not a little robot under a long-peaked green cap'.

It also gave rise to a rumour that he would reverse his decision to retire. Did he care enough about the century average to come back and try again? So easily did the runs flow from Bradman's bat in the games after the fifth Test that newspaper reports began to speculate on his playing in the next Ashes series, in 1950–51. Fred Root wrote in the *Sunday Pictorial* that Keith Johnson had told him the 1948 tour had 'rejuvenated' Bradman. Root concluded, 'I can see the maestro scoring many more centuries before he finally hangs his boots on the pegs of a Sydney museum.'

The truth was that Bradman never considered changing his mind. This was partially the nature of the man. Once he had decided, he had decided. He also had enough self-knowledge to accept that at forty he was no longer the batsman he used to be, and could not expect to take Australia's next tour, to South Africa, and automatically take his average back over 100.

In England, all summer, comparing the Bradman of 1948 with the prewar version had become almost an obsession, and his final duck seemed to settle the matter. 'Is he still the Bradman of old?' Arlott asked. 'Of course he damned well wasn't. Any man in possession of all his faculties must develop and change in ten years. D.G. Bradman of the 1948 Australian team was a great batsman in his 1948 right.' The difference was his lack of hunger to go after records. He had 'a different general aim'.

Yet Bradman in 1948, forty years old, was still playing strokes impossible to any other cricketer in the world. He stood at the crease perfectly immobile until the ball was on its way to him, then his steps flowed like quicksilver out of trouble or into position to attack. He could still pull the ball outside the off-stump accurately wide of mid-on's right hand to avoid a packed off-side field. He still played the ball off his back foot past mid-off before that fieldsman could bend to it. He still hit through the covers with the grace of a swooping bird. He could cut and glance, drive, hook and pull, and he could play unbelievably late in defence. He often made a shaky start – the shakiest starts of all before his biggest scores.

Sometimes he 'stooped like a very tired man' in the field, but he had his old 'dancing alertness' at The Oval.

He was as interesting to watch as ever, if not as exciting. *The Times*'s correspondent, Major Beau Vincent, said that in 1948, after watching Bradman bat for some time, people tended to go and have a beer. He said they wouldn't have done that in the 1930s.

O'Reilly admired Bradman's effort, compensating for his diminishing eye and fluency by concentrating 'more than I had ever seen him concentrate before'. Otherwise, fieldsmen were allowed to stand in places where it would have been foolhardy in the 1930s. '[N]o one in his proper senses could compare the Bradman of 1948 with the one of 1930 to 1938. He was slow to follow the moving ball. Spin bowlers, whenever he met one, found him allergic to the ball which moved away from his bat . . . [But he] had the self-possession to evaluate his own post-war ability better than most other people did. He knew that it was better to bide his time.'

As well as his nine first-class centuries, Bradman played three innings of substance in the 1948 Tests. Each was tailored to circumstance. The 138 at Trent Bridge, withstanding Yardley's leg theory, was a masterpiece of patience. The 89 at Lord's was second fiddle to Barnes's 141, but crucial in driving home Australia's advantage. The unbeaten 173 at Headingley was, if overshadowed by Morris's 182, one of Bradman's greatest days. He only scored

another 108 runs in his six other innings, including the ducks at
Trent Bridge and The Oval, but was still third in the aggregates
behind Morris and Compton.

R.C. Robertson-Glasgow put his finger on the difference in
Bradman's batting:

> In [prewar] days, you saw where he scored most of his runs;
> wide of mid-on, say; square-cuts, say; and so on. Nowadays,
> you don't seem to see him run-getting; it just happens. He bats
> and, behold a hundred pops up on the board against his name.
> But he doesn't murder any more; her persuades; persuades
> Fate to let him survive those early-middle-age gropings and
> soundings at the start of his innings, persuades the ball away
> from the best-placed fields, persuades himself back, almost, to
> a miracle-lad.

In self-summary, Bradman said he was sounder in defence, more
orthodox but less aggressive, and slower in the field to avoid
risking injury.

But you don't ask the sun why it shines. Lindwall, as a teammate,
said Bradman's impact on the 1948 series far transcended the
runs he scored. 'His deeds and consistency were nothing short of
amazing, but of equal value was the feeling of supreme confidence
his presence gave to the rest of the eleven. Even in moments of
crisis the atmosphere in the Australian dressing-room was always
that "everything is bound to work out right, the Don is playing".'

When Bradman had become Australian captain in 1936–37, he
was accused of being a selfish player, putting his batting needs on
a higher plane than would, say, a self-sacrificing captain such as
Bill Woodfull. At 0–2 down in his first series in charge, Bradman
had moved himself down to number seven to avoid batting on a
sticky wicket in the third Test at Melbourne. He agreed that this
was selfish: but in his case, he argued, his needs and the team's were
synonymous. The greatest service he could do his team, in the

interest of winning Test matches, was to score runs. That day he scored 270 and put on a world-record 345 for the sixth wicket. His partner was Fingleton. Australia won the Test, and, miraculously, the series 3–2.

Identifying his own batting interest with the team's was not as necessary in 1948. Morris, Barnes, Hassett, Miller, Harvey and Loxton were all able to make big scores. Morris was the first Australian in twenty years to outscore Bradman in a Test series. Bradman's captaincy now rested on more than runs. As Cardus wrote of him in 1948, 'He is the brain and the vertebra of Australian cricket, Government and executive . . . Bradman bestrides them all; he bestrides the entire history of the game.'

A few hours after his duck, Bradman attended a concert at the Albert Hall by the Australian pianist Eileen Joyce, who had fallen from a horse during the week. During her performance, she collapsed, having to be carried to her dressing room. Bradman met her backstage, and 'reflected that perhaps I understood better than most people in the audience the mental strain she had endured to get through. The human nervous system is so marvellous in its ability to produce untold reserves of energy until the moment of the climax is reached.'

When they resumed on Monday at 2/153, Morris and Hassett knuckled down to the task of batting England into oblivion. There was no hand-wringing over Bradman's average. Morris confirmed his standing as the Australian batsman of the series. Simple and effective, he set out with Hassett to 'squeeze the heart out of the losing side', Arlott said. Hassett made 37, and Miller fell forward from his crease to be stumped for 5, but Harvey, Loxton and Tallon helped Morris grind towards 400. Bradman said Morris's 196 'was the innings of a young master who had steadily gone from strength to strength until he stood that day firmly entrenched as not only the greatest contemporary left-hand bat, but in my opinion the greatest left-hander I have ever seen'.

Some praise from a man who had seen Woolley and Leyland.

Dewes, who also fielded to a Morris century in the Middlesex match, says: 'I learnt a lot about batting from watching Morris's innings. He was so steady, the ball never got past him. He was also extremely determined. As a left-hander, he showed me how to use the back foot. We were mostly front-foot players, and it hampered us against Lindwall and Miller.'

Right on top of the bowling now, Morris gave his unorthodoxy full play, forcing the bowlers to change their line by hitting off-stump balls through the leg side.

Harvey, who had not seen a great deal of Morris before the tour, was now a convert. 'Everything he tried seemed to come off and he out-scored even the mighty Bradman . . . He could cut, drive and pull the bowling about at will once he settled down, and he was never dull to watch. Any spectator who didn't relish watching Arthur at the wicket just didn't like watching cricket.'

The bowlers could not get him out. Tallon played Hollies to short third man and Morris, trying to protect his teammate from the leg spinner, went for a tight run. 'It was my call, my fault,' Morris says. 'Reg Simpson threw it in. I was just trying to keep the strike, because Hollies was having a lot of success.'

England had nearly a session to survive Lindwall and Miller that afternoon. Dewes, still trying to come to terms with fast bowling for which there was no preparation in English cricket, tried to poise his stance on his back foot to force himself to come forward to meet the ball. 'But there were one or two short balls an over,' he says. 'Lindwall skidded it through, it pitched and went zoom.'

Dewes played what Arlott recorded as 'one remarkable stroke: it was a perfectly executed hook, to a ball from Lindwall rising over his leg-stump. Everyone looked to square-leg, and then, bewildered, looked back to see that the ball had gone all along the ground, off the middle of the meat of the bat for four – to third man.' As in the first innings, the full-pitched inswinger beat him and he was out for 10, trying to pull his bat away. Yardley was again a strong supporter of Dewes's contentious selection, saying he 'was very unlucky to get out to a ball which went from his bat to his pads and so on to the wicket . . . [B]ut for misfortune, he might have made a solid score.'

Edrich played some optimistic attacking strokes, but a fast one from Lindwall bowled him for 28 early on the Tuesday. Compton made an uncertain 39 before snicking Johnston's away-floater, Lindwall snapping up a freakish slips catch, and then Crapp, who earned respect for his doughtiness, took a Miller bouncer on his head. The ball ricocheted past point for four leg byes. An admiring Lindwall said: 'Jack just shook his head and settled down for the next ball.' Arlott said Crapp resumed 'under the handicap of a headache, which was still with him when he caught the Bristol express on Wednesday afternoon'.

O'Reilly loved this kind of thing, all the more so in England's bleakest moment. 'The manner in which the Gloucester man "took" this painful knock was the most stoical I have seen on a cricket field. He just stood there with his head bent to one side and did not take the trouble even to rub the spot. The Australian in-fieldsmen, however, came in to carry out this job for him.'

Miller, after a spell of off spin, attacked the batsmen with bouncers, and then dismissed Hutton and Crapp with pitched-up deliveries. Hutton would later say that he valued his runs against the 1948 Australians more highly than any others in his eighteen-year Test career:

> Lindwall, Miller and Johnston were the most formidable combination it was my lot to face and almost a generation of shell-shocked England batsmen can testify to their skill and belligerence. The runs I made against them really counted, and my abilities and experience were stretched to the limit. I would look at Bradman conferring with Lindwall, Miller or Big Bill and wonder what they were hatching up, and I resolved if

ever I became captain I would endeavour to implant the same curious doubts in the minds of my opponents.

Hutton's 64 was, in Arlott's opinion, as good as his 364 on the same ground a decade earlier. 'Then he had been the successful batsman: in this later day he stood as the solid rock without whom the side must collapse.'

But collapse they did. Doug Ring finally got a bowl and took his first Test wicket, the hapless Watkins, who had received eight painkilling injections. He pulled Ring and thought, '"That's four runs." But it went straight down Lindsay Hassett's throat. He didn't have to move.'

The light faded early, making England's struggle all the harder. When Evans came in, 'a dark cloud passed over the ground. I saw Ray Lindwall at the other end wave the ball in the air as he was preparing to run up. I thought this was a signal to Don Tallon that his bouncer was coming. But it wasn't. I hardly saw the ball as it shattered my wicket. My dismissal was the signal for all the players to return to the pavilion, the umpires having called a halt because of the light.'

When Evans asked Lindwall why he had waved, he replied: 'I was trying to get you to appeal against the light.'

The Australians were making every effort to be good sports, now that the contest was over. Yardley later apologised to Evans for not having appealed. But it was too late now. It had been too late, for England, ever since the rain cancelled out their comeback in Manchester.

On the Wednesday morning, Johnston clipped the tail, finishing the series equal with Lindwall on twenty-seven wickets, the same as Ted McDonald's record from 1921. The ambitious Lindwall said he 'never tried harder' to get his twenty-eighth. But the last wicket was Johnston's, a skied slog from Hollies, landing with Australia's batsman of the series, Morris. As they walked off, Johnston consoled Lindwall, saying wicket-taking 'was much easier when the bowler was trying not to take them'.

England were, in this match, dire, an unfortunate regression after their fightback in Manchester and Leeds. Fingleton said the Test 'could well be remembered as the poorest Test ever between England and Australia – or better still, it could well be forgotten altogether'. That was never going to happen, but it was Bradman's duck, rather than the heroics of Morris, Lindwall and Johnston, that etched the game in memory.

The Australians were, in victory, able diplomats. Throughout the Oval Test they had made gestures of sportsmanship: Loxton shaking Dewes's hand, Hassett refusing to run Compton out, Lindwall hinting to Evans that he should appeal against the light. As the winners came off, Miller, who'd claimed a bail, threw it to a group of small boys in the outer. Fingleton observed: 'A little lad in front of the Press-box could hardly believe his eyes when he saw it tumbling to him. The pleased look on his face as he clasped the bail in his two hands was one of the sights of the game.'

Before a crowd of 5000, there was a presentation and some speeches. Bradman said: '[W]hatever you have read to the contrary, this is definitely the last Test match in which I shall ever play. I'm sorry my personal contribution was so small, but that was thanks to the generosity of the reception from the public and the English players and the very fine ball which Hollies bowled me.' He said Yardley had been 'a very lovable opposition skipper . . . Norman has been in an unfortunate position because the captain of a losing side has a very difficult job, a task I know only too well. I think he has been up against one of the strongest Australian sides ever to visit this country.'

The English were miserable about their loss, Dewes says. 'We were very disappointed, not just with losing but losing so easily. We didn't have a strong bowling attack but we expected better of our batting.'

Always a gentleman, Yardley made a gracious reply to Bradman's speech: 'Future Australian sides will seem strange without Don

Bradman. The only people who can be happy about his Test retirement are those who face the task of getting him out.'

The crowd sang 'For He's a Jolly Good Fellow', and that was it for Don Bradman, Test cricketer. Not, however, as a tourist. Ashes tours were not, as they are now, focused entirely on the international matches. County and invitational fixtures retained their traditional importance, and Bradman's team still had to play five first-class and two second-class opponents. This was where Armstrong, in 1921, had stumbled. Bradman was determined to be different.

11

THE IRRESISTIBLE PULL

While the clouds of a new war hung over Britain – the Berlin airlift had taken place the week after the second Test, and the Soviet Union's first atom bomb was just months from detonation – Australia was looking to a new era. Indeed, the countries were diverging at an unprecedented rate. Britain had nationalised coal, railways and electricity; the Australian public had rejected a referendum to nationalise banks. Britain was surrendering its mandate in Palestine, its empire in Asia, and owed nearly £1 billion to the United States. Australia's economy and population were entering a decade-long boom. The forty-hour week had been introduced in early 1948, and paid sick leave and long-service leave were soon to follow. Wool was moving towards a record price, all rationing was soon to end, and the Snowy Mountains Scheme, the most ambitious single infrastructure project in Australian history, would commence in 1949. So appealing had Australia become to gloom-stricken Britons that in the months after the Invincibles returned, the 100 000th postwar British migrant would arrive.

In victory, Bradman's team felt the irresistible pull of their journey home. Two weak counties, Kent and Somerset, awaited, plus three composite XIs: the Gentlemen, the South of England, and Leveson-Gower's XI in the banana-skin Scarborough Fair game that had felled Armstrong's team in 1921 and Bradman's in 1938. The tour would conclude with two second-class games in Scotland, which Bradman, unerringly neat, would not countenance losing.

After a bonus day off, the Australians travelled to Canterbury. Brown made his seventh century of the tour, pulling level with Morris, and Bradman was in imperious form, pulling three consecutive balls from Fred Ridgway into the same peg of the mayor's tent.

Evans had never caught or stumped Bradman while keeping to more than 1400 runs off his bat in Australia and England. But when Bradman was in his fifties, he chopped down on a ball from Eddie Crush. Evans stifled an appeal.

Later, Bradman said, laughing, 'You are a fool, Godfrey; you've been trying to get me all these years and you threw away the perfect chance out there.'

'Did you hit it then, Don?'

'Of course I did . . . I hit it hard. There was your chance, and when you got it, Godfrey, you didn't take it.'

On the rest day, Loxton broke his teetotal rule, volunteering to accompany Bradman, Johnson and Hamence to a party at Kent captain Brian Valentine's house. The alcohol was supplied by a sponsor, Shepherd Neame. 'The hosts had invited friends and so on, and there was magnificent glassware in the table with this Taylor '08 port in it,' Loxton said. 'Forty years old – jeez, it was lovely! It undid me, I tell you.'

He had to be assisted back to the hotel, where he was sent to his room in a service lift. 'Perhaps I needed servicing. I was no good the next day. Not even Harv would help me. I tried to get up the next morning and the little bastard wouldn't help me.'

During the match, Australia's Foreign Minister H.V. Evatt visited Canterbury to track Bradman down over an outstanding matter. The Australian government had asked Bradman to hand over a cheque for £10 000 from the State of New South Wales for the restoration of Canterbury Cathedral. When Evatt found

Bradman at the Kent game to ask him what had become of the cheque, Bradman's first words were, 'What have you done about that taxation matter for me?' He wanted a tax break on royalties for his forthcoming *Farewell to Cricket*. Fingleton told the story as an example of Bradman's looming post-retirement priorities.

On the Monday, a new ground record of 23 000 saw twenty-six wickets fall. Evans's Kent teammates had said, after England's debacle at The Oval, 'At least when we play the Aussies we'll get more than 52 runs.' As it turned out, they got one fewer.

The Australians were running out of enthusiasm and good temper, however. This was why the last phase posed so many risks to a perfectionist like Bradman. The team started to grow tetchy, and Kent's first innings saw the only occasion Miller knew Johnston to 'go crook' on a cricket field. 'Ray Lindwall has always been allowed to choose the bowling end he preferred. After a couple of overs at Canterbury, Ray asked to be switched to the other end. Bill, who had taken a couple of cheap wickets, intervened angrily, "Why? Is the game made for one man?" He soon calmed down, and so far as I know this was the only time he has ever said a word out of place.'

Tempers were fraying after four months on tour, but the Australians were not stress-tested by Kent, whose first innings only lasted eighty-five minutes. Their 41-year-old opener, Les Todd, was hit on the toe by Lindwall's first ball. Todd told the umpire he should be given out lbw. The umpire declined. Todd let himself be bowled next ball, and refused to bat in the second innings. Kent suspended him for the rest of the season.

A greater controversy, if a private one, was a mysterious request sent to Lindwall.

> I received an unsigned telegram suggesting that I bowl bumpers to Leslie Ames, [the Kent and England wicketkeeper who had been on the Bodyline tour]. The sender apparently forgot that the wire would bear the name of the district from which it was dispatched. Now this was such a small place that I knew the

wire could have come from only one man, someone so high up in English cricket that his name would cause a sensation if I revealed it. I purposely did not bowl a single bumper to Les but the next time I met the 'VIP' I challenged him with sending the wire, remarking that I thought it a very silly thing to do. He confessed he meant it only as a joke. To me the joke was not very funny, especially as the sender of the telegram was not the type of individual who appreciates leg-pulling at his own expense.

The identity of the sender? Every clue – the relish to see batsmen challenged by bouncers, the distinctive rural address, the questionable sense of humour, the personal history with Ames (they were teammates for England in the 1930s) – leads to the same man: Bradman's mate, R.W.V. Robins.

Many of the Australians questioned Robins's ability as a selector, and during a drink in the Kent match, they ventured to tell Evans what they thought the English Test team should have been. It was: Hutton, Washbrook, Edrich, Compton, Jack Robertson, Reg Simpson, Evans, Bedser, Pollard, Wright, and Hollies (or Young). Notable is the absence of Yardley – presumably Edrich, the best-qualified amateur, or the professional Hutton would have been captain – and their inclusion of two leg spinners. O'Reilly would have been proud. Interestingly, in no Test match of the actual series did the English selectors get more than seven of that eleven onto the field.

Perhaps it was only to be expected that when Bradman offered his own ideas about the ideal England team, Yardley took offence: 'Don Bradman amazed me, after the Tests had ended, by writing some articles purporting to tell me how we ought to have selected our team! There would have been some very funny Test matches if we had been able to follow his advice.'

What Yardley did not know was how much of Bradman's advice, via Robins, the England selectors had already taken.

*

The Gentlemen, who had last beaten Australia in 1878, were not, of course, what they had once been. They could have done with a Grace or two. The Gentlemen's annual fixture against the Players was slipping into irrelevance, too one-sided to hold the public's interest. Amateurism, as an idea, was in its last throes as Britain entered a modern social-democratic age. Professional cricket, correspondingly, did not carry the below-stairs stigma it had had in the nineteenth century. The amateurs of 1948 were a shell, featuring only two Test-class English batsmen, Edrich and Simpson, plus the New Zealander Donnelly, the Worcestershire schoolteacher Charles Palmer, and a long bolt of captaincy material in Yardley, George Mann, Robins, Wilfred Wooller and Freddie Brown. Trevor Bailey, still in his fast-bowling guise, took the new ball.

Brown and Bradman made centuries, Bradman surpassing Warren Bardsley by becoming the only man to pass 2000 runs on four tours of England, while Hassett came back to form with an unbeaten 200. A fifteen-year-old Kentish boy in the crowd, Michael Colin Cowdrey, watched Bradman bat and never forgot what he saw. 'As he walked back to the pavilion for the last time, having made 150, he turned to the crowd, hung his gloves round his bat handle, raised them aloft and bowed farewell. I don't think I have ever seen a more moving moment than this on the cricket field . . .' In a speech in Adelaide in October 1948, Bradman said batting at Lord's in that match had been his biggest thrill of the tour.

By the end of August, tiredness was pervading the squad. Barnes had endured a frustrating tour, without a century since the second Test match. He had set out to compete with Bradman for runs and celebrity, and was feeling peeved enough to criticise Bradman for, at this stage of the tour, not giving Hamence a turn at number three at Lord's.

I felt very sorry for Ronnie Hamence . . . Don just wouldn't alter his batting list and Hamence had a disappointing time. He . . . didn't even get the chance of batting when the men above him had been scoring heavily in other games. This aggregate and average business is bad on an English tour. A lot of people say so-and-so got so many runs at such-and-such an average on an English trip, but such figures leave me cold. I have seen too many big scores made at a time when they are not wanted.

Hamence never complained. Most likely, Barnes was projecting his own frustrations.

When the Gentlemen had their turn to bat, the spinners Johnson and Ring prevented a competitive score. Lindwall and Miller took it easy – except for one target, as Lindwall recalled.

Robins – the suspected sender of the Ames telegram – had been loudly criticising the England batsmen for 'their timidity against fast bowling and for not hooking the bumper. This prompted several of the England team to suggest that Keith Miller and I should bowl one or two bumpers to him in the Lord's game to see whether he would employ the methods he advocated so strongly. We decided that each should test him with one bumper. The intention was to drop it short enough for it to fly harmlessly over his head.'

But the soft pitch kept the ball down. Robins ducked into Lindwall's first bumper and was hit on the back of his neck. Miller's knocked his cap off. 'On returning to the dressing-room after his innings,' Lindwall said, 'Robins retracted all his previous criticisms.'

Miller told the story similarly, albeit placing himself at the centre: 'More than one of the England players hinted to us that [Robins] might not shape so well against them himself. We decided to try him with one and I was selected as the man to do it. Accordingly I think almost everyone on the ground knew I was going to give Robins a bumper first ball. I did – it was one of the fastest I have ever bowled. It did not rise as much as I intended and it nearly "sconed" poor Robbie. I am sure it parted his hair. Bradman laughed heartily at his pal's discomfort.'

Miller said this incident, and Bradman's laughter, was his justification for bouncing Bradman in his Melbourne benefit match in 1949. 'Only this time "Braddles" did not laugh.' Instead, he omitted Miller from the next Australian team.

On the third day of the Gentlemen's match, 27 August, a celebration was arranged for Bradman's fortieth birthday. Pelham Warner presented him with a copy of his history of Lord's and a birthday cake, eighteen inches square, in the shape of an open book, made by the MCC caterer George Portman, who had been at the club for six years longer than Bradman had been alive. One leaf was iced: 'To Don Bradman. Many Happy Returns of the Day from All at Lord's.' On the other was a bouquet of roses, a photo of Bradman, and on each corner of the base was a kangaroo in marzipan.

Bradman noted: 'I see it's not closed. We still have a few games after this one.' He remained in a competitive mood. His team sang him 'Happy Birthday'; the crowd followed with a reprise and 'Auld Lang Syne'. Bradman, somewhat ungraciously, or perhaps showing his dislike for being the centre of attention, would write: 'This sentimental angle which had crept into the final matches was proving a great strain. I felt physically and mentally tired. Moreover, my emotions had been stirred and I found great difficulty in keeping myself up to concert pitch.'

Fingleton was emotionally moved by the scenes at the end of the match:

> England adored him and bore no resentment against him for what he did to the country's bowlers. He was, if anything, even more popular there than in his native Australia. He was cheered to the echo whenever he appeared on a ground, and

the people's faces lit up as if they had seen a miracle when they recognised him in the street. He was seen for the last time on an English field at Lord's in 1948 and thousands stood on the field for him to make an almost Royal appearance on the Australian balcony. But he never came again nor was seen there in flannels. There comes a time when the Pavilion swallows up all players for the last time, but the thousands at Lord's did not comprehend that Bradman would come no more. That seemed unbelievable.

The following day Bradman rested in London while Hassett took the team to Taunton. When the 1948 team's credibility as the greatest to tour England is questioned, it is on the basis of matches such as this. Somerset were barely first-class standard, scoring 115 and 71 in response to Australia's 5/560. Only Yorkshire, Hampshire, Warwickshire and Lancashire had given them anything like a challenge, though Glamorgan might also have done so if not for rain. The rest of the counties were making up the numbers. Any final assessment of the 1948 tour would have to acknowledge that while England fielded a team of some strength, the majority of the counties did not.

Two first-class matches against composite teams remained. Bradman's nerves jangled, while many of his team clocked off. Twenty thousand in Hastings for the September Festival turned out to see Bradman lead Australia against a South of England side containing Edrich, Doggart, Compton and Bailey but a suspect bowling attack. Bradman, lucky with tosses in the run-home phase of the tour, was able to bat again.

Bradman, Hassett and Harvey made centuries, but poor Colin McCool, who had contained his frustration all tour, finally lost his temper. The second day brought, he said, the only occasion when he ever snapped at Bradman.

Our blokes were playing with their eyes shut. The hard stuff was over, they were thinking of going home and everybody was wandering round in a semi-conscious state – as exemplified by Sidney Barnes, who fielded at cover with a faraway look on his face and his hands in his pockets. During the course of one over off my bowling Lindsay Hassett woke up to the fact that he could have made a catch – five minutes after the ball hit the ground – and then I beat the batsman with a googly only to find Don Tallon stranded on the off-side of the wicket while the ball went down the leg-side. He'd given up reading the hand for the day! At the end of the over I was walking moodily away from the wicket when Bradman said as he passed: 'Well bowled, Col.'

I boiled over. I'd had a disappointing tour, and, in any case, a cricket match was always something to be played hard in my reckoning.

'Well bowled, my foot,' I snarled.

'What's the matter?' asked Bradman, genuinely taken aback.

'The matter,' I said, 'is that I'm the only one out here who gives a damn. I'm the only one who's trying.'

'I'm trying,' he said, hurt that anyone should think he wasn't giving 100 per cent.

'Oh, not you,' I said. 'But do you think that little fella's trying' – nodding at Hassett. 'And what about him?' – looking at Barnes. 'He hasn't taken his hands out of his pockets since I began bowling.'

Bradman said no more. He ran across to Barnes, said half a dozen words, and from then on Sid and the rest of the side fielded as if the devil was just one pace behind them.

Rain shut down the match, if not the demands. A London schoolboy waited for hours in the rain to get Bradman to sign something for him. He later told his mother, 'I didn't get Bradman's autograph but he trod on my toe, though.' It was a rare oversight by Bradman, who was scrupulous in responding to children's requests. One English girl had sent him a birthday card, and her friends laughed at her – until she received a personal letter of thanks from him with signatures of the entire team.

A five-day break in Paris did not distract Bradman from the knowledge that ahead, in the Scarborough Festival game, lay a trap. It was here that Archie MacLaren, twelve years into retirement, had ambushed Armstrong's unbeatables of 1921. The Scarborough team, chosen by 'Shrimp' Leveson-Gower, was always close to Test-strength. It would be wrong to say Bradman's desire to go through England undefeated was unique to 1948. This had certainly also been his aim in 1938, and their stumble, only three weeks from the end, still rankled. The Leveson-Gower team that beat Australia then included Hutton, Herbert Sutcliffe, Maurice Leyland, Ken Farnes, Bill Bowes and Hedley Verity. Their ten-wicket win is not hard to explain.

How important was it to be undefeated? How much did it mean to Bradman, or the others, to not lose a game?

He was sensitive about his ambition, as he showed when he reacted against Fingleton's *Daily Mail* leader in April. Bradman, always motivated by some perceived or real slight, wanted to exceed Armstrong. Participants on the tour had no doubt that Bradman was, as Flanagan put it, 'intensely loyal to his purpose of completing it undefeated'. Harvey says Bradman was most tense about achieving that goal 'when only a few matches were left after the completion of the Test series'.

The ambition was not unanimously held. Miller was irked by Bradman's constant urgings during minor county games. He recalled Bradman saying: 'When you get in front, nail 'em into the ground. When you get 'em down, never let up.'

In county matches, team members, wanting a day off, would ask, 'Haven't we got enough now?' Bradman 'would give a crooked little smile and say in his thin, piping voice, "I remember when England made 900 against us and kept us in the field for three days"'.

It was, Miller thought, an unseemly vengefulness; as if the events between 1938 and 1948 had slid across the surface of Bradman's soul.

The Australians moved into the Royal Hotel at Scarborough, owned by Tom Laughton, the actor Charles's brother, but for Bradman there was no partying. 'The one [Bradman] was really scared about was the Scarborough game,' Barnes said. 'This was the last first-class game of the tour and the star men of our side were tired of the game by now. We were all feeling the effect of a long tour and looking forward to the finish.'

When he heard that Leveson-Gower was intending to field a Test-strength XI – one last chance to knock the Aussies off – Bradman protested, saying 'that we would not relish a "Test" at Scarborough and would fight every inch of the way to preserve our reputation'. Leveson-Gower chose six current England players plus Fishlock, Donnelly, Robins, Brown and Pritchard.

Bradman said he was unjustly accused by a report saying that even though he had got Leveson-Gower to agree to select only six current England Test players, he countered by choosing a Test-strength Australian XI.

'The facts?' he wrote. 'Well, firstly I was not responsible for the Australian Team. It was chosen by a Selection Committee, not by me alone. Secondly, no such "arrangement" existed. Leveson-Gower was perfectly free to choose whatever players he wished.'

His account is contradicted by every witness. Morris, as the third tour selector, says Bradman 'always got whatever team he wanted . . . He *was* the tour selection committee.' And Bradman had admitted to Barnes that he had spoken to Leveson-Gower about his selection. Barnes said 'there was a whisper of the Don dictating to the powers that run such games that, if the game were to be a Festival one, Leveson-Gower's team at Scarborough should include no more than six Test men from the series just past. With that granted, Don's worries about the unbeaten record were almost wiped out.'

Morris agrees that Bradman intervened in the home team's selection.

> The thing was, in 1938 Don was very annoyed that Leveson-Gower picked fast bowlers in what was meant to be a festival match. It was to relax after the Tests, for people to play their shots and entertain the crowd. Bradman had been cranky that on previous tours the English treated it as a sixth Test. He read the riot act to Leveson-Gower, and said this wasn't meant to be a Test match. We didn't know that this was the one match Armstrong's team had lost, but you can bet that Bradman did.

Flanagan, always a Bradman supporter, put it bluntly: 'Bradman cautiously requested that the names of the players invited to play in the Leveson-Gower XI be first submitted to him. The officials graciously complied, and Bradman promptly objected to some of the real strength in the proposed side; these players were omitted. Then to make doubly sure Bradman selected a Test team to represent Australia.'

Fingleton also wrote that Bradman dictated Leveson-Gower's selection, and Edrich felt the whole episode was another instance of Bradman's lack of fellow-feeling for the English cricketers. 'I don't think I shall ever forgive him for his attitude towards the Scarborough Festival match in 1948,' he wrote.

> [It would be] a postscript to a season in which we had been chivvied and chased by the Australians. We needed to relax. But Festival cricket was alien to Bradman ... He told his

players to get 'stuck in'. The record had to be kept straight at all costs. Keith Miller, whose approach to the game is the right one, was incensed by the decision. But then friction between the unpredictable Miller and his captain was no new thing. Actual clashes between the two were rare, but that was mainly because Miller had no time for 'the little man', as he called him. Miller went his own sweet way.

Every Australian player wanted Hamence to have one last chance to score a hundred, but Bradman would not relent. Barnes wrote: 'Hamence, anxious to get up as many runs as possible so that he would not return to Australia a failure, was the keenest in our party to play in this game, but he was stood down.' Bradman 'wanted that record and he got it'.

Miller called the whole Scarborough excursion 'an incredible incident'.

'We had won the series. We had not been beaten through the long course of an English season, and we had reached the Scarborough Festival for the last first-class fixture against H.G. Leveson-Gower's Eleven. Bradman refused to announce the team until five minutes before the game started. So every player in the party had to go to the ground prepared to play. Why he did so remains to this day a mystery to me.'

There was no mystery to it. Bradman was in a fever of anxiety. He had the pitch completely covered during rain breaks, so there would be no risk of getting caught on a sticky. No doubt his disclaimers of having had any control over Leveson-Gower's selection, or – quite laughably – his own, were due simply to the fact that he did not always want to appear so baldly as he was: a control freak obsessed, by this stage, with remaining undefeated.

As usual, he turned out to have worried too much. Robins won the toss and batted, but from the moment Lindwall bowled Hutton with his fourth ball, Australia could not lose. Lindwall took 6/59 as the home team crumbled for 177. There was nothing festive about Australia's response, though Morris was drinking more than his customary one or two beers the night before a match. 'When I was making more runs than him,' Don said, jokingly, "Don't have too much of that, it won't do you any good!" He was only joking: he knew bloody well at that stage that nothing was going to stop us going to the pub.'

Barnes and Bradman churned out 150s in what, for wildly divergent reasons, would be the last first-class game for Australia for both men.

Loxton went in at number four but promptly swept a ball from Freddie Brown into his own nose. He would need surgery in Edinburgh days later. 'It was the only time I ever tried to play the sweep shot,' Loxton said. 'I didn't want to retire hurt. I only needed 27 more runs to get to the thousand [for the tour]. But Braddles said, "You've broken your nose, Sam!" I said, "No I haven't." But there was blood all over my glove, and I went off.'

In the dressing room, Bradman had joked to Hassett that to average 100 in England, he'd have to make 500 not out, 'and this game, you know, is limited to three days'. So, having reached 151, he chose to give his wicket away to the deserving Bedser, skying a catch to Hutton. 'By the time that Hutton's two safe hands had closed on the ball,' Fingleton said, 'Bradman was half-way to the pavilion. He did not turn to see whether the catch had been taken. He continued running, gloves, cap and bat fluttering from his hands, and almost before this huge Yorkshire crowd at the Scarborough Festival had had time to warm its hands in appreciation to him, Bradman was lost to view for ever as a first-class batsman on an English ground.'

A band struck up 'For He's a Jolly Good Fellow'. Fingleton said: 'This was a most significant moment in cricketing history.'

Miller, down the order at number seven, showed no sentiment, remarking to Laker: 'This is no way to play festival cricket. I'm buggered if I am going to support this "heads-down" idea.' He told Laker not to think 'all the Australians were as prim as this little man'.

Miller had reason to reflect on an unfulfilling tour. In the Tests, he scored fewer runs, at a lower average, than Lindwall – let alone the recognised batsmen, and he only took six Test wickets after his heroics at Nottingham. 'It would be ridiculous to suggest that Miller's overall performance on that tour worthily reflected his ability,' Whitington wrote. 'A great deal of iron clearly had entered his soul and nobody in the Australian camp doubted that the "Blacksmith" had been Don Bradman.'

Did Bradman destroy Miller in 1948? Bradman's own rating of Miller's tour was damning with faint praise: 'One of the most volatile cricketers of any age . . . Altogether a crowd-pleasing personality of the Jack Gregory type whose limitations were caused mainly by his own failure to concentrate.'

Miller's many supporters lined up to corroborate Whitington's image of the iron-souled 'Blacksmith'. Miller was, in O'Reilly's opinion, 'a problem to both captains, Yardley and Bradman'. After Nottingham 'he seemed to lose all desire to settle down to run-getting'. O'Reilly thought Bradman didn't understand Miller, and 'missed out completely in his responsibility as touring captain in this regard'.

'A cricketer who has any pretensions at all to successful captaincy must remember that friendliness and frankness are more necessary attributes than spectacular shrewdness. A captain must go out of his way to get to know each member of his team individually. He must not regard his men as a flock of sheep to be yarded and shorn at will.'

Compton, Miller's friend, said Bradman's captaincy limited Miller's effectiveness: 'I cannot say that I felt drawn to [Bradman's] approach to the game of cricket, though I must admire the consistency and determination, almost the ruthlessness, of his attitude and its effectiveness. I am not sure that he brought the best out of Keith Miller. In a way we were grateful that he did not, because Keith was quite formidable enough as it was.'

Even Harvey, loath to criticise Bradman, admitted that by

contrast Hassett, bowling Miller in shorter spells, got more out of him. In 1953, Harvey thought, Miller was 'a far more menacing bowler' than in 1948.

But can Bradman be blamed for not sharing Miller's egocentricity? Is it Bradman's fault if he knew he had enough batting in the 1948 team but needed Miller's bowling more? Here can be seen the method in Bradman's ruthlessness. While antagonising Miller, he also got some match-winning efforts out of him. Had the 1948 tour been staged for Miller's personal glory, no doubt he would have batted at number four and bowled sparingly. But Bradman harnessed his explosive talents for the good of the team. Ian Johnson, the fellow air-force pilot who would become Miller's rival for the Australian captaincy after Hassett's retirement in 1953 ('I find that there are times when I like Keith immensely. There are also times when I dislike him intensely'), put forward a convincing case in support of Bradman's use of Miller. Johnson didn't think Bradman over-bowled Miller in 1948, because 'his bowling has always been of greater value to Australia than his batting'. Johnson thought Miller always had more match-winning impact as a bowler.

> Under pressure, Keith is a devastating bowler. As a batsman, he is unreliable and often fails under the same pressure. Probably the reason for this lies in his temperament. He is exceptionally highly strung and, to a great extent, he lives upon his nerves. When the pressure is on his batting, this condition causes him to be tense and strained, and so interferes with his natural approach to the job on hand. Bowling, on the other hand, offers an outlet for his pent-up nervous energy; this provides a driving force which lifts him well above the ordinary.

So – Miller was a better bowler than he thought he was, and not as good a batsman. Bradman's assessment seems fair. The ticklish thing was how to communicate this to Miller without losing him completely. Johnson, as a captain, struggled with it, for 'You can never be certain, on the field, whether he will put his heart into the job or act like a mechanical automaton. He is a bad example to young players. Yet he can be such a help to them. All of which adds up to a rather complex character who is essentially an individualist rather than a team man.'

Edrich knew that Miller saw himself as Bradman's competitor as a batsman, and believed Bradman over-bowled him because, as a batsman, he felt threatened by him. Miller's amour-propre had few limits. He said: 'A fast bowler should not bat higher than number six. I thought that neither Bradman nor Hassett completely realised that after a long spell of bowling a fast bowler is physically and mentally spent for a while.' At first, this might seem a sensible appeal from a fast bowler to bat lower, to get more time to rest. But it is actually the converse: Miller thought so highly of himself as a batsman that he should not have been asked to open the bowling as well.

On this issue, Miller was wrong and Bradman was right, in 1948 at least. Bradman was able to deploy Miller to his greatest effect. His bowling at Trent Bridge won the match. His catching in slips there and at Lord's turned the series Australia's way. His innings at Headingley was a highpoint of the summer. Left to his own devices, Miller would have scored unnecessary centuries and bowled little. Under Bradman's captaincy, he may not have racked up the statistics, but he helped Australia win matches.

The romantic Arlott summarised:

> Here was a great cricketer – when he was needed to be a great cricketer. Here was that rare cricketer without conceit, without respect for averages, who never cared what the crowd thought of him. Yet he was as human as the man in the next hospital bed; he was as gay as a sparrow; he never dogmatised; he knew cricket inside out and loved the game. Although he could give of his transcendent best only when the moment demanded it,

he was desperately keen for Australia to win the Tests; he never relaxed for a single ball; he never failed to appeal for anything. Keith Miller did not care who had a personal success so long as Australia won.

Arlott possibly gilded the lily here. Miller did care for personal success. But under the hand of the 'Blacksmith' Bradman, Miller was forced to become a team player, and it is a measure of Bradman's captaincy that he got what he wanted.

After all the behind-the-scenes controversy and angst, rain vitiated the Scarborough game. As it petered out, even Bradman had a bowl, his one concession to light-heartedness. Even then he felt the need to justify his late declaration: 'There was criticism of my action but I have no apology to make. I would do the same again. Only those who have toured know the great strain upon Australian players after the last Test is over.'

That night, he said, 'The sun went down just as usual. Apart from the feeling of personal satisfaction, I freely admit to the great pleasure of achieving one ambition – to lead an Australian team through an English tour undefeated. No other Australian side in history had been able to avoid defeat.'

Finally, he could reflect and celebrate. A crowd in the Royal Hotel gave him a standing ovation as he came down the staircase to dinner. Rosenwater wrote that he 'was certainly embarrassed – but at the same time deeply moved. It was a rare tribute, normally reserved for Hollywood film scenarios, and a form of tribute that may well be unique for a first-class cricketer.'

He – his team – had done it. Or had they? Always, there was more cricket. Three days after the Scarborough match, they were due at the Raeburn Place ground in Edinburgh. Bradman thought their record might still be questioned if they lost to Scotland, so he decided to play and ensure nothing went wrong. Afterwards,

he played a round of golf with Lindwall and Miller, and Miller
went to Edinburgh's Usher Hall to hear the sixty-voice Glasgow
Orpheus Choir. He had no ticket but, after pleading that he was
an Australian of Scottish descent, he was allowed to sit on the
stairs. The Scottish *Daily Express* reported his pleasure at 'Bonnie
Dundee' and 'Jesu, Joy of Man's Desiring', and said he took a
'flaxen-haired lass' by the hand to sing 'Auld Lang Syne'. Miller
told the reporter: 'I missed my dinner for that concert. But it was
worth it!'

In the final match of the tour, on 17 and 18 September at
Mannofield in Aberdeen, Bradman scored a century, 123 not out
in eighty-nine minutes, to please the 10 000 who had come to see
him off. The show never seemed to stop. He said: 'As a spectacle, it
must have been my best effort on the trip.'

Bradman was an involved cricketer, to the end. He even found
time to comment on a controversial matter in the Aberdeen game.
The light was bad, he said, and 'justified an appeal' when the Scots
were batting a second time, but the Scottish captain, William
Laidlaw, 'said his team was obviously beaten, nobody was in any
danger, they wanted to learn, and the public had come to watch
Australia play and he wished to continue to the end'. Bradman
praised this attitude, comparing it favourably to an incident way
back in Perth, against Western Australia at the very beginning of
the tour, when the local batsmen appealed against the light to save
a draw, even though Johnson and McCool were bowling. Bradman
thought there was something wrong with that. He played every
game, no matter how inconsequential, as seriously as every other.
He was even feeling stressed in Aberdeen.

Another chap and I tried to go shopping one morning in
Aberdeen. I had never been in Aberdeen before, yet I was
stopped some twenty times in little more than half an hour by
people of all ages, usually seeking autographs. On one occasion
a woman wheeling a baby in a pram asked me to sign an

autograph because he would like it when he grew up. He wasn't interested. She had neither pencil nor paper. The sentimental folk will say, 'What a compliment.' That is probably so, but try it yourselves for twenty years and see what it does to your nervous system. Remember, you can't turn this thing on or off like a tap. It goes on perpetually in trains, trams, buses and ships all over the world. If I tried to walk anywhere in London I was often followed by a crowd of small boys.

It was a good time to retire.

Sectors of the English cricket community, too, had had enough of him. At the end of the Scottish leg, the team was invited to Balmoral Castle. At the King's insistence, the scorer-baggageman Ferguson and the press corps were also asked along.

Ian Johnson set the scene:

> It was a lovely autumn day in Scotland; a thin veil of mist hung low on the Highlands, there was a scent of heather in the air. There was also a feeling of excited anticipation among Bradman's men. The tour was over, and we were the first team ever to go through England undefeated. Some of the games had been close, in some we had been lucky – but all that was now past history . . . Our team coach nosed its way towards the white, regal building ahead of us. It looked magnificent, with its background of hills, its terraced gardens, its rolling lawns. Yet there was a homely touch, too, for two corgis were gambolling on the lawns.

As they approached, 'we noticed, framed in one of the windows on the second floor, a girl in blue – Princess Margaret.'

The Queen, who greeted them, 'looked lovely beyond description. As she approached Don Bradman, our suspense was great. But our thrill and relief which followed was enormous, for the Queen immediately broke all formality by saying, "Hallo, Mr Bradman. It's so nice that we have all met before. It's rather like a reunion of old friends."'

Johnson was enchanted. 'As for the Royal ladies – well, photographs have never done them justice. For instance Princess Margaret, who is positively beautiful, like an exquisite Dresden figure.' The Duke of Edinburgh was 'an absolute cracker' who thought England had been better in the series than the margin indicated, and spent half an hour talking with Tallon and Johnson about sailing, shooting and the pleasures of Balmoral. Johnson then had a long conversation with Princess Elizabeth. 'I have never before, or since, felt so very much at ease with anybody on first acquaintance. She said that she had not liked cricket a great deal before her marriage, but added: "When you have a husband who plays the game, you just have to like it, and I am rather surprised now to find that I do."'

And so it went. The humble scorer, Ferguson, was beside himself.

> On previous occasions when I had met royalty, I had invariably had to be content with a handshake and a brief 'How are you?' so it was with a little trepidation that I tried to answer the King's questions as he spoke to me. 'Do you carry an adding machine around with you to use when Bradman is batting?' he asked me. I told him that it was not really necessary!
>
> 'And do you never make any mistakes in your scoring?' was the King's next enquiry. 'Plenty, Your Majesty,' I answered, 'but I always correct them before anyone notices.'
>
> Later we were given tea in the buffet, being again joined by the Royal Family – a very real family, I decided – who moved among us, chatting with the players, making us all imagine that the occasion was nothing more significant than any afternoon tea party with a gathering of nice people . . .

Princess Margaret I liked enormously, thinking that she, of all the Royal Family, provided the perfect answer to critics of the monarchy who still believe that the rulers of this nation are not ordinary people. Margaret would roar with laughter when the chaps cracked jokes with her. A jolly girl, though – like her father – she did not seem very strong physically.

These exercises were of mutual public relations benefit, as long as the public knew about them. That was where the press came in. The Australian media were as seduced as the players and officials, but a photo was taken of Bradman in his three-piece suit walking alongside the King. George VI wore a kilt, and Bradman had his hands in his pockets. Finding a new excuse to attack him, the British media hopped in. He had been 'disrespectful' in the extreme. Bradman did not react publicly, though he was deeply hurt, as he confided a week later on the *Orontes*, in the captain's cabin for a pre-lunch cocktail.

'What was all this trouble, Don, about you having your hands in your pockets when walking with the King at Balmoral?' Captain Winfield asked.

Flanagan observed: 'Bradman betrayed feeling and emotion as he answered slowly and precisely, "Well, in the first place, the Press had no right to be there. In the second place the photo should never have been published. And in the third place, the visit was completely informal and the only reason the King didn't have his hands in his pockets was because he was wearing kilts."'

Bradman recalled the 1934 tour when Bill Woodfull's team had been criticised for wearing their hats while visiting the King, even though His Majesty had asked them to. Bradman joked by quoting a country newspaper: 'it is at least clear that no serious harm can come to those who keep their hands in their own pockets, and that only the income tax collector is permitted by law to put his hands in someone else's.'

Hassett quipped: 'Pocket billiards was not a royal sport.'

Bradman felt every wound. He could never understand why he was criticised. What he missed was that the hands-in-pockets affair was a proxy for pent-up grievances against the way he had conducted the tour. The merciless treatment of county teams, the warlike use of short-pitched bowling, the deployment of Barnes close to the bat, the seeming inability to understand that, after the 1939–45 war, perhaps sport could rediscover a lighter tone . . . The criticism of the hands-in-pockets affair at Balmoral was the release of a five-month accumulation of feeling.

On 20 September, *The People* hosted a farewell luncheon at the Savoy, presenting Bradman with a 378-ounce silver replica of the Warwick Vase, paid for by a shilling fund campaign the newspaper had run during the fourth Test. He donated leftover funds for the construction of concrete wickets in England. Larwood was there, and had his first social chat with Bradman since 1933. Lindwall was thrilled to meet his hero: 'my mind flashed back to those hot December days of 1932 when, from my perch on the Hill, I saw him storm through the pride of Australian batting.' Jardine was not invited.

Three days later, the Piccadilly Hotel was a scene of chaos as players tried to clean up and pack. Not Room 326, however. As Rosenwater wrote: 'While others could not find shoes or shaving brushes, [Bradman] was the first to be ready in a neat lounge suit.'

Yardley and Robins farewelled the team from Tilbury, and Bradman replied to their speeches before stepping onto P&O's *Orontes*. 'As I watched the pier gradually recede, the handkerchiefs waving – not all of them dry – I really felt here was the end of a mission,' he wrote. 'It had been without doubt in every sense the grandest tour of all.'

*

The return voyage, never as well documented as the outgoing one, was a time of great carousing. 'Doc' Roland Pope, who had travelled with earlier Ashes teams, had told Bradman that 'seasickness is something you grow out of after 20 years'. Eighteen years and eight voyages since his first trip, Bradman, finally, was not seasick.

O'Reilly and Hassett spent their evenings in the saloon conducting rival singing groups, said Johnson, 'each trying to drown the other in volume. There was bedlam. O'Reilly's long arms beat the air, and his savagely flushed face and raucous bellowing voice proved too powerful for the Hassett "choir". Suddenly, Lindsay had an inspiration. He led his crowd off in "Danny Boy", the Tiger's favourite. The strains of the melody drifted faintly to O'Reilly as he paused for breath . . . He suddenly burst into "Danny Boy" and then, more loudly than the others, led his own followers in the song.'

Harvey celebrated his twentieth birthday on the *Orontes*. 'The boys gave me a party in the dining room. I didn't drink in those days, but they made up for it. Generally speaking that voyage was a relaxing time after six months of playing six days a week. We were worn out, really. It wasn't easy.'

The RAF in Aden sent a wireless message challenging the team to a cricket game, or, if not, a drink and a meal. When the *Orontes* docked, an air-force launch took nearly all the Australians ashore – but not Bradman. Miller called it 'another "gaffe". The RAF sent him a second invitation to a special lunch in his honour, but he still did not go. Even the "true blue" Bradman boys in the party thought it a bit stiff.'

But Bradman was finished – not with cricket, but with being an Australian cricketer. He would arrive in Australia one stone lighter than when he had left, and he was only a small man to begin with.

12

THE LEGACY

How good were they? Comparisons between eras are absurd, of course, but that has never stopped cricket followers. Within a year, Fingleton and O'Reilly were measuring the 1948 team not only against the teams of the 1930s that they had been a part of, but with the giants of the more distant past.

Fingleton was ready to write, in 1949, that it 'was a good side; it was a grand side and I am sure a more popular Australian side has never visited England, but one must never forget the calibre of the opposition'. He thought Woodfull's 1930 side was better – mainly because Bradman in 1930 was a far superior player to Bradman in 1948, and a team with the Bradman of 1930 was close to unbeatable.

Woodfull's team won the Ashes 2–1 and did not lose to a county. Their only defeat was against the bowling of Maurice Tate and Walter Robins on a poor wicket at Lord's. That team of Woodfull's, dubbed the 'Children's Crusade' because six were aged twenty-three or less, interrupted an eight-year streak of English superiority. The 1930 team's claim to greatness is based on the opposition they faced: England's first Test team was Hobbs, Sutcliffe, Hammond, Woolley, Hendren, Chapman, Larwood, Robins, Tate, Tyldesley and Duckworth. During the series England also used Duleepsinhji, Gubby Allen, Jack White, George Geary, Maurice Leyland, Ian Peebles, Bob Wyatt and Tom Goddard. Has English cricket ever been stronger? Either side of the 1930 series, that set of Englishmen trounced Australia 4–1 twice in Australia. The 1948 Englishmen were barely a shadow of that team, and for that reason Fingleton had many supporters in staking the earlier side's superiority.

O'Reilly looked with similar favour upon the teams of the 1930s. 'It would be kind to pretend that Bradman and his men [of 1948] were world-beaters, too strong for any opposition, but it would not be true,' O'Reilly said. 'As an old player, I am open to the charge that I am necessarily biased in favour of teams with which I myself was actively engaged, but I think I can sidestep any such suspicion.'

Satisfied with his own 'objectivity', O'Reilly thought that in 1948 Bradman, Brown and Hassett were all inferior to the batsmen they were in 1938. In spin bowling, O'Reilly (1934 and 1938) and Clarrie Grimmett (1930 and 1934) were vastly better than the twirlers of 1948. O'Reilly did acknowledge that Lindwall exceeded in pace, accuracy and sheer wicket-taking ability any of the fast bowlers of the prewar era. But that was the only department in which the 1948 team was superior.

The English agreed on the supremacy of Lindwall. Compton sought the opinions of those who could remember Gregory, McDonald and Larwood. 'Lindwall, the majority said, was the most graceful, the greatest fast bowler they had ever seen.'

Bradman concurred: 'The man who so often broke the back of England's batting was this fine athlete. He went on from strength to strength until it became a question whether Australia ever had a better fast bowler.'

Bill Ferguson, who had toured England with every team since 1909, declined to make comparisons. But in his all-time best Anglo–Australian team, he found space for only two of the 1948 series: Bradman and Hutton. The others in his top XI were Noble,

Trumper, Hammond, Hobbs, Rhodes, Grimmett, Larwood, McDonald and Oldfield.

Notwithstanding all the comparisons with the teams of the 1930s, however, the most widely acknowledged benchmarks were Armstrong's team of 1921 and Darling's of 1902. Armstrong's, as has been noted, only lost to MacLaren's ambush at Scarborough in the tour's dying breath. Armstrong's team, which won the Ashes 3–0, was undoubtedly strong in all departments. Its batting strength lay in Herbie Collins, Charlie Macartney, Warren Bardsley and Armstrong. Oldfield was the wicketkeeper, the Gregory–McDonald fast-bowling partnership compared well with Lindwall–Miller, and Arthur Mailey was a better leg spinner than anyone Bradman took in 1948.

Like the 1948 team, however, Armstrong's near-invincibles were playing war-weakened opponents. After both wars, England fielded many old players desperate to extend their careers, and after both wars they took precisely eight years to regain the Ashes.

Armstrong himself said his 1921 team would have been slaughtered by Darling's 1902 team, in which the Big Ship had played as a young man. The 1902 team took on England at its best. Golden Age heroes studded the international and county fixtures: MacLaren, Ranjitsinhji, Jackson, Fry, Jessop, Hirst, Barnes, Rhodes, Lockwood. Australia's team was outstanding in batting, with Darling, Hill, Trumper, Duff, Noble, Gregory and Armstrong, and in bowling, with Jones, Noble, Armstrong, Trumble and Saunders. In a wet summer, the 1902 Australians won the Ashes 2–1, with some of the most exciting Test finishes ever seen. If Australian tours were judged purely by the quality of the opposition they overcame, the 1902 team stands out, followed closely by that of 1930. The opposition faced by Bradman's 1948 team didn't come near.

It was on this basis that Ted Swanton rated the 1902 Australians the best ever. 'The thing to remember is that English cricket at the turn of the century was in the middle of the Golden Age. It was immensely strong. This may seem a romantic judgement by an old dodderer, but, for what it is worth and with deep respect all round, I award the palm to the men of 1902.'

It's also worth considering the star-studded 1882 team that won the inaugural 'Ashes' Test match at The Oval. Here was a tour squad that had the best bowling attack of Test cricket's first quarter-century – Spofforth, Boyle, Palmer, Giffen – and also the best batting – Murdoch, McDonnell, Alec Bannerman, Giffen, Horan and Bonnor. They also played counties and representative teams that had a historic superiority over Australia, and set a standard of credibility for Australian cricket that convinced English cricket followers that the international version exceeded what they were used to seeing domestically.

Of course, that comparisons across eras are academic did not stop Bradman from having a go.

In *Farewell to Cricket*, he said he had performed some statistical analysis comparing the teams of 1948, 1921 and 1902. His team had won 72 per cent of their games, compared with 58 per cent for Armstrong's team and 59 for Darling's. He said that Darling's team had scored 8 runs per wicket more than they conceded, compared with 16 for Armstrong's and 30 for his own. But the variables between tours make such statistical whitewashing farcical, and the most sensible remark Bradman made about the comparison was: 'History may decide whether it was the greatest Australian team ever. I can't. For me, I'm satisfied to say it was a really great team, whose strength lay in its all-round ability, versatility and brilliance allied to bulldog courage. You can often get some of these things; to get the lot is a rarity.'

Reg Hayter, writing in accord, gave Bradman's team *Wisden*'s imprimatur: 'When . . . Bradman claimed that the 1948 side bore comparison with any of its predecessors, he accurately reflected the majority of opinion.'

The sense of greatness that accumulated around the 1948 team over the years has owed as much to romance as to statistics. It was the New South Wales Cricket Association secretary, Bob Radford, who claimed to coin the term 'Invincibles' at a reunion in 1978. Certainly no team since 1948 had matched them. Australian teams won or retained the Ashes in England in 1961, 1964, 1968 and 1975, but none had marched through the kingdom as irresistibly – as invincibly – as the team of 1948. Neil Harvey said that the 1948 team was 'probably the greatest side Australia ever sent to visit England – at least it was far superior to any other side I have travelled with in nine international jaunts'. Ian Chappell's 1975 team only conducted a short tour of England, combined with the inaugural World Cup, and by the end of the 1970s the full six-month tour by Australian teams of England, a tradition going back to 1878, was in eclipse. Certainly the great Australian teams led to England by Allan Border, Mark Taylor and Steve Waugh between 1989 and 2001 could stand beside Bradman's in any purely cricketing comparison, but their tours were not the marathons of Test and first-class cricket that had previously existed, and they did not manage to get through without losing a match. There is, and always will be, only one team of 'Invincibles'.

Given their record, it is surprising how many did not rate 1948 as their happiest tour.

For one thing, as Flanagan recorded, there was a unique kind of pressure in playing under Bradman. 'When the serious part of the tour begins, the strain on the players becomes acute for they are either worrying about their form, about team selections, or whether they will make the Test side. There is really little relaxation.'

Morris, Harvey, Miller, Hassett, Ring, Tallon, Lindwall and Johnston went to South Africa in 1949–50 and England in 1953. Their recorded consensus is that, for all the unrepeatable magnificence of the 1948 tour, those that followed were more fun.

Morris says that in 1953, under Hassett, his batting had a greater 'light-heartedness' than in 1948. 'It was very intense in 1948 and

I put a lot more pressure on myself.'

Lindwall wrote pointedly that Hassett was 'the best leader of men under whom I have played'. The 1953 team fell one match short of invincibility, and unfortunately for them that match was the decider in the Test series. But they were playing against a much-improved England, led at last by a professional in Hutton, and drew greater crowds than even the 1948 record-setters. There was probably no more popular Australian team of the era than Hassett's in 1953. Whitington wrote that when Hassett became Australian captain, he 'restored cricket between his country and England to a game'.

Harvey inherited Bradman's mantle as Australia's champion batsman in 1949–50, when he plundered the South African bowling. He remained his country's batting keystone throughout the 1950s, finishing his career in 1963 with an aggregate second only to Bradman's. Harvey, who toured England in 1948, 1953, 1956 and 1961, wrote: 'In every way the 1961 side [led by Richie Benaud] was the happiest with which I have ever toured. There was complete harmony throughout the five months and more firm friendships were formed among the players than on any previous tour . . . There had been no common room on previous tours and if players wanted to group together they usually had to cram into somebody's bedroom and huddle around in a very limited space.'

Harvey, who has a great nostalgia for his short time under Bradman, also played for Australia under Hassett, Johnson, Morris, Ian Craig and Benaud. 'Bradman was a far less emotional leader than Benaud; he rarely proffered advice to his players and stayed more aloof from the team.'

It is underestandable that for Harvey, as a nineteen-year-old, the 1948 tour contained stresses he outgrew on later tours. But even those who were elder statesmen in 1948 confessed that it was not their favourite tour. Looking back, Bill Brown wrote to Fingleton after the 1948 tour: 'As for team spirit, I feel it didn't come anywhere near the '34, '38 and South African [1935–36] sides.'

The reason for this is undoubtedly the tension exerted by Bradman, both through his demands for an unbeaten tour and through his mere presence. The Invincibles loved winning, of course, but it is unimaginable that Bradman would have done what Hassett did in 1953 and manufactured Bill Johnston's tour so that he would only get out once for a total of 102 runs – a cheeky 'Bradmanian' century average. This is not to say the 1948 tour was unhappy. It was frustrating for players like McCool, Ring and Hamence, it was unfulfilled personally for the vaulting ambitions of Miller and Barnes, but as a team effort it was unanimously satisfying. It just wasn't as light in spirit as other tours.

In 1948 (and since), judging the relative greatness of Bradman's team did not occupy English minds. The tour instead opened a debate about what was wrong with their own cricket.

In batting, wicketkeeping, swing and spin bowling, England's Test team matched Australia. Where they were dramatically outplayed was in fast bowling. The fastest bowlers in England in 1948 were Trevor Bailey, the New Zealander Tom Pritchard, and Derbyshire's Les Jackson. The fastest bowler used in the Test series was Edrich. Colin McCool said: 'What surprised us most was to find that [Bailey] and Tom Pritchard . . . were rated by Englishmen as fast bowlers. Yet they weren't as quick as Sam Loxton, and Sam's pace didn't frighten anybody in Australia.' McCool thought Jackson was 'by far the fastest English bowler' and should have been Bedser's partner all series.

The result of such a scarcity of fast bowling was twofold. First, as Dewes found out whenever he played Miller and Lindwall, 'we didn't have a chance to practise against that kind of pace, so it took us by surprise'. Arlott said that after Hutton and Washbrook had been 'manifestly uneasy' in the first Test, 'No practice could be found . . . anywhere in England against bowling of comparable speed. They took their practice only in matches against Australia.'

Nor could England retaliate, either with wicket-taking or threat. Lindwall's response to the criticism of his bouncers was that England's 'only regret, sometimes expressed publicly and often in private, has been that England possessed no one capable of bowling the same type of ball'. Australia's bouncer attacks could, then, proceed with impunity.

Compton was not alone in believing that Lindwall – and Miller when fit and in the mood – proved the difference between the teams. (Although Bedser, it has to be said, blamed the loss on England's batsmen: 'I do not consider the England attack was exactly overwhelmed . . . England's batting failures did not give the bowlers a decent total to bowl to.') In Compton's view, England's batting in 1948 was better than in their Ashes-winning 1954–55 and 1956 teams. The figures give him some support. Even amid their Ashes frustrations, Washbrook, who averaged 93 in county games, and Hutton, who averaged 92, were enjoying bountiful seasons – when not facing Australia's bowlers. In the Tests, said Compton, they had to bat 'when the Miller-Lindwall attack was at its greatest and most unrelenting, and was being used with consummate skill by Bradman. It was a major part of the greatest attack Australia has ever had. If we had had a fast attack I think we could easily have won that series.'

In its review of the 1948 season, the MCC said the standard of English cricket had not improved as quickly as expected after the war because of the continuation of national service; the ongoing postwar economic crisis leading to the 'Control of Engagement Order', which 'created a serious difficulty over the recruitment of younger players'; the existence of full employment, deterring young men from making cricket their career; and that 'a period of post-war reaction in England instead of getting less has if anything become intensified and this may account for some uncertainty in the players' outlook towards the game'. This was Lord's way of sniffing at the rise of social democratic politics. The ascent of Attlee's Labour Party, they felt, was corroding the old stability of the amateur–professional cricket economy.

The war's impact on English cricket showed mostly in the scarcity of fast bowlers. As Compton said, 'In a fast bowler's life six years is a long time – indeed it may be the whole of his effective career – and that means many a potential pace bowler never got his chance because of the war.'

Whitington had asked the same question when the English toured Australia in 1946–47: 'I've often wondered how differently cricket history may have evolved had Voce, Pollard and Compton been used to good food in 1939 through to 1945, instead of being confronted with it for a month in Perth for the first time in six years.'

Ken Farnes, who would have been in his late thirties by 1948, was the only known top-class England express bowler to die in the war, but the war years militated against fast bowlers building themselves up over time. Lindwall and Miller were in active service, the best place to get a good feed. The effect of poor nutrition was also felt in the overall culture of English cricket. When the game resumed after the war, not only were there no strapping young fast bowlers who had reached their physical maturity in the early 1940s, as had Lindwall and Miller, but county cricket was full of older men prolonging their careers to make up for lost time, and the spirit of postwar England was hardly conducive to the risks inherent in tearing in and bowling fast. The standard of county cricket, generally, was lower than at any time since 1921.

O'Reilly observed the sharp decline of county cricket since 1938: 'English cricket cannot do itself justice when the standard of county cricket is so low . . . the Australians had a fairly hollow round of victories against a range of spent volcanoes which masqueraded under the name of English county clubs.'

What was most inopportune for England in 1948 was the mechanism the MCC used to address the fast-bowling scarcity. The experimental rule of allowing a second new ball after fifty-five six-ball overs, meant to encourage fast bowling, decimated spin bowling and flooded county cricket with medium-pace inswing bowlers imitating Bedser. McCool, its chief victim on the Australian side, said, 'All it did was to send England plunging to humiliating defeat, and to put the game of cricket as a whole on its sick-bed.' Halfway through the 1948 series, at its 16 July meeting, the MCC was already discussing changing the law to extend the first ball's life to sixty-five overs. The 55-over rule was long abandoned by the time English fast bowling renewed itself in the mid 1950s, in Frank Tyson, Fred Trueman, Peter Loader and Brian Statham. 'I think,' said Compton, 'and have always thought, that the decision was a stupid one – perhaps the fact that it was so quickly changed proves my point.'

In the 1948 Tests, the 55-over rule gave Bradman's Australians a decisive advantage. On lush English grounds and uncovered wickets, the ball was never allowed to grow old. 'I have always had the impression that we saw very little of the old ball,' Compton said. 'You seemed constantly to be facing Miller and Lindwall with the new one.' Sometimes it got wet, or Lindwall, Johnston and Miller needed a rest, but this was where Bradman exploited the rule by using Toshack and Johnson cynically with slow leg theory.

'Their function was to close the game down until the new ball was due, and they closed it down completely: right down,' Compton said. 'It was an unattractive but tactically effective way of playing the game. I never thought that Toshack was a great bowler, although he was an efficient one, and was just what Bradman needed under the circumstances.' He had five men on the leg side and 'it was very difficult indeed to get after him'.

Johnson, one of the containment bowlers, agreed – albeit from a winner's perspective. 'Often when Lindwall and Miller returned with the new ball little over a hundred runs were on the board – a miserable prospect for the batting side.'

Leg theory as a defensive tactic, which had flourished before World War I, was revived in 1948 and persisted into the 1950s. The success of the Bedser–Hutton trap against Bradman gave defensive leg theory a life that survived his retirement: the placement of three short legs and a man deep on the square-leg fence remained common in the next three Ashes series. 'Negative cricket started in [1948] and has continued since, and seems a very difficult weed to uproot,' said a frustrated Compton. 'It is somewhat ironical that Bradman, now the greatest advocate of brighter cricket, should have started it, for start it he did.'

But McCool did not blame Bradman for using it to his best advantage; nor, for that matter, did he believe Bradman had initiated the change. 'Despite many claims to the contrary, the suggestion that an experimental rule should be tried was made by England, not Australia . . . Quite unjustly and irrationally, Bradman has been labelled as the man responsible for this depressing trend. What Bradman did was to devise a way of making Australia unbeatable. And that he did uncommonly well, without once stretching the rules or bruising the spirit of the game.'

In 1950, Bradman was optimistic that the wheel would soon turn for English cricket. 'Throughout cricket's history the standard of play has fluctuated. One era was termed "The Golden Age". Since then we have gone off the gold standard. Cricket in England is at this very moment surrounded by great difficulties, not the least being of an economic character. Even so, great players still exist. They will continue to develop. The heart of cricket is sound and still beats strongly as a symbol of British character and tradition.'

It must also be remembered that the Test series of 1948 was considerably closer than the 4–0 scoreline suggests. An irritated Compton said: 'I feel that although the Australians were a greater side than we were, we have never quite had the fair assessment of our abilities which the England players of that year deserved.'

Washbrook wouldn't go so far as to say the Australians were lucky to win, 'but it must not be forgotten that rain robbed us of nearly the whole of the last two days' play at Manchester . . . If we had won then we might also have won at Leeds . . . and who can tell what would have happened in the last Test if we had gone to The Oval all-square instead of three down?'

In a wetter English summer, Washbrook speculated, the Australian batsmen would have struggled to score heavily. Yorkshire, in Bradford, had shown their limitations on soft wickets; Washbrook considered Barnes their only comfortable soft-wicket player, and his absence accounted for their batting failures in the Old Trafford Test match. Washbrook thought Australia's success was due to the majority of matches being played on pace-friendly wickets.

This sounds like a stretch, and it is, but it shows that the series should never be regarded as one-sided. The teams were antagonists, no less than the teams of later eras. Big cricket was never a gentlemen's game.

Few could doubt Bradman's singular contribution, as a captain, to the success of the Invincibles. Johnson remembered his first Test, when Bradman stayed with him while he ate his breakfast despite having numerous other duties. '[H]e came back so that I, a young player new to the strain and tension of international cricket, would not be left alone with my thoughts. In many respects that may seem a small thing but it was typical of Bradman and something which I appreciated more than I could say.'

Johnson was, it is true, something of a favourite of Bradman. But he was an accurate and perceptive observer, and as a bowler had first-hand experience of the most important of a captain's skills.

'On the field, Bradman handled his bowlers very humanly and, if he wanted to move a fieldsman from one position to another, he would explain his reasons for the move to the bowler. If the bowler wished to move a fieldsman, Don would want to know the reason. The bowler's explanation would be met either with, "Well, yes, it's a very good idea, let's try it," or, "I don't like it very much, but let's try it if you want to.'"

Johnson's description of Bradman's on-field enthusiasm squares with that of every other watcher. 'Bradman, on the field, was very much an extrovert and allowed what was almost a boyish enthusiasm to reveal his various reactions to events.'

His zest complemented his tactical nous, Johnson said:

> I think that he, possibly more than any captain before him, set different fields for each different batsman . . . In only one phase of captaincy did Bradman's genius fall below the level he set for himself. That was in his ability to decide how a wicket would play. In this he was no more knowledgeable than most players of comparable experience . . . Contrary to general opinion, Don was not a disciplinarian. He relied upon the individual's common sense and rarely did his players let him down. All Bradman asked was that you were fit each day to take the field. Apart from that, he had no objection to anything the players did in their leisure time.

From the press box, Arlott could find nothing to fault in Bradman's captaincy:

> As a captain he did the right thing almost automatically, for the idiom of the game [has] become his native language. High-shouldered, shirt collar turned up to the chin, cap pulled well on, he walked backwards to his position in the field as the bowler walked to his mark. His eyes moved alertly as a blackbird's, and he would stop the game while, back cautiously turned to the batsman, he passed his latest intelligence to the bowler. He set the defensive field with true Australian mastery. He nursed his bowlers wisely and received magnificent service from his fieldsmen.

Bradman's opponents felt as if he, personally, encircled them. Compton said that 'he seemed to know almost all that was to be known about each individual player, and he used his knowledge with powerful effect . . . Batting against a side captained by him always gave you the feeling that you had been carefully examined, studied and thought about, and that the attack was organised accordingly. This was never more apparent than in 1948.' The Englishmen sensed the way in which Bradman 'seemed to be able to spread his cricketing skill through his team, and so give a lift to their competence and their confidence'. For Compton, Bradman's captaincy was as vital a weapon as Lindwall's outswinger or Miller's bumper.

Though a captain is rarely better than the quality of his bowlers, Yardley, who only had one Bedser to Bradman's quartet of top-line seamers, still acknowledged his counterpart's tactical prowess:

> Hardly ever have I known him miss the crucial moment of a game; yet the greatest captains in cricket history have sometimes done so. He sees his chance and takes it dispassionately; and he is just as quick to rob an opponent of any opportunity. He is relentless; having got you down, he will strive with every ounce of power that is in him to grind you down, so that you shall never forget it and, if possible, never feel confident against him again. He is what you might call a psychological cricketer. He never relaxes, even though your chance of victory may have hopelessly gone long ago.

Yardley could not articulate his admiration without it beginning to shade towards suspicion and criticism. A gentleman on the field, regarded as too soft to be a good Test captain, Yardley showed a sharper edge in his memoir. At bottom, he did not feel that he quite understood Bradman.

'Does anyone know Bradman? Has anyone ever got under his cool, armoured surface? Certainly not I; and I doubt if even the men who have served in his own sides longest really know their Bradman.'

But then, Yardley said, what could you understand of, or how could you quite forgive, Bradman's inability to recognise the limits to healthy competitiveness?

'I personally enjoyed playing against him and his team in 1948,' Yardley concluded. '[T]here were no disagreements or serious incidents whatever during the whole series. At the same time I felt that he let his relentless determination to win sometimes run away with him. For a captain to appeal vehemently for lbw from cover-point or the gully is, to my mind, inexcusable.'

There it was, again: among the English cricketers, the Bradman of 1948 left a sour taste. They admired and respected him, but players like Yardley, Compton and Edrich just didn't like the way he led Australia.

Said Compton: 'Bradman, to put it mildly, had some qualities which were difficult to like or admire . . . one never had the impression that he forgave easily, and in one instance, at least, he hardly spoke to an opponent for twenty years after a comment, admittedly not a very kind one, but probably just, made on the field during the progress of a Test in Australia.'

He was referring, most likely, to Jack White, the spin bowler who had called Bradman his 'bunny' in 1928–29, when Bradman was a boy. By 1948, as a middle-aged man, even after six years of war, he was still hell-bent on making Englishmen pay.

Arlott found that 1948 was a summer from which it took a long time to recover. Sport as war by another means was back.

> It has not been a soft season. The season of the Australian visit is a business season. English county cricket must rise early, polish its buttons and go on parade . . . The tourists, whether they like it or not – and usually they do not – make a procession, rather than a tour, round England. Every county ground they visit is packed until its pre-war wooden fences bulge and creak.

For their match only, in all the season, the pavilion is over-full, the specators uncomfortable, the caterers conscious of inadequate resources. The dust of cramped crowds permeates the quietest of provincial cricket fields, and the atmosphere is changed by those who come to see the Australians, but not, necessarily, to see the cricket. The unfortunate Australian dare not put his nose outside his hotel without being surrounded by a posse of autograph hunters who feel as little respect as they show for their victims . . .

Test matches also fray the nerves more than cricket . . . No, it has not been a soft season.

Bradman, in the years after his retirement, was not the unimpeachable cricket god he later became. He was a figure of great controversy and no little criticism. His 1950 autobiography seems excessive in its self-justification. But in 1950, he felt he had a lot of enemies to answer.

Bradman's unpopularity may be measured by the stridency of his self-defence, and by the others who rushed to his aid. Bill Ferguson wrote:

[I]t is surprising how many people imagine that Don – as a man – did not enjoy the confidence, or the affection of those who served under him. This legend of Bradman's unpopularity is quite unearned . . . Aloof? If such a charge were true, Don Bradman would never have consulted his colleagues after winning the toss, asking for their views about whether he should bat or bowl – but I have often seen him do it. Unpopular? In 1948, Bradman's last tour of England, he was desperately keen to go through the trip undefeated and, knowing all about the normal 'looseness' which follows the final Test, appealed to his team to keep up the good work, not only against the counties, but also in the festival games. Their response, at a time when laxity and carelessness could

have been condoned, is the finest testimony to the popularity
of the 'unpopular' Don.

Andy Flanagan alluded to the criticisms when he wrote: 'In some
quarters Bradman has been accused of being a relentless captain,
and I am among those who subscribe to the belief that Bradman
plays to win, but to win fairly. Surely no one can cavil at that.
Sport knows no greater insult than to patronise an opponent.'

Bradman himself gave a well-worn response: 'Very early in my
career, a friend passed on a piece of advice. "You cannot make
people love you," he said, "but you can make them respect you." If
I have been able to do the latter – and I believe I have – my efforts
have not been in vain.'

Most of the reasons for Bradman's unpopularity have already
been canvassed here. Taken as individual issues, they are all
debatable. His exploitation of the 55-over rule, his deployment of
negative fields, his hypocritical condonement of bumper attacks, his
probable white-anting of Hutton through the Robins connection,
his merciless pursuit of victory in the county games, his brutal use
of Miller and his manipulation of the Leveson-Gower selection are
controversies that have two sides, and one could reasonably take
Bradman's side in each of them. He certainly took care of that in
his autobiography. But there was an overarching pattern here, with
ramifications far beyond the individual issues. It goes to the way
cricket could have been played after the war, and how Bradman
stopped that from happening, redirecting it on a route that it has
followed ever since.

Rosenwater, a fair but mostly admiring biographer of Bradman,
noting that Australia didn't lose one of its first twenty Tests after
the war (the first loss was in the last Test of the 1950–51 series),
says their cricket 'was characterised by efficiency approaching
ruthlessness . . . Much of this ruthlessness stemmed directly from
the influence of Bradman. He liked to win, and he liked even
more not to lose . . . His influence in this respect has never left

Australian cricket. Australians were formidable opponents before Bradman, but never quite so consistently ruthless as they were after he emerged.'

This is the key issue when assessing the legacy of 1948, and it broaches the great taboo of Bradman's war years. There is no doubt that when the war ended, the spirit of the Victory Tests augured a new era for cricket, in which men who had seen the worst of mankind could play a game in a way that celebrated the best. Cricket could be a direct antidote and response to warfare. Whitington said the essential message of the Victory Tests was that 'Cricket was meant for making friends, not enemies; for making fun and friendly fight, not money.'

Bill Brown's Australian tour of New Zealand in 1945–46, the tour when, Johnson said, 'we partied our way around the country', also embodied this postwar spirit. Warrior-cricketers could bring a new joy to the game – they could renew the meaning of 'sport'. But when Bradman came back in 1946, he brought back his old bitter competitiveness; his way of playing sport was war by another name. O'Reilly (another non-participant in the war) supported him fully. But those who had fought saw things a different way. Whitington wrote after 1948: 'I doubt whether Don could help doing that which was not so magnificent or good. It was in him and had to come out. But when the bright sun that was Bradman the batsman ceased shining, the army-general of a captain, the behind-the-scenes manipulator that was Bradman left a lot of night.'

Bradman did not experience the war as a soldier. He spent it on his wife's parents' farm at Bowral, and stockbroking for a crook in Adelaide. The war seemed somehow to have left his approach to cricket untouched. From Hammond's 'That's a bloody fine way to start' in Brisbane in 1946, right through to the last game of the 1948 tour, Bradman played cricket as the 'army-general' he had never been in the services.

Those who saw the war closest have a privileged voice in these matters. Edrich, the man who was nearest to the action – as a

DFC-winning pilot who lost many mates to the Germans, as a batsman who hooked Lindwall off his nose, and as the retaliating 'pea-shooter' – expressed his hope for a change when Bradman 'retired to the Olympian heights of cricket control'. He deserves to be quoted at length:

> Do not for one moment suppose that I am blaming Don because a new bitterness has come into the game around his figure and performances . . . A batsman so supremely great, so much above his contemporaries, was bound to be the mark of every Test bowler, the particular study of every fieldsman, the cynosure of all Press cameras, the flashpoint of cricket criticism so that every word he spoke and every word he omitted to say, on or off the field, was taken, boomed, twisted, misinterpreted, sent echoing round the world. Don's personality, whatever it may have been when he was just the boyish Bowral Wonder, became a little soured, a little super-sensitive to such a position; and no wonder. Certainly, when 'bodyline' limelighted him years ago, he had plenty to say about 'boots and all' Test match tactics; but nearly all cricketers agree that, since 1945, Australia under his captaincy had shown more ruthlessness, more cold-blooded determination to win, even at the cost of happy relationships, than any country has displayed, in 1932–3 or on any other occasion at all . . .
>
> I rate him as the best captain of a cricket team since 1914 – and perhaps ever. At the same time, I much prefer playing against a captain who allows cricket to remain a game. I am not trying to give Don a knock; it is simply a question of a different outlook and approach, and judged on results his are better than anyone's; but I know most cricketers, Australians as well as English, feel as I do.

No other participant has given a more moving and durable epitaph to 1948.

*

Bradman elucidated two aims for his captaincy: to foster attacking cricket and to promote goodwill. He believed he had done both, and when he wanted to bring forward evidence in support of his case, he had trunks full of admiring letters from the public. Here, Bradman felt, was his true constituency: the thousands who wrote to him. No doubt his unbending habit of responding personally to his mail was the result of a natural and admirable courtesy. But his correspondence would also have provided a shrine of greatness in which he could shelter every night. Imagine, a man retreating from his team to spend hour after hour, night after night, reading letter after letter from common folk telling him how magnificent he was. Little wonder he trusted his judgements, and little wonder he felt, always, that he had right on his side. He cited a letter written to him while he was in England:

> Myself, I write as an ordinary English workman who has been privileged to witness the displays of your team and you at Trent Bridge and Lord's, and what a feast of enjoyment and a tonic they have been to me in these rather exacting times. Also on returning home from a hard day's work the radio commentaries have been so full of interest that we (and I know I speak for other workers) have forgotten about the little less sugar we now have in our tea and the shortage of meat on our plate!!

Bradman's prestige among the English public, the multitudes who felt the same way about him as that 'ordinary English workman', created an atmosphere that had no parallel in the sporting world. Flanagan observed: 'Bradman, in England, almost disputes popularity with Royalty. He is the absolute monarch of cricket.'

Dignitaries were as effusive as the common man. The British Minister of State, Philip Noel-Baker, said in 1948, 'No team has ever done so much to stimulate and to create good feeling.' Sir

Norman Birkett, who gave the charming speech of welcome to
Bradman in London in April, wrote a foreword to Fingleton's
1949 book in which he had had time to reflect on the meaning of
the tour.

> There is sometimes a tendency when writing of cricket to
> use the language of unreality, and to ascribe to cricket moral
> qualities and perfections that are not its sole prerogative . . .
> But I also like to think that the tour of 1948, because of certain
> exceptional circumstances, has brought us nearer to each
> other than ever before . . . The nature of the welcome given
> to the Australian team in all parts of the country was quite
> remarkable. Conventional language scarcely does justice to
> it. It was, I believe, much more than the traditional welcome
> to our brethren from overseas; it was in some measure a
> thanksgiving that one of the great institutions of our common
> life had been restored. The great crowds . . . did more than
> testify to their love of cricket; they did more than pay their
> affectionate tribute to a consummate captain of a great team;
> they did more than give expression to their joy in seeing
> that team once more in their midst; they gave utterance to
> their deep-seated satisfaction, after years of darkness and
> danger, that cricket had once more come into its kingdom in
> these great and historic encounters. For not the least of the
> deprivations of war is that the glory and the grace of cricket
> depart for a season . . . To see the Australian team emerging
> once more from the pavilion after the years of war was to be
> filled with thankfulness and pride and happiness, and not a
> little emotion.

Whatever the debates about Bradman's captaincy on the cricket
field, and whatever view is taken on his ethics and motivations
in destroying his opponents, there can be no gainsaying the
ambassadorial value of his appearance in England in 1948.

Yet it continued to take the personal toll that it had exacted
in the 1930s. Bradman did not welcome fame. It drove him back
into himself. His need for privacy put him inside his hotel room,
or in the home of friends such as Robins, so that he could not be
a captain to his men in the fullest sense of the word – as captains
such as Hassett, Benaud and Ian Chappell would be – and he also
missed out on the camaraderie sport offers the less-exalted.

Arlott, among others, was greatly sympathetic. 'Because he is
"a success", because he is a public figure, because he is Bradman,
he has missed much of the best of cricket. He has never been a
temporary failure among other temporary failures, never shared
with ten others, neither appreciably greater nor appreciably less
than himself, that sympathy and mutual delight in temporary
success which the other cricketer knows.' Of the 1948 tour,
Arlott summarised: 'From late April until late September 1948,
in England, Donald George Bradman played cricket, captained a
cricket team, made speeches, was polite to bores, ignored the spite
of those who grudged him that he had earned, kept his temper and
consolidated a great public reputation. He gained more of respect
than of envy from those who sought to understand.'

O'Reilly and Fingleton, who have been misrepresented as
implacable enemies of Bradman (not least by Bradman himself,
who exaggerated their enmity), showed a deep sympathy and
understanding for the isolation into which celebrity drove him. At
the end of the 1948 tour, O'Reilly wrote:

> I have seen him be recognised in Regent Street, London, and a
> crowd of people gathered in split seconds to have a good look
> at him. When the team is due to leave its hotel to go off to a
> Test match ground . . . thousands of people congregate outside
> and block the traffic in their eagerness to see the 'Great Don'.
> That type of glory might appeal to the boy fresh from school,
> but to Bradman and any man who has been through the mill
> it is nauseating, to say the least. Bradman has never been free

from it since his first glorious trip to England. That explains
why it is that I have always been extremely sorry for him.

Aside from Bradman, being an Invincible was to be its own reward,
materially. Broadcast rights were not what they are now: the tour
was the first to be seen on television, and the BBC had paid the
MCC £250 for the rights. There was good reason for such a small
fee: the signal only reached a radius of fifty miles around Alexandra
Palace, and just 4.3 per cent of the adult population had a television
set. Gate receipts remained cricket's main source of income, but
not one that flowed to the players. The Australians' share of the
tour gate was 82 675, more than double the previous record. The
Australian players were each paid £600, including £150 that the
Board retained until after the tour as a bond for 'good conduct',
plus a silver cigarette case. Keith Johnson's expense account for the
1948 tour totalled seventy-five pounds. 'It is incredible, but it is
true', said Flanagan, and it 'proves the niggardliness and pettiness
of the men controlling this great organisation'. After expenses, the
Australian Board netted £54 172 from the tour.

The hotels, moreover, were far from top-class. Of the twenty-
four hotels the Australians used, Bradman reported that those in
Worcester, Leicester, Bradford, Nottingham, Bristol, Leeds and
Birmingham should be rejected on future tours. For the Piccadilly,
the team's home away from home in London, he noted: 'Bad, get
another'. Only fifteen of the twenty-four were rated 'Good'.

The £600 tour fee included expenses and was taxable. For the
same period, an Australian on the lowest legal Commonwealth
wage would have earned approximately £200. But it cost a player
such as Lindwall about £400 to keep his family during his time
away, and 'my own expenses were extremely high. I had to pay
for my own cricket clothes and equipment, my ordinary clothes,
smokes, drinks, entertainment and any travel not made with the
official party.' Players were allowed 7s 6d for breakfast, 10s 6d for

dinner, but paid out of their own pocket anything above that. Prices were high in London and costs were always above the allowance. In 1953, Lindwall estimated he broke even on the tour but 'some of my colleagues throught they would be as much as £200 to £250 down.'

Of the 1948 team, he wrote, 'Not all the team suffered complete loss of wages through undertaking the tour but only a few, such as those with their own business, did not have to take a very substantial salary cut while away, and those with Government jobs had to be reconciled to falling eight months behind in the service seniority lists.'

Johnson thought a single man 'can make a nice profit' from the tour but a married man with a family 'saves little, if anything. After all, when he is away he is virtually keeping two homes going . . . I venture to say most of them at the end of a tour are worse off financially than at the start.'

This state of affairs had led Bradman to seek individual deals outside cricket. Writing for newspapers had got him into trouble with the Board in the 1930s, but by 1948 he was doing nicely enough from sponsorships and gifts.

His example could only lead the entrepreneurially minded to try to do the same. No cricketer could command the endorsements and gifts of Bradman, but some could try.

On his return to Australia, Barnes had so much commercial cargo, mainly English cloth, that he was worried about breaching customs regulations. When he heard customs officers were awaiting him in Sydney, he disembarked in Melbourne and went home by train. His biographer Rick Smith wrote: 'The move succeeded and he was able to sell all his stock at a substantial profit, supplementing his tour fees. No one but Sid knew just how much he made, but the most conservative estimate is that it was at least equal to his fee for making the tour.'

Barnes also made a film from the footage he shot during the tour, and in 1949 toured it around Australia. Sometimes the crowds of thousands were so big that people fainted in the crush.

He said he made £10 000 'for charity and sporting organisations', but Barnes wouldn't have been Barnes if he hadn't taken a little off the top.

At the end of the film he made a cheeky remark about how, having 'been playing solidly for five and a half months, six days a week, early in the morning to late in the afternoon, we were unbeaten and we had made record profits. The Board of Control decided that we had fully earned a rest . . . And so, after 48 hours' holiday, we said farewell to England.'

Barnes could not afford to take the 1949–50 tour of South Africa, for which the players received £450 each. He did not play for Australia again, leaving his career, of thirteen Tests with an average of 63, an 'unfinished symphony' like his second innings at Trent Bridge. In 1952, after continual non-selection in Australian teams, Barnes went to court, ostensibly in a defamation case against a member of the public, J.L. Raith, who had had a letter published that denigrated Barnes's character, but effectively against the Board of Control, which had to defend the assertion that Barnes had been kept out of the Test team for non-cricketing reasons. Keith Johnson, by then a director of the Board, took the stand. Surprisingly, he brought up various Barnes 'misdemeanours' from the 1948 tour: asking for permission to travel alone to see his wife, shooting movie pictures, and distracting Toshack from his twelfth man duties to play tennis at Northampton. Johnson's written report to the Board at the end of the 1948 tour had said 'the team behaved in a manner befitting worthy representatives of Australia. On and off the field their conduct was exemplary and I feel that they have contributed something to our Empire relations.' But in 1952, he said that he would make an exception of Barnes, admitting that he gave the Board verbal reports that conflicted with the written report. Johnson agreed with Barnes's barrister that he was misleading the state associations by giving separate verbal opinions. Johnson admitted that he had consented to Barnes shooting films and travelling alone in 1948. He disputed how close the Northampton tennis court was to the pavilion. Johnson said he had opposed Barnes becoming New South Wales captain in 1951–52 as he was 'temperamentally unsuitable'.

Barnes won the case, but the affair left him on the outer with many of his 1948 teammates. It also affected Keith Johnson, who, Loxton said, 'took the rap for others' by standing up in the 1952 case. As always, Johnson was prepared to put personal considerations aside for what he perceived to be a greater good.

On the way home from the 1948 tour, during the Melbourne stopover, Lindwall 'became involved in a merry party' and nodded off in a garden. A teammate told him to get out of the pouring rain. Lindwall staggered to his feet, only to find 'a crowd of guests, enjoying the joke tremendously. When I peered through the mists in front of my eyes I saw that the moon was shining brightly and not a cloud was to be found anywhere!'

The 1948 Australians enjoyed their success as much as any other group of young men. But then there were jobs to be resumed, families to be supported, and, within a month, a new cricket season to be played.

Bradman appeared in two testimonial matches before retiring. He was knighted in 1949, although, he said, 'No man ever had less ambitions in that direction. I neither desired nor anticipated any recognition of my services. They had been spontaneously given. There was no thought of reward. However, it was clear that I was the medium through which was to be expressed England's appreciation of what Australian cricket has meant to the British Empire.'

He came under some pressure to stand for parliament – the first rumours of which had reached him while he was coming home on the *Orontes*. The question was asked and an answer recorded in parliamentary Hansard. But for what side? When the *Orontes* berthed at Fremantle, a docker called out, 'If you're going into parliament, Don, you'd better stand for the Labor Party.' Another message came from a senator who asked Jessie to use her influence to keep Don out of politics – citing the example of Churchill, reduced from a 'world idol to a political stooge by the same people who would exploit the affection and respect that is held by all Australians for your husband'.

Bradman, sensibly, reserved his ambitions for private business and a lengthy career as a director, chairman and selector for the Australian and South Australian cricket administrations.

In Australia's next Test tour, to South Africa, nine Invincibles remained: Hassett, Morris, Harvey, Johnson, Johnston, Lindwall, Loxton, McCool and Saggers. Miller was later added after being left out. Tallon was picked but withdrew with injury. The other six were Bradman, Toshack and Brown (all retired), Barnes (unavailable), Hamence and Ring.

Hassett only won the Test captaincy ahead of Morris by one vote. Ray Robinson said this was 'an act of disgusting ingratitude' after Hassett's vice-captaincy in England in 1948. 'With Bradman absorbed by the duties and interests of an active businessman-captain, Hassett never spared himself in keeping the side ticking over as a companionable party.'

Neil Harvey, who amassed 663 runs at 137 in the series in South Africa, was a great admirer of Hassett's captaincy over the next four years. Hassett, he wrote, 'must go down as one of Australia's most astute captains ever'. Harvey praised him as a tactician and field setter, 'always thinking out ways to whittle down the opposing batting strength. He was never afraid to experiment and knew how to make the most of a particular batsman's weakness.' His batting thrived on captaincy responsibilities, often opening with Morris when needed.

> [And he] was one of the greatest characters in sport. He had a
> wonderfully wry sense of humour and believed in enjoying life

to the full . . . For all his humour and sense of fun, however, Lindsay was a serious little bloke once he got out in the middle, directing an attack or keeping the opposition at bay with his sweet footwork and straight-flowing blade. He was never a strong disciplinarian, yet everything he ever suggested was done immediately. His decisions were always clear-cut and thoughtful.

Morris, edged out as captain, would lead Australia in two Tests in the early 1950s as a stand-in. The 1948 tour would prove to be his peak as a batsman, but he continued as arguably Australia's greatest postwar opener until, in 1955, he retired when he learnt that his first wife, Valerie, had a terminal cancer. As Harvey wrote of him, 'Modest and mild of disposition he won friends even more easily than he made runs. He was never a selfish player and if his side was out of danger he was always prepared to toss his innings away and let one of the middle order batsmen have a knock.'

Morris covered cricket tours as a journalist for a short period, which Miller recalled as being a peculiar challenge for him. 'Arthur Morris rarely watched a ball from the dressing-room. Usually he read a book or magazine after getting out. Or maybe he would have a rub down or write a letter, or take forty winks. Then he took a job as a newspaper correspondent and had to watch every ball that was bowled!'

Later, Morris was a member of the Sydney Cricket Ground Trust and remains a courteous, well-loved torch-bearer for Australian cricket. His sense of humour has remained intact in his home on the Central Coast of New South Wales. Asked, for instance, if he ever played lawn bowls, he shakes his head and says, 'I couldn't afford the wreaths.'

In 1948, John Arlott said of him, 'he is virtually infallible, temperament and technique are so blended in his play as to make it difficult to imagine any possible ground for improvement.

He is infallibly thoughtful, infallibly good-mannered, infallibly considerate, infallibly purposeful.'

Harvey played Test cricket until 1963, when in most opinions he had surpassed Morris and Clem Hill as Australia's greatest left-handed batsman. He owned his own sales businesses and served Australia as a selector in the 1970s. Now the 83-year-old baby of the tour continues to live in Sydney. His comments on cricket, sometimes stringent, are uttered in a tone rich with love for the game.

Sam Loxton became a member of the Victorian parliament after retiring from cricket, and was also a Test selector in the 1970s. He lost a wife and son in separate tragic accidents in recent years, and in 2010 a stroke robbed him of his sight. But he continued supporting and attending cricket from the home he shared on the Gold Coast with his son Peter, until he died in late 2011.

Barnes was the first Invincible to pass away, from an overdose of pills in 1973. By the time of the fiftieth-anniversary reunion in 1998, McCool, Saggers, Hassett, Lindwall and Tallon had also died. Between the fiftieth and sixtieth anniversaries, Ring, Johnston, Toshack, Miller, Johnson, Bradman and Brown had gone too.

Len Hutton made a wonderful recovery from the travails of 1948. He became England's first professional captain since 1886–87 and led his country to Ashes wins in 1953 and 1954–55. Limiting him had always been the secret to Bradman's success in 1948, and Lindwall acknowledged as much when he said: 'Len Hutton must come next to Bradman for skill allied to certainty. I have bowled to Len scores of times and occasionally I have taken his wicket, but I cannot truthfully say that I have been anything but surprised when I have done so.'

If only Hutton had known that in 1948, he might have had a better time. But pessimism was his nature. Johnson, who was his opposing captain in 1954–55, said:

[Hutton] is by nature dour and suspicious of all opponents . . .
I respect him for it, but I feel that he tends to carry his intensity
to play to win – an intensity with which I entirely agree on
the field – far too much off the field, so that he cannot relax.
The Australian approach is, 'The day's play is over, now let's
enjoy ourselves.' Len never seemed able to do that. When one
day's play ended, he settled down to plan out the next and
fraternisation with the opposition did not enter his scheme of
things at all.

Bedser, Compton and Evans also went on to prosper in Test cricket
through the 1950s. In one way, though, the defeat of 1948 was
a blessing to England. The older generation had reached its use-
by date, and from the early 1950s youth was given its head. This
resulted in England's winning three straight Ashes series from 1953
to 1956, as the pendulum of regeneration swung their way.

At time of writing, the only surviving England Test player from
1948 is John Dewes, who lives with his wife Shirley in Bath. His
memory is not flawless on the past five minutes, but he remembers
1948 clearly. A number of county players who faced the Invincibles,
including Hubert Doggart, Doug Insole and Tony Pawson, also
survive. Allan Watkins, who made his debut at The Oval in 1948
and suffered the pain of a Lindwall bruiser to his shoulder, passed
away in August 2011.

For the Australians of 1948, being an Invincible meant more and
more as time went by. Loxton, whose Test career was over within
two years, became a champion of the team's legacy. Bill Johnston
said, over-modestly as always, that he would have been forgotten
if not for his association with that team. Morris and Harvey were
great Australian Test batsmen for years after 1948, but since their
teammates began to pass away in numbers, the pair have become
spokesmen for the generation of '48.

The effect of so many lives passing away is to obscure the way the team was seen in its own time. In the years after the war, cricket audiences were looking for a new start; a way of playing the game that might reflect new hopes for an equitable society. The war could not have been worth fighting if it did not yield a just social dividend.

But Test cricket disappointed these ideals. In the years after the war it was played as 'boots and all' as it had been in the 1930s. It remained a hostile game, a ritualisation of conflict between nations. For those who did well in it, this was the way it should have been played, and they were glad that it had lost none of its hostility. But that brief moment of hope, embodied in the Victory Tests and the Australian tour of New Zealand in 1945–46, was snuffed out by a reality just as crushing as that which, in the form of the Cold War, snuffed out a generation's ideals of a peaceful postwar world. Old habits died hard.

For the relationship between Australia and England, there was another sense in which 1948 was not a new beginning, but the beginning of the end. Tom Keneally has written of the Invincibles that 'All our desires for national validity were tied up with this extraordinary team.' Remnants of that desire may have animated Australia in 1948, but it was less true then than it had been in the 1930s, which was less true than it had been in the early 1900s, which in turn was less true than it had been in the 1880s. Australians had validated themselves as a country through cricket even before the nation of Australia existed. In the late nineteenth century, to excel on the cricket fields of England was to prove that the race had not degenerated, and to advertise the colonies as attractive soil for immigration. Our desire for national validation, through cricket, was overwhelmingly needy between 1878 and 1912. Thereafter, as Australia matured as a society and an economy, the need began to ebb. In truth, by 1948, Australia did not need cricket to show that it could produce greatness.

Culturally, by 1948 Australia was shedding its dependence on

England. The fall of Singapore and the Pacific war had turned our faces to the east. Less than two years after the Invincibles returned home, Australia sent ground troops and aircraft to a war, in Korea, that for the first time in our history had nothing to do with defending the British Empire. In 1948, Australia's popular-cultural ties to Britain were entering their long decline. 'Bodgies' and 'widgies', harbingers of a new kind of popular culture, were emerging. Over the next decade, the teenager, an American invention exported in whole cloth to Australia, would not scream at the feet of cricketers, but at those of rock and roll performers and movie stars. Cricket would become a dour affair in the 1950s and 1960s, as it was overtaken by more colourful cultural attractions – American ones. Our first drive-in cinema was five years away in 1948, our first motel two years later. As a sporting attraction, cricket in the 1950s would yield to the great American–Australian tennis rivalry in the Davis Cup, and the global spectacle of the Olympic Games in Melbourne. Obsessive children in the 1950s would be hula-hooping and riding surfboards, not just hitting a golf ball against a water-tank stand. Not until the advent of non-Anglo–Australian cricketing gods would the game discover a new identity and break out of what became, in the 1950s, perceived as a prewar Anglocentric fustiness. The cricket that regenerated from the 1970s was a game of West Indians, Pakistanis and Indians just as much as, and eventually even more than, a game of Englishmen and Australians.

This can be seen, finally, as the legacy of 1948. The Invincibles are what they are, in our imagination, because they were the last of their kind. After Bradman's retirement, Ray Robinson wrote, cricket was 'a room with the light turned out'. But the game's loss of lustre went far beyond Bradman. Ashes cricket would never again be what it had been before World War II, and the 1948 tour was that era's final flourishing. Forces were gathering, on and off the field, which made 1948 a year not of welcome return to cricket between England and Australia, but of farewell.

TOUR STATISTICS

THE ASHES TESTS

1ST TEST

Trent Bridge, Nottingham, 10–12, 14–15 June
Australia won by 8 wickets

ENGLAND 1ST INNINGS		R	M	B	4s	6s	SR
L Hutton	b Miller	3	12		0	0	
C Washbrook	c Brown b Lindwall	6	41		0	0	
WJ Edrich	b Johnston	18	74		1	0	
DCS Compton	b Miller	19	60		2	0	
J Hardstaff jnr	c Miller b Johnston	0	2	2	0	0	0.00
CJ Barnett	b Johnston	8	16		1	0	
NWD Yardley*	lbw b Toshack	3	26		0	0	
TG Evans†	c Morris b Johnston	12	18		2	0	
JC Laker	c †Tallon b Miller	63	101		6	0	
AV Bedser	c Brown b Johnston	22	89		2	0	
JA Young	not out	1	8		0	0	
Extras	(b 5, lb 5)	10					
Total	(all out; 79 overs)	165 (2.08 runs per over)					

FALL OF WICKETS 1–9 (Hutton), 2–15 (Washbrook), 3–46 (Edrich), 4–46 (Hardstaff), 5–48 (Compton), 6–60 (Barnett), 7–74 (Evans), 8–74 (Yardley), 9–163 (Bedser), 10–165 (Laker)

BOWLING	O	M	R	W	ECON
RR Lindwall	13	5	30	1	2.30
KR Miller	19	8	38	3	2.00
WA Johnston	25	11	36	5	1.44
ERH Toshack	14	8	28	1	2.00
IWG Johnson	5	1	19	0	3.80
AR Morris	3	1	4	0	1.33

AUSTRALIA 1ST INNINGS		R	M	B	4s	6s	SR
SG Barnes	c †Evans b Laker	62	153		6	0	
AR Morris	b Laker	31	121		3	0	
DG Bradman*	c Hutton b Bedser	138	290	321	10	0	42.99
KR Miller	c Edrich b Laker	0	6		0	0	
WA Brown	lbw b Yardley	17	58		1	0	
AL Hassett	b Bedser	137	354		20	1	
IWG Johnson	b Laker	21	38		3	0	
D Tallon†	c & b Young	10	39		1	0	
RR Lindwall	c †Evans b Yardley	42	121		7	0	
WA Johnston	not out	17	27		2	0	
ERH Toshack	lbw b Bedser	19	18		3	0	
Extras	(b 9, lb 4, w 1, nb 1)	15					
TOTAL	(all out; 216.2 overs)	509 (2.35 runs per over)					

FALL OF WICKETS 1–73 (Morris), 2–121 (Barnes), 3–121 (Miller), 4–185 (Brown), 5–305 (Bradman), 6–338 (Johnson), 7–365 (Tallon), 8–472 (Hassett), 9–476 (Lindwall), 10–509 (Toshack)

BOWLING	O	M	R	W	ECON
WJ Edrich	18	1	72	0	4.00
AV Bedser	44.2	12	113	3	2.54
CJ Barnett	17	5	36	0	2.11
JA Young	60	28	79	1	1.31
JC Laker	55	14	138	4	2.50
DCS Compton	5	0	24	0	4.80
NWD Yardley	17	6	32	2	1.88

ENGLAND 2ND INNINGS		R	M	4s	6s
L Hutton	b Miller	74	168	11	0
C Washbrook	c †Tallon b Miller	1	10	0	0
WJ Edrich	c †Tallon b Johnson	13	43	2	0
DCS Compton	hit wicket b Miller	184	413	19	0
J Hardstaff jnr	c Hassett b Toshack	43	101	6	0
CJ Barnett	c Miller b Johnston	6	33	0	0
NWD Yardley*	c & b Johnston	22	66	4	0
TG Evans†	c †Tallon b Johnston	50	124	8	0
JC Laker	b Miller	4	16	0	0
AV Bedser	not out	3	20	0	0
JA Young	b Johnston	9	8	2	0
Extras	(b 12, lb 17, nb 3)	32			
TOTAL	(all out; 183 overs)	441 (2.40 runs per over)			

FALL OF WICKETS 1–5 (Washbrook), 2–39 (Edrich), 3–150 (Hutton), 4–243 (Hardstaff), 5–264 (Barnett), 6–321 (Yardley), 7–405 (Compton), 8–413 (Laker), 9–423 (Evans), 10–441 (Young)

BOWLING	O	M	R	W	ECON
KR Miller	44	10	125	4	2.84
WA Johnston	59	12	147	4	2.49
ERH Toshack	33	14	60	1	1.81
IWG Johnson	42	15	66	1	1.57
SG Barnes	5	2	11	0	2.20

AUSTRALIA 2ND INNINGS (target: 98 runs)		R	M	B	4s	6s	SR
SG Barnes	not out	64	87		11	0	
AR Morris	b Bedser	9	32		1	0	
DG Bradman*	c Hutton b Bedser	0	12	10	0	0	0.00
AL Hassett	not out	21	39		2	0	
Extras	(lb 2, w 1, nb 1)	4					
TOTAL	(2 wickets; 28.3 overs)	98 (3.43 runs per over)					

DID NOT BAT KR Miller, WA Brown, IWG Johnson, D Tallon†, RR Lindwall, WA Johnston, ERH Toshack

FALL OF WICKETS 1–38 (Morris), 2–48 (Bradman)

BOWLING	O	M	R	W	ECON
AV Bedser	14.3	4	46	2	3.17
JA Young	10	3	28	0	2.80
WJ Edrich	4	0	20	0	5.00

CLOSE OF PLAY

THU, 10 JUN – day 1 – Australia 1st innings 17/0 (SG Barnes 6*, AR Morris 10*)

FRI, 11 JUN – day 2 – Australia 1st innings 293/4 (DG Bradman 130*, AL Hassett 41*)

SAT, 12 JUN – day 3 – England 2nd innings 121/2 (L Hutton 63*, DCS Compton 36*)

SUN, 13 JUN – rest day

MON, 14 JUN – day 4 – England 2nd innings 345/6 (DCS Compton 154*, TG Evans 10*)

TUE, 15 JUN – day 5 – Australia 2nd innings 98/2 (28.3 ov) – end of match

2ND TEST

Lord's, London, 24–29 June

Australia won by 409 runs

AUSTRALIA 1ST INNINGS		R	M	B	4s	6s	SR
SG Barnes	c Hutton b Coxon	0			0	0	
AR Morris	c Hutton b Coxon	105	209		14	1	
DG Bradman*	c Hutton b Bedser	38	115	104		0	36.53
AL Hassett	b Yardley	47	175			0	
KR Miller	lbw b Bedser	4				0	
WA Brown	lbw b Yardley	24	84			0	
IWG Johnson	c †Evans b Edrich	4				0	
D Tallon†	c Yardley b Bedser	53				0	
RR Lindwall	b Bedser	15				0	
WA Johnston	st †Evans b Wright	29				0	
ERH Toshack	not out	20				0	
Extras	(b 3, lb 7, nb 1)	11					
TOTAL	(all out; 129.3 overs)	350 (2.70 runs per over)					

FALL OF WICKETS 1–3 (Barnes), 2–87 (Bradman), 3–166 (Morris), 4–173 (Miller), 5–216 (Hassett), 6–225 (Brown), 7–246 (Johnson), 8–275 (Lindwall), 9–320 (Tallon), 10–350 (Johnston)

BOWLING	O	M	R	W	ECON
AV Bedser	43	14	100	4	2.32
A Coxon	35	10	90	2	2.57
WJ Edrich	8	0	43	1	5.37
DVP Wright	21.3	8	54	1	2.51
JC Laker	7	3	17	0	2.42
NWD Yardley	15	4	35	2	2.33

ENGLAND 1ST INNINGS		R	M	B	4s	6s	SR
L Hutton	b Johnson	20				0	
C Washbrook	c †Tallon b Lindwall	8				0	
WJ Edrich	b Lindwall	5	70			0	
DCS Compton	c Miller b Johnston	53				0	
HE Dollery	b Lindwall	0		2	0	0	0.00
NWD Yardley*	b Lindwall	44				0	
A Coxon	c & b Johnson	19				0	
TG Evans†	c Miller b Johnston	9				0	
JC Laker	c †Tallon b Johnson	28				0	
AV Bedser	b Lindwall	9				0	
DVP Wright	not out	13				0	
Extras	(lb 3, nb 4)	7					
TOTAL	(all out; 102.4 overs)	215 (2.09 runs per over)					

FALL OF WICKETS 1–17 (Washbrook), 2–32 (Hutton), 3–46 (Edrich), 4–46 (Dollery), 5–133 (Compton), 6–134 (Yardley), 7–145 (Evans), 8–186 (Coxon), 9–197 (Laker), 10–215 (Bedser)

BOWLING	O	M	R	W	ECON
RR Lindwall	27.4	7	70	5	2.53
WA Johnston	22	4	43	2	1.95
IWG Johnson	35	13	72	3	2.05
ERH Toshack	18	11	23	0	1.27

AUSTRALIA 2ND INNINGS		R	M	B	4s	6s	SR
SG Barnes	c Washbrook b Yardley	141	277		14	2	
AR Morris	b Wright	62				1	
DG Bradman*	c Edrich b Bedser	89	185	162	13	0	54.93
AL Hassett	b Yardley	0	1	1	0	0	0.00
KR Miller	c Bedser b Laker	74				1	
WA Brown	c †Evans b Coxon	32				0	
RR Lindwall	st †Evans b Laker	25				0	
IWG Johnson	not out	9				0	
Extras	(b 22, lb 5, nb 1)	28					
TOTAL	(7 wickets dec; 130.2 overs)	460 (3.52 runs per over)					

DID NOT BAT D Tallon†, WA Johnston, ERH Toshack

FALL OF WICKETS 1–122 (Morris), 2–296 (Barnes), 3–296 (Hassett), 4–329 (Bradman), 5–416 (Brown), 6–445 (Miller), 7–460 (Lindwall)

BOWLING	O	M	R	W	ECON
AV Bedser	34	6	112	1	3.29
A Coxon	28	3	82	1	2.92
WJ Edrich	2	0	11	0	5.50
DVP Wright	19	4	69	1	3.63
JC Laker	31.2	6	111	2	3.54
NWD Yardley	13	4	36	2	2.76
DCS Compton	3	0	11	0	3.66

ENGLAND 2ND INNINGS (target: 596 runs)

		R	B	4s	6s	SR
L Hutton	c Johnson b Lindwall	13			0	
C Washbrook	c †Tallon b Toshack	37			0	
WJ Edrich	c Johnson b Toshack	2		0	0	
DCS Compton	c Miller b Johnston	29			0	
HE Dollery	b Lindwall	37			0	
NWD Yardley*	b Toshack	11			0	
A Coxon	lbw b Toshack	0	2	0	0	0.00
TG Evans†	not out	24			0	
JC Laker	b Lindwall	0		0	0	
AV Bedser	c Hassett b Johnston	9			0	
DVP Wright	c Lindwall b Toshack	4			0	
Extras	(b 16, lb 4)	20				
TOTAL	(all out; 78.1 overs)	186 (2.37 runs per over)				

FALL OF WICKETS 1–42 (Hutton), 2–52 (Edrich), 3–65 (Washbrook), 4–106 (Compton), 5–133 (Yardley), 6–133 (Coxon), 7–141 (Dollery), 8–141 (Laker), 9–158 (Bedser), 10–186 (Wright)

BOWLING	O	M	R	W	ECON
RR Lindwall	23	9	61	3	2.65
WA Johnston	33	15	62	2	1.87
IWG Johnson	2	1	3	0	1.50
ERH Toshack	20.1	6	40	5	1.98

CLOSE OF PLAY

THU, 24 JUN – day 1 – Australia 1st innings 258/7 (D Tallon 25*, RR Lindwall 3*)

FRI, 25 JUN – day 2 – England 1st innings 207/9 (AV Bedser 6*, DVP Wright 8*)

SAT, 26 JUN – day 3 – Australia 2nd innings 343/4 (KR Miller 22*, WA Brown 7*)

SUN, 27 JUN – rest day

MON, 28 JUN – day 4 – England 2nd innings 106/3 (DCS Compton 29*, HE Dollery 21*)

TUE, 29 JUN – day 5 – England 2nd innings 186 (78.1 ov) – end of match

3RD TEST
Old Trafford, Manchester, 8–9, 12–13 June
Match drawn

ENGLAND 1ST INNINGS		R	M	4s	6s
C Washbrook	b Johnston	11	30	1	0
GM Emmett	c Barnes b Lindwall	10	47	0	0
WJ Edrich	c †Tallon b Lindwall	32	170	5	0
DCS Compton	not out	145	324	16	0
JF Crapp	lbw b Lindwall	37	115	4	1
HE Dollery	b Johnston	1	5	0	0
NWD Yardley*	c Johnson b Toshack	22	83	3	0
TG Evans†	c Johnston b Lindwall	34	76	4	0
AV Bedser	run out	37	145	7	0
R Pollard	b Toshack	3	26	0	0
JA Young	c Bradman b Johnston	4	10	0	0
Extras	(b 7, lb 17, nb 3)	27			
TOTAL	(all out; 171.5 overs)	363 (2.11 runs per over)			

FALL OF WICKETS 1–22 (Washbrook), 2–28 (Emmett), 2–33* (Compton, retired not out), 3–96 (Crapp), 4–97 (Dollery), 5–119 (Edrich), 6–141 (Yardley), 7–216 (Evans), 8–337 (Bedser), 9–352 (Pollard), 10–363 (Young)

BOWLING	O	M	R	W	ECON
RR Lindwall	40	8	99	4	2.47
WA Johnston	45.5	13	67	3	1.46
SJE Loxton	7	0	18	0	2.57
ERH Toshack	41	20	75	2	1.82
IWG Johnson	38	16	77	0	2.02

AUSTRALIA 1ST INNINGS		R	M	B	4s	6s	SR
AR Morris	c Compton b Bedser	51	218		6	0	
IWG Johnson	c †Evans b Bedser	1	7		0	0	
DG Bradman*	lbw b Pollard	7	9	7	1	0	100.00
AL Hassett	c Washbrook b Young	38	101		5	0	
KR Miller	lbw b Pollard	31	75		4	0	
SG Barnes	retired hurt	1	25		0	0	
SJE Loxton	b Pollard	36	77		6	0	
D Tallon†	c †Evans b Edrich	18	30		1	0	
RR Lindwall	c Washbrook b Bedser	23	106		3	0	
WA Johnston	c Crapp b Bedser	3	13		0	0	
ERH Toshack	not out	0	1		0	0	
Extras	(b 5, lb 4, nb 3)	12					
TOTAL	(all out; 93 overs)	221 (2.37 runs per over)					

FALL OF WICKETS 1–3 (Johnson), 2–13 (Bradman), 3–82 (Hassett), 4–135 (Miller), 5–139 (Morris), 5–139* (Barnes, retired not out), 6–172 (Tallon), 7–208 (Loxton), 8–219 (Johnston), 9–221 (Lindwall)

BOWLING	O	M	R	W	ECON
AV Bedser	36	12	81	4	2.25
R Pollard	32	9	53	3	1.65
WJ Edrich	7	3	27	1	3.85
NWD Yardley	4	0	12	0	3.00
JA Young	14	5	36	1	2.57

ENGLAND 2ND INNINGS		R	M	4s	6s
C Washbrook	not out	85	208	11	0
GM Emmett	c †Tallon b Lindwall	0	3	0	0
WJ Edrich	run out	53	138	8	1
DCS Compton	c Miller b Toshack	0	6	0	0
JF Crapp	not out	19	55	2	0
Extras	(b 9, lb 7, w 1)	17			
Total	(3 wickets dec; 69 overs)	174 (2.52 runs per over)			

DID NOT BAT HE Dollery, NWD Yardley*, TG Evans†, AV Bedser, R Pollard, JA Young

FALL OF WICKETS 1–1 (Emmett), 2–125 (Edrich), 3–129 (Compton)

BOWLING	O	M	R	W	ECON
RR Lindwall	14	4	37	1	2.64
WA Johnston	14	3	34	0	2.42
SJE Loxton	8	2	29	0	3.62
ERH Toshack	12	5	26	1	2.16
IWG Johnson	7	3	16	0	2.28
KR Miller	14	7	15	0	1.07

AUSTRALIA 2ND INNINGS (target: 317runs)		R	M	B	4S	6S	SR
AR Morris	not out	54	156		9	0	
IWG Johnson	c Crapp b Young	6	32		1	0	
DG Bradman*	not out	30	122	146	6	0	20.54
Extras	(nb 2)	2					
TOTAL	(1 wicket; 61 overs)	92 (1.50 runs per over)					

DID NOT BAT AL Hassett, KR Miller, SG Barnes, SJE Loxton, D Tallon†, RR Lindwall, WA Johnston, ERH Toshack

FALL OF WICKETS 1–10 (Johnson)

BOWLING	O	M	R	W	ECON
AV Bedser	19	12	27	0	1.42
R Pollard	10	8	6	0	0.60
WJ Edrich	2	0	8	0	4.00
JA Young	21	12	31	1	1.47
DCS Compton	9	3	18	0	2.00

CLOSE OF PLAY

THU, 8 JUL – day 1 – England 1st innings 231/7 (DCS Compton 64*, AV Bedser 4*)

FRI, 9 JUL – day 2 – Australia 1st innings 126/3 (AR Morris 48*, KR Miller 23*)

SAT, 10 JUL – day 3 – England 2nd innings 174/3 (C Washbrook 85*, JF Crapp 19*)

SUN, 11 JUL – rest day

MON, 12 JUL – day 4 – no play

TUE, 13 JUL – day 5 – Australia 2nd innings 92/1 (61 ov) – end of match

4TH TEST

Headingley, Leeds, 22–24, 26–27 June 1948 (5-day match)

Australia won by 7 wickets

ENGLAND 1ST INNINGS		R	M	4s	6s
L Hutton	b Lindwall	81	187		0
C Washbrook	c Lindwall b Johnston	143	317	22	0
WJ Edrich	c Morris b Johnson	111	314	13	1
AV Bedser	c & b Johnson	79	177	8	2
DCS Compton	c †Saggers b Lindwall	23	55		0
JF Crapp	b Toshack	5			0
NWD Yardley*	b Miller	25			0
K Cranston	b Loxton	10			0
TG Evans†	c Hassett b Loxton	3		0	0
JC Laker	c †Saggers b Loxton	4			0
R Pollard	not out	0		0	0
Extras	(b 2, lb 8, w 1, nb 1)	12			
TOTAL	(all out; 192.1 overs)	496 (2.58 runs per over)			

FALL OF WICKETS 1–168 (Hutton), 2–268 (Washbrook), 3–423 (Bedser), 4–426 (Edrich), 5–447 (Crapp), 6–473 (Compton), 7–486 (Cranston), 8–490 (Evans), 9–496 (Laker), 10–496 (Yardley)

BOWLING	O	M	R	W	ECON
RR Lindwall	38	10	79	2	2.07
KR Miller	17.1	2	43	1	2.50
WA Johnston	38	12	86	1	2.26
ERH Toshack	35	6	112	1	3.20
SJE Loxton	26	4	55	3	2.11
IWG Johnson	33	9	89	2	2.69
AR Morris	5	0	20	0	4.00

AUSTRALIA 1ST INNINGS		R	M	B	4s	6s	SR
AR Morris	c Cranston b Bedser	6				0	
AL Hassett	c Crapp b Pollard	13				0	
DG Bradman*	b Pollard	33	59	56		0	58.92
KR Miller	c Edrich b Yardley	58				2	
RN Harvey	b Laker	112	188		17	0	
SJE Loxton	b Yardley	93	135		8	5	
IWG Johnson	c Cranston b Laker	10				0	
RR Lindwall	c Crapp b Bedser	77				0	
RA Saggers†	st †Evans b Laker	5				0	
WA Johnston	c Edrich b Bedser	13				0	
ERH Toshack	not out	12				0	
Extras	(b 9, lb 14, nb 3)	26					
Total	(all out; 136.2 overs)	458 (3.35 runs per over)					

FALL OF WICKETS 1–13 (Morris), 2–65 (Hassett), 3–68 (Bradman), 4–189 (Miller), 5–294 (Harvey), 6–329 (Johnson), 7–344 (Loxton), 8–355 (Saggers), 9–403 (Johnston), 10–458 (Lindwall)

BOWLING	O	M	R	W	ECON
AV Bedser	31.2	4	92	3	2.93
R Pollard	38	6	104	2	2.73
K Cranston	14	1	51	0	3.64
WJ Edrich	3	0	19	0	6.33
JC Laker	30	8	113	3	3.76
NWD Yardley	17	6	38	2	2.23
DCS Compton	3	0	15	0	5.00

ENGLAND 2ND INNINGS		R	B	4s	6s	SR
L Hutton	c Bradman b Johnson	57			1	
C Washbrook	c Harvey b Johnston	65			1	
WJ Edrich	lbw b Lindwall	54			1	
DCS Compton	c Miller b Johnston	66			0	
JF Crapp	b Lindwall	18			0	
NWD Yardley*	c Harvey b Johnston	7			0	
K Cranston	c †Saggers b Johnston	0	2	0	0	0.00
TG Evans†	not out	47			0	
AV Bedser	c Hassett b Miller	17		4	0	
JC Laker	not out	15			0	
Extras	(b 4, lb 12, nb 3)	19				
TOTAL	(8 wickets dec; 107 overs)	365 (3.41 runs per over)				

DID NOT BAT R Pollard

FALL OF WICKETS 1–129 (Washbrook), 2–129 (Hutton), 3–232 (Edrich), 4–260 (Crapp), 5–277 (Yardley), 6–278 (Cranston), 7–293 (Compton), 8–330 (Bedser)

BOWLING	O	M	R	W	ECON
RR Lindwall	26	6	84	2	3.23
KR Miller	21	5	53	1	2.52
WA Johnston	29	5	95	4	3.27
SJE Loxton	10	2	29	0	2.90
IWG Johnson	21	2	85	1	4.04

AUSTRALIA 2ND INNINGS (target: 404 runs)		R	M	B	4s	6s	SR
AR Morris	c Pollard b Yardley	182	291		33	0	
AL Hassett	c & b Compton	17	74		1	0	
DG Bradman*	not out	173	255	292	29	0	59.24
KR Miller	lbw b Cranston	12	30		2	0	
RN Harvey	not out	4			1	0	
Extras	(b 6, lb 9, nb 1)	16					
TOTAL	(3 wickets; 114.1 overs)	404 (3.53 runs per over)					

DID NOT BAT SJE Loxton, IWG Johnson, RR Lindwall, RA Saggers†, WA Johnston, ERH Toshack
FALL OF WICKETS 1–57 (Hassett), 2–358 (Morris), 3–396 (Miller)

BOWLING	O	M	R	W	ECON
AV Bedser	21	2	56	0	2.66
R Pollard	22	6	55	0	2.50
K Cranston	7.1	0	28	1	3.90
JC Laker	32	11	93	0	2.90
NWD Yardley	13	1	44	1	3.38
DCS Compton	15	3	82	1	5.46
L Hutton	4	1	30	0	7.50

CLOSE OF PLAY

THU, 22 JUL – day 1 – England 1st innings 268/2 (WJ Edrich 41*, AV Bedser 0*)

FRI, 23 JUL – day 2 – Australia 1st innings 63/1 (AL Hassett 13*, DG Bradman 31*)

SAT, 24 JUL – day 3 – Australia 1st innings 457/9 (RR Lindwall 76*, ERH Toshack 12*)

SUN, 25 JUL – rest day

MON, 26 JUL – day 4 – England 2nd innings 362/8 (TG Evans 47*, JC Laker 14*)

TUE, 27 JUL – day 5 – Australia 2nd innings 404/3 (114.1 ov) – end of match

5TH TEST
Kennington Oval, London, 14, 16–18 June ⸱ *August?*
Australia won by an innings and 149 runs

ENGLAND 1ST INNINGS		R	M	B	4s	6s	SR
L Hutton	c †Tallon b Lindwall	30	124	147	1	0	20.40
JG Dewes	b Miller	1	6	5	0	0	20.00
WJ Edrich	c Hassett b Johnston	3	20	20	0	0	15.00
DCS Compton	c Morris b Lindwall	4	9	11	0	0	36.36
JF Crapp	c †Tallon b Miller	0	19	23	0	0	0.00
NWD Yardley*	b Lindwall	7	31	33	0	0	21.21
AJ Watkins	lbw b Johnston	0	16	16	0	0	0.00
TG Evans†	b Lindwall	1	9	4	0	0	25.00
AV Bedser	b Lindwall	0	3	5	0	0	0.00
JA Young	b Lindwall	0	4	5	0	0	0.00
WE Hollies	not out	0	12	8	0	0	0.00
Extras	(b 6)	6					
TOTAL	(all out; 42.1 overs)	52 (1.23 runs per over)					

FALL OF WICKETS 1–2 (Dewes), 2–10 (Edrich), 3–17 (Compton), 4–23 (Crapp), 5–35 (Yardley), 6–42 (Watkins), 7–45 (Evans), 8–45 (Bedser), 9–47 (Young), 10–52 (Hutton)

BOWLING	O	M	R	W	ECON
RR Lindwall	16.1	5	20	6	1.23
KR Miller	8	5	5	2	0.62
WA Johnston	16	4	20	2	1.25
SJE Loxton	2	1	1	0	0.50

AUSTRALIA 1ST INNINGS		R	M	B	4s	6s	SR
SG Barnes	c †Evans b Hollies	61	126			0	
AR Morris	run out	196	406		16	0	
DG Bradman*	b Hollies	0	1	2	0	0	0.00
AL Hassett	lbw b Young	37	134			0	
KR Miller	st †Evans b Hollies	5				0	
RN Harvey	c Young b Hollies	17				0	
SJE Loxton	c †Evans b Edrich	15				0	
RR Lindwall	c Edrich b Young	9				0	
D Tallon†	c Crapp b Hollies	31				0	
DT Ring	c Crapp b Bedser	9				0	
WA Johnston	not out	0	1	2	0	0	0.00
Extras	(b 4, lb 2, nb 3)	9					
Total	(all out; 158.2 overs)	389 (2.45 runs per over)					

FALL OF WICKETS 1–117 (Barnes), 2–117 (Bradman), 3–226 (Hassett), 4–243 (Miller), 5–265 (Harvey), 6–304 (Loxton), 7–332 (Lindwall), 8–359 (Morris), 9–389 (Tallon), 10–389 (Ring)

BOWLING	O	M	R	W	ECON
AV Bedser	31.2	9	61	1	1.94
AJ Watkins	4	1	19	0	4.75
JA Young	51	16	118	2	2.31
WE Hollies	56	14	131	5	2.33
DCS Compton	2	0	6	0	3.00
WJ Edrich	9	1	38	1	4.22
NWD Yardley	5	1	7	0	1.40

ENGLAND 2ND INNINGS		R	M	B	4s	6s	SR
L Hutton	c †Tallon b Miller	64				0	
JG Dewes	b Lindwall	10				0	
WJ Edrich	b Lindwall	28				0	
DCS Compton	c Lindwall b Johnston	39				0	
JF Crapp	b Miller	9				0	
NWD Yardley*	c Miller b Johnston	9				0	
AJ Watkins	c Hassett b Ring	2			0	0	
TG Evans†	b Lindwall	8				0	
AV Bedser	b Johnston	0	5	5	0	0	0.00
JA Young	not out	3	10	7	0	0	42.85
WE Hollies	c Morris b Johnston	0	1	1	0	0	0.00
Extras	(b 9, lb 4, nb 3)	16					
Total	(all out; 105.3 overs)	188 (1.78 runs per over)					

FALL OF WICKETS 1–20 (Dewes), 2–64 (Edrich), 3–125 (Compton), 4–153 (Hutton), 5–164 (Crapp), 6–167 (Watkins), 7–178 (Evans), 8–181 (Bedser), 9–188 (Yardley), 10–188 (Hollies)

BOWLING	O	M	R	W	ECON
RR Lindwall	25	3	50	3	2.00
KR Miller	15	6	22	2	1.46
WA Johnston	27.3	12	40	4	1.45
SJE Loxton	10	2	16	0	1.60
DT Ring	28	13	44	1	1.57

CLOSE OF PLAY

SAT, 14 AUG – day 1 – Australia 1st innings 153/2 (AR Morris 77*, AL Hassett 10*)

SUN, 15 AUG – rest day

MON, 16 AUG – day 2 – England 2nd innings 54/1 (L Hutton 19*, WJ Edrich 23*)

TUE, 17 AUG – day 3 – England 2nd innings 178/7 (NWD Yardley 2*)

WED, 18 AUG – day 4 – England 2nd innings 188 (105.3 ov) – end of match

FIRST-CLASS MATCHES

WORCESTERSHIRE V AUSTRALIANS (County Ground, New Road, Worcester) 28–30 April: Worcestershire 233 (Palmer 85, Cooper 51, Johnson 3/52), Australians 462 dec. (Morris 138, Bradman 107, Jackson 6/135), Worcestershire 212 (Outschoorn 54, McCool 4/29, Johnson 3/75). Australians won by an innings and 17 runs.

LEICESTERSHIRE V AUSTRALIANS (Grace Road, Leicester) 1–4 May: Australians 448 (Miller 202 n.o., Bradman 81, Jackson 5/91), Leicestershire 130 (Ring 5/45), Leicestershire 147 (Johnson 7/42). Australians won by an innings and 171 runs.

YORKSHIRE V AUSTRALIANS Bradford Park Avenue Cricket Ground) 5–6 May: Yorkshire 71 (Miller 6/42, Johnston 4/22), Australians 101 (Smailes 6/51), Yorkshire 89 (Johnston 6/18), Australians 63. Australians won by 4 wickets.

SURREY V AUSTRALIANS (Kennington Oval, London) 8–11 May: Australians 632 (Barnes 176, Bradman 146, Hassett 110, Bedser 4/104, McMahon 4/210), Surrey 141 (Fishlock 81 n.o., Johnson 5/53, Ring 3/34), Surrey 195 (Squires 54, Johnston 4/40, Johnson 3/40). Australians won by an innings and 296 runs.

CAMBRIDGE UNIVERSITY V AUSTRALIANS (FP Fenner's Ground, Cambridge) 12–14 May: Cambridge University 167 (Miller 5/46), Australians 414 (Brown 200, Hamence 92, Hassett 61 n.o.), Cambridge University 196 (Bailey 66 n.o., McCool 7/78). Australians won by an innings and 51 runs.

ESSEX V AUSTRALIANS (Southchurch Park, Southend-on-Sea) 15–17 May: Australians 721 (Bradman 187, Brown 153, Loxton 120, Saggers 104 n.o., Smith 4/193), Essex 83 (Toshack 5/31, Miller 3/14), Essex 187 (Pearce 71, Smith 54, Johnson 6/37). Australians won by an innings and 451 runs.

OXFORD UNIVERSITY V AUSTRALIANS (Christ Church College Ground, Oxford) 19–21 May: Australians 431 (Brown 108, Loxton 79 n.o., Morris 64, Mallett 3/110), Oxford University 185 (Kardar 54, Toshack 3/34), Oxford 156 (McCool 3/29, Toshack 3/37). Australians won by an innings and 90 runs.

MARYLEBONE CRICKET CLUB V AUSTRALIANS (Lord's, London) 22–25 May: Australians 552 (Miller 163, Bradman 98, Barnes 81, Young 4/147, Laker 3/127), Marylebone Cricket Club 189 (Hutton 52, Miller 3/28), Marylebone Cricket Club 205 (Hutton 64, McCool 4/35, Johnson 3/37). Australians won by an innings and 158 runs.

LANCASHIRE V AUSTRALIANS (Old Trafford, Manchester) 26–28 May: Australians 204 (Hilton 4/81, Pollard 3/37, Roberts 3/57), Lancashire 182 (Edrich 55, Johnston 5/49, Lindwall 3/44), Australians 259 (Harvey 76 n.o., Loxton 52). Match drawn.

NOTTINGHAMSHIRE V AUSTRALIANS (Trent Bridge, Nottingham) 29 May–1 June: Nottinghamshire 179 (Simpson 74, Lindwall 6/14), Australians 400 (Brown 122, Bradman 86, Jepson 4/109, Woodhead 3/92), Nottinghamshire 299 (Hardstaff jnr 107, Ring 4/104, Johnson 3/78). Match drawn.

HAMPSHIRE V AUSTRALIANS (County Ground, Southampton) 2–4 June: Hampshire 195 (Johnston 6/74), Australians 117 (Knott 5/57, Bailey 4/27), Hampshire 103 (Miller 5/25, Johnston 5/43), Australians 182 (Brown 81 n.o., Johnson 74). Australians won by 8 wickets.

SUSSEX V AUSTRALIANS (County Ground, Hove) 5–7 June: Sussex 86 (Lindwall 6/34), Australians 549 (Morris 184, Bradman 109, Harvey 100 n.o.), Sussex 138 (Parks 61, Lindwall 5/25, Ring 3/42). Australians won by an innings and 325 runs.

NORTHAMPTONSHIRE V AUSTRALIANS (County Ground, Northampton) 16–18 June: Northamptonshire 119 (Johnson 3/13, Johnston 3/24), Australians 352 (Hassett 127, Morris 60, Nutter 5/57), Northamptonshire 169 (Ring 4/31, Johnston 4/49). Australians won by an innings and 64 runs.

YORKSHIRE V AUSTRALIANS (Bramall Lane, Sheffield) 19–22 June: Australians 249 (Bradman 54, Coxon 4/66, Wardle 3/37), Yorkshire 206 (Toshack 7/81, Johnston 3/101), Australians 285 (Brown 113, Bradman 86), Yorkshire 85. Match drawn.

SURREY V AUSTRALIANS (Kennington Oval, London) 30 June–2 July: Surrey 221 (Parker 76, Ring 3/51), Australia 389 (Hassett 139, Bradman 128), Surrey 289 (Parker 81, Fishlock 61, McCool 6/113), Australians 122 (Harvey 73 n.o.). Australians won by 10 wickets.

GLOUCESTERSHIRE V AUSTRALIANS (Ashley Down Ground, Bristol) 3–6 July: Australians 774 (Morris 290, Loxton 159 n.o., Cook 3/147), Gloucestershire 279 (Crapp 100 n.o., Johnson 6/68), Gloucestershire 132 (Johnson 5/32, Ring 5/47). Australians won by an innings and 363 runs.

MIDDLESEX V AUSTRALIANS (Lord's, London) 17–20 July: Middlesex 203 (Compton 62, Loxton 3/33, Johnston 3/43), Australians 317 (Loxton 123, Morris 109, Sims 6/65), Middlesex 135 (Dewes 51, McCool 3/27), Australians 22. Australians won by 10 wickets.

DERBYSHIRE V AUSTRALIANS (County Ground, Derby) 28–30 July: Australians 456 (Brown 140, Bradman 62, Jackson 4/103, Gothard 3/108), Derbyshire 240 (Elliott 57, Miller 3/31, Johnston 3/41), Derbyshire 182 (Smith 88, McCool 6/77, Loxton 3/16). Australians won by an innings and 34 runs.

GLAMORGAN V AUSTRALIANS (St Helen's, Swansea) 31 July–3 August: Glamorgan 197 (Ring 3/34, Johnson 3/58), Australians 215 (Miller 84, Hassett 71 n.o.). Match drawn.

WARWICKSHIRE V AUSTRALIANS (Edgbaston, Birmingham) 4–6 August: Warwickshire 138 (Lindwall 3/27, Johnson 3/29), Australians 254 (Hassett 68, Lindwall 45, Hollies 8/107), Warwickshire 155 (Johnston 4/32, McCool 4/56), Australians 41. Australians won by 9 wickets.

LANCASHIRE V AUSTRALIANS (Old Trafford, Manchester) 7–10 August: Australians 321 (Barnes 67, Roberts 6/73), Lancashire 130 (Johnson 3/5, Lindwall 3/32), Australians 265 (Bradman 133, Barnes 90, Pollard 3/58), Lancashire 199 (Ikin 99, Lindwall 4/27). Match drawn.

DURHAM V AUSTRALIANS (Ashbrooke, Sunderland) 11–12 August: Australians 282 (McCool 64, Miller 55, Jackson 5/76, Herbert 3/80), Durham 73. Match drawn.

KENT V AUSTRALIANS (St Lawrence Ground, Canterbury) 21–23 August: Australians 361 (Brown 106, Bradman 65, Dovey 4/90, Ridgway 3/119), Kent 51 (Johnston 3/10, Loxton 3/10), Kent 124 (Lindwall 4/25, Johnson 2/15). Australians won by an innings and 186 runs.

GENTLEMEN OF ENGLAND V AUSTRALIANS (Lord's, London) 25–27 August: Australians 610 (Hassett 200 n.o., Bradman 150, Brown 120), Gentlemen of England 245 (Simpson 60, Johnson 4/60, Ring 3/74), Gentlemen of England 284 (Edrich 128, Ring 5/70, Johnson 3/69). Australians won by an innings and 81 runs.

SOMERSET V AUSTRALIANS (County Ground, Taunton) 28–30 August: Australians 560 (Harvey 126, Johnson 113 n.o., Hassett 103, Redman 3/78), Somerset 115 (McCool 4/21, Johnston 3/34), Somerset 71 (Johnston 5/34, McCool 4/23). Australians won by an innings and 374 runs.

SOUTH V AUSTRALIANS (Central Recreation Ground, Hastings) 1–3 September: Australians 522 (Hassett 151, Bradman 143, Harvey 110, Perks 3/92), South 298 (Compton 82, Edrich 52, Brown 4/16). Match drawn.

HDG LEVESON-GOWER'S XI V AUSTRALIANS (North Marine Road Ground, Scarborough) 8–10 September: HDG Leveson-Gower's XI 177 (Lindwall 6/59, Johnson 3/45), Australians 489 (Bradman 153, Barnes 151, Bedser 3/72, Brown 3/171), HDG Leveson-Gower's XI 75. Match drawn.

AUSTRALIA AND ENGLAND
TEST MATCH AVERAGES

AUSTRALIA BATTING

PLAYER	M	I	NO	R	HS	AVE	100	50	0
AR Morris	5	9	1	696	196	87.00	3	3	0
SG Barnes	4	6	2	329	141	82.25	1	3	1
DG Bradman	5	9	2	508	173*	72.57	2	1	2
RN Harvey	2	3	1	133	112	66.50	1	0	0
ERH Toshack	4	4	3	51	20*	51.00	0	0	0
SJE Loxton	3	3	0	144	93	48.00	0	1	0
AL Hassett	5	8	1	310	137	44.28	1	0	1
RR Lindwall	5	6	0	191	77	31.83	0	1	0
D Tallon	4	4	0	112	53	28.00	0	1	0
KR Miller	5	7	0	184	74	26.28	0	2	1
WA Brown	2	3	0	73	32	24.33	0	0	0
WA Johnston	5	5	2	62	29	20.66	0	0	0
IWG Johnson	4	6	1	51	21	10.20	0	0	0
DT Ring	1	1	0	9	9	9.00	0	0	0
RA Saggers	1	1	0	5	5	5.00	0	0	0

AUSTRALIA BOWLING

PLAYER	M	I	O	MN	R	W	BBI	BBM	AVE	E	SR	5	CT	ST
RR Lindwall	5	9	222.5	57	530	27	6/20	9/70	19.62	2.37	49.5	2	3	0
KR Miller	5	7	138.1	43	301	13	4/125	7/163	23.15	2.17	63.7	0	8	0
WA Johnston	5	10	309.2	91	630	27	5/36	9/183	23.33	2.03	68.7	1	2	0
ERH Toshack	4	7	173.1	70	364	11	5/40	5/63	33.09	2.10	94.4	1	0	0
DT Ring	1	1	28.0	13	44	1	1/44	1/44	44.00	1.57	168.0	0	0	0
SJE Loxton	3	6	63.0	11	148	3	3/55	3/84	49.33	2.34	126.0	0	0	0
IWG Johnson	4	8	183.0	60	427	7	3/72	3/75	61.00	2.33	156.8	0	5	0
SG Barnes	4	1	5.0	2	11	0	-	-	-	2.20	-	0	1	0
AR Morris	5	2	8.0	1	24	0	-	-	-	3.00	-	0	4	0
DG Bradman	5	-	-	-	-	-	-	-	-	-	-	-	2	0
WA Brown	2	-	-	-	-	-	-	-	-	-	-	-	2	0
RN Harvey	2	-	-	-	-	-	-	-	-	-	-	-	2	0
AL Hassett	5	-	-	-	-	-	-	-	-	-	-	-	6	0
RA Saggers	1	-	-	-	-	-	-	-	-	-	-	-	3	0
D Tallon	4	-	-	-	-	-	-	-	-	-	-	-	12	0

M Matches   **I** Innings   **NO** Not outs   **R** Runs   **HS** High score   **AVE** Average   **O** Overs   **MN** Maidens
W Wickets   **BBI** Best bowling in an innings   **BBM** Best bowling in a match   **E** Economy   **SR** Strike rate
5 5-wicket innings   **CT** Catches   **ST** Stumpings

ENGLAND BATTING

PLAYER	M	I	NO	R	HS	AVE	100	50	0
DCS Compton	5	10	1	562	184	62.44	2	2	1
C Washbrook	4	8	1	356	143	50.85	1	2	0
L Hutton	4	8	0	342	81	42.75	0	4	0
WJ Edrich	5	10	0	319	111	31.90	1	2	0
TG Evans	5	9	2	188	50	26.85	0	1	0
JC Laker	3	6	1	114	63	22.80	0	1	1
AV Bedser	5	9	1	176	79	22.00	0	1	2
J Hardstaff	1	2	0	43	43	21.50	0	0	1
JF Crapp	3	6	1	88	37	17.60	0	0	1
DVP Wright	1	2	1	17	13*	17.00	0	0	0
NWD Yardley	5	9	0	150	44	16.66	0	0	0
HE Dollery	2	3	0	38	37	12.66	0	0	1
A Coxon	1	2	0	19	19	9.50	0	0	1
CJ Barnett	1	2	0	14	8	7.00	0	0	0
JA Young	3	5	2	17	9	5.66	0	0	1
JG Dewes	1	2	0	11	10	5.50	0	0	0
K Cranston	1	2	0	10	10	5.00	0	0	1
GM Emmett	1	2	0	10	10	5.00	0	0	1
R Pollard	2	2	1	3	3	3.00	0	0	0
AJ Watkins	1	2	0	2	2	1.00	0	0	1
WE Hollies	1	2	1	0	0*	0.00	0	0	1

ENGLAND BOWLING

PLAYER	M	I	O	MN	R	W	BBI	BBM	AVE	E	SR	5	CT	ST
NWD Yardley	5	7	84.0	22	204	9	2/32	4/71	22.66	2.42	56.0	0	1	0
WE Hollies	1	1	56.0	14	131	5	5/131	5/131	26.20	2.33	67.2	1	0	0
AV Bedser	5	9	274.3	75	688	18	4/81	5/159	38.22	2.50	91.5	0	1	0
R Pollard	2	4	102.0	29	218	5	3/53	3/59	43.60	2.13	122.4	0	1	0
JC Laker	3	5	155.2	42	472	9	4/138	4/138	52.44	3.03	103.5	0	0	0
A Coxon	1	2	63.0	13	172	3	2/90	3/172	57.33	2.73	126.0	0	0	0
JA Young	3	5	156.0	64	292	5	2/118	2/67	58.40	1.87	187.2	0	2	0
DVP Wright	1	2	40.3	12	123	2	1/54	2/123	61.50	3.03	121.5	0	0	0
K Cranston	1	2	21.1	1	79	1	1/28	1/79	79.00	3.73	127.0	0	2	0
WJ Edrich	5	8	53.0	5	238	3	1/27	1/35	79.33	4.49	106.0	0	5	0
DCS Compton	5	6	37.0	6	156	1	1/82	1/97	156.00	4.21	222.0	0	2	0
AJ Watkins	1	1	4.0	1	19	0	-	-	-	4.75	-	0	0	0
L Hutton	4	1	4.0	1	30	0	-	-	-	7.50	-	0	5	0
CJ Barnett	1	1	17.0	5	36	0	-	-	-	2.11	-	0	0	0
JF Crapp	3	-	-	-	-	-	-	-	-	-	-	-	6	0
JG Dewes	1	-	-	-	-	-	-	-	-	-	-	-	0	0
HE Dollery	2	-	-	-	-	-	-	-	-	-	-	-	0	0
GM Emmett	1	-	-	-	-	-	-	-	-	-	-	-	0	0
TG Evans	5	-	-	-	-	-	-	-	-	-	-	-	8	4
J Hardstaff	1	-	-	-	-	-	-	-	-	-	-	-	0	0
C Washbrook	4	-	-	-	-	-	-	-	-	-	-	-	3	0

RECORDS INCLUDES THE FOLLOWING CURRENT OR RECENT MATCHES:

England v Australia at The Oval, 5th Test, Aug 14–18, 1948. England v Australia at Leeds, 4th Test, Jul 22–27, 1948. England v Australia at Manchester, 3rd Test, Jul 8–13, 1948

AUSTRALIAN SECOND-CLASS AVERAGES
(V SCOTLAND)

BATTING

PLAYER	M	I	NO	R	HS	AVE	100	50	0
DG Bradman	2	2	1	150	123*	150.00	1	0	0
CL McCool	2	2	0	160	108	80.00	1	1	0
AR Morris	2	2	0	122	112	61.00	1	0	0
IWG Johnson	2	2	0	95	95	47.50	0	1	1
RR Lindwall	1	1	0	15	15	15.00	0	0	0
RA Hamence	2	2	0	21	15	10.50	0	0	0
RA Saggers	1	1	0	8	8	8.00	0	0	0
KR Miller	1	1	0	6	6	6.00	0	0	0
D Tallon	2	1	0	6	6	6.00	0	0	0
SG Barnes	1	1	0	5	5	5.00	0	0	0
RN Harvey	1	1	0	4	4	4.00	0	0	0
WA Johnston	2	1	0	0	0	0.00	0	0	1
WA Brown	1	1	1	24	24*	-	0	0	0
DT Ring	2	1	1	3	3*	-	0	0	0

BOWLING AND FIELDING

PLAYER	M	I	O	MN	R	W	BBI	BBM	AVE	E	SR	5	CT	ST
AR Morris	2	3	18.0	3	35	8	5/10	5/10	4.37	1.94	13.5	1	0	0
RN Harvey	1	1	5.0	0	13	2	2/13	2/13	6.50	2.60	15.0	0	0	0
WA Johnston	2	4	33.5	9	66	8	6/15	6/18	8.25	1.95	25.3	1	0	0
WA Brown	1	1	5.0	0	9	1	1/9	1/9	9.00	1.80	30.0	0	1	0
IWG Johnson	2	4	40.2	21	58	6	3/18	3/26	9.66	1.43	40.3	0	2	1
D Tallon	2	2	17.0	6	25	2	2/15	2/15	12.50	1.47	51.0	0	0	0
DT Ring	2	4	39.2	8	101	8	4/20	4/29	12.62	2.56	29.5	0	4	0
CL McCool	2	4	37.3	8	89	5	3/31	3/50	17.80	2.37	45.0	0	1	0
SG Barnes	1	1	9.0	7	9	0	-	-	-	1.00	-	0	1	0
RA Hamence	2	1	5.0	1	13	0	-	-	-	2.60	-	0	0	0
KR Miller	1	2	10.0	4	18	0	-	-	-	1.80	-	0	0	0
RR Lindwall	1	2	14.0	5	28	0	-	-	-	2.00	-	0	1	0
DG Bradman	2	-	-	-	-	-	-	-	-	-	-	-	0	0
RA Saggers	1	-	-	-	-	-	-	-	-	-	-	-	2	5

RECORDS INCLUDES THE FOLLOWING CURRENT OR RECENT MATCHES:
Scotland v Australians at Aberdeen, Sep 17–18, 1948. Scotland v Australians at Edinburgh, Sep 13–14, 1948. Ceylon v Australians (Colombo Cricket Club Ground) 27 March 1948 (One-day match): Australians 184 dec. (Barnes 49 ret., Coomaraswamy 4/45), Ceylon 46. Rain stopped play, match drawn.

NOTES ON SOURCES

I have drawn on several collections of cricket material in my research for this book, but wish to thank three in particular: Neil Robinson and the staff of the MCC Library at Lord's, Ronald Cardwell and Mike Coward.

I would also like to thank the three remaining Test players from the 1948 series, who generously offered their time for interviews: John Dewes, Neil Harvey and Arthur Morris. My thanks go, as well, to Peter Loxton, for his assistance in my interviews with the late Sam Loxton. Thanks also to Hubert Doggart and Doug Insole, who played first-class cricket in England against the 1948 Australians, for making themselves available.

Rather than footnoting the text, which can be a labour for readers, I have pointed to the use of sources as follows:

INTRODUCTION

Bradman's autobiography: Bradman, D.G., *Farewell to Cricket*

Alan Gibson's commentary: Gibson, Alan, *The Cricket Captains of England*

Miller's omission from the 1949–50 tour and the Sid Barnes defamation case: Miller,
    Keith, *Cricket Crossfire*; Miller, Keith and Whitington, R.S., *Cricket Caravan*;
    Smith, Rick, *Cricket's Enigma: The Sid Barnes Story*; Barnes, Sid, *It Isn't Cricket*

McCool's reflections on Bradman: McCool, Colin, *Cricket is a Game*

Arlott's comments: Arlott, John, *Gone to the Test Match*

Fingleton's comments: Fingleton, J.H., *Brightly Fades the Don*

Yardley's comments: Yardley, Norman, *Cricket Campaigns*

Edrich's comments: Edrich, W.J., *Cricket Heritage*

CHAPTER 1

The Australian War Memorial's records were used to verify Australian players' service
    in World War II.

Hassett's war experience and the Victory Tests: Whitington, R.S. *Lindsay Hassett:*
    The Quiet Australian

Loxton's war experience is drawn from his interviews with the author.

Miller's war experience: Whitington, R.S., *Keith Miller: The Golden Nugget* and
    Cricket Crossfire, *Cricket Caravan*, Perry, Roland, *Miller's Luck*

Compton's war experience: Compton, Denis, *End of an Innings*; Heald, Tim,
    Denis Compton: The Life of a Sporting Hero; Peebles, Ian, *Denis Compton:*
    The Generous Cricketer

David Kynaston's *Austerity Britain 1945–51* was a useful source on British life
    and society in 1948.

Edrich's war experience: *Cricket Heritage*

Washbrook's war experience: Washbrook, Cyril, *Cricket: The Silver Lining*

Hutton's war experience: Thomson, A.A., *Hutton & Washbrook*; Trelford, Donald
    (ed), *Len Hutton Remembered*; Howat, Gerald, *Len Hutton: The Biography*;

Hutton, Len with Alex Bannister, *Fifty Years in Cricket*; Hutton, Len, *Cricket is My Life*; Hutton, Len, *Just My Story*

Barnes's war experience: *Cricket's Enigma: The Sid Barnes Story* and *It Isn't Cricket*

Bradman's wartime experiences are drawn from many Bradman sources, including *Farewell to Cricket*. The most authoritative biography is Rosenwater, Irving, *Sir Donald Bradman: A Biography*. More intimate, if less impartial, is Moyes, A.G., *Bradman*.

Lindwall's war experience: Lindwall, Ray, *Flying Stumps*

Ian Johnson's war experience and the 1945-46 tour of New Zealand: Johnson, Ian, *Cricket at the Crossroads*

CHAPTER 2

ICC's and Lord's meetings in the postwar years: minutes of the Marylebone Cricket Club, MCC Library

Bradman's deliberations on whether to continue playing: *Farewell to Cricket*

Recollections from Morris: interview with author

Compton's recollections: *End of an Innings*

Johnson's recollections: *Cricket at the Crossroads*

Conversation between Hutton and Washbrook: *Hutton & Washbrook*

Howat's observations of Hutton: *Len Hutton: The Biography*

Miller's comments on bouncers: *Cricket Crossfire*

Ring's comments on Tallon: Philip Derriman, *The Life and Artistry of Don Tallon*

Barnes's recollections: *It Isn't Cricket*

Fingleton on the 1946–47 series: Jack Fingleton, *Batting from Memory*

Edrich's conversation with Bradman in Australia: *Cricket Heritage*

Yardley's plans: Norman Yardley, *Cricket Campaigns*

CHAPTER 3

Harvey's recollections are drawn mostly from the author's interviews with Harvey, but some (those which he wrote) are from Neil Harvey, *My World of Cricket*.

Loxton's recollections are from the author's interviews with Loxton.

Bradman's recollections on the Indian series: *Farewell to Cricket*

Whitington on Hassett: *The Quiet Australian*

Moyes' and Jeanes' conversations with Bradman about his availability for the tour: *Bradman*

Rosenwater on the Melbourne club election: *Sir Donald Bradman: A Biography*

Fingleton on Bradman's new attitude: Jack Fingleton, *Brightly Fades the Don*

Barnes on the pre-tour horrors: *It Isn't Cricket*

McCool's nerves: *Cricket is a Game*

CHAPTER 4

Bedser's comments are mainly drawn from Mike Coward's 2001 documentary for the ABC/Roadshow Entertainment, *Bradman and the Invincibles*.

McCool on the new-ball rule: *Cricket is a Game*

MCC Minutes on the new-ball rule are in the MCC library, Lord's

Bradman's jitters: *Farewell to Cricket*

Loxton's recollections: interviews with author

Fingleton's shipboard observations: *Brightly Fades the Don*

Flanagan's shipboard observations: Andy Flanagan, *On Tour with Bradman*

Morris's recollections: interview with author

Johnson's recollections: *Cricket at the Crossroads*

Barnes's recollections: *It Isn't Cricket*

Bradman discussing Fingleton with Loxton and Harvey: author interviews
    with Loxton

O'Reilly's recollections: Bill O'Reilly, *Cricket Conquest*

Miller's comments on Bradman not going ashore in Bombay: *Cricket Crossfire*

Bradman's discussions with Lindwall on the drag: *Farewell to Cricket* and
    Ray Lindwall, *Flying Stumps*

Ring's recollections: *Bradman and the Invincibles*

CHAPTER 5

Kynaston's observations, Anthony Heap's diary entry, Weldon's and Isherwood's
    views of postwar England: *Austerity Britain*

Fingleton's observations of arriving in England and the early functions:
    Brightly Fades the Don

Harvey's observations: interviews with author

O'Reilly's predictions, comments on the Essex match, on the MCC match,
    on McCool's finger, on Malcolm Hilton: *Cricket Conquest*

Bradman on Bedser: *Farewell to Cricket*

Bedser on Bradman, on The Oval: Alec and Eric Bedser, *Our Cricket Story*

Harvey on the food, on Barnes, on the Yorkshire match, on his catch at The Oval:
    interviews with author

Bedser on his diet: *Bradman and the Invincibles*

Bradman on getting caught in the crowd, on golf, on writing letters, on meeting
    the umpires, on Harvey's catch at The Oval: *Farewell to Cricket*

Morris on Barnes: interview with author

Flanagan on Barnes, on Harvey, on the facilities in Yorkshire, on the Essex match:
    On Tour with Bradman

Barnes on his domestic arrangements, on Lord's, on his conversations with Bradman:
    It Isn't Cricket

Arlott on anticipation, on the Essex match, on Hutton: John Arlott,
    Gone to the Test Match

Watkins on watching Toshack: Douglas Miller, *Allan Watkins: A True All-Rounder*

Fingleton on Toshack, the weather, Bradman at The Oval, the dog and Skelding,
    the Essex match, on Lord's, on Bradman playing Hilton: *Brightly Fades the Don*

Miller on Skelding, on the Essex match: *Cricket Crossfire*

Brown on 'sausage meat', on London: *Bradman and the Invincibles*

Whitington on Dewes: *The Quiet Australian*

Dewes' recollections: interview with author

Doggart's recollections: interview with author

Bailey on playing the Australians: Trevor Bailey, *Wickets, Catches and the Odd Run*

Loxton on Bailey: interviews with author

Johnson on Bailey, on Miller at Southend: *Cricket at the Crossroads*

Bradman on Essex: *Farewell to Cricket*

Barnes on Bradman, on fielding close to the bat, on the plan for Hutton:
   It Isn't Cricket

Ferguson on the Essex match: WH Ferguson, *Mr Cricket*

Compton on Barnes's fielding position: *End of an Innings*

Edrich on Barnes: *Cricket Heritage*

Bradman on the Chapman letter, McCool's finger, Malcolm Hilton, Welbeck Abbey:
   Farewell to Cricket

Kitchin at Lord's: Laurence Kitchin, *Len Hutton*

Miller's encounter with Princess Margaret: Johnson, *Cricket at the Crossroads*

McCool on his suffering: *Cricket is a Game*

Whitington on Old Trafford: *The Quiet Australian*

Washbrook on playing the Australians: *Cricket: The Silver Lining*

Geoffrey Edrich on stumping Bradman: *Cricket Heritage*

Lindwall on Nottingham, on bruising his chest, on Bradman's captaincy:
   Flying Stumps

Miller on Johnston, Johnson: *Cricket Crossfire*

CHAPTER 6

Arlott on England's prospects: *Gone to the Test Match*

Dewes on playing with professionals: interview with author

Rosenwater on Robins: *Sir Donald Bradman: A Biography*

Gibson on Robins, on Hutton and Compton: *The Cricket Captains of England*

Foot on Robins: *Fragments of Idolatry*

Harvey on Bradman and Robins, on the first Test match: interviews with author

Yardley on planning, on the first Test match: *Cricket Campaigns*

Flanagan on the Victoria: *On Tour with Bradman*

Bradman on the first Test: *Farewell to Cricket*

Arlott's commentary on the first Test: *Gone to the Test Match*

Hutton on Lindwall: Len Hutton, *Cricket Is My Life*

Lindwall on Washbrook, on Bradman's advice, on his injury, on Miller's bouncers:
   Flying Stumps

Fingleton's commentary on the first Test: *Brightly Fades the Don*

Miller on warming up, on bowling to Hutton and Compton, on the bouncer
   incident, on the bath with Johnston: *Cricket Crossfire*

O'Reilly's commentary on the first Test: *Cricket Conquest*

Morris on fielding: interview with author

Bedser on Laker's batting, on leg theory, on the Black Boy Hotel conversation with
O'Reilly: *Our Cricket Story*

Flanagan's commentary on the first Test: *On Tour with Bradman*

Evans on his catch of Barnes, on Bradman's captaincy, on batting against Miller:
Godfrey Evans, *Behind the Stumps*

O'Reilly on Hassett: Whitington, *The Quiet Australian*

Barnes on England's leg theory: *It Isn't Cricket*

Edrich's conversation with Bradman on leg theory: *Cricket Heritage*

Compton on Bradman's advice, on facing Miller's bouncers, on Bradman's response:
End of an Innings

Thomson on Hutton's batting: *Hutton & Washbrook*

Johnson on the Trent Bridge crowd, on Chester: *Cricket at the Crossroads*

Loxton on the Trent Bridge crowd: interviews with author

CHAPTER 7

Barnes on Northampton, on the second Test match: *It Isn't Cricket*

Bradman on Sheffield, on the second Test match: *Farewell to Cricket*

Flanagan on Yorkshire: *On Tour with Bradman*

O'Reilly on Bradman's batting, on the second Test match: *Cricket Conquest*

Fingleton on the Yorkshire people, on the second Test match:
Brightly Fades the Don

Arlott on the second Test match: *Gone to the Test Match*

Lindwall on the second Test match: *Flying Stumps*

Wright's comment to Evans: *Behind the Stumps*

Bedser on the second Test match: *Our Cricket Story*

Morris on his century: interview with author

Miller on the second Test match: *Cricket Crossfire*

Edrich on Miller and Bradman, on 'Yorkshire Annie': *Cricket Heritage*

Johnson on the Miller–Bradman incident: *Cricket at the Crossroads*

Yardley on the Miller–Bradman incident: *Cricket Campaigns*

Evans on his conversations with Barnes: *Behind the Stumps*

Loxton photographing the Queen: Loxton, interviews with author; Ring and
Johnson in *Bradman and the Invincibles*

Fingleton's report on the Bradman–Miller 'fibrositis' incident: Greg Growden,
Jack Fingleton: The Man Who Stood Up To Bradman

Kitchin on Hutton's batting: *Len Hutton*

CHAPTER 8

Arlott on Loxton, on Crapp, on the selectors, on Hutton, on the third Test match:
Gone to the Test Match

Bradman on The Oval, on Hutton's omission, on the third Test match:
Farewell to Cricket

Loxton on conversations with Bradman, going to the tennis, on solving Harvey's
   problems, on Barnes, on the third Test match: interviews with author

Morris on Brown, on Gloucestershire, on Barnes, on Hutton, on Bradman and
   Robins: interview with author

McCool on Goddard, on Wright, on the joke played on Tallon, on Lindwall:
   Cricket is a Game

Harvey on his difficulties, on Hutton, on Bradman and Robins: interviews
   with author

O'Reilly on Emmett, on England's selections, on the third Test match: *Cricket Conquest*

Bedser on Holmes, on the third Test match: *Our Cricket Story*

Edrich on Hutton's omission, on the third Test match: *Cricket Heritage*

Hutton on being dropped, on playing the Australians: *Just My Story*

Washbrook on Hutton's omission, on the third Test match: *Cricket:
   The Silver Lining*

Fingleton on Hutton's omission, on the third Test match: *Brightly Fades the Don*

Yardley on Hutton's omission: *Cricket Campaigns*

Flanagan on the third Test match: *On Tour with Bradman*

Batchelor on Edrich: Denzil Batchelor, *Days without Sunset*

Compton on batting against Miller, on Barnes's injury, on batting:
   End of an Innings

Derriman on Tallon: *The Life and Artistry of Don Tallon*

Barnes on getting hit: *It Isn't Cricket*

Ferguson on Barnes's injury: *Mr Cricket*

Rosenwater on Bradman's dismissal by Pollard: *Sir Donald Bradman: A Biography*

Evans on Barnes's injury: *Behind the Stumps*

Johnson on batting with Morris: *Cricket at the Crossroads*

CHAPTER 9

Miller and crew dropping in on the nobleman: Johnson, *Cricket at the Crossroads*
   also in Ray Robinson, *On Top Down Under*

Miller on drinking: *Cricket Crossfire*

Lindwall on living with Miller: *Flying Stumps*

Dewes on playing Australia: interview with author

Loxton on being picked, playing in the fourth Test match: interviews with author

O'Reilly on the fourth Test match: *Cricket Conquest*

Kitchin on Hutton: *Len Hutton*

Arlott on the fourth Test match: *Gone to the Test Match*

Fingleton on the fourth Test match: *Brightly Fades the Don*

Flanagan on the fourth Test match: *On Tour with Bradman*

Harvey on playing in the fourth Test match: interviews with author

Yardley on the fourth Test match: *Cricket Campaigns*

Morris's conversation with Edrich: Jack McHarg, *An Elegant Genius*

Edrich on the fourth Test match: *Cricket Heritage*

Thomson on Hutton: *Hutton & Washbrook*

Bradman on the fourth Test match: *Farewell to Cricket*

Bedser on the fourth Test match: *Our Cricket Story*

McCool on Edrich: *Cricket is a Game*

Harvey on eight years later: *My World of Cricket*

Harvey on Bradman signing his bat: interview with author

Johnson on Bradman's motivational speech: *Cricket at the Crossroads*

Evans on the last day: *Behind the Stumps*

Batchelor on Bradman's century: *Days Without Sunset*

Ferguson on Bradman's century: *Mr Cricket*

Rosenwater on Bradman as manipulator of fate: *Sir Donald Bradman: A Biography*

Laker on Bradman: Jim Laker, *Over to Me*

CHAPTER 10

Bradman on travelling to Derby, on the fifth Test match: *Farewell to Cricket*

Miller on Barnes: *Cricket Crossfire*

Compton on Barnes: *End of an Innings*

Loxton on Bradman, on the fifth Test match: interviews with author

Arlott on Bradman in Wales, on the fifth Test match: *Gone to the Test Match*

Fingleton on joining the team, on visiting Larwood, on the fifth Test match: *Brightly Fades the Don*

Rosenwater on Hollies: *Sir Donald Bradman: A Biography*

O'Reilly on Hollies, on the Lancashire match, on the fifth Test match: *Cricket Conquest*

Lindwall on the Lancashire match, on the fifth Test match: *Flying Stumps*

Barnes on batting with Bradman at Old Trafford, on the fifth Test match: *It Isn't Cricket*

Toshack's knee: see Flanagan, *On Tour with Bradman*

Yardley on the fifth Test match: *Cricket Campaigns*

Watkins on the fifth Test match: Miller, *Allan Watkins: A True All-Rounder*

Duckworth on Hollies: Leslie Duckworth, *Story of Warwickshire Cricket*

Dewes on playing in the fifth Test: interview with author

Miller on the fifth Test match: *Cricket Crossfire*

Kitchin on Lindwall: *Len Hutton*

Doggart on being in the crowd: interview with author

Evans on the fifth Test match: *Behind the Stumps*

CHAPTER 11

Evans on his encounter with Bradman at Canterbury: *Behind the Stumps*

Loxton on the celebrations: interviews with author

Fingleton on the aftermath of the Test series: *Brightly Fades the Don*

Johnston's one blow-up: Miller, *Cricket Crossfire*

Lindwall on the mysterious telegram, on bouncing Robins: *Flying Stumps*

Yardley on the Australians' advice: *Cricket Campaigns*

Barnes on the final weeks: *It Isn't Cricket*

Miller on bouncing Robins: *Cricket Crossfire*

Bradman on the last weeks: *Farewell to Cricket*

McCool on boiling over: *Cricket is a Game*

Morris on Bradman and the Scarborough game: interview with author

Edrich on the Scarborough game, on Miller: *Cricket Heritage*

Compton on Miller and Bradman: *End of an Innings*

Johnson on Miller, on Balmoral: *Cricket at the Crossroads*

Arlott on Miller: *Gone to the Test Match*

Ferguson on Balmoral: *Mr Cricket*

Flanagan on Balmoral: *On Tour with Bradman*

Harvey on the trip home: interviews with author

CHAPTER 12

O'Reilly's final summation: *Cricket Conquest*

Bradman on the team, on individual players: *Farewell to Cricket*

Ferguson's all-time eleven: *Mr Cricket*

Flanagan on the stresses of touring: *On Tour with Bradman*

Lindwall on Hassett: *Flying Stumps*

Harvey on the 1961 tour: *My World of Cricket*

Brown's letter to Fingleton: Growden, *Jack Fingleton: The Man Who Stood
   Up to Bradman*

McCool on England's bowling: *Cricket is a Game*

Dewes on batting against fast bowlers: interview with author

Compton's summary: *End of an Innings*

MCC''s summary: Minutes of the Marylebone Cricket Club, MCC Library, Lord's

Johnson's summary: *Cricket at the Crossroads*

Washbrook's summary: *Cricket: The Silver Lining*

Yardley's summary: *Cricket Campaigns*

   Arlott's summary: *Gone to the Test Match*

Ferguson on Bradman: *Mr Cricket*

Flanagan on Bradman: *On Tour with Bradman*

Rosewater's summary of Bradman's captaincy: *Sir Donald Bradman: A Biography*

Whitington on the Victory Tests: *The Quiet Australian*

Edrich's summary: *Cricket Heritage*

Birkett's foreword: *Brightly Fades the Don*

Lindwall on the money, on Hutton: *Flying Stumps*

Barnes's troubles: Rick Smith, *Cricket's Enigma: The Sid Barnes Story*

Harvey on Hassett's captaincy and on Morris: *My World of Cricket*

Johnson on Hutton: *Cricket at the Crossroads*

Tom Keneally on the Invincibles: See Peter Allen, *The Invincibles: The Legend
   of Don Bradman's 1948 Australians*

BIBLIOGRAPHY

Allen, Peter, *The Invincibles: The Legend of Bradman's 1948 Australians* (ABC Books, Sydney 1998)

Arlott, John, *Gone to the Test Match* (Longmans, Green and Co, London 1949)

Bailey, Trevor, *Wickets, Catches and the Odd Run* (Willow Books London 1986)

Barnes, Sid, *It Isn't Cricket* (Collins, London 1953)

Batchelor, Denzil, *Days Without Sunset* (Eyre & Spottiswoode London 1949)

Bedser, Alec and Bedser, Eric, *Our Cricket Story* (Evans Brothers Limited, London, 1951)

Bose, Mihir, *Keith Miller: A Cricketing Biography* (George Allen & Unwin, London 1979)

Bradman, D.G., *Farewell to Cricket* (T. Brun, London 1950)

Compton, Denis, *End of an Innings* (Oldbourne, London 1958)

Derriman, Philip, *The Life and Artistry of Don Tallon* (The Cricket Publishing Company, Sydney 2000)

Edrich, W.J., *Cricket Heritage* (Stanley Paul & Co, London 1948)

Evans, Godfrey, *Behind the Stumps* (Hodder and Stoughton London 1951)

Evans, Godfrey, *The Gloves Are Off* (Hodder and Stoughton London 1960)

Ferguson, W.H., *Mr Cricket* (Nicholas Kaye, London 1957)

Fingleton, J.H., *Brightly Fades the Don* (Collins, London 1949)

Fingleton, Jack, *Batting From Memory* (Collins, London 1981)

Flanagan, Andy, *On Tour with Bradman* (Halstead Press, Sydney 1950)

Foot, David, *Fragments of Idolatry* (Fairfield Books, Bath 2001)

Gibson, Alan, *The Cricket Captains of England* (Cassell, London 1979)

Growden, Greg, *Jack Fingleton: The Man Who Stood Up to Bradman* (Allen & Unwin, Sydney 2008)

Haigh, Gideon, *Silent Revolutions: Writings on Cricket History* (Black Inc, Melbourne 2006)

Haigh, Gideon and Frith, David, *Inside Story: Unlocking Australian Cricket's Archives* (News Custom Publishing, Melbourne 2007)

Harte, Chris, *A History of Australian Cricket* (Andre Deutsch, London 1993)

Harvey, Neil, *My World of Cricket* (Hodder & Stoughton, London 1963)

Heald, Tim, *Denis Compton: The Life of a Sporting Hero* (Aurum Press, London 2006)

Howat, Gerald, *Len Hutton: The Biography* (Heinemann Kingswood, London 1988)

Hutton, Len with Alex Bannister, *Fifty Years in Cricket* (Stanley Paul & Co, London 1984)

Hutton, Len, *Cricket is My Life* (Hutchinson & Co, London 1949)

Hutton, Len, *Just My Story* (Hutchinson, London 1956)

Johnson, Ian, *Cricket at the Crossroads* (Cassell & Co, London 1957)

Kilburn, J.M., *Cricket Decade: England v Australia 1946 to 1956* (The Windmill Press, London 1959)

Kitchin, Laurence, *Len Hutton* (Phoenix House Limited, London 1953)

Knox, Malcolm, *The Captains* (Hardie Grant Books, Melbourne 2011)

Kynaston, David, *Austerity Britain 1945–51* (Bloomsbury, London 2007)

Lindwall, Ray, *Flying Stumps* (Stanley Paul, London 1954)

McCool, Colin, *Cricket is a Game* (Stanley Paul, London 1961)

McHarg, Jack, *Arthur Morris: An Elegant Genius* (ABC Books, Sydney 1995)

Miller, Douglas, *Allan Watkins, A True All-Rounder* (Association of Cricket Statisticians and Historians, Cardiff 2007)

Miller, Keith, *Cricket Crossfire* (Oldbourne Press, London 1956)

Miller, Keith and Whitington, R.S., *Cricket Caravan* (Latimer House, London 1950).

Moyes, A.G., *Bradman* (Angus and Robertson, Sydney 1948)

O'Reilly, W.J., *Cricket Conquest* (Werner Laurie, London 1949)

Peebles, Ian, *Denis Compton: The Generous Cricketer* (Macmillan London 1971)

Perry, Roland, *Bradman's Invincibles* (Hachette, Sydney 2008)

Perry, Roland, *Captain Australia* (Random House Australia, Sydney 2000)

Perry, Roland, *Miller's Luck* (Random House Australia, Sydney 2006)

Robinson, Ray, *On Top Down Under: Australia's Cricket Captains* (Cassell, London 1981)

Rosenwater, Irving, *Sir Donald Bradman: A Biography* (B.T. Batsford Ltd, London 1978)

Smith, Rick, *Cricket's Enigma: The Sid Barnes Story* (ABC Books, Sydney 1999)

Thomson, A.A., *Hutton & Washbrook* (The Sportsmans Book Club, London 1966)

Trelford, Donald (ed), *Len Hutton Remembered* (H.F. & G. Witherby Ltd, London 1992)

Washbrook, Cyril, *Cricket: The Silver Lining* (Sportsguide Publications, London 1950)

West, Peter, *Denis Compton: Cricketing Genius* (Stanley Paul & Co, London 1989)

Whitington, R.S., *Keith Miller: The Golden Nugget* (Rigby, Sydney 1981)

Whitington, R.S., *Lindsay Hassett: The Quiet Australian* (William Heinemann, London 1969)

Wisden Cricketers' Almanack 1949 (John Wisden & Co, London 1949)

Wisden Book Of Obituaries

Yardley, Norman, *Cricket Campaigns* (Stanley Paul & Co, London, 1950)

200 Years of Australian Cricket 1804–2004, (Macmillan Sydney 2004)

Bradman to Chappell (ABC Books, Sydney 1974)

ACKNOWLEDGEMENTS

When the Fiftieth Anniversary of the Invincibles' tour was celebrated in 1998, the majority of the Australian and English Test cricketers from 1948 were alive. When I started my research for this book in 2010, just three Australians – Neil Harvey, Arthur Morris and Sam Loxton – and three Englishmen – John Dewes, Allan Watkins and Alec Bedser – remained. Sam, Allan and Alec are no longer with us. I wish to offer my sincere gratitude to Neil, Arthur and John for sparing the time to talk about the postwar era (again!). To see them reliving the past was a privilege. I don't have adequate words to thank Shirley Dewes for bringing her husband John and me together in Bath. I would also like to thank Hubert Doggart for a very enjoyable lunch and enlightening conversation in Chichester. The late Sam Loxton's son Peter was a great help in getting Sam and me to the Southport Labrador cricket club one summer afternoon, and at other times for getting Sam on (and off) the phone.

This book also benefited from the great generosity of Mike Coward, Ronald Cardwell, Matthew Engel and Stephen Chalke. Ben Ball had the idea for a different kind of book about the Invincibles; his continuing drive and excellent ideas have achieved as much as a publisher can do. I would like to thank Ben and his staff at Penguin, particularly Michael Nolan. Those people are responsible for this book's strengths. The weaknesses are down to the author.

INDEX

knee injury 304
Lord's pre-test match 133
New Zealand v Australia 1945-46 30
nicknames 109
Northampton mid-tests match 192
Second Test, Lord's 196, 205, 207, 213,
 215–18
Sheffield mid-tests match 193
Third Test, Old Trafford 235–6, 238,
 242, 249–50
voyage to England 73, 75
war service 26
Worcester pre-test match 107, 109–10
Travers, Basil 'Jika' 133
Trent Bridge *see* First Test, Nottingham;
 Nottingham pre-test match
Trumble, Hugh 57, 355
Trumper, Victor 54, 64, 99, 355
Tyldesley, Richard 353

U

Ulyett, George 33
umpires 107

V

Valentine, Brian 229–30, 313
Van Ryneveld, Clive 133
Verity, Hedley
 bowling success 66
 Bradman dismissals 11
 death 11
 England v Australia 1938 264, 338
 pre-war cricket career 11, 34
 war service 11
Victory Tests 10–11, 13–15, 19, 26, 35,
 121, 370, 383
Vigar, Frank 127
Vincent, Beau [Major] 321
Voce, Bill
 Australia v England 1946-47 40
 bowling success 66
 pre-war cricket career 34, 146, 176, 181
von Nida, Norman 17, 198, 208

W

Walcott, Clyde 95
Walker, Charlie 4, 48
Wallace, Johnny 38
Walsh, Jack 112
Walters, Doug 215
Wardle, John 115–16
 Sheffield mid-tests match 193

Warner, Pelham 226, 257, 303, 335
warrior-cricketers 370
Warwickshire mid-tests match 299–301
Washbrook, Cyril
 assessments of tour 363–4
 Australia v England 1946-47 36, 43, 158
 benefit match at Old Trafford 301–2
 on Bradman 247–8
 county success 360
 cricket career 95
 First Test, Nottingham 152, 158–60
 on First Test, Nottingham 173
 forces cricket 13
 Fourth Test, Leeds 264–7, 271, 284, 290
 on Hutton 226
 Lancashire mid-tests match 301–2
 Lancashire pre-test match 143–4
 post war attitude to cricket 26
 pre-war cricket career 14
 respect for Australian bowlers 247
 Second Test, Lord's 205, 207, 210,
  214–16, 218
 strengths of English team 94
 Third Test, Old Trafford 233–4,
  246, 248–51
Watkins, Allan
 on Bradman's 5th Test dismissal 318
 death 382
 Fifth Test, The Oval 305–6, 311, 313,
  316–17, 326
 on Glamorgan mid-tests match 298
 spectator at Worcester 109
 Test selection 195
Waugh, Steve 298, 357
Weekes, Everton 95
Weldon, Fay 92
West Indes v England 1948 95
Whitcombe, Phil 153
White, Allan 107
White, Crawford 131
White, Jack 354, 367
White, Ted 3
Whitington, Dick
 and Bradman 53
 on Bradman 35, 56, 129, 144, 206,
  343, 370
 on Dewes 121
 on effects of war on cricket 361
 on First Test, Nottingham 166
 forces cricket 3, 5–6, 27
 on forces cricket 10, 15–16, 18, 25
 on Hassett 4, 56, 358
 on Lord's pre-test match 134